# Sarajevo 1914

*Sparking the First World War*

EDITED BY
MARK CORNWALL

BLOOMSBURY ACADEMIC
LONDON • NEW YORK • OXFORD • NEW DELHI • SYDNEY

BLOOMSBURY ACADEMIC
Bloomsbury Publishing Plc
50 Bedford Square, London, WC1B 3DP, UK
1385 Broadway, New York, NY 10018, USA
BLOOMSBURY, BLOOMSBURY ACADEMIC and the Diana logo are trademarks of
Bloomsbury Publishing Plc

First published in Great Britain 2020

Copyright © Mark Cornwall and Contributors 2020

Mark Cornwall has asserted his right under the Copyright, Designs and Patents Act, 1988, to be identified as Editor of this work.

Cover design: Tjaša Krivec
Cover image: Archduke Franz Ferdinand and his wife in Sarajevo just before their assassination, June 1914. (© Science History Images / Alamy Stock Photo)

All rights reserved. No part of this publication may be reproduced or transmitted in any form or by any means, electronic or mechanical, including photocopying, recording, or any information storage or retrieval system, without prior permission in writing from the publishers.

Bloomsbury Publishing Plc does not have any control over, or responsibility for, any third-party websites referred to or in this book. All internet addresses given in this book were correct at the time of going to press. The author and publisher regret any inconvenience caused if addresses have changed or sites have ceased to exist, but can accept no responsibility for any such changes.

A catalogue record for this book is available from the British Library.

Library of Congress Cataloging-in-Publication Data

Names: Cornwall, Mark, editor.
Title: Sarajevo 1914: Sparking the First World War / edited by Mark Cornwall.
Identifiers: LCCN 2020019746 (print) | LCCN 2020019747 (ebook) |
ISBN 9781350093201 (paperback) | ISBN 9781350093218 (hardback) |
ISBN 9781350093195 (ebook) | ISBN 9781350093188 (epub)
Subjects: LCSH: World War, 1914-1918–Balkan Peninsula. | Franz Ferdinand, Archduke of Austria, 1863-1914–Assassination. | Balkan Peninsula–History, Military– 20th century. | Serbia–History–1804-1918. | Yugoslavia–History–1918-1945.
Classification: LCC D560 .S27 2020 (print) | LCC D560 (ebook) | DDC 940.3/11–dc23

LC record available at https://lccn.loc.gov/2020019746
LC ebook record available at https://lccn.loc.gov/2020019747

ISBN: HB: 978-1-3500-9321-8
PB: 978-1-3500-9320-1
ePDF: 978-1-3500-9319-5
eBook: 978-1-3500-9318-8

Typeset by Deanta Global Publishing Services, Chennai, India
Printed and bound in Great Britain

To find out more about our authors and books visit www.bloomsbury.com and sign up for our newsletters.

# Sarajevo 1914

## CONTENTS

'Six powers appalled by war': The July crisis and the limits of crisis management  *T. G. Otte*  163

The British elite and the Sarajevo assassinations  *F. R. Bridge*  184

## PART III  Regional blaze  205

11  Between Budapest and Belgrade: The road to pragmatism and treason in 1914 Croatia  *Mark Cornwall*  207

12  The outbreak of war in Habsburg Trieste  *Borut Klabjan*  233

13  The inner enemy in wartime: The Habsburg state and the Serb citizens of Bosnia-Herzegovina, 1913–18  *Heiner Grunert*  253

14  Remembering Franz Ferdinand and Sarajevo in interwar Czechoslovakia  *Dagmar Hájková*  274

Selected further reading  293
Index  295

# CONTENTS

*List of illustrations* vii
*List of contributors* viii
*Acknowledgements* xi

1 Introduction: The Southern Slav Question
  *Mark Cornwall* 1

## PART I  Tinder and spark 15

2 Franz Ferdinand: Power and image  *Alma Hannig*
3 Great expectations: The Habsburg heir apparent a Southern Slavs  *Andrej Rahten* 39
4 Noblesse oblige: The outlook of the Croatian arist on the eve of the First World War  *Iskra Iveljić* 56
5 Bosnian-Croatian-Serbian-Serbo-Croatian: Friction over language terminology in pre-war Bosnia-Herzegovina  *Tamara Scheer* 82
6 *Mlada Bosna*: The educational and cultural context  *Robin Okey* 102

## PART II  International blaze 123

7 Why did nobody control Apis?: Serbian military intelligence and the Sarajevo assassination  *Danilo Šarenac* 125
8 Why fight a Third Balkan War?: The Habsburg mindset in 1914  *Lothar Höbelt* 149

# ILLUSTRATIONS

Portrait of Franz Ferdinand as Emperor Franz II, by Wilhelm Vita (c. 1910) xii

1.1 The South Slav (Yugoslav) lands in 1913 4
2.1 'Military conference chaired by Emperor Franz Joseph', by Felician von Myrbach-Reinfeld (1908) 20
2.2 'Archduke Franz Ferdinand and Conrad von Hötzendorf on manoeuvres at the Dukla Pass', 1911 22
4.1 'Baron Pavao Rauch. Ban of the kingdom of Croatia, Slavonia and Dalmatia'. Official heliogravure by Rudolf Mosinger 63
4.2 Hunting diary of Stjepan Erdödy 71
7.1 Dragutin T. Dimitrijević ('Apis') 131
11.1 Count István Tisza enters Zagreb 214
11.2 Tisza as the Croatian Pégoud 215
11.3 Frano Supilo speaks to the crowds in Sušak 217
12.1 The arrival of the bodies in Trieste 236
12.2 The procession on Trieste's main square, today Piazza Unità d'Italia 237
12.3 Detail of the procession on the Corso in Trieste 238
13.1 Anti-Serb riots and the devastation of Serb property 256
14.1 Castle and hunting lodge of the Konopiště estate, 1901 282
14.2 The Archduke Franz Ferdinand Bridge in Prague, opened in 1914 285

# CONTRIBUTORS

**F. R. Bridge** is Emeritus Professor of International History at the University of Leeds and a leading authority on Habsburg foreign policy. His many publications include *Great Britain and Austria-Hungary 1906-1914: A Diplomatic History* (1972); *From Sadowa to Sarajevo: The Foreign Policy of Austria-Hungary* (1972); *Austro-Hungarian Foreign Documents on the Macedonian Struggle 1896-1912* (1976); *The Habsburg Monarchy among the Great Powers, 1815-1918* (1991); *The Great Powers and the European States System 1815-1914* (2nd ed. 2005).

**Mark Cornwall** is Professor of Modern European History at the University of Southampton, specializing in modern East-Central Europe. His publications include *The Last Years of Austria-Hungary: A Multinational Experiment in Early Twentieth-Century Europe* (2nd ed. 2002); *The Devil's Wall: The Nationalist Youth Mission of Heinz Rutha* (2012); *Sacrifice and Rebirth: The Legacy of the Last Habsburg War* (ed. with John Paul Newman, 2016); and *The Undermining of Austria-Hungary: The Battle for Hearts and Minds* (new ed. 2018). He is writing a history of treason in the late Habsburg Monarchy.

**Heiner Grunert** is a research assistant to the chair of Eastern European history at Ludwig-Maximilians University in Munich. His work has focused on religious and linguistic diversity in South-Eastern Europe. His publications include *Glauben im Hinterland. Die Serbisch-Orthodoxen in der habsburgischen Herzegowina 1878–1918* (2016) and 'Interreligiöse Konkurrenz und Kooperation im Imperium. Orthodoxe, Muslime und Katholiken in Bosnien-Herzegowina unter habsburgischer Verwaltung', in Jana Osterkamp (ed.), *Kooperatives Imperium. Politische Zusammenarbeit in der späten Habsburgermonarchie* (2018). He is now researching agrarian ideas in early twentieth-century Poland and Yugoslavia.

**Dagmar Hájková** is a senior researcher in the Masaryk Institute and Archive of the Czech Academy of Sciences in Prague. She specializes in Czechoslovak/Czech political and cultural history. She is an author, co-author and editor of several monographs and document collections from the First World War and interwar Czechoslovakia. Among her recent publications are a major biography of a wartime Czech spy: *Emanuel Voska. Špionážní* *legenda první světové války* (2014); *Republika československá: 1918-1939* (2018) and *Sláva republice! Oficiální svátky a oslavy v meziválečném Československu* (2018).

**Alma Hannig** works as a museum and exhibition curator in Vienna and Dresden, and was also for a decade based at Bonn University. Her research focuses on Austrian and German political and diplomatic history of the nineteenth and twentieth centuries and the history of the German aristocracy. Besides many recent articles on these themes, she has written the standard life of Franz Ferdinand, *Franz Ferdinand. Die Biografie* (2013), and is also co-editor of *Die Familie Hohenlohe im 19. und 20. Jahrhundert. Eine europäische Dynastie* (2013).

**Lothar Höbelt** is Associate Professor of Modern History at the University of Vienna and has published extensively on the reign of Emperor Franz Joseph, the First World War and modern Austrian political history. His books include *Kornblume und Kaiseradler. Die deutschfreiheitlichen Parteien Altösterreichs 1882-1918* (1993); *Franz Joseph I. Der Kaiser und sein Reich. Eine politische Geschichte* (2009); *'Stehen oder fallen?' Österreichische Politik im Ersten Weltkrieg* (2015) and a reappraisal of the Austrian *Heimwehr* movement: *Die Heimwehren und die österreichische Politik 1927-1936* (2017).

**Iskra Iveljić** is Professor of Croatian Nineteenth-Century History at the University of Zagreb, her research focusing on aspects of modernization, the middle-class elite and the Croatian aristocracy. Her publications include *Memoari bana Pavla Raucha* (2009); *Banska Hrvatska i Vojna krajina od prosvijećenog apsolutizma do 1848. godine* (2010); *Anatomija jedne velikaške porodice Rauchovi* (2014); and, as editor, *The Entangled Histories of Vienna, Zagreb and Budapest* (2015). She is the principal investigator of an international project financed by the Croatian Science Foundation, *The Transition of Croatian Elites from the Habsburg Monarchy to the Yugoslav State*.

**Borut Klabjan** is Marie Skłodowska Curie Fellow at the European University Institute in Florence, Senior Research Fellow at the Science and Research Centre in Koper and Associate Professor of History at the University of Ljubljana. His research focuses on political and cultural history with a special emphasis on the northern Adriatic and Central Europe. He has edited and authored four multilingual volumes, and his monograph *Czechoslovakia in the Adriatic* has been published in Slovene (2007) and Czech (2014). His last edited volume was *Borderlands of Memory: Adriatic and Central European Perspectives* (2019).

**Robin Okey** is Emeritus Professor of History at Warwick University, where he taught from 1966 to 2007. His main interests have centred on East-Central Europe in the nineteenth and twentieth centuries with research specialization on relations between the Habsburg Monarchy and the South Slavs in the dualist period. His major publications are *Eastern Europe 1740-1985* (2nd ed.1986); *The Habsburg Monarchy c. 1765-1918: From Enlightenment to Eclipse* (2000); *The Demise of Communist East Europe: 1989 in Context* (2004) and *Taming Balkan Nationalism: The Habsburg 'Civilizing Mission' in Bosnia, 1878-1914* (2007).

**T. G. Otte** is Professor of Diplomatic History at the University of East Anglia and has published widely on European diplomatic and political history. His books include *The Foreign Office Mind: The Making of British Foreign Policy 1865-1914* (2011); *July Crisis: The World's Descent into War, Summer 1914* (2014); *An Historian in Peace and War: The Diaries of Harold Temperley 1900-1939* (2014); *The Age of Anniversaries: The Cult of Commemoration 1895-1925* (2017); and *Sir Edward Grey: Statesman of Europe* (2020).

**Andrej Rahten** is Senior Research Fellow at the Research Centre of the Slovenian Academy of Sciences and Arts (ZRC SAZU) in Ljubljana. He is also Full Professor for Contemporary History at the University of Maribor and a Corresponding Member of the Austrian Academy of Sciences. He is the co-founder of the *Studia Diplomatica Slovenica* book series and president of the Ljubljana-based Coordination Committee for the Research of Diplomatic History. Many of his publications have focused on the Southern Slav Question, including a biography of Ivan Šusteršič (2012), and books about the assassination of Franz Ferdinand (2014) and late wartime Slovenian politics (2016).

**Danilo Šarenac** is a senior research fellow at the Institute for Contemporary History in Belgrade. His research has mainly focused on the First World War in the Balkans. His publications include *Top, vojnik i sećanja. Prvi svetski rat i Srbija 1914-2009* (2014) and *The Forgotten Admiral: Extracts from the Diary of Sir Ernest Troubridge 1915-1919* (2017). He has also contributed articles to several international volumes about the Great War, and is now researching banditry and the state in the early twentieth-century Balkans.

**Tamara Scheer** is a lecturer and research associate at the Institute for East European History at the University of Vienna. Her many publications include *Zwischen Front und Heimat. Österreich-Ungarns Militärverwaltungen im Ersten Weltkrieg* (2009); *Die Ringstraßenfront – Österreich-Ungarn, das Kriegsüberwachungsamt und der Ausnahmezustand während des Ersten Weltkriegs* (2010); *'Minimale Kosten, absolut kein Blut!': Österreich-Ungarns Präsenz im Sandžak von Novipazar (1879-1908)* (2013) and with Clemens Ruthner, *Österreich-Ungarn und Bosnien-Herzegowina, 1878-1918. Annäherungen an eine Kolonie* (2018). She is currently completing a book on language diversity in the late Habsburg imperial army.

# ACKNOWLEDGEMENTS

This volume has had a long preparation, and I am deeply indebted to all the contributors for their patience with the editing process. The concept for the book emerged from many roots but was accelerated through a symposium on *Sarajevo 1914*, held at the University of Southampton on 28 June 2014. Unlike several conferences organized for that anniversary, this proved to be a very harmonious and positive venture, bringing together scholars from half a dozen countries to assess critically the spark and impact of the Sarajevo assassinations. I am most grateful to all who took part and aided that success, especially Christopher Clark, Robert Evans, Lothar Höbelt, Dominic Lieven, Annika Mombauer, Jasna Dragović-Soso and H. E. Emil Brix (then Austrian ambassador to the UK). The Austrian Cultural Forum and a grant from the British Academy helped to fund the event. In my own long engagement with the Southern Slav Question, I have also learnt much from notable historians in the field and pay tribute to them here: Dragovan Šepić, Janko Pleterski, Andrej Mitrović, Iskra Iveljić, Stjepan Matković and Petra Svoljšak. At Southampton, my head of department, Sarah Pearce, was the terrier urging me to persist with this project; and I have had a wise and most encouraging editor at Bloomsbury in Rhodri Mogford.

Mark Cornwall
April 2020

*Portrait of Franz Ferdinand as Emperor Franz II, by Wilhelm Vita (c. 1910).*

# CHAPTER 1

# Introduction

# The Southern Slav Question

## Mark Cornwall

In 1914, many people living in Austria-Hungary – the vast conglomeration of lands that stretched across East-Central Europe as the Habsburg Empire – expected that Franz Joseph, their eighty-three-year-old monarch, would soon die, to be succeeded by the fifty-year-old heir apparent Archduke Franz Ferdinand. Some anticipated the latter's accession as Emperor Franz II with optimism, others with anxiety. He was rumoured to have a radical reform programme in mind, but he was also notoriously reactionary and nurtured deep resentment against anyone he felt to have damaged the prestige of the Habsburg dynasty. This accession to the throne of course never took place. For on 28 June 1914 in the Bosnian capital of Sarajevo it was Franz Ferdinand who died, murdered along with his wife by the Bosnian Serb, Gavrilo Princip. It was the old emperor Franz Joseph who survived and who a month later led the Habsburg Monarchy into a disastrous European war which would cost the lives of a million of his subjects.

The significance of the Sarajevo assassination was recognized immediately by those contemporaries who knew what was really at stake. In Vienna on 28 June, Josef Redlich recorded in his diary, 'This day is the day of a world historical event ... the fateful hour of the Habsburg approaches.'[1] In Prague, the Czech university professor Josef Pekař greeted his students dressed in black, observing that the death of the Habsburg prince had damaged the Monarchy in 'deep and unforeseen ways'.[2] Others in the public eye agreed that there were bound to be very unpredictable results from the 'ghastly end of the heir apparent'.[3] Some in hindsight would claim to have predicted an inevitable war, even if they were not clear whether Austria-Hungary would be enmeshed in a Serbian, a Balkan or a European conflict.[4]

Most historians would agree with Vladimir Dedijer, still the leading chronicler of the assassination, that 'no other political murder in modern history has had such momentous consequences'.[5] Proverbially, as every school pupil knows, it was the spark that ignited the First World War, the trigger that led on to mass slaughter. Not surprisingly it has produced ever since a huge historiographical industry, embracing myths, hypotheses and partisanship – what exactly happened, why it happened and who was really responsible.[6] After the collapse of the Habsburg Empire in 1918, there were always some who eulogized Franz Ferdinand as a hero and martyr for the dynasty.[7] Others – not least some Serbian historians – portrayed him as a warmonger and tyrant who had even been planning the war of which he was the first victim. It was a debate reactivated around 2014 on the centenary of Sarajevo, when some Serbian academics strongly objected to the work of Christopher Clark who, in portraying the Serbia of 1914 as a 'rogue state' in the Balkans, had implied that their country too bore some responsibility for the catastrophe.[8] It is clear then that, with the myriad perspectives on 'Sarajevo 1914', the controversy over it will take a long time to die.

Yet this focus on the spark itself has often obscured the more significant underlying tinder that the spark ignited. Behind Franz Ferdinand's demise lay the intricate context of the Balkans, that European region which observers by 1914 had variously constructed as exotic, chaotic and barbaric.[9] For many contemporaries the Balkans was also synonymous with the intractability of the so-called Southern Slav Question. As one historian has vividly argued, this late imperial era was in fact an 'age of questions'; politicians or commentators regularly asserted that some social or geopolitical issue was of international significance, demanding a speedy solution if it was not to escalate and cause havoc.[10]

The 'Southern Slav Question' was one such thorny problem. In essence, it meant the suggestion widely discussed in European educated society that the South Slav peoples – notably Serbs, Croats and Slovenes – could or should be fused together into some new territorial unit. Any student who wishes seriously to explain the Sarajevo assassinations has to navigate this South Slav labyrinth and will soon realize that there was no one Southern Slav question. There were numerous interpretations of what it meant, and numerous 'correct' solutions being proffered on all sides. That it was portentous and needed a solution, however, was clear to anyone in authority. Writing just a month before Franz Ferdinand was killed, the Viennese newspaper *Reichspost* (always close to the archduke's thinking) warned that among the many problems facing the Monarchy 'the Southern Slav has become the greatest danger'; it needed to be fixed calmly but energetically.[11] Reminiscing much later, one Hungarian politician would stress the decisive role of this Southern Slav Question in causing the Great War; it was, he added, 'a thoroughly prepared, consciously and systematically directed political action'.[12]

As this suggests, to some contemporaries there was a sense of real momentum and purpose behind the Southern Slav project. There seemed to be something organic, something inevitable, about the rise of a modern South Slav (Yugo-Slav) nation to challenge the existing geopolitical order. The Habsburg regime based in Vienna increasingly saw this as a fundamental threat to its existence. After all, in the 1860s, the empire had lost most of its Italian lands and its German sphere of influence, thanks to the creation of new national Italian and German states sponsored by Piedmont and Prussia respectively. In the wake of those disasters, Austro-Hungarian foreign policy from the 1870s turned to focus on south-east Europe – the Balkans – but immediately encountered there the rising nationalist states of Serbia, Montenegro and Romania (each of which secured full independence from the Ottoman Empire in 1878).

The Habsburg elite was increasingly anxious that Serbia in particular would be another Piedmont.[13] For it was well known that Serbian rulers had long aspired to expand their territory into Bosnia or even Croatia, incorporating the large Serb diaspora and recreating a 'Greater Serbia' in the Balkans. Partly to anticipate that national advance, Austria-Hungary in 1878 managed to occupy the Ottoman provinces of Bosnia and Herzegovina and thirty years later annexed them in the face of fierce Serbian opposition. Until the mid-1890s, thanks to an Austro-Serbian alliance (1881–95), Vienna had successfully managed to rein in a restless Serbian kingdom and reduce it to a satellite state of the Monarchy. But thereafter, under its last Obrenović king, Serbia became increasingly erratic in its foreign policy and suspect in its intentions. In the early years of the new century a prosperous and liberal Belgrade would also become a mecca for many Serbs or South Slavs from the Habsburg Empire who were dissatisfied with conditions at home.[14]

But in the Habsburg mindset we must note, too, a deeper international dimension to Serbia's instability. The warning, sounded back in 1870, that Serbia might one day become a stalking horse for Russia seemed to be ever more credible.[15] For a century, Austro-Russian rivalry in the Balkans had caused international crises – indeed, it was at the heart of the so-called Eastern Question about the fate of the Ottoman Empire. If Russia managed to gain overwhelming influence in the Orthodox states of Serbia or Montenegro, then a Russian noose would begin to tighten around Austria-Hungary. Montenegro was always a potential Russian satellite; from 1900, Serbia also seemed to be drifting in that direction. It was a geopolitical nightmare for Vienna, conjuring up the wild possibility that Russia would eventually control the states bordering the Habsburg Monarchy and even gain access to the Adriatic Sea.[16]

In this light, for the Habsburg elite, the Southern Slav Question was largely synonymous with the menace of a Greater Serbia. Belgrade seemed to be pushing a nationalist agenda that threatened the very standing of the

Monarchy as a European Great Power. Hawks in the Habsburg army like Franz Conrad von Hötzendorf (chief of the general staff) duly felt that only a military solution would pre-empt Serbia's ambitions and force it back into its correct satellite status. Yet a potentially more constructive solution did also beckon after 1900.[17] For by the twentieth century just as fundamental for the Habsburg Monarchy was the question of whether its own domestic South Slavs might be fused into some new national unit, allowing Vienna (not Belgrade) to dominate the Southern Slav agenda. To this as a solution, however, the empire's very structure presented a major obstacle. For in 1867 through the empire's dualist system, the Monarchy had been divided into two halves – Austria and Hungary.[18] It was a division that cut straight across the Southern Slav lands, allotting Slovene territories and Dalmatia to Austria, while Croatia and a substantial Serb population were left within the Hungarian half of the empire (Figure 1.1). The annexation of Bosnia-Herzegovina in 1908 added more Serbs and Croats to the empire and theoretically implied that some Southern Slav unit 'within' would be viable.

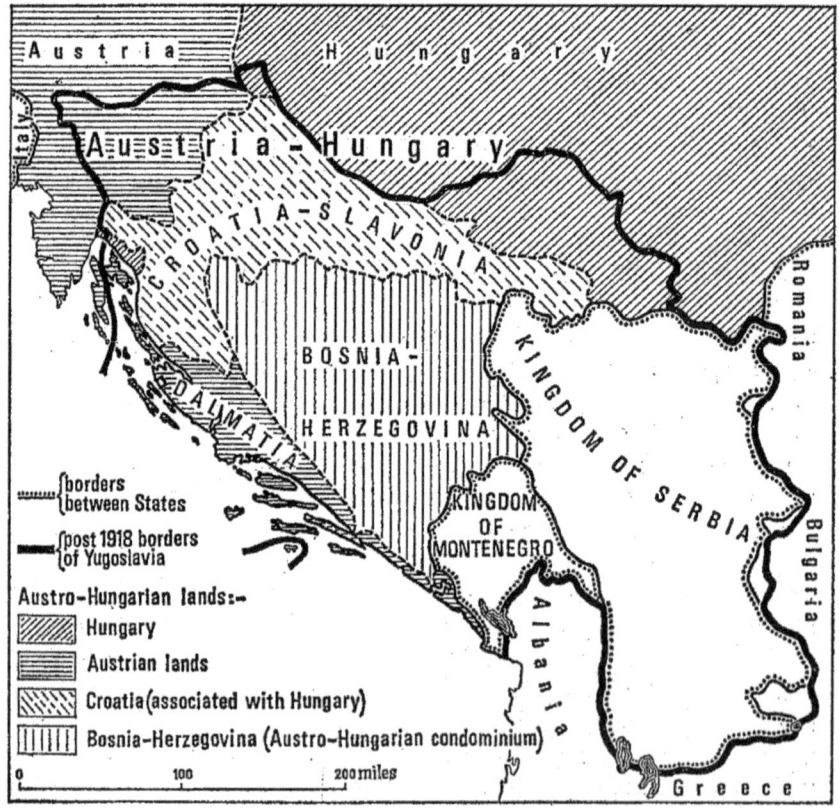

FIGURE 1.1 *The South Slav (Yugoslav) lands in 1913.*

In fact, it brought another layer of complexity, for the new provinces were not subsumed into Austria or Hungary but treated as a colony, a *corpus separatum* with their own governor and a special ministry supervising them from Vienna.[19]

It was therefore an enormous challenge (or headache) for any Habsburg statesman to solve the Southern Slav riddle, particularly since the Hungarian regime in Budapest was absolutely wedded to the dualist system. But we should emphasize in turn the multifaceted interpretations of Southern Slav unity which also exacerbated any resolution.[20] To many intellectuals in the southern Habsburg lands, it was never about achieving Serb unification, but a case of some 'Greater Croatian' or 'Yugoslav' vision. The stance of Croat nationalists for decades had been to join Habsburg South Slavs together in one Greater Croatia with Zagreb as the capital. The core territory of Croatia-Slavonia would be united again with Dalmatia and Bosnia, and perhaps even the Slovene lands. Thereby they would fulfil that historic crusade for Croatian 'state right' (the *pravaši* ideology), recreating a fully sovereign Croatian territory. 'Trialism' would be the result: the dualism of Austria-Hungary converted through a special Croatian unit into a trialist empire.

Parallel to this Greater Croatia was a distinctly 'Yugoslav' interpretation of trialism and the Southern Slav Question. Its adherents promoted the unity of Serbs and Croats within the empire on an equal basis, and with a progressive agenda of social and constitutional reform. A wholly new and modern nationality was said to be emerging, characterized by civic inclusivity rather than the nationalist exclusivity of a Greater Serbia or Greater Croatia. Popular particularly in Dalmatia due to the vibrant example of the Italian Risorgimento, this 'Yugoslav' approach to the Southern Slav problem gained ground especially after 1903. A new generation of younger politicians created a Croat-Serb Coalition of sympathetic political parties in Croatia and Dalmatia, loosely allied across the dualist border and seeking a 'New Course' for the new century.[21] In retrospect it was perhaps the most idealistic of solutions, for it worked from the assumption that linguistic unity – a common language between Serbs and Croats – would make inevitable a successful fusion of the two peoples into one modern nation.

In the years leading up to 1914, this 'just solution' was championed by many youthful idealists across the region (including Gavrilo Princip himself). A notable enthusiast too was the British historian and commentator, R. W. Seton-Watson. In his classic work *The Southern Slav Question* (1911), Seton-Watson emphasized that 'Croato-Serb Unity must and will come'. He prioritized the rough linguistic uniformity of the region over any historic diversity: 'a homogeneous population, speaking a single language, has been split up by an unkindly fate into a large number of purely artificial fragments.'[22] In his view, a natural unstoppable evolution was occurring towards Serbo-Croat unity on the model of Germany and Italy, so the main question to solve was how the Habsburg Empire could best manage and control the 'aspirations of its eight million Southern Slavs'. Seton-Watson, at least until 1913, excluded any solution involving 'uncivilized' Serbia, arguing that any 'Pan-Serb' dream could only be achieved through a European conflagration. His ideal instead was a trialist but Yugoslav solution centred on Zagreb and based firmly within the empire. Grouped into one state territory would be the Serbs and Croats of Croatia, Bosnia-Herzegovina, and most South Slav lands of Austria (notably Dalmatia and Istria). Yet for this to occur, he admitted, it needed an Austrian statesman possessing 'genius and courage', someone who could 'identify the movement for Croato-Serb Unity with the requirements of Austrian patriotism'.[23] In 1911 – but even more by 1914 – Seton-Watson envisaged that Franz Ferdinand, as the next Habsburg emperor, could well be the man to achieve this, thereby blocking a Greater Serbia and stabilizing the Balkans. It was therefore a crushing blow to him when the archduke was assassinated at Sarajevo.[24]

In hindsight, of course, we might query the whole premise that Southern Slav unification was inevitable, or that any solution in the south had to involve a major restructuring of the Habsburg state. Yet in the years before 1914, observers within and without the Monarchy felt there was ample evidence to prove that the status quo was under threat, and they loosely ascribed much of the discontent to some aspect of the 'Southern Slav Question'. At home it was manifest in the clamour for radical reform, the populist rallies and the prevalence of assassination attempts on Habsburg officials in Croatia and Bosnia – almost on a par with those in late Tsarist Russia. From abroad, the dangers or opportunities seemed to be mounting as Serbia – supposedly backed by Russia – grew in confidence and then, in the wake of the Balkan Wars of 1912–13, managed to double the size of its territory.

Alarmed by this and by the South Slav momentum at home, the Habsburg authorities could respond with reform or repression. Both avenues in fact were tried in the decade before 1914. Evidence of reform was certainly there in the universal male suffrage introduced into Austria, in the 1910 constitution granted to Bosnia-Herzegovina and in a slightly widened franchise for Croatia. Yet it was repression that tended to dominate the news in this final decade of peace. There was the official tendency to censor and ban political meetings, the years of unconstitutional rule and political trials in Croatia, and the anti-Serb security measures during the Balkan Wars that effectively produced a 'militarist-police regime' in Bosnia.[25] All these tactics clashed with a burgeoning civil society, suggesting rightly to many contemporaries that their Habsburg government was insecure and prone to violence. In short, pre-war Austria-Hungary in its South Slav territories was a long way from being 'inherently calm and predictable' or the ideal European *Rechtsstaat*.[26]

The regime's response to the Sarajevo assassinations confirmed this tendency. Those advocating a forceful solution now prevailed completely: Serbia had to be crushed militarily at all costs, and the irritating kingdom either extinguished or incorporated into the empire. Historians have often claimed that the Habsburg decisions for war in July 1914 were based largely on matters of dynastic and imperial prestige – a primacy of foreign policy in the decision making. Yet while true in essence, we cannot ignore the unspoken assumptions behind those decisions, the deep-seated elite anxiety (shared by Franz Ferdinand) that a Greater Serbian menace was out of control in the Balkans. In other words, Serbia but also the Southern Slav Question had to be settled once and for all. That 'question' now entered a new phase with wartime making feasible a really radical solution. In Seton-Watson's view, there were two stark options ahead towards 'inevitable' Yugoslav unity. Either the Habsburg Monarchy, in challenging Greater Serbia, would proceed violently to force through a unification of all South Slavs within the empire, or Serbia would act as 'the Southern Slav Piedmont', liberating and uniting the South Slavs in a completely new state. Out of the conflagration, he felt, it was the latter which must prevail.[27]

It might well be posited – and Seton-Watson certainly did – that the murder of Franz Ferdinand by a Bosnian Serb soon became a subject of minor importance, a 'side issue' compared to settling the far more significant Southern Slav problem. Yet it is impossible to underestimate the tremors emanating from this single violent event, which the Viennese elite unanimously interpreted as a brutal attack by Greater Serbia on the Habsburg dynasty's present and future.[28] It set in motion a course – otherwise not at all inevitable – of war against Serbia, which then spiralled out of control across Europe. We know that the assassination had not been planned by the Serbian government as Vienna always insisted, but certainly it had been indirectly facilitated through Serbian soft power – propaganda as well as arms smuggling. Serbia had not lived as a 'good neighbour', as Austria-Hungary had patronizingly demanded after the Bosnian crisis of 1908–9.[29] Many Habsburg officers, cognizant at least to some degree of this context, saw the atrocity befalling their future Emperor Franz II as a red rag; it was the signal that fully justified a brutal army campaign against Serbia in 1914, and its military occupation in the years 1916–18.[30]

Meanwhile, within the empire, the Sarajevo act of violence immediately provided the justification and licence for widespread violence against anyone deemed an accessory to the Greater Serbian project. While Croat nationalists could target 'Serb murderers' with vicious rhetoric and the destruction of property, the state security services proceeded to arrest thousands of 'unreliable' South Slavs and dispatch them to internment camps. In October 1914, the Sarajevo assassination was naturally the focal point in the trial of Gavrilo Princip and his accomplices, for their conviction would justify the ongoing war against Serbia. But from that treason trial many others mushroomed across Bosnia and Croatia in 1915–16. In all of them the prosecutors used as their main evidence the previous dissemination across the Monarchy of Greater Serbian propaganda, whose cumulative effect had supposedly been the murder of the Habsburg heir apparent.[31]

In these ways the imperial authorities in wartime continued to fight the battle over the Southern Slav (or Greater Serbian) Question, with a key focus on violently eradicating its pernicious elements from the map. Yet, as before 1914, destruction was not the only way forward. The Habsburg elite did not entirely forsake discussions about some constructive Southern Slav resolution for the post-war empire. Here, the impetus stemmed especially from the issue of how to treat Serbia after its conquest, but also a realization that the Southern Slav idea was ever present and could not simply be wished away. Many Croatian politicians, for example, continued to clamour for some form of 'trialism', and in 1917–18, Slovene politicians would manage to mobilize a new grassroots movement for Southern Slav unity across the region.[32]

With the Southern Slav Question periodically surfacing, the Habsburg elite was endlessly conflicted on how to proceed. The Hungarian premier, István Tisza, was determined to maintain the empire's dualist structure, only conceding that there could be Southern Slav unity – preferably disunity – under Hungarian auspices. The chief of staff, Conrad von Hötzendorf, meanwhile repeatedly demanded that all South Slavs lands, including an exterminated Serbia, be forced into a new trialist unit: 'I have always stressed that solving the Southern Slav Question is the Monarchy's most important problem and emphasized that Yugoslav unification is an unavoidable fact that will take place, either inside the Monarchy or outside it to its detriment' (May 1915). Most of the elite felt this as an ongoing migraine, a major reason for the war of 1914, and many duly wailed about the constant procrastination. Thus in May 1918, the military governor of Bosnia, Stjepan Sarkotić, noted with frustration in his diary, 'The Southern Slav Question is a Gordian knot which can only be cut by someone with intense determination backed by force (the army).'[33]

In the end, the Alexander who cut this Gordian knot came not from the Habsburg Empire but from a resurgent Serbia in the person of Crown Prince Aleksandar.[34] As the war ended and the Habsburg state disintegrated, it was the Serbian kingdom that rose victorious from the Southern Slav struggle; Croatian and Slovenian politicians duly turned to Serbia and sought security for their lands in a new Yugoslav state. Yet if this implied that the Greater Serbian ideal had triumphed in the Balkans, the hydra-headed nature of the pre-1914 Southern Slav problem would remain to exasperate the new rulers. For those entering Yugoslavia brought with them their own historic interpretations and prejudices, ensuring that the much vaunted ideal of Southern Slav unity would be far easier to proclaim than to practice in interwar Europe. The Yugoslav state experiment would face constant challenges in its cohesion, from its inception in 1918 through to its disintegration in the 1980s.

\* \* \*

There are two red threads running through this book. First is the assassination of Archduke Franz Ferdinand, its causes and its repercussions; the second is the Southern Slav context in all its complexity. Our aim is not to assess how the memory of the Sarajevo assassination was constructed and utilized in different cultural milieux over the past century, for that has been done well by many others.[35] Rather, the purpose is to provide more clarity and context to an allegedly well-worn topic, illustrating both the geopolitical landscape in which 'Sarajevo 1914' occurred and the waves this violent event could create – locally, regionally and internationally. The chapters bring together fresh research and thinking, demonstrating at the same time a wide variety of disciplinary approaches from historians who hail from seven different European countries (including Austria, Serbia, Croatia and Slovenia). In each case, the subject is approached from an expert viewpoint, mirroring the diversity of mindsets that assessed the Southern Slav conundrum of the early twentieth century.

Although the book is structured into three parts, many of the chapters stray beyond a strict delimitation. Those in Part I, 'Tinder and Spark', introduce the controversial personality of Franz Ferdinand, his allies and his plans, and the potential for a South Slav or trialist restructuring of the empire. We then explore various frameworks in which to situate the Southern Slav Question, not least the mentality of the pre-war generation of young men in Bosnia (*Mlada Bosna*). While the Sarajevo assassination is the 'backdrop' to all these chapters, those on the Croatian aristocracy or on the language policy in Bosnia delve into unresearched aspects of everyday life in the Habsburg south, where conservative mindsets struggled to adapt in an era of fast-moving social change. There Habsburg governance could often seem to be either authoritarian or drifting. There individuals often encountered some 'Southern Slav problem', but thoughts of violence or imminent disaster were far from being to the fore in their lives.

Parts II and III of the book assess how and why the spark of Sarajevo became both a regional and an international blaze. Many of the chapters examine 'Sarajevo 1914' as a watershed moment after which attitudes and policies changed abruptly across Europe. But clear too are the many continuities felt by officials or keen observers; the Sarajevo thunderclap both confirmed and accentuated existing prejudices, giving licence to more radical courses of action. For all those – regionally or internationally – who were totally surprised by the sharp turn of events, there were many – not least among the Habsburg elite, the regional nationalists or journalists – who had long predicted some catastrophe arising from the Southern Slav problem. Part II explores the potential for an international disaster as well as the actual repercussions of the Sarajevo assassination. Danilo Šarenac and Lothar Höbelt reassess respectively the mindsets of those with influence in Belgrade and Vienna, with Šarenac digging deep into the complex power struggle of pre-war Serbia. Two further chapters deal directly with the waves spreading out from Sarajevo across the continent, revealing that although the event was shocking for all the European Great Powers, it offered some regimes a singular opportunity to transform the international political map to their liking.

The regional blaze, how it fired up and then continued to smoulder in the Habsburg lands, is the theme addressed in Part III of the book. In case studies from Trieste, Croatia and Bosnia-Herzegovina, three chapters analyse the impact of the Sarajevo murders and the wave of anti-Serb(ian) or South Slav violence it unleashed at an official and grassroots level. After initial chaos in the months after Sarajevo, how the authorities managed that violence was not uniform. It depended on the empire's territorial divisions as well as on a region's proximity to the 'war zone'. Thus, for instance, Croatia managed to retain some rule of law far more effectively than Bosnia or the Austrian lands. The case studies show how 'Greater Serbia' was being brutally eradicated on the ground – through stigmatization, arrests, trials or even executions – while at the same time the Habsburg elite in Vienna was vacillating over any comprehensive Southern Slav solution. Even if some virulent nationalists or Habsburg loyalists felt a sense of catharsis in this anti-Serb campaign, they were dangerously likely to lose control of the radical spiral of events. Not least, a major consequence was that, in the eyes of many Serbs, the Habsburg regime irrevocably lost its legitimacy – already shaky to some South Slavs before 1914 – due to the official and military excesses in the early war years. By 1917, fuelled by famine and war weariness, there was a swathe of popular animosity stirring against Austro-Hungarian rule; many citizens were becoming highly receptive to non-Habsburg (eventually Yugoslav) solutions to the old Southern Slav Question.

In this wartime power struggle, the 'spark' of Franz Ferdinand's murder was soon lost amid the regional and international flames. Yet this spark periodically flickered during the war years and thereafter, since it served variously as a totem of Habsburg power, a justification for the conflict, or – to Austria-Hungary's enemies – a strike against alien tyranny. In Sarajevo itself on 28 June 1917, a huge monument to the murdered couple was finally unveiled. Two years later, however, it was torn down after power had passed to the Yugoslav state; by 1930, with new memories embedded and old loyalties forgotten, it was Gavrilo Princip and his struggle against Habsburg tyranny that was commemorated with a plaque on the site of the assassination.[36] Dagmar Hájková's final chapter offers us a case study in how 'Sarajevo 1914' could be remembered, or the memory of Franz Ferdinand exploited, in those ex-Habsburg lands where he remained a highly contentious figure. For his assassination, unlike any other assassination of the twentieth century, had resulted in mass slaughter and a radical reconfiguration of the European map. Equally, in the post-war world, his personality and his demise usefully embodied the old patronizing and 'militarist' Austria-Hungary, on the ashes of which a completely 'New Europe' was supposedly being built.

This book therefore offers both students and general readers a range of new ways of understanding the 'spark' of the First World War. It also reasserts the importance of the Southern Slav Question as a major cause of that war: something highlighted in the 1920s, but then so often neglected by historians through their overwhelming focus on Germany. A century after the events took place, many dimensions of the Southern Slav labyrinth are only now being uncovered or divested of their nationalist myths. This offers historians many new avenues for collaborative research on the Southern Slav Question, particularly to study the mindsets in Austria-Hungary and the Balkans that did so much to transform the European map of the early twentieth century.

## Notes

1  Josef Redlich, *Schicksalsjahre Österreichs. Die Erinnerungen und Tagebücher Josef Redlichs 1869-1936*, eds Fritz Fellner and Doris A. Corradini, 2 vols (Vienna: Böhlau, 2011), I, 609–10.
2  Martin Kučera, *Rakouský občan Josef Pekař* (Prague: Karolinum, 2005), 81.
3  István Burián, *Báró Burián István naplói 1907-1922* (Burián diary), eds Erzsébet Horváth and Sándor Tenke (Budapest: Ráday, 1999), 105.
4  Zdeněk V. Tobolka, *Můj deník z první světové války*, ed. Martin Kučera (Prague: Karolinum, 2008), 7.
5  Vladimir Dedijer, *The Road to Sarajevo* (London: Macgibbon & Kee, 1967), 17.
6  A still useful early study is R. W. Seton-Watson, *Sarajevo: A Study in the Origins of the Great War* (London: Hutchinson, 1925). For a recent survey that plays with the myths and memory of the past century, see Paul Miller, '"The First Shots of the First World War": The Sarajevo Assassination in History and Memory', *Central Europe* 14:2 (2016): 141–56.
7  Ottokar Czernin, *Im Weltkriege* (Berlin and Vienna: Ullstein, 1919), 63.
8  Christopher Clark, *The Sleepwalkers: How Europe Went to War in 1914* (London: Allen Lane, 2012), 452. For a recent example of a very pro-Serbian stance, see John Zametica, *Folly and Malice: The Habsburg Empire, the Balkans and the Start of World War One* (London: Shepheard-Walwyn, 2017); for a critical review of this, see Mark Cornwall, 'Who Caused the War: A Pro-Serbian Polemic', *Times Literary Supplement*, 6002 (April 2018), 27.
9  See Maria Todorova, *Imagining the Balkans* (Oxford: Oxford University Press, 1996); and for a lively first-hand account, stereotypically derogatory: M. Edith Durham, *Twenty Years of Balkan Tangle* (London: Allen and Unwin, 1920).
10 Holly Case, *The Age of Questions* (Princeton and Oxford: Princeton University Press, 2018). Case does not analyse the Southern Slav Question per se, but her theories are an intriguing commentary on that subject as one of the 'burning questions' of the day.
11 30 May 1914: quoted in Mirjana Gross, 'Hrvatska politika velikoaustrijskog kruga oko prijestolonasljenika Franje Ferdinanda', *Časopis za suvremenu povijest* 2/2 (1970), 68–9.
12 József Szterényi, *Régmult idők emlékei. Politikai feljegyzések* (Budapest: Pesti könyvnyomda részvénytársaság, 1925), 179.

13 For this trend, see, for example, Ian D. Armour, *Apple of Discord: The 'Hungarian Factor' in Austro-Serbian Relations, 1867-1881* (West Lafayette: Purdue University Press, 2014).

14 Still useful for Serbian policy at this crucial turning point is Wayne Vucinich, *Serbia between East and West: The Events of 1903-1908* (Stanford: Stanford University Press, 1954). See also the study in Serbian of the last Obrenović king: Suzana Rajić, *Aleksandar Obrenović. Vladar na prelazu vekova. Sukobljeni svetovi* (Belgrade: SKZ, 2014). And for the vibrant culture in pre-war Serbia, see for instance Jelena Milojkovic-Djuric, *Tradition and Avant-Garde: Literature and Art in Serbian Culture 1900-1918* (New York: Columbia University Press, 1988).

15 F. R. Bridge, *The Habsburg Monarchy among the Great Powers, 1815-1918* (New York: Berg, 1990), 92: the warning of Austrian chancellor Beust.

16 For Russia's policy in the Balkans, see the work of Dominic Lieven: most recently, *Towards the Flame: Empire, War and the End of Tsarist Russia* (London: Penguin, 2015).

17 An incisive contemporary commentary on Austria-Hungary's Southern Slav policy is that of one German-Austrian politician who regularly visited the region: Joseph M. Baernreither, *Fragmente eines politischen Tagebuches. Die südslawische Frage und Österreich-Ungarn vor dem Weltkrieg* (Berlin: Verlag für Kulturpolitik, 1928).

18 The so-called Compromise of 1867 was an agreement between the monarch and Hungary, conceding to the latter substantial autonomy with its own government and parliament in Budapest. The rest of the empire – not officially termed 'Austria' until 1915 – then had to organize its own parliament and government in Vienna.

19 See Edin Hajdarpasic, *Whose Bosnia? Nationalism and Political Imagination in the Balkans, 1840-1914* (Ithaca, NY: Cornell University Press, 2015); Robin Okey, *Taming Balkan Nationalism: The Habsburg 'Civilizing Mission' in Bosnia, 1878-1914* (Oxford: Oxford University Press, 2007).

20 For the variety of approaches that came together in the new Yugoslav state after 1918, see Ivo Banac, *The National Question in Yugoslavia: Origins, History, Politics* (Ithaca and London: Cornell University Press, 1984).

21 See Rene Lovrenčić, *Geneza politike 'novog kursa' u Hrvatskoj* (Zagreb: Institut za hrvatsku povijest, 1972).

22 R. W. Seton-Watson, *The Southern Slav Question and the Habsburg Monarchy* (London: Constable, 1911), 336, 343.

23 Ibid., 343. The book was dedicated to the Austrian statesman who had the 'genius and courage' to achieve this.

24 Hugh and Christopher Seton-Watson, *The Making of a New Europe: R.W. Seton-Watson and the Last Years of Austria-Hungary* (London: Methuen, 1981), 101.

25 Baernreither, *Fragmente*, 275: his observations in October 1913.

26 Cf. the recent exaggerated claims in John Deak and Jonathan E. Gumz, 'How to Break a State: The Habsburg Monarchy's Internal War, 1914-1918', *American Historical Review*, 122/4 (October 2017): 1118, 1125.

27 R. W. Seton-Watson, J. Dover Wilson, Alfred E. Zimmern and Arthur Greenwood, *The War and Democracy* (London: Macmillan, 1914), 158, 255ff.
28 Ibid., 159. Also Clark, *The Sleepwalkers,* 379–80.
29 See Austria-Hungary's justification for war as set out in 'The Austro-Hungarian Red Book', in *Collected Diplomatic Documents Relating to the Outbreak of the European War* (London: H.M.S.O, 1915), 443–7; and for the Serbian government's own stance in July 1914, see Mark Cornwall, 'Serbia', in Keith Wilson (ed.), *Decisions for War, 1914* (London: UCL Press, 1995), 55–96.
30 The best study is Jonathan E. Gumz, *The Resurrection and Collapse of Empire in Habsburg Serbia, 1914-1918* (Cambridge: Cambridge University Press, 2009).
31 Notably the Banjaluka trial of 1915–16 that arraigned 156 Bosnian Serb intellectuals. See the excellent essays in *Veleizdajnički proces u Banjaluci. Zbornik radova s Medjunarodnog naučnog skupa 'Veleizdajnički proces u Banjaluci 1915–16'*, ed. Galib Šljivo (Banjaluka: Institut za historiju, 1987).
32 See Mark Cornwall, 'The Great War and the Yugoslav Grassroots: Popular Mobilization in the Habsburg Monarchy, 1914-1918', in Dejan Djokić and James Ker-Lindsay (eds), *New Perspectives on Yugoslavia* (London and New York: Routledge, 2011), 32–42.
33 Mark Cornwall, 'The Habsburg Elite and the Southern Slav Question 1914-1918', in Lothar Höbelt and T. G. Otte (eds), *A Living Anachronism? European Diplomacy and the Habsburg Monarchy* (Vienna: Böhlau, 2010), 239–70. Quotations: 253, 265.
34 As Holly Case has noted, the 'Gordian knot' regularly appeared as a metaphor for intractable questions at this time: Case, *The Age of Questions,* 172.
35 Most recently, the forty varied essays in Vahidin Preljević and Clemens Ruther (eds), *Sarajevski dugi picnji 1914. Događaj – narativ – pamćenje* (Zenica: Vrijeme, 2015).
36 See Selma Harrington, 'Djevojka Bosna, carević i Baš-Čelik. Kako smo se sjećali Sarajevsko atentata', in ibid., 567–84.

# PART I
# Tinder and spark

## CHAPTER 2

# Franz Ferdinand
# Power and image

*Alma Hannig*

One of the most frequently quoted literary works about the day of the assassination of the Austro-Hungarian heir to the throne, Franz Ferdinand, is the autobiography of Stefan Zweig. The famous Viennese author was spending some days in Baden near Vienna when he heard about the assassination that, in his words, 'aroused no profound sympathy'.[1] Almost thirty years later, Zweig recalled the reaction of people on the streets:

> To be honest, there was no particular shock or dismay to be seen on their faces, for the heir apparent was not at all well-liked. ... Two hours later signs of genuine mourning were no longer to be seen. The throngs laughed and chattered and, as the evening advanced, music was resumed at public resorts. There were many on that day in Austria who secretly sighed with relief that this heir of the aged emperor had been removed in favour of the much more beloved young Archduke Karl.[2]

This description of the atmosphere became part of general cultural memory about the outbreak of the Great War, at least in the German-speaking world. Despite the fact that Zweig wrote these lines in 1940 during his years of exile without 'any aids to his memory' (no notes or documents),[3] and although he idealized the olden times which naturally seemed 'golden' compared to the Nazi regime, most historians treat *The World of Yesterday* as akin to a scientific treatise or at least as one of the most trustworthy and authentic sources for late imperial Austria.

Zweig's negative portrait of the 'man with his bulldog neck and his cold, staring eyes' has, together with other literary works, shaped the image of Franz Ferdinand until the present day: 'Franz Ferdinand lacked everything that counts for real popularity in Austria; amiability, personal charm and easygoingness. ... He was never seen to smile, and no photography showed him relaxed. He had no sense for music, and no sense of humour, and his wife was equally unfriendly.'[4] As with most of the young authors of the pre-war period, Zweig did not like the conservative, bigoted archduke and took a critical stance. There is nothing unusual about modern literati lacking sympathy for the ruling class and vice versa, but it is unusual that many historians have simply believed Zweig's assertion that his opinion was 'shared by the entire nation'.[5] In reality, most people rarely share the opinion of modern authors. Inversely, no one would treat Franz Ferdinand's statements about modern literature or the arts as the prevalent opinion of the upper classes in Austria-Hungary. A review of the newspaper articles and private sources of many contemporaries after the assassination reveals that Zweig's description was not only very subjective but in some points completely false.[6]

The leading liberal newspaper in Vienna, the *Neue Freie Presse*, described the situation quite differently:

> No proclamation, but a kind of paralysis. With their eyes wide open the people stand there, in groups of ten or twenty bend over the paper sheets and murmur a dull horrific sound. ... Vienna is silent. No theatre opens its gates, the music from the summer gardens is nowhere to be heard, life has been frozen and turned into muffled sorrow.[7]

Despite their poor relations with the archduke, the *Neue Freie Presse* as well as the socialist *Arbeiter-Zeitung* asserted in posthumous comments that Franz Ferdinand was not a 'replaceable archduke of mean value', but a 'source of energy', so his death buried all hopes for the future.[8] The Austro-Hungarian foreign minister Leopold von Berchtold noted similarly in his diary: 'He was the compass, towards which everyone devoted to old Austria and confident about the Habsburg Monarchy's dignified future was already beginning to orientate.'[9] Numerous other examples from the press and private documents attest that many people from across the empire were desperate after the death of Franz Ferdinand, since for them he symbolized their hopes for reform and a better future for the multinational state.[10] When he was murdered, he was not only a representative of the main pillar of the Monarchy, the House of Habsburg, but also officially the second figure of power in the state.

Other historians have explored Franz Ferdinand's political ideas, his intervention in cultural and educational issues, or his plans for reform of the state structure.[11] The purpose of this chapter is to detail how the heir apparent consolidated his position by using a variety of personal networks to guarantee a smooth transition after the death of Franz Joseph. These networks and their way of operating are crucial, for they raise the question of how successful and influential the archduke was in promoting to the public his vision for politics and the military. We will also be asking whether or not his contemporaries realized his power. What was his public image during his own lifetime? Obviously, there was a discrepancy between modern men of letters, ruling classes and public opinion. My objective is not only to point out these differences but also to explain why they existed and still exist even in the literature of today.

## Belvedere – a parallel government?

Belvedere, the official seat of the Habsburg heir to the throne in Vienna, was often used as a synonym for the powerful military chancellery of Franz Ferdinand. It was called *Nebenregierung* (parallel or shadow government) or *Gegenregierung* (counter-government) in opposition to Emperor Franz Joseph and his court at Schönbrunn. For some contemporaries Belvedere was a symbol for the unknown, negatively characterized heir apparent and his erratic policy that many feared. For others it epitomized the change, reforms and plans through which the Monarchy would be remodelled in order to secure its survival in an era of nationalism and national states. According to the veteran bank director Rudolf Sieghart, all of this generated 'cross-eyed' politicians and soldiers who tried to meet the expectations of both the emperor and his successor. Franz Joseph personified the present and Franz Ferdinand the future, so most careers were reliant on both of them.[12] Or as the German historian Günther Kronenbitter has noted, Franz Ferdinand's influence was based on the expectations that people connected with him.[13] Kronenbitter as well as the Austrian historian Ludwig Jedlicka have underlined another function of the Belvedere, namely as a 'watchdog': from 1906 the archduke gained insight into all political and military documents and intervened with the emperor when decisions appeared to be unreasonable.[14] There was of course no legal basis for this, but Schönbrunn tolerated it.

But how and when did the Belvedere attain so much power? The military chancellery was situated in the Lower Belvedere, whereas Franz Ferdinand stayed at the Upper Belvedere when he resided in Vienna.[15] The two magnificent palaces had been built in the eighteenth century as the summer residence of one of the most important generals, Prince Eugen of Savoy. Although he had become heir apparent after the death of Crown Prince Rudolf in 1889, Franz Ferdinand was recognized as such by official bodies only in 1898, when the emperor put him at the 'disposal of the supreme command'. Now he was to gain insight into military affairs, taking part in official consultations and receiving information about all important activities from the military ministries (Austrian, Hungarian and the Common War Ministry). Finally, an aide-de-camp was assigned to him. Until then he had mainly performed representative functions, receiving an education in (constitutional) law and completing the military training that enabled him to move up the military career ladder. Fifteen years later, in 1913, he became inspector general of the armed forces, a triumph that marked the zenith of his career. The old emperor, appreciating his nephew's military knowledge and experience, increasingly gave him a free hand to form and reform the Austro-Hungarian army.[16] As long as Emperor Franz Joseph lived, Franz Ferdinand could not hold any higher office (Figure 2.1).

In contrast to the military, there was no basis for a political engagement by the heir, and for many years the emperor did not tolerate Franz Ferdinand's attempts at political interference. He expected him to follow the instructions concerning official and ceremonial duties and represent the monarch's views in public. Several times the heir apparent acted differently and provoked public antagonism, notably when he expressed his desire for a more rigorous treatment of Hungary as well as his commitment to the Catholic School Association. By contrast, the emperor expected strict neutrality and equal treatment for all nationalities and religions in the Monarchy.[17]

**FIGURE 2.1** *'Military conference chaired by Emperor Franz Joseph', by Felician von Myrbach-Reinfeld (1908), with Franz Ferdinand sitting to the right of the emperor (Austrian National Library, Vienna).*

Franz Ferdinand's first successful foray in political and military policy was connected to personnel policy. In 1906, several important posts became occupied by his favourites. Alois von Aehrenthal, the former ambassador to St Petersburg, became foreign minister and Conrad von Hötzendorf, the archduke's most highly valued military officer, was appointed as chief of the general staff (CGS). In anticipation of military reforms, Franz Ferdinand also enforced the appointment of General Franz von Schönaich as minister of war. And his most important political adviser and intimate Max Wladimir von Beck became Austrian prime minister, a concession probably by the emperor to his nephew. Over time, Franz Ferdinand became politically active, placing increasing numbers of his followers and favourites in key positions. When a post was vacant in politics, diplomacy, culture or the military, he was asked his opinion, and more than once he blocked the appointment of unwelcome individuals or forced their resignation.[18] Thanks to some clever networking, the last two years of his life saw him at his zenith.

The rise of Franz Ferdinand's military chancellery began in 1905–6, when Major Alexander Brosch von Aarenau became his aide-de-camp and chief of his chancellery. This was the man who played the key role in the archduke's advancement and had the greatest influence upon him. Franz Ferdinand appreciated Brosch's skills: somebody who was clever, well educated, reliable, ambitious and assertive. Brosch in turn tried to arbitrate between Franz Joseph and his nephew and composed all the memoranda promoting the latter's ideas.[19] Brosch also gave audiences, as Franz Ferdinand hated them.[20] All information that the archduke received was 'filtered' by the chief of his chancellery. Shortly after his appointment, Brosch engaged competent consultants from different professions and nationalities for various tasks. Some of them worked on a reform programme for the Belvedere while others were asked for their specialized knowledge in foreign or economic affairs, domestic or regional policy. They were politicians, experts in constitutional and international law, journalists, military officials as well as representatives of different nationalities. They hoped for key positions under Emperor Franz II and at least partly, they shared the archduke's agenda.

## The archduke's network: Advisers and disciples

Who then were the most important of these advisers, experts and disciples who worked either directly with the heir apparent or via the military chancellery?[21] One of the most influential was Franz Conrad von Hötzendorf who became his main consultant and assistant in expanding and modernizing the Austro-Hungarian army, both in terms of personnel and technical matters.[22] The archduke had noticed Conrad's talent during military inspections and manoeuvres, and continued to follow his career progression with great interest. He placed high hopes in Conrad when recommending him as CGS; the emperor approved, and the official appointment took place in November 1906. Conrad and Franz Ferdinand largely shared the same vision: a strong common army and the concept of a united state (*Gesamtstaatsgedanke*). Yet if Conrad's main enthusiasm was as a fellow campaigner for the reforms and the development of strategies, in his function as CGS he still pursued his own interests, sometimes contradicting the plans of politicians or the navy. Besides, his political engagement often compromised his impartiality (Figure 2.2).[23]

**FIGURE 2.2** *'Archduke Franz Ferdinand and Conrad von Hötzendorf on manoeuvres at the Dukla Pass', 1911 (Austrian National Library, Vienna).*

Indeed, Conrad was probably one of the most aggressive militarists of the era, endlessly demanding a war against Serbia and Italy.[24] Despite some inconsistencies, the archduke adhered to the general, and although Conrad was deposed at the instigation of Foreign Minister Aehrenthal in 1911, Franz Ferdinand enforced his reappointment at a critical point in the First Balkan War. Later, however, the archduke had to restrain Conrad and warned the Ballhausplatz (foreign ministry) about his warmongering against Serbia and Italy. Conrad was of course not the Belvedere's only military expert. In his daily business, the archduke consulted two others: his chief of the chancellery Brosch and, from December 1911, Brosch's successor Carl von Bardolff. In addition to securing most of his information on foreign policy from the Ballhausplatz, he also appreciated the reports of military attachés, which sometimes differed from those of the empire's ambassadors abroad. Generally, he put more trust in the competence and reliability of military men than in diplomats and wished to appoint more military attachés as ambassadors.[25]

On all political and constitutional questions, Franz Ferdinand relied for many years on the expertise of Max Wladimir von Beck, his former teacher in constitutional and international law. Beck had been taken into his favour after helping in 1900 to find a compromise with the emperor and a legal solution for his marriage to Sophie Chotek, a woman below his social station. From that point Beck wrote and reported on all debatable questions, gave Franz Ferdinand advice and prepared him for important audiences with the emperor. Beck also sketched out a kind of future political programme in memoranda that were presented to Franz Joseph.[26] Yet when Beck became Austrian prime minister, the former teacher suddenly fell into disgrace with his imperial student. Having expected Beck to become the Belvedere's own prime minister, Franz Ferdinand failed to appreciate Beck's willingness to work under Franz Joseph. Even worse, Beck now showed himself loyal to the monarch: in 1906, he not only supported franchise reform in Austria but tried to find a compromise with Hungary by combining the military with the economic agenda. All this was contrary to what Franz Ferdinand had expected. For that reason, he severed his ties and intervened successfully to have Beck dismissed in November 1908.[27]

In the years after Beck, Franz Ferdinand was advised by several experts on constitutional law and domestic policy, including among Austrian university professors, Heinrich Lammasch, who would later become the last Austrian prime minister.[28] Two constitutional law experts, Gustav Turba and Edmund Bernatzik, as well as Johann Eichhoff, head of department at the Ministry of the Interior, were often consulted and worked on the programme for state reform. In economic and financial issues the Belvedere also relied on acknowledged experts: Alexander von Spitzmüller, governor general of the *Kreditanstalt* (credit bank) and later Austria-Hungary's last common finance minister, and Richard Riedl, head of department at the Ministry of Trade.

A similar fate to Beck was suffered by the energetic Habsburg foreign minister Alois von Aehrenthal (1906–12). Although he was Franz Ferdinand's favourite and shared his notion of stronger cooperation with Russia, their relationship deteriorated.[29] One reason was Aehrenthal's autonomous and resolute actions without consulting or even informing the archduke, for example, during the annexation of Bosnia-Herzegovina in 1908; later the conflicts intensified when Aehrenthal increasingly criticized Conrad and demanded his dismissal. By contrast, Aehrenthal's successor, Count Leopold Berchtold, was able to establish and keep good relations with the heir apparent until the end. Berchtold sent him copies of important records, and experts and officials were sometimes even dispatched from the Ballhausplatz to Franz Ferdinand's residences to report on recent developments. Thereby, the archduke secured a very high level of intelligence and benefited from the expertise of informed diplomats. Berchtold also involved the Belvedere in the decision-making process, not least because of similar views on foreign policy.

In the foreign arena, the most important adviser, however, was the Bohemian count Ottokar Czernin, who in the critical period after the Second Balkan War in 1913 became Habsburg envoy to Romania.[30] Franz Ferdinand expected this confidant to find ways to improve and strengthen ties between Romania and Austria-Hungary but this proved impossible – Czernin failed. He had belonged to the Belvedere circle since 1905, and his memoranda on foreign and personnel policy dated back to 1908. When he claimed that the prerequisite for progress was a Hungarian-Romanian agreement and talks between the archduke and the Hungarian prime minister István Tisza, however, Czernin simply angered the Magyarophobe heir apparent. It resulted, according to Robert A. Kann, in a sharp reduction of Czernin's influence on the eve of Sarajevo.[31]

Perhaps surprisingly, Franz Ferdinand did realize rather early on the significance of public opinion for a constitutional monarchy. Brosch supplied him daily with reviews of the international press to be carefully read and annotated. For the archduke understood the necessity of good connections to the press for the successful public promotion of his ideas. Brosch therefore acquired several journalists as Belvedere collaborators in political campaigns. The most important was Friedrich Funder, chief editor of the *Reichspost* (newspaper of the Christian Social Party), which gradually became the Belvedere's main organ. Another three influential journalists who supported the archduke's ideas and cooperated closely were Leopold von Chlumecky (*Österreichische Rundschau*), Carl M. Danzer (*Armee-Zeitung*) and Theodor von Sosnosky (political writer and historian). Although all of them belonged to conservative and military-related groups, with their help the archduke was able to disseminate his ideas to the public. It was, however, a mixed success. Brosch failed in his attempt to buy up some newspapers, for example, the liberal *Zeit*, or to create a new one through which to transmit the Belvedere's agenda.[32] There is also no proof that the chancellery ever tried to establish positive relations with the Hungarian press, for it was almost overwhelmingly hostile towards the heir apparent.[33]

Yet another important group of disseminators were the numerous representatives of different nationalities. This was doubtless the largest and most diversified group in the Belvedere circle. Franz Ferdinand appreciated both the enormous power of the nationalist movements and their potentially dangerous effect on a multinational state such as Austria-Hungary. Although most of his consultants were German Austrians, he secured advisers from different regions of the Monarchy, men who were usually members of the intellectual elite. These included Josip Frank and Pavao Rauch, both notorious political figures in Croatia. Then there was Ivan Žolger, a Slovene expert on constitutional law – and as Slovak representatives, Milan Hodža and Cornel Stodola. For the Belvedere, Croats, Slovenes and Slovaks were deemed the most loyal nationalities, for supposedly their Catholic faith and culture required protection from Hungarian aggression. In the Croats, Franz Ferdinand particularly saw something of a counterbalance to the 'treacherous' Serbs, presuming that a Croatian kingdom could act as a counter-attraction for the Monarchy's South Slavs and an alternative to the Serbian kingdom.[34] In the Belvedere circle, there were also two notable Romanian politicians, Alexandru Vaida-Voevod and Iuliu Maniu, as well as the Romanian clergyman Miron Cristea and the university professor Aurel Popovici (also a Hungarian MP and author of the famous book *United States of Greater Austria*). Lastly, there was the leader of the Pan-Germans, Professor Paul Samassa. Although we require more research on the relative significance of these individuals, they offered the Belvedere some valuable, if skewed, insights into different regions of the Monarchy.

Indeed, the archduke was genuinely interested in how the national delegates viewed his future reforms as well as their analysis of the contemporary political situation. He also expected them to promote his politics among their own ethnic groups. Yet we might ask why they would cooperate with the Belvedere at all. It was well known that the heir apparent planned to reform the Monarchy, yet it remains unclear whether he wished to transform it into a federal, trialistic or centralistic state. What is fairly certain is that he intended to introduce equal rights for all nationalities. And this was exactly what most of the national advisers hoped for, since they already had their own programmes for imperial reform.[35] Franz Ferdinand's main purpose, however, in proposing equal rights was to break Magyar hegemony in the kingdom of Hungary. From all that we know about him, his impetus was not the self-determination of peoples but a monarchical, autocratic system with federal, supranational structures and a powerful position for the monarch – comparable to the Holy Roman Empire of the German Nation.[36] For the representatives of the nationalities, who aspired to equality as well as political participation, the archduke was simply the only one who seemed to embody their own vision.

Despite his antipathy towards the Magyar ruling gentry, the archduke still did acquire some Hungarian consultants. In this regard the most important were József Kristóffy, the former Hungarian minister of the interior, and

Bishop József Lányi, the heir's confessor and teacher of the Magyar language. But apart from Slovaks and Romanians, the other main advisers from Hungary were, interestingly, German politicians: Edmund Steinacker, leader of the German Hungarian People's Party and an expert in nationalities issues and constitutional law; and Rudolf Brandsch and Georg Linder, who were both deputies in the Hungarian parliament. Certainly it was a mistake that Franz Ferdinand did not consult more influential Magyars and – even more astonishing – that he failed to involve any Polish, Italian, Czech, Serb or Bosnian advisers in his long-term reform plans.[37] His personal animosity towards Magyars, Poles, Italians, Serbs or Jews was proverbial, but one might still expect from a future emperor some neutrality of treatment, or at least an attempt to establish contacts and networks in certain politically sensitive areas.

With Austrian political parties Franz Ferdinand also failed to establish good relations. Putting this positively, he manoeuvred and played them off against each other, using different parties as a political weapon when trying to enforce his ideas or prevent some developments in the Austrian Reichsrat (the parliament). Often he acted like an opposition politician, promising everything in order to secure support for his ideas without any need to keep the promise. Certainly, he respected Karl Lueger, the leader of the Christian Social Party, and his general political views were largely reflected in that party. But at times he feared its social component – interpreting it as socialist – and therefore, when it was opportune, he was prepared to work with other parties against the Christian Socials.[38] This lack of continuous cooperation with any influential political party resulted in him having a marginal influence on Austrian domestic affairs. And needless to say, despite his group of Hungarian advisers, his influence on Hungarian domestic affairs was even more limited. His conduct in this question was the logical consequence of his general disdain for parliaments, democracy and universal male suffrage.

Since the Catholic Church and the aristocracy were always two of the strongest pillars of the Habsburg dynasty, it is unsurprising that the heir apparent also tried to network closely with them. The Catholic Church and Franz Ferdinand could always rely on each other, though without becoming instruments of the other party. His contacts with the Vatican were very good, but he never paid an official visit there; his most reliable agent in Rome was the director of the Austrian Institute, Ludwig Pastor, a historian and theologian.[39] As for his network of aristocratic and diplomatic circles, most were recruited from the Bohemian feudal aristocracy. Some were his closest friends, intimates and consultants: Heinrich Clam-Martinic, who advised on domestic policy and later became a wartime Austrian prime minister; Vinzenz Latour, who was an expert on military issues; Karl Schwarzenberg, Ernst Silva-Tarouca and Jaroslav Thun, with whom he discussed politics in general and the Bohemian question in particular; and Franz Thun, who was a former governor of Bohemia and in 1896 the head of his court household – in 1914 he was the executor of the archduke's will.[40] Being the closest friends of Franz Ferdinand and Sophie, Jaroslav Thun and his wife (Sophie's sister) became the guardians of their children after the Sarajevo assassinations.

Among aristocratic diplomats, we have already mentioned Ottokar Czernin who advised not only on foreign affairs but also on domestic and personnel policy, as well as the foreign ministers Aehrenthal and Berchtold. Konrad and Gottfried Hohenlohe as representatives of the German-Austrian aristocracy were close favourites too. Gottfried was one of Franz Ferdinand's early intimates as was Clam-Martinic, since both had accompanied him in 1891 on his first official visit to Russia. Later, Gottfried Hohenlohe was designated the ambassador to Berlin and eventually to St Petersburg, his career benefiting enormously from the archduke's support. His appointment to Berlin came in April 1914, and he only took office after the Sarajevo assassinations; he stayed there until the end of the war, becoming an important mediator between the German and Austro-Hungarian governments.[41] Gottfried's brother Konrad advanced in turn to be *Obersthofmeister* (head of the court household) under the young Emperor Karl.

Franz Ferdinand and his military chancellery had exact plans for the distribution of posts among his intimates and advisers upon his accession, although some modifications were conceivable if somebody fell in disgrace.[42] Among the most frequently mentioned was Brosch as imperial chancellor, a position to be created after the empire's reform. Czernin was designated as foreign minister; Kristóffy and Clam-Martinic for the posts respectively of Hungarian and Austrian prime ministers; Spitzmüller as the common minister of finance. While most of these men were indeed later appointed by Emperor Karl, some of the national advisers would become significant politicians or diplomats after 1918 in the successor states of the Habsburg Monarchy.[43]

Due to these networks we can conclude that Franz Ferdinand before his death was becoming an extremely well-informed man. The members of the Belvedere circle sent him elaborate memoranda on all points of interest or they reported in private audiences. With their support, he was well prepared for any kind of discussions with the emperor, representatives of the government or the military. On the one hand he secured relevant intelligence from his advisers, and on the other he used them to propagate his ideas more widely. During his lifetime, Franz Joseph also conceded to him a larger scope in military and personnel decisions and even some say in foreign policy. Thereby, with enormous influence over key posts in the military, politics and diplomacy, it became almost impossible to appoint a diplomat or high-ranking politician without his approval.

Why then did Franz Joseph give such wide latitude to his nephew?[44] Due to his old age, the emperor had to delegate some tasks for practical reasons. But Franz Joseph also began to appreciate Franz Ferdinand's military expertise and increasingly tolerated his interferences in foreign policy and official appointments, not least because of the nephew's monarchical networks that offered some confident perspective for the future. His friendship with the German emperor Wilhelm II became the strongest pillar of Franz Ferdinand's position among the power structures of the Habsburg Empire. This close relationship with one of the most powerful individuals in Europe defined Franz Ferdinand's image both in and outside Austria-Hungary. Their exchange of private and official visits, their common enthusiasm for the navy and hunting as well as similar ideas on autocratic rule and the shaping of foreign policy, provided a sound basis for good cooperation. They often discussed foreign affairs where they largely shared the same opinions for instance on Bulgaria, Romania, Great Britain, France and, to some extent, even Serbia.[45]

In the last years before the war, as relations with Wilhelm became closer, Franz Ferdinand was taken much more seriously by Franz Joseph and influential Austro-Hungarian political groups. For example, in late 1912 Franz Joseph let the archduke take the first steps towards preparation of a war against Serbia, and was impressed by the quick agreement between Franz Ferdinand and the Kaiser that guaranteed German support in the case of Russian involvement. The plan, however, failed when the Berlin civilian government opposed any German involvement in the Balkan Wars. The archduke understood probably better than anyone else that for definite German support the approval of Germany's Kaiser, its government and its military was necessary. As this was almost impossible to achieve over the conflict-riddled Balkans, he finally realized that any involvement in the Balkan Wars might lead to isolation and lack of German support in a possible conflict with Russia. From that point he exclusively supported Berchtold's policy of keeping the peace.[46] Yet an important point of disagreement was Wilhelm's attitude towards Russia. The Kaiser, fearing Russian Panslavism and imperialism, believed that a conflict between Teutons and Slavs was inevitable, whereas Franz Ferdinand hoped to restore the traditional alliance of the three most conservative monarchies in Europe.

There were a few situations where the Kaiser gave unsolicited advice to Franz Ferdinand over domestic political or nationality issues. The most controversial subject was Hungary. Wilhelm revealed an understanding and even sympathy for leading Hungarian politicians; notably he appreciated Prime Minister István Tisza whom Franz Ferdinand treated as his greatest foe. As it became obvious that Tisza was very influential in foreign affairs, Franz Ferdinand asked the Kaiser for help, counting on his friendship and loyalty, and hoping that Wilhelm's authority might help him tame the Magyar. This was one of the topics that the two discussed during their last conversation, only a fortnight before Sarajevo.[47] Moreover, over time, Franz Ferdinand increasingly adopted Germany's Balkan policy, contradicting and even undermining the Ballhausplatz plans for new political constellations such as closer cooperation with Bulgaria.[48]

Apart from Wilhelm II, the archduke felt closest to the Romanian king Carol, who was also a German prince (Hohenzollern-Sigmaringen). In 1909, the warm reception of Franz Ferdinand's wife Sophie during her first official visit to Romania, when Carol ignored traditional protocol that would have marginalized her, built an excellent basis for cordial relations. The loyalty and integrity of King Carol as well as common political interests regarding Bulgaria or the situation of the Romanian minority in Hungary strengthened their cooperation.[49] By contrast, the Bulgarian Tsar Ferdinand, despite his German origin (Saxony-Coburg), was persona non grata. The archduke as well as the Kaiser distrusted and detested him, both politically and privately. They were both convinced that Ferdinand would cooperate with Russia – which in fact did not happen in contrast to Carol's later apostasy.

With other Balkan monarchs, Franz Ferdinand maintained no real relationship, mistrusting them or viewing them as insignificant. And in view of his well-known Italophobia, it is not surprising that he belittled the Italian king, a monarch who treated the pope as a prisoner and had even married a Montenegrin princess. France, as the only republic among the Great Powers and because of its secularity, seemed to be the least interesting state for any kind of cooperation. However, as F. R. Bridge's chapter shows us, in 1913 there was an important approach towards the British king George V. While sceptical about England for many years, Franz Ferdinand changed his opinion after he and Sophie paid two visits to the British court. Conversely, the British public as well as the royal family took a largely positive view of the princely couple from the Danube Monarchy.[50] A further improvement of relations was anticipated from a reciprocal British royal visit, planned for autumn 1914 to the archduke's castle in Konopiště near Prague.

Yet perhaps the most curious and inconsequential relationship was with the Russian Tsar. Franz Ferdinand and Nicholas II had met several times in their earlier years. Although the former was keen on renewing the Three Emperors' Alliance of the 1880s, he did not cultivate a personal relationship with Nicholas, despite the fact that they had some similar characteristics. For instance, they both preferred to spend time with their families or hunting than with state affairs or official duties. In 1903, they met for the last time, after which neither of them planned a visit to the opposite imperial capital. This is astonishing in view of the frictions developing between the two empires in the context of the annexation crisis of 1908–9. Franz Ferdinand criticized Aehrenthal's decision to annex Bosnia-Herzegovina, fearing correctly that this would result in further alienation between Austria-Hungary and Russia. However, he at least tried to send his favourites as ambassadors and attachés to St Petersburg in the hope that they would implement his pro-Russian policy.[51]

Summing up the archduke's networks, we can conclude that since he was only an heir apparent he managed to build up a remarkably strong national and international power base within a few years. Brosch transformed the chancellery into a think tank and vibrant instrument of power, which within a very short time gained increasing influence in political, military and even cultural spheres. Franz Joseph could hardly ignore it, and with increasing age, he seemed willing to delegate more tasks and responsibilities to his nephew. Thus, Heinrich von Tschirschky, the German ambassador in Vienna, could conclude after the Sarajevo assassination: 'The hand of the Archduke was noticeable everywhere, not only in the army and navy, but in every ministry, in every provincial government and in the missions abroad.'[52]

Yet Franz Ferdinand in his networking also made cardinal mistakes, characteristic not only in his private relations but also in the vision he held for his reign. Although important aristocratic and royal, military and political, clerical and journalistic groups and individuals belonged to the Belvedere circle, supporting and propagating his ideas, he neglected to integrate his opponents or at least interact with them in order to manage that smooth transition which might incorporate his reform programme. Furthermore, he hardly had any influence on domestic issues in Austria or Hungary. His animosity towards different nationalities and political groups as well as some foreign countries and their heads of state was not only irrational but dangerous and blinkered. This included his blatant refusal to give an audience to Hungarian prime ministers, as well as suspecting almost the complete Magyar ruling elite of disloyalty and treason. The same applied to the Poles, Czechs, Serbs and Italians, despite the fact that major reforms could hardly be implemented against the will of the larger nationalities.

Implementing equal rights for smaller nationalities might have reduced the power of the larger national elites, but it could not reverse the circumstances completely. At the same time, it might have caused perilous instability bordering on revolution in such a conservative Monarchy, or provoked aggression from states such as Serbia, Romania and Italy, each of whom had irredentist aspirations on Austro-Hungarian territory.[53] Like many of the Habsburg elite, Franz Ferdinand obviously failed to recognize the signs of the times; he refused to cooperate with broader social and political circles, relying instead on the old feudal structures and a strong army. It remains open to question whether this kind of autocratic rule, which implied a reduction of democratic and constitutional rights, could have been implemented, or whether it could have prevented a catastrophic war and the Monarchy's disintegration.

## Franz Ferdinand – a 'Sphinx'?[54]

When in 1913 Franz Ferdinand celebrated his fiftieth birthday, most newspapers in Austria published articles or even special editions about his private life as well as his activities in political, military and cultural affairs. It is striking that one of 'his' journalists, Carl M. Danzer, described him as follows: 'He is regarded as the big mystery, the enigmatic X, which lets the mathematical equation of the European Great Powers appear insoluble.'[55] By 1913 the archduke had been heir to the throne for almost a quarter of a century. How was it possible that to the public and many newspapers, he was still a 'big mystery'?[56] Less surprising are Sigmund Freud's words in 1898 that Franz Ferdinand 'probably did not have a profile'.[57] At that time, only those who had direct contact to the archduke could have described him more precisely. For example, Bernhard von Bülow, Germany's foreign secretary, credited him with exceptional will power and intellect.[58] It must be stressed that there was a huge difference in the perception of Franz Ferdinand between those who directly interacted with him and the wider public. Nonetheless, how was it possible that such a public figure could remain 'unknown' to such a large audience?

Due to the special circumstances of him becoming heir apparent, in 1889 after Crown Prince Rudolf's suicide, and his long period of illness with tuberculosis, the press for a decade paid no more attention to Franz Ferdinand than to other archdukes. Then in 1898, after his complete convalescence, he was put at the 'disposal of the supreme command'; and in 1900, on the occasion of his marriage to Sophie Chotek, newspaper readers became more familiar with him for the first time. The press throughout the Monarchy reported the unconventional love match in a very positive way, though some nationalist Czech and Hungarian papers took advantage of the situation and discussed the constitutional problem that arose from the diverse treatment of Sophie's unequal rank in different regions of Austria-Hungary.[59] Since positive stories were published about his private life and official duties, they could have provided a sound basis for a positive image to develop. However, Franz Ferdinand wished to protect his privacy and actually never strove to become a charming heir apparent. His aim was to popularize his political views and not his personality.[60] His decision to spend most of his time at home in his different residences, far away from Vienna, was motivated by the unequal treatment of his wife and children due to their lower rank. The consequence of this absence from Vienna was that only a few people maintained regular contact with him, and his subjects rarely saw him. All this proved to be fatal for cultivating his image.

Many rumours circulated about the couple's stinginess and bigotry. However, their intimates described the archduke as an extraordinarily warm and loving father and husband, his family life as harmonious and happy.[61] To a certain extent the different perceptions resulted from differing pictures and photographs. All official photos and paintings showed an earnest and formal family, with Franz Ferdinand as a frosty and unapproachable individual (exactly how Zweig later described him); yet private and unpublished photos recorded a smiling heir to the throne, even in official functions, and a happy family that enjoyed their time together.[62]

Although there was a consensus about Franz Ferdinand's high intellectual abilities and will power, his character polarized many people. On the one hand he was described as amiable, friendly, attentive, open-minded, diligent, disciplined, self-critical and loyal, with an ability to learn quickly; on the other hand, critics saw him as distrustful, superficial, pedantic and resentful towards individuals who had disappointed him.[63] His entourage had varied experiences with him, as reflected in those controversial adjectives. Some former supporters and friends were dropped and antagonized due to their 'disloyalty', while others like Czernin or Conrad mostly experienced support and confidence despite their misconduct.[64] Foreign Minister Berchtold stated that Franz Ferdinand's 'sense for fidelity towards his few real friends was as strong as his hatred for everyone once they had aroused his suspicions'.[65] Even those close to him, who estimated him positively, tended to criticize his interference in too many areas and his erratic changes of mind.[66] For this reason, some of them questioned his qualities as a future ruler.[67]

Two biographies were published during Franz Ferdinand's lifetime, showing him in the best light and ignoring all sensitive issues.[68] His commitment to reforming and expanding the armed forces as well as his friendship with Kaiser Wilhelm were outlined as future oriented. His status as a 'Sphinx' – unknown and enigmatic – was explained by the fact that, as the second figure in the state, his public presence should not be too dominant out of deference to the old emperor.[69] Everyone knew that he was ambitious and eager to reign. Many contemporaries duly characterized him as a tyrant and an autocratic 'renaissance man'.[70] However, even his opponents agreed that he was 'a personality' with talents[71] – and probably the only one who could have 'rescued' the Monarchy.[72] This ambivalent public discourse was typical; although his ideas could be met with scepticism and he had many negative critics, public opinion in different parts of the empire had hopes for state reform which he seemed to personify like nobody else.[73]

Historians have yet to analyse in depth his image abroad, but even at first glance it becomes obvious that it differed in the various European states. While German and British politicians, diplomats and journalists mostly portrayed him positively, in Serbia, Russia, France and Italy his image was largely negative.[74] He was deemed a dangerous warmonger and leader of the Viennese war party – almost the opposite of how he was seen among much of the Austro-Hungarian public.[75] There are isolated statements in a few studies which indicate that, especially in Russia and Serbia, he was viewed as a powerful second man in the state, an 'enemy of the Slavs' and a threat to peace,[76] and finally, that his death was a 'direct consequence of oppressive policy towards the Slavs', which he had supposedly inspired.[77] A single sample from the official Serbian diplomatic documents, recently published in forty-two volumes, confirms his negative image in the world of Serbian diplomacy: there he was 'the head of a war party', a bellicose individual whose death was a 'relief' to most European diplomats.[78] A more systematic analysis of press articles and diplomatic material would help us evaluate and explain these differences across the various European states.

## Conclusion

After the death of Franz Ferdinand, representatives of Slovaks and Romanians from Hungary laid wreaths on his catafalque with the inscription, 'To our last hope, in loyal devotion'.[79] Many people, especially members of the smaller nationalities, felt this way, and there were numerous outbreaks of sorrow and frustration in different regions of the empire. It was clear to all that an important authority as well as the main symbol for the Monarchy's future had been eliminated. Moreover, the prime centre for the archduke's influence and power – his military chancellery in the Belvedere – was dissolved within three days. For almost a decade, it had been a key instrument of power, a highly diversified institution, with numerous official and unofficial associates and experts enabling him, alongside varying networks, to extend his influence into military, foreign and personnel spheres of policy. We have shown the strengths and weaknesses of this wide spectrum of networks, but it remains an open question whether this imposing entity could have guaranteed a smooth transition from Franz Joseph to Emperor Franz II. What is clear is that with its help the archduke had become one of the main protagonists and decision makers in the late Habsburg Empire – and at the same time probably the most influential heir apparent in Europe.

Yet despite all rumours, the extent of his influence and power was hardly identifiable to most people in Austria-Hungary, as it was rarely mentioned in public. Only those political, social and military elites who were directly involved could observe and experience his impact. Usually, an heir to the throne was a highly visible figure, representing a system of rule and its continuity. In Franz Ferdinand's case, he personified the traditional and most conservative side of the Habsburg dynasty and, at the same time, the concept of reforming the state. His concrete plans for the future however were obscure, causing fear and insecurity, while his absence from Vienna and wish for privacy resulted in a lack of familiarity and popularity. He expected only respect and obedience, not love from his subjects. And he made no real effort to deny reports about his antipathy towards certain nationalities or being a warmonger. Yet for many people, his energetic manner offered at least a hope for reforms and improvement of the Monarchy's stability. This ambivalent public image continued after his death and continues into the present.

Even the memorial ceremony for Franz Ferdinand and his wife led to controversial public debates. While some of his intimates considered it appropriate, most newspapers criticized his burial ceremony as too simple, referring to it as a 'third-class-funeral'. One thing is certain: the Viennese decision not to invite European heads of state was a mistake. In July 1914 the Habsburg Monarchy failed to seize the opportunity to demonstrate monarchical solidarity, and even more important, to consult with the other Great Powers in order to preserve peace.

## Notes

1. Stefan Zweig, *Die Welt von Gestern. Erinnerungen eines Europäers* (Frankfurt am Main: Fischer, 2002), 249.
2. Ibid., 248–9.
3. Ibid., 12.
4. Ibid., 248. Compare Alma Hannig, *Franz Ferdinand. Die Biografie* (Vienna: Amalthea, 2013), 260–5.
5. Ibid., 249. See also the critical comments of Oliver Matuschek in the annotated edition of Stefan Zweig, *Die Welt von Gestern. Erinnerungen eines Europäers* (Frankfurt am Main: S. Fischer, 2017), 465–638.
6. For example, when Zweig (ibid., 250) claimed that the young Archduchesses and Prince Alfred Montenuovo had decided to bury Franz Ferdinand and his wife in Artstetten, and not in the Viennese Capuchin crypt. It was well known that Franz Ferdinand and Sophie had made this decision by themselves in 1908.
7. *Neue Freie Presse*, 29 June 1914, 4. For similar descriptions, see *Wiener Zeitung, Fremdenblatt, Zeit, Reichspost* from 29 June 1914. See also Jan Galandauer, *Franz Fürst Thun. Statthalter des Königreiches Böhmen* (Vienna, Cologne and Weimar: Böhlau, 2014), 304.
8. *Neue Freie Presse*, 29 June 1914, 1 and *Arbeiter-Zeitung*, 29 June 1914, 1. Most Austrian newspapers published more pathetic and positive obituaries. See Alma Hannig, '"Wer uns kränkt, den schlagen wir nieder": Die Wiener Tagespresse in der Julikrise 1914', in Georg Eckert, Peter Geiss and Arne Karsten (eds), *Die Presse in der Julikrise 1914. Die internationale Berichterstattung und der Weg in den Ersten Weltkrieg* (Münster: Aschendorff, 2014), 25.
9. Berchtold diary, 28 June 1914, in Leopold Berchtold MSS, Haus-, Hof- und Staatsarchiv Vienna (hereafter HHStA), karton 4.
10. See Hannig, *Franz Ferdinand*, 205–10, 217–18.
11. For Franz Ferdinand's enhanced engagement in culture and education, see Theodor Brückler, *Thronfolger Franz Ferdinand als Denkmalpfleger. Die 'Kunstakten' der Militärkanzlei im Österreichischen Staatsarchiv (Kriegsarchiv)* (Vienna, Cologne and Weimar: Böhlau, 2009). For his political vision see Robert A. Kann, *Erzherzog Franz Ferdinand Studien* (Vienna: Verlag für Geschichte und Politik, 1976); Samuel R. Williamson, 'Influence, Power, and the Policy Process: The Case of Franz Ferdinand, 1906-1914', *The Historical Journal* 17 (1974): 417–34.
12. Rudolf Sieghart, *Die letzten Jahrzehnte einer Großmacht. Menschen, Völker, Probleme des Habsburger-Reiches* (Berlin: Ullstein, 1932), 235.
13. Günther Kronenbitter, 'Verhinderter Retter? Erzherzog Franz Ferdinand und die Erhaltung der Habsburgermonarchie', in Ulrich E. Zellenberg (ed.), *Konservative Profile. Ideen und Praxis in der Politik zwischen FM Radetzky, Karl Kraus und Alois Mock* (Graz: Stocker, 2003), 272.

14  Ibid.; Ludwig Jedlicka, 'Erzherzog Franz Ferdinand (1863-1914)', in Hugo Hantsch (ed.), *Gestalter der Geschichte Österreichs* (Innsbruck, Vienna and Munich: Tyrolia, 1962), 531–2.

15  For Franz Ferdinand's different residencies, see Jean-Paul Bled, *Franz Ferdinand. Der eigensinnige Thronfolger* (Vienna, Cologne and Weimar: Böhlau, 2013), 163–8.

16  Rudolf Kiszling, *Erzherzog Franz Ferdinand von Österreich-Este. Leben, Pläne und Wirken am Schicksalsweg der Donaumonarchie* (Graz and Cologne: Böhlau, 1953), 63–72, 155–60, 171.

17  Ibid., 60–1, 80–5; Theodor von Sosnosky, *Franz Ferdinand. Der Erzherzog-Thronfolger. Ein Lebensbild* (Munich and Berlin: Oldenbourg, 1929), 45, 106–8.

18  Günther Kronenbitter, 'The Opposition of the Archdukes: Rudolf, Franz Ferdinand and the Late Habsburg Monarchy', in Frank Lorenz Müller and Heide Mehrkens (eds), *Sons and Heirs: Succession and Political Culture in Nineteenth-Century Europe* (Basingstoke: Palgrave Macmillan, 2015), 221.

19  Martha Sitte, *Alexander Brosch von Aarenau, der Flügeladjutant und Vorstand der Militärkanzlei des Thronfolgers Franz Ferdinand* (PhD diss., University of Vienna, 1961).

20  See 'Brosch über den Thronfolger als Mensch und Soldat', in Leopold von Chlumecky, *Erzherzog Franz Ferdinands Wirken und Wollen* (Berlin: Verlag für Kulturpolitik, 1929), 358.

21  The following arguments are based on Georg Franz, *Erzherzog Franz Ferdinand und die Pläne zur Reform der Habsburger Monarchie* (Brünn, Munich and Vienna: Rohrer, 1943), 26–39, 69–75.

22  Peter Broucek, 'Erzherzog Franz Ferdinand und sein Verhältnis zum Chef des Generalstabes Franz Freiherr Conrad von Hötzendorf', in *Ab Sarajewo zum Großen Krieg* (Prague: Österreichisches Kulturinstitut, 1995), 19–33.

23  Günther Kronenbitter, *'Krieg im Frieden': Die Führung der k.u.k. Armee und die Großmachtpolitik Österreich-Ungarns 1906-1914* (Munich: Oldenbourg, 2003), 88–96, 145–78.

24  Holger Afflerbach, *Der Dreibund. Europäische Großmacht- und Allianzpolitik vor dem Ersten Weltkrieg* (Weimar, Vienna, Cologne: Böhlau, 2002), 824. Compare biographies on Conrad by Lawrence Sondhaus, *Franz Conrad von Hötzendorf: Architect of the Apocalypse* (Boston, Leiden and Cologne: Brill, 2000); and Wolfram Dornik, *Des Kaisers Falke. Wirken und Nach-Wirken von Franz Conrad von Hötzendorf* (Innsbruck: Studienverlag, 2013).

25  Kann, *Erzherzog*, 44.

26  Kiszling, *Erzherzog*, 12, 20, 36, 76, 83–6, 91–9.

27  J. Chr. Allmayer-Beck, *Ministerpräsident Baron Beck. Ein Staatsmann des alten Österreich* (Munich: Oldenbourg, 1956), 136–8, 241–6. Cf. Chlumecky, *Erzherzog*, 296–305.

28  Marga Lammasch and Hans Sperl (eds), *Heinrich Lammasch. Seine Aufzeichnungen, sein Wirken und seine Politik* (Vienna and Leipzig: Deuticke, 1922), 77–95.

29 Solomon Wank, 'The Archduke and Aehrenthal: The Origins of a Hatred', *Austrian History Yearbook* 33 (2002): 77–104.

30 Ottokar Czernin, *Im Weltkriege* (Berlin and Vienna: Ullstein 1919), 105; Kann, *Erzherzog*, 157–205.

31 Kann, *Erzherzog*, 159, 163, 197.

32 Chlumecky, *Erzherzog*, 290–3.

33 Friedrich Funder, *Vom Gestern ins Heute. Aus dem Kaiserreich in die Republik* (Vienna: Herold, 1952), 377–83; Hannig, *Franz Ferdinand*, 115–21.

34 Mirjana Gross has shown how difficult it was for the Belvedere to find influential Croatian politicians for cooperation and that Franz Ferdinand's view of Rauch and Frank remained ambivalent: Mirjana Gross, 'Erzherzog Franz Ferdinand und die kroatische Frage. Ein Beitrag zur groß-österreichischen Politik in Kroatien', *Österreichische Osthefte* 8 (1966): 277–99.

35 Peter Broucek, 'Reformpläne aus dem Beraterkreis Erzherzog Franz Ferdinands und Kaiser Karls', in Richard Plaschka et al. (eds), *Mitteleuropa-Konzeptionen in der ersten Hälfte des 20. Jahrhunderts* (Vienna: Verlag der Österreichischen Akademie der Wissenschaften, 1995), 111–21. Compare Franz, *Erzherzog*, 82–99; Sosnosky, *Franz Ferdinand*, 66–78.

36 Franz, *Erzherzog*, 22–3; Sosnosky, *Franz Ferdinand*, 238.

37 Kann, *Erzherzog*, 100–126.

38 Lothar Höbelt, 'Der Thronfolger und die politischen Parteien', *Études Danubiennes* 27 (2011): 13–23.

39 Wilhelm Wühr (ed.), *Ludwig Freiherr von Pastor. Tagebücher, Briefe, Erinnerungen* (Heidelberg: Kerle 1950), 535–49, 573–5, 604–7. Friedrich Engel-Janosi, *Österreich und der Vatikan 1846-1918*, vol. 2 (Graz, Vienna and Cologne: Styria, 1960), 153–62.

40 Galandauer, *Thun*, 119–31, 304–6; Kann, *Erzherzog*, 127–56.

41 Alma Hannig, 'Prinz Gottfried zu Hohenlohe-Schillingsfürst (1867-1936). Ein Liebling der Kaiserhöfe', in Alma Hannig and Martina Winkelhofer (eds), *Die Familie Hohenlohe. Eine europäische Dynastie im 19. und 20. Jahrhundert* (Vienna, Cologne and Weimar: Böhlau, 2013), 229–68.

42 As noted earlier, Kann argued that Czernin, after he had failed in Romania, was probably out of the race. See Kann, *Erzherzog*, 159, 163, 197. However, no one else was considered as a better candidate.

43 Broucek, 'Reformpläne', 111–21.

44 In contrast, for example, to his own son, Crown Prince Rudolf, who in the 1880s 'never got anywhere near to exerting the level of influence enjoyed by Franz Ferdinand' (Kronenbitter, 'The Opposition of the Archdukes', 222). Rudolf never had any influence on the army or foreign policy, and possessed no network of informants.

45 Kann, *Erzherzog*, 47–85.

46 Hannig, *Franz Ferdinand*, 176–90.

47 Hugo Hantsch, *Leopold Graf Berchtold. Grandseigneur und Staatsmann*, 2 vols (Graz, Vienna and Cologne: Styria, 1963), II, 544–5.

48  Hannig, *Franz Ferdinand*, 165–71.
49  Czernin, *Im Weltkriege*, 105.
50  Hannig, *Franz Ferdinand*, 159–61.
51  Ibid., 157–9.
52  Tschirschky to Bethmann Hollweg, 2 July 1914, in Imanuel Geiss (ed.), *Julikrise und Kriegsausbruch. Eine Dokumentensammlung*, vol. 1 (Hannover: Verlag für Literatur und Zeitgeschehen, 1963), nos 10, 66. Compare also Kiszling, *Erzherzog*, 38.
53  Franz, *Erzherzog*, 87.
54  Chlumecky, *Erzherzog*, 63.
55  *Danzer´s Armee-Zeitung*, 18 December 1913, 1.
56  See, for example, *Deutsches Volksblatt*, 18 December 1913, 1. Although after the death of Crown Prince Rudolf, Franz Ferdinand's father was legally next in line to the throne, due to his old age nobody expected him to become the next emperor.
57  Sigmund Freud to Wilhelm Fließ, 7 July 1898, in Jeffrey M. Masson (ed.), *Sigmund Freud. Briefe an Wilhelm Fliess 1887-1904* (Frankfurt am Main: S. Fischer 1986), 349.
58  Bernhard Fürst von Bülow, *Denkwürdigkeiten*, vol. 1 (Berlin: Ullstein, 1930), 167.
59  Hannig, *Franz Ferdinand*, 67–70.
60  Franz, *Erzherzog*, 59; Sosnosky, *Franz Ferdinand*, 242.
61  Franz Conrad von Hötzendorf, *Aus meiner Dienstzeit 1906-1918*, vol. 2 (Vienna, Leipzig, Munich: Rikola, 1922), 95; Carl Freiherr von Bardolff, *Soldat im alten Österreich* (Jena: Diederichs, 1938), 132. Cf. *Die Fackel* 4 (August 1902), 13–15; Sieghart, *Die letzten Jahrzehnte*, 234; Pastor, *Tagebücher*, 606: entry for 5 July 1914; Czernin, *Im Weltkriege*, 51.
62  Hannig, *Franz Ferdinand*, 73–4.
63  Funder, *Vom Gestern*, 493–6; Pastor, *Tagebücher*, 497, 589: entries for 1 December 1908, 31 January 1914; Hohenlohe to Aehrenthal, 13 November 1907, in Solomon Wank (ed.), *Aus dem Nachlaß Aehrenthal. Briefe und Dokumente zur österreichisch-ungarischen Innen- und Außenpolitik 1885-1912*, 2 vols (Graz: Neugebauer, 1994), II, 555; Edmund Glaise-Horstenau, 'Erzherzog Franz Ferdinand (1863–1914)', in *Neue Österreichische Biografie 1815-1918*, vol. 3 (Vienna: Amalthea, 1926), 16–18.
64  Sieghart, *Die letzten Jahrzehnte*, 237; Conrad, *Aus meiner Dienstzeit*, vol. 3, 435–6, 470.
65  Berchtold diary, 28 June 1914, in HHStA, Berchtold MSS, karton 4.
66  Czernin, *Im Weltkriege*, 45; Sieghart, *Die letzten Jahrzehnte*, 234, 237, 241; Bardolff, *Soldat,*136; Chlumecky, *Erzherzog*, 355–7.
67  Hohenlohe to Aehrenthal, 11 November 1906, in Wank, *Aus dem Nachlaß Aehrenthal*, I, 417.
68  Baron von Falkenegg, *Erzherzog Franz Ferdinand von Österreich-Este. Was hat man von seiner zukünftigen Regierungstätigkeit zu erwarten?* (Berlin: R.

Boll, 1908); Hermann Heller, *Erzherzog Franz Ferdinand, der Thronfolger Österreichs. Nach authentischen Quellen* (Brünn: Winiker, 1911).

69  Theodor von Sosnosky, 'Erzherzog Franz Ferdinand', and Leopold von Chlumecky, 'Unser Thronfolger', in *Österreichische Rundschau*, Illustriertes Sonderheft 1913, 7, 8, 26–30.

70  HHStA, Mensdorff MSS, karton 4: Mensdorff diary, 2 July 1914; Franz, *Erzherzog*, 16.

71  Mensdorff diary, 2 July 1914; HHStA, Berchtold MSS, karton 4: Berchtold diary, 28 June 1914; Karl Kraus, 'Franz Ferdinand und die Talente', *Die Fackel*, 10 July 1914, 1–4.

72  Pastor, *Tagebücher*, 819: entry for 28 February 1925. Cf. Engel-Janosi, *Österreich*, vol. 2, 154.

73  Mensdorff diary, 2 July 1914; Pastor, *Tagebücher*, 601–2: entries for 28 June 1914, 5 July 1914.

74  Even after his death, the French press 'reminded' its readers that the archduke had been a warmonger: Peter Geiss, '"Das unsterbliche Frankreich, der Soldat des Rechts": Französische Zeitungen in der Julikrise 1914', in Eckert, Geiss and Karsten (eds), *Presse in der Julikrise*, 89. For Great Britain, see Georg Eckert's article in ibid., 115–16; D.C. Watt, 'The British Reactions to the Assassination at Sarajevo', *European History Quarterly* 1:3 (1971): 234–47; and F. R. Bridge's chapter in this volume.

75  An exception was the Austrian Peace Movement and Bertha von Suttner who did consider the archduke a warmonger: see Brigitte Hamann, *Bertha von Suttner. Ein Leben für den Frieden* (Munich: Piper, 1986), 467–9, 495–6.

76  Jörg Baberowski, '"Der Nationalismus ist ein mächtiges Gefühl": Die russische Presse und der Ausbruch des Ersten Weltkrieges', in Eckert, Geiss and Karsten (eds), *Presse in der Julikrise*, 67–8.

77  See, for example, Elena G. Kostrikova, 'Russian Support to Serbia in July 1914', in Dragoljub R. Živojinović (ed.), *The Serbs and the First World War 1914-1918* (Belgrade: Serbian Academy of Sciences and Arts, 2015), 206. Cf. also Husnija Kamberović, 'Ubojstvo Franza Ferdinanda u Sarajevu 1914. – devedeset godina poslije', *Prilozi* 34 (Sarajevo, 2005): 21.

78  *Dokumenti o spoljnoj politici Kraljevine Srbije 1903-1914*, vol. 3.3, 569 (19 November 1908); and vol. 7.2, 428 (5 July 1914): http://diplprepiska.mi.sanu.ac.rs/wb/Serbia-Forum/knjige/3_3#page/569/mode/1up, http://diplprepiska.mi.sanu.ac.rs/wb/Serbia-Forum/knjige/7_2#page/424/mode/1up (downloaded 15 January 2018).

79  Arthur J. May, *The Passing of the Hapsburg Monarchy 1914-1918*, 2 vols. (Philadelphia: University of Pennsylvania Press, 1968), I, 39.

# CHAPTER 3

# Great expectations

# The Habsburg heir apparent and the Southern Slavs

*Andrej Rahten*

Historiography still remains divided on why the Habsburg Archduke Franz Ferdinand was chosen as a target of the Sarajevo conspirators. Was it punishment for his ambitions to strengthen the role of Austria-Hungary in the Balkans? Were his adversaries perhaps resentful of the fact that he was surrounded by high army officers designing grand military plans? Or did the advocates of Greater Serbia feel threatened not so much by his alleged rattling of guns as by his expert knowledge of the Southern Slav Question? Was there a general belief that the archduke's protective relationship with the Croats would thwart the efforts of the statesmen in Belgrade to find a solution to the Southern Slav Question? Undoubtedly, Franz Ferdinand was well aware of how vulnerable the Habsburg Monarchy was due to unsolved domestic political conflicts, and as long as the latter had not been settled, the Monarchy was not able to conduct a more engaged policy in the Balkans. Nevertheless, a legend spread in Serbian political circles before the First World War that Franz Ferdinand was the leader of the 'Viennese war party', something which would later serve to justify his assassination. Yet the real power of the notorious 'Belvedere circle' was hidden in its reform plans for the creation of a Southern Slav unit within the Habsburg Monarchy, which might be able to undermine aspirations to create Greater Serbia. Therefore, the story about the motives for the assassination of the Habsburg archduke is also a study of the concepts for reconstructing Austria-Hungary.

The today largely forgotten booklet of Ivanka Klemenčič, the first Slovene professional female journalist, published in Ljubljana immediately after the Sarajevo assassination, portrayed Franz Ferdinand as the great supporter of the Southern Slavs: 'The Archduke was well aware of the value that our loyalty to the Habsburg throne had for the state, and if he had any say in it, times would already have been different for us down here. Now he's dead; woe betide us Slovenes and Croats!' The role of the Slovenes and the Croats as the 'iron bulwark in the sea' was deemed to be perfect for realizing the heir apparent's grandiose plans to develop the Austro-Hungarian navy.[1] Thus Slovene and Croatian politicians were also among the most adamant advocates of the heir apparent's plans for the Habsburg navy as the best guarantee against Italian ambitions in the Adriatic. Franz Ferdinand, as is well known, loved to visit the Brijuni Islands, where he enjoyed the health benefits of the balmy climate for his pulmonary ailments. However, this was not the only reason that he took an interest in places along the northern Adriatic, as he was also very active in Istria as a patron of the 'Central Commission for the Study and Preservation of Art and Historical Monuments'. With his purchases, he saved many Istrian works of art from dealers in antiquities, especially those from Italy whom he found the most annoying.[2]

## Franz Ferdinand's trialist Monarchy

Most interesting, at least according to Southern Slav politicians – both within and outside the Habsburg Monarchy – were the heir apparent's views of the Southern Slav Question. In 1911, his military chancellery drew up the famous Programme for the Succession to the Throne (*Programm für den Thronwechsel*).[3] Pursuant to this plan, dualism would, for foreign policy reasons (appeasement of Germany), temporarily remain in place, but the heir apparent decided to postpone his pledge to the Hungarian constitution. This would give him full power to implement planned reforms, notably to introduce universal and equal suffrage in Hungary and to form a central imperial government led by a *Reichskanzler*. It was further envisaged that the new ruler would issue only one manifesto instead of two. If Hungary resisted, three congruent manifestos would be issued – one for Austria, one for Hungary and a special one for Bosnia and Herzegovina. Some historians interpret this move as the archduke's plan for executing his Greater Austrian programme by way of a carefully camouflaged and temporary trialist arrangement, where the *Reichsländer* of Bosnia and Herzegovina would be raised in status to be the third constitutional element in the empire.[4] But most have seen this programme as proof that Franz Ferdinand was not really in favour of trialism. Such a position was most vigorously maintained by the well-known Yugoslav scholar Vladimir Dedijer. In his opinion, the propaganda of 'trialism' by the archduke's confidants like Karl Schwarzenberg was merely tactical, used to intimidate the Magyars and provoke Croatian-Serbian conflicts. At the same time, it could be seen as a move to lead the nationalist circles in Belgrade to believe that the archduke actually hoped for the creation of a Southern Slav state unit within the boundaries of the Habsburg Monarchy that would prevent Serbia from playing the role of a 'Yugoslav Piedmont'.[5]

Franz Ferdinand was indeed no Slavophile, and as a Habsburg he was most partial to the Germans among all nationalities of the Monarchy. Therefore, explanations that sprang up after his death that he intended to establish two Slav kingdoms for his sons are hardly credible.[6] In his hierarchy of nations, the Austro-Hungarian South Slavs had an inferior role in relation to the presumably culturally superior Germans. But that was not a good enough reason for him not to support a constitutional unification of the Southern Slavs, if the latter would help to consolidate the Monarchy and create a much-desired Greater Austria which could then pursue a stronger foreign policy. This is also confirmed by memoir literature, especially the account of the emperor's adjutant Baron Albert Margutti.[7]

Franz Ferdinand most likely envisaged the third state unit as a sort of Greater Croatia.[8] His Belvedere circle maintained regular contacts with Croatian politicians of 'state right' provenance (*pravaši*) and supported their plans. The Croatian Count Marko Bombelles was one of the archduke's hunting companions and a kind of ambassador to the Belvedere court.[9] As evident from their surviving correspondence, Bombelles did not confine himself in his letters to praising the heir apparent's hunting prowess but also criticized Hungarian and Serbian politics. He continuously warned the heir apparent that even the proverbial Croatian dynastic loyalty had its limits and that Habsburg policy towards the Croats required drastic changes.[10] Finally, it was in this connection that, after the annexation of Bosnia-Herzegovina in 1908, the archduke sent Bombelles a famous message asking him to urge his Croatian people to demonstrate their traditional loyalty just once more; when his time came to take over the throne, he would redress all their wrongs.[11] The heir apparent thus proclaimed himself patron of the Croats, and many Croatian politicians relied on him to produce their long-desired Greater Croatia.[12]

It was no later than 1905 that Vjekoslav Spinčić and other Croat deputies to the Vienna parliament (Reichsrat) had opened a discussion of the archduke's reform plans with the influential Prince Alois Liechtenstein. Then Spinčić learnt that the old Emperor Franz Joseph would not hear of any constitutional changes, while the opposite was true of his heir. According to Spinčić, 'Franz Ferdinand intends to rule on the foundations of equality of all nations and give to every man his due.'[13] In 1907, similar assurances were given to the Croatian vice-ban (vice-governor) Vladimir Nikolić.[14] Irrespective of occasional doubts about Croatian loyalty, as, for instance, in the wake of the 'Rijeka Resolution' of 1905 when Croatian politicians started turning towards Budapest, Franz Ferdinand seems never to have completely abandoned his trialist plans. Even in a conversation at the end of 1913 with the editor of the newspaper *Österreichische Rundschau*, Baron Leopold von Chlumecky, he assured him that Croatia-Slavonia, Dalmatia and Bosnia-Herzegovina belonged together.[15]

Trialism is generally known to have had multiple meanings. It was most often considered to be a Greater Croatian concept, but occasionally, the term was also used to denote some older plan to elevate the Bohemian lands to become a third constitutional element in the empire on a par with Hungary and Austria.[16] Franz Ferdinand certainly opposed this Czech variant of trialism, as it would 'completely sunder the already loosened structure of the Monarchy'.[17] The heir apparent and the Greater Austrian trialists recognized clear threats to the Monarchy in Magyar nationalism, and in the concepts of Greater Serbia or Czech Neo-Slavism, but by no means in the trialism advocated by Croatian politicians. Despite these facts, Vladimir Dedijer exhibited a very pronounced tendency to justify the Sarajevo assassination as the 'murder of a tyrant'. Yet his interpretation, of the assassins as heroic fighters for the rights of Southern Slav peoples 'oppressed' by the Monarchy, in no way corresponds to the picture of Franz Ferdinand as an advocate of trialism and Croat national aspirations.

Franz Ferdinand clearly had no intention of further decentralizing the already loosened dualist system by adding new analogue political institutions of a third state unit to the Austrian and Hungarian units, without simultaneously strengthening the central state bodies. In such a trialist monarchy, reorganized as a mere multiplication of dualism, Hungary would surely lose control of Croatian-Slavonia. But even in such a decentralized system, the Magyars could continue to be strong political players, not to mention the fact that the archduke's protégés, the Romanians, Slovaks and Hungarian Germans would continue to remain under Magyar hegemony. Such a situation would in the long run undoubtedly be intolerable for the heir apparent.

Even so, Franz Ferdinand never lost interest in the idea of trialism for three reasons. Coupled with the threat of introducing universal suffrage into Hungary, it was a Sword of Damocles hanging over the Magyars. Similarly, the fulfilment of state-right demands by the Monarchy's Southern Slavs in the form of trialism would serve as an effective weapon in the struggle against the idea of a Greater Serbia. The third argument in favour of a trialist reorganization stemmed from the archduke's views of how such constitutional reform should take place. The ideal of Greater Austria was, at least according to key figures in his circle, best attainable in gradual steps, through trialism, rather than through using radical methods to eliminate the old borders of the crown lands at a single stroke. On the one hand, concessions would be made for dividing the state into three major units, the Austrian, Hungarian and a newly formed South Slav entity; and on the other, a strong centralized government and parliament would simultaneously be created in Vienna for all provinces of the Monarchy. Each of the three state units of the Monarchy would then be further divided into smaller crown lands and all nations would be ensured some autonomy in national and cultural matters.[18] For Franz Ferdinand and his adherents, trialism was therefore, first and foremost, a means to dismantle the dualist system and, as such, an important integral part of his programme to establish Greater Austria rather than any alternative ideal.[19] The establishment of the third state unit would weaken Hungary and simultaneously allow Franz Ferdinand to build strong central institutions in Vienna. The Monarchy would thereby consolidate itself and strengthen its status as a Great Power, finally enabling it to pursue a more active policy in the Balkans.

## Slovene and Croatian support for trialism

In the Slovene ethnic territory, the main advocate of trialism was the Pan-Slovene People's Party (*Vseslovenska ljudska stranka*) led by Ivan Šušteršič, the 'uncrowned Duke of Carniola', who did everything in his power to unite his party and the Croats into a combined trialistic force. Šušteršič, being the same age as Franz Ferdinand, was the only figure in the Slovene-speaking provinces with a sound enough political power base for his constitutional plans to attract Vienna's attention. His ideal was a Greater Austria as 'a great monarchic Switzerland, a steadfast stronghold securing the development of all its nations on the inside, as well as a supreme factor of European equilibrium and peace on the outside'.[20] In 1909, Šušteršič managed to bring together 'Catholic Patriots' from across the entire Slovene ethnic territory from Trieste to the Drava River under the banner of the Pan-Slovene People's Party. In the last elections to the Reichsrat before the First World War, his party won no less than 87 per cent of all Slovene seats. The realization of his trialist vision, however, required the indispensable support of the heir apparent.

In the decade prior to the Great War, particularly after the annexation of Bosnia-Herzegovina in 1908, 'trialism' had become the magic word in Slovene politics. However, it should be borne in mind that a trialist programme was in fact also developed by Croatian politicians and that it existed in various versions. The Slovene version of trialism provided for the unification of Bosnia-Herzegovina, the Triune Kingdom (Croatia-Slavonia-Dalmatia), Vojvodina and the Slovene ethnic territory into one large state with its capital in Zagreb. The central idea of its advocates was that the only solution to the Southern Slav Question was the preservation of the Dual Monarchy as a Great Power. In order to strengthen its influence in the Balkans, it was imperative for the Monarchy to establish a 'vast, administratively united Southern Slav territory'.[21] Should the Monarchy eventually undergo reconstruction, the main and unconditional demand of many Slovene politicians was therefore to unite with the Croats in a new Southern Slav formation. A form of trialism that merely entailed the unification of the Croatian provinces posed a danger to the Slovenes, by allowing the possibility that they, and the Czechs, would become isolated in a German-dominated Austrian state.

How some of the Croatian advocates of trialism (namely the *pravaši*) envisaged the internal organization of a Greater Croatian trialist unit can be gathered from the brochures of the Dubrovnik-native journalist Nikola Zvonimir Bjelovučić. His most notable political publication appeared in 1911 under the title *Trializam i hrvatska država* (Trialism and the Croatian State). Therein, Bjelovučić meticulously described his vision of Greater Croatia within the trialist Monarchy. 'The Croatian state' was to encompass all Croatian and Slovene provinces divided into counties. The Trieste County was the only one to have not only Croatian but also Italian as the official language. The Habsburg monarch would appoint a nine-member Croatian government headed by the ban (governor) and based in Zagreb. Bjelovučić envisaged common ministries for the entire Monarchy for the navy (based in Pula), the army and foreign affairs. The Common Finance Ministry would be dissolved, but the current system of 'Delegations' would remain.[22] To the Delegations each of the three parliaments would send forty delegates, and their sessions would be held alternately in Vienna, Budapest and Zagreb.[23]

Many Croatian politicians were well aware that sacrifices would have to be made on the path towards creating Greater Croatia. In exchange for the unification of all Croatian provinces, including Bosnia-Herzegovina, they were willing to support the establishment of a strong pan-national parliament and a reconstruction of the Monarchy in the sense of the 'centralised federalism' advocated by Franz Ferdinand.[24] On the other hand, Slovene politicians were aware that Franz Ferdinand recognized the Croats as the most loyal defenders of the dynasty and was willing to respond to their national demands. Therefore, in order to be granted due consideration in the archduke's reform plans, it was imperative for Slovene politicians to establish the closest possible affiliation with the Croats. This could, for instance, explain the burning zeal with which the Pan-Slovene People's Party leadership tried to build a firm alliance with the Croats. And finally, this is also why it tirelessly repeated 'that the Slovenes were nothing more than Alpine Croats'.[25]

In the party of the Slovene Catholic Patriots, the most radical vision for collaborating with the Croats was set out by its main ideologist Aleš Ušeničnik in 1913 in an analysis entitled *Slovenci in Hrvati* (The Slovenes and the Croats).[26] This study above all expressed his apprehension that the Slovene nation might be lost in the flurry of major nationalisms appearing. He examined appropriate steps to be taken in case 'the Slovenes themselves did not enjoy adequate living conditions and were not able to sustain themselves as an independent cultural unit'. This would imply that they were not a nation in the full sense of the term: they could only become a nation 'through assimilation with other ethnic groups'. According to Ušeničnik, the best solution for the Slovenes was to unite with the Croats 'in one administrative unit and in one of the federal states of Great Austria'. A 'United Slovenia' as an autonomous entity pursuant to the principle of national federalism was, in his view, a 'very theoretical' possibility, given that the Germans and the Italians were unwilling to sacrifice their own minorities. However, with regard to any federalism of the historic crown lands, Ušeničnik claimed that it would certainly be 'national death' for the Slovenes to abandon their national minorities in Carinthia, Styria and the Littoral to the mercy of German or Italian nationalists. Given that 'the Slovenes alone were too weak to take on the Germans', their 'political and cultural ideal' should be to unite with the Croats. Ušeničnik was well aware that this 'form of Yugoslav unity', for which the term 'trialism' had been adopted, was opposed by many elements in the Monarchy, especially by the Hungarian political elite and by German nationalists. The former feared that the formation of a Southern Slav administrative body would cost them the port of Rijeka (Fiume); the latter were unwilling to give up the 'German bridge to Trieste'. Ušeničnik had serious doubts that the Germans would ever sacrifice their outlet to the sea at Trieste. He nevertheless hoped that the Croatian-Slovene administrative unit would at least secure Rijeka, a port 'which has long since belonged not only to Croatia but to Carniola as well'.[27]

Clearly, the leaders of the Pan-Slovene People's Party readily understood that the dogma of one 'Croatian-Slovene nation', which they tirelessly declared with much *éclat* at various gatherings, also had negative implications. However, in the face of a political situation where German nationalism was rapidly gaining ground, there was a general consensus that that represented a much greater danger to the small Slovene nation. Only a few could anticipate that the armour of Croatian state right, which Slovenes tried to buckle on to protect themselves from the blows of 'Teutonic' swords, would perhaps prove too tight and fatally suffocating.

The influential prince bishop of Ljubljana, Anton Bonaventura Jeglič, felt that Franz Ferdinand was an ally of the Slovenes in their trialist ambitions. Unlike Franz Joseph, who once scolded the prince bishop because of the obstruction of Šusteršič's Catholic Patriots in the Carniolan Provincial Diet, Franz Ferdinand was of a different opinion. He reportedly once said to Jeglič: 'Congratulations on your upstanding clergy.'[28] In any event, the list of Slovene and Croatian politicians who hoped that Franz Ferdinand would reform the state was most certainly an extensive one. Among them was Anton Korošec, who succeeded Šusteršič in heading the South Slav deputies in the Vienna Reichsrat and who in March 1910 defended the heir apparent against attacks from the Social Democratic leader Viktor Adler. Adler had described the Belvedere circle as a gang of inactive flatterers and bigots, who would destroy the administration bit by bit. Korošec, on the other hand, stated that every shoemaker's apprentice had the right to state his opinion about politics, while the same right was being denied to the heir apparent.²⁹

After the First World War, Korošec admitted to one of his confidants that the Belvedere circle had even drawn up a speech for one of his appearances in the Delegations, so that he could challenge the arguments of Hungarian politicians. Other deputies at the time had wondered where this Slovene politician had obtained such precise data. On that occasion, Korošec had also allegedly had a conversation with Franz Ferdinand, from which he most remembered the archduke's exclamation: 'Wir werden den Widerstand der madjarischen Gentry niederstampfen!' ('We will stamp upon the Magyar gentry's resistance!').³⁰ According to Korošec, therefore, Slovene deputies had had plenty of contacts with the exponents of the Greater Austrian idea, including Prince Karl Schwarzenberg who had assured them that he had 'great plans for the Southern Slavs'.³¹

An interesting record preserved in memoir literature confirms that Šušteršič also met the archduke in person. The meeting took place in the summer of 1909, when Šušteršič paid a visit to Franz Ferdinand in the company of Moric Hruban and Count Jaroslav Thun.³² Even though Šušteršič was not a member of the Belvedere circle, this cannot change the fact that his policy essentially followed the Greater Austrian course, a direction in which he deliberately steered the entire political activity of his party to benefit from the heir apparent's patronage. Not coincidentally, he consistently argued that through trialism the Monarchy would consolidate and strengthen its status as a Great Power.

Music to Franz Ferdinand's sensitive ears was also Šušteršič's blatant declaration of dynastic loyalty. In late July 1909, Šušteršič sent to the archduke an extensive memorandum clarifying his vision of the trialist reorganization of the Monarchy. The memorandum, dated 25 July 1909 from Toblach in Tyrol, is known to us solely from Šušteršič's booklet compiled in 1922, while the original version has still not been found. The undeniable existence of such a document is proven by Šušteršič's accompanying text to the memorandum and a letter of gratitude from the heir apparent's military chancellery, both preserved in the War Archives in Vienna. The letter of gratitude states that Franz Ferdinand 'took note' of the aforementioned memorandum 'with keen interest'.³³ In the memorandum, Šušteršič explained that 'dynastic interest ... corresponds entirely with the national interest of the Southern Slavs', because the future of the dynasty stood side by side with the Southern Slav peoples in the Balkan-Adriatic region. But in order for the Monarchy to gain ascendancy over the Balkans, Šušteršič maintained that it first had to fully implement a trialist programme:

> The unification of the Southern Slav lands and provinces into a third state within the Monarchy is imperative for the dynasty, for only in this way can a successful counterweight be provided against the three mortal enemies of the dynasty: Magyar chauvinism, and Italian and Serbian

Irredentism. A Southern Slav state within the Monarchy, encompassing Croatia-Slavonia, Bosnia and Herzegovina, the Serb provinces in Hungary, together with Slovene and Croatian lands and provinces in Cisleithania [Austria], particularly Dalmatia, the Littoral, Carniola and Slovene Styria, would put the ever-growing Southern Slav national movements at the service of a dynastic world policy. The Habsburg Southern Slav state would lay a sound foundation for the Monarchy's future policy in the Balkans and the Adriatic. ... Contrary to the present situation, when small neighbouring Southern Slav states often have a strong national appeal for Southern Slavs of the Monarchy, it will be the Great Habsburg Southern Slav state that will attract small states to itself.[34]

In his speeches in the Austrian Reichsrat, Šuteršič often drew from the vocabulary used by the heir apparent's followers, even excelling them in emphasizing Austrian dynastic patriotism. In November 1911, he sent to Franz Ferdinand via Bishop Jeglič the wording of one of his parliamentary speeches in which he extolled the power of the 'Austrian spirit'; he later received a letter of gratitude.[35] On 12 October 1912, the Croatian-Slovene Club in the Reichsrat sent a statement to the editorial board of the newspaper *Groß-Österreich* stressing that, throughout the recent parliamentary sessions, all its deputies had advocated an imperial and Greater Austrian orientation.[36]

Nevertheless, of all the Slovenes, it was Ivan Žolger, a lawyer from Styria, who seemed to be the closest to Franz Ferdinand. Žolger's major work was published in 1911 under the title *Der staatsrechtliche Ausgleich zwischen Österreich und Ungarn* (The Constitutional Compromise between Austria and Hungary). While researching this he had learnt Hungarian, and for that purpose even taken up temporary residence in Debrecen. As he then demonstrated, the Hungarian and German texts of the 1867 Compromise were not wholly compatible.[37] Žolger duly attracted the attention of Franz Ferdinand, who asked him to write a manifesto in which he would repudiate Magyar ambitions to extend Hungary's jurisdiction at the expense of imperial unity.[38]

Despite these examples, Vladimir Dedijer was indeed correct in establishing that Franz Ferdinand accorded the Slovenes a subordinate role compared to the Croats. This in itself was not an issue – in a way it even made sense – considering the existence of Croatian state right to which many Slovene leaders wanted to subject themselves for lack of a similar historic tradition of their own. But this is not to suggest that Franz Ferdinand did not perceive a role for the Slovenes in the burning Southern Slav Question. While he always failed to mention them in his statements concerning trialism, this does not imply that he excluded them from his trialist concept. There are enough memoirs (quoted for example by Dedijer) that demonstrate his ambition to include the Slovenes in any future third constitutional unit.

Interestingly, Dedijer's impressively comprehensive list of sources and literature did not contain a book by Edmund von Horváth, a Habsburg diplomat of Croatian descent, best known as the father of the famous writer Ödön Horváth. His statements regarding trialist plans make the work of Horváth Senior particularly notable. Not only due to his Croatian descent but also because of his superior knowledge of Serbia (as a diplomat, he spent several years in Belgrade), he was undoubtedly a go-to expert in discussions on the Southern Slav Question. During a visit to the Bavarian Court on 21 April 1914, Franz Ferdinand summoned the diplomat, who was then serving in Munich. The subject of their conversation was the Southern Slav Question, which, as Franz Ferdinand told him, was the Monarchy's most critical domestic and foreign political issue. It required an immediate solution or else there would be the worst possible consequences for Austria-Hungary; he also mentioned that the Magyars opposed any settlement of this question for domestic political reasons. In other words, reservations came from Hungary which, in a worst case scenario, would be forced to relinquish two provinces – Croatia and Slavonia. In the archduke's opinion, however, those territories had already essentially been lost to Budapest due to their cultural autonomy. As for Austria, he maintained that it should, as always, make greater sacrifices by relinquishing three southern crown lands: Carniola, Istria and Dalmatia.[39]

In the same conversation with Horváth, Franz Ferdinand accused the Magyars of using their policy to shake the once unwavering dynastic loyalty of Serbs and Romanians, who were beginning to turn towards Belgrade and Bucharest. Both capitals had now become the gravitational centres for their citizens, and there was a noticeable 'great conquering spirit', especially among the Serbs. The archduke particularly stressed the need to reform the franchise in Hungary. The days of gradual concessions were over; it was time to act swiftly and 'damn the Serbian flood'. He even contemplated preventing a potential 'Serbian invasion' by creating a new military frontier stretching from Zemun on the Serbian border to Kotor on the Adriatic. In this regard, he also remembered the merits of military commanders of Serbian descent in the imperial armies over the previous centuries. While explicitly rejecting any 'violent suppression of the loyal Serb element living in Austria-Hungary', he stressed that the Serbs should not enjoy a privileged position vis-à-vis other Southern Slavs. In the Habsburg Monarchy, he maintained, this also had much to do with the proportion of their population, which was approximately 1:3 against the Croats and Slovenes. The envisaged Southern Slav unit was to have its centre in Zagreb, but he was convinced that it could easily be included in the constitutional structure of the Monarchy.[40] On the basis of Horváth's account, it may again be concluded that Franz Ferdinand was considering the possibility of including at least some Slovenes in his trialist plans. This was only two months before his death in Sarajevo.

Yet the ultimate goal of Franz Ferdinand and his circle was still the establishment of Greater Austria and consolidation of the power of the imperial throne and the central government. He recognized one authentic criterion not just for the Southern Slavs but for all other peoples in the Monarchy: loyalty to the Habsburg dynasty. In his view, Catholic Croats and Slovenes were not only faithful to their Austrian dynastic tradition but were also his allies against Hungary's political preponderance as well as any idea of establishing a Greater Serbia. The Croatian and Slovene politicians who remained loyal to the dynasty undoubtedly stood as important pieces on his Belvedere chessboard, on which he would combine various scenarios to reform the Monarchy. Such was also the opinion of Anton Mahnič, bishop of Krk, who with his own ears in 1912 had heard the heir apparent say that he 'wished to establish our unit in the south'.[41]

## Pre-1914 and the Serbian dimension

The German-Austrian Christian Social Party had initially also pursued such a pro-Croatian policy, but it ended in 1910 with the death of their notorious leader Karl Lueger and at the same time they withdrew their support for trialism as well. German nationalist parties meanwhile were continuously opposed to any form of trialism whatsoever. Their antagonistic stance mainly stemmed from their fear that with the incorporation of Slovenes into a possible third state unit, the Germans would lose access to Trieste and the Adriatic. However, it would be wrong to identify their position with the views of the Greater Austrian advocates of trialism. Prince Heinrich Hanau, for instance, in the famous trialist maps which he issued in 1909 and 1912, charted how Slovene territory could fit within the boundaries of the Southern Slav state unit. For Hanau, Slovene incorporation was no argument against a trialist reconstruction of the Monarchy.[42]

The consolidation of a Slovene-Croatian political alliance undoubtedly reached its peak with the convocation of the 'First Croatian-Slovene Assembly' (Sabor), which was held on 20 October 1912 in Ljubljana.[43] The gathering was a remarkable manifestation of Slovene-Croatian fidelity towards the trialist idea. The Ljubljana Sabor also attracted major attention outside the Slovene and Croatian provinces. If any leading statesmen in Vienna and Budapest had until then remained in the dark about what Croatians and Slovenes meant by trialism, it must have surely dawned on them after the gathering in Ljubljana. Seen as a sign of dynastic loyalty by the Southern Slavs, the unification of the Pan-Slovene People's Party and the Croatian *pravaši* under the leadership of the 'extremely loyal' Šusteršič was even welcomed by Franz Ferdinand himself in a memorandum to the emperor.[44] But Šusteršič, the uncrowned duke of Carniola, was not destined to enjoy his triumph for long: the first shots fired by the Orthodox Christian armies in the Balkan Wars ushered in a new era in the development of the Southern Slav Question.

It is now generally accepted that the diplomatic games during the Balkan Wars were a kind of a prelude to the fateful events surrounding the Sarajevo assassination of 28 June 1914.[45] Even though Austro-Hungarian diplomacy enjoyed a fairly good starting position at the outbreak of the wars, this case, too, revealed the disastrous influence that domestic national-political relations had on the empire's functioning in the outside world. The statesmen in Vienna failed to heed the arguments of Slovene and Croatian politicians that protecting the interests of domestic South Slavs would ensure the protection of the Monarchy's interests regarding South Slavs abroad. For too long in particular Vienna had ignored the suspension of the constitution in Croatia, something which the Hungarian authorities then exacerbated by backing the notorious Cuvaj regime in 1912. While the clash between the league of the Balkan Orthodox states and the Ottoman Empire in the Balkan Wars brought disunity within the leading Slovene and Croatian parties, the aversion of German nationalists and the Habsburg elite to Southern Slav unification within the Monarchy grew even stronger.

In dealing with the Southern Slav challenge, Habsburg foreign policy indeed seemed to be without a clear concept. Instead of trying to find a solution for Serbian pretensions with regard to access to the sea at the outbreak of the Balkan hostilities, the Habsburg elite tried to appease Belgrade with concessions that would hardly have satisfied the Austrophile Obrenović dynasty of the 1880s, let alone the Russophile house of Karadjordjević. The assumption that Nikola Pašić, the master of Serbian diplomacy, might have been prevented from playing the role of Piedmont's Camillo Cavour is, of course, merely an assumption. But the fact is that despite its undoubtedly dominant role in the peninsula, Austro-Hungarian diplomacy gained very little from the Balkan Wars. The result in 1913 was a Romania with expanded borders but estranged from its former Habsburg ally; an Austrophile but defeated Bulgaria; a disgruntled Serbia without access to the sea; and a volatile Albania with a long stretch of coastline, ideal for the realization of the Italian thesis about the Adriatic as *mare nostro*. The growing Slovene and Croatian criticism, targeting Habsburg foreign policy, and present both in the press and private correspondence, was clearly well founded.

Thus, Franz Ferdinand and his think tank in the Belvedere remained the only hope in the eyes of the loyalist Southern Slav elites within the Habsburg Monarchy. And it appears that the secrets of the Belvedere circle were not hidden either from some leading Serbian diplomats and politicians. One of them was Miroslav Spalajković. He firmly believed that the Bosnians were the 'noblest part of the Serbian race' and that their blood had been preserved as the 'purest from foreign influences'. This was why Bosnia-Herzegovina proved a perfect place for him to find a wife – and one with a prominent standing among the local Bosnian Serb elite. For her father was Gligorije Jeftanović, president of the Orthodox Church municipality, who in 1904 had attended the coronation of Petar Karadjordjević in Belgrade as head of the Bosnian delegation and on that occasion had also met with Serbian prime minister Nikola Pašić. Jeftanović opposed the Habsburg annexation of Bosnia-Herzegovina and drew up a 'National Programme' (*Narodni program*) in collaboration with Spalajković, the then secretary general of the Serbian Foreign Ministry. With this tactical manoeuvre, the Serbian elite endorsed the idea of creating an autonomous Bosnian-Herzegovinian state unit as part of the Ottoman Empire. Since Jeftanović won financial support from Belgrade, the Bosnian delegation was then able to travel to London and St Petersburg and present its programme to foreign diplomats.[46] Spalajković, who before the First World War held some of the most prestigious positions in the diplomatic service of the kingdom of Serbia, was – partly via his father-in-law and his circle of friends – extremely well informed about the situation in the Habsburg Monarchy.

One can even note Spalajković's expert knowledge about the Greater Austrian plans. This was evident in a conversation he had in May 1912, when Serbian minister to Bulgaria, with his French colleague Hector André de Panafieu. It was Spalajković's opinion that in order to overcome its domestic political problems, Austria-Hungary should replace dualism with trialism. He stressed that Franz Ferdinand was 'an acknowledged supporter of trialism', 'his emissaries circle around all Slav provinces, spreading appealing slogans', and that one of his first steps after assuming the throne would be 'the establishment of a third state'. Spalajković believed that a Southern Slav state within the Habsburg empire would subsequently embrace not only Serbia and Montenegro but also Macedonia. Particularly interesting is Spalajković's conclusion that Serbia had to prevent Austria from delivering on its trialist plans, for otherwise Serbia would fail to survive as a sovereign entity in international relations. This was why, as Spalajković assured the French minister, Serbia had concluded a pact with Bulgaria and entered the Bulgarian-Serbian-Greek alliance under Russian patronage in order to stand against Austro-Hungarian ascendancy in the Balkans.[47] The conclusions from De Panafieu's dispatch were also confirmed by the French chargé d'affaires in Belgrade, Louis Frédéric Clément-Simon, when he realized that the idea of 'Austro-Hungarian-Slav trialism' had indeed been in the air for quite some time. And to all appearances, it even found some sympathizers in Serbia.[48]

This must have been clear also to the notorious Colonel Dragutin Dimitrijević-Apis and his conspiratorial Black Hand organization. In order to justify the terrorist methods of his organization, he would later describe Franz Ferdinand with the following words: 'By uniting South Slavs of the Monarchy under a uniform, co-ordinated administration [trialism], the archduke might halt the erosion of Austrian power and envelop Serbia.'[49] Some of the Sarajevo assassins certainly thought that Franz Ferdinand had been planning to reorganize the Monarchy and then incorporate into it both Serbia and Montenegro. They were also familiar with his protective stance towards the Croats. Gavrilo Princip in October 1914 stated that 'as future sovereign [Franz Ferdinand] would have prevented our union by carrying through certain reforms'.[50] Ivan Kranjčević, another of those accused at the Sarajevo trial, repeatedly claimed that Franz Ferdinand was 'a friend of the Croats' and 'a friend of all Slavs'.[51]

## Conclusion

It might therefore be argued that for Serbia the gravest menace was coming not from Conrad von Hötzendorf's notorious sabre rattling but from the supposed programme of Franz Ferdinand. Later, during the First World War, Nikola Pašić, who consistently believed in the triumph of the Greater Serbian idea and envisaged the demise of Austria-Hungary as only a question of time, repeatedly admitted to the Italian envoy on Corfu that he had been afraid only once in his life – when 'he was awaiting the outcome of the Archduke's ideas'.[52]

Unlike the rigid regime of Franz Joseph, Franz Ferdinand at least tried to provide solutions to the 'Austrian state problem'. This was often in a brusque, awkward and old-fashioned manner, but no one can deny his will to reform, his preparedness to merge Central European cultural diversity into a firmer state unity. Another question is what the real chances were for the realization of his plans. Rudolf Wierer, who in 1960 published what is still today perhaps the most detailed analysis of concepts of federalism in the modern Danube region, believed that the archduke's reform plans could have had good chances of success, if only he had been willing to strike some compromises on assuming the Habsburg throne.[53]

The historian Robert A. Kann was more sceptical that Franz Ferdinand's plans could really have meshed with the rapidly increasing national consciousness in the Habsburg Monarchy at the beginning of the twentieth century. But as he himself stated, some of the archduke's contemporaries thought otherwise.[54] R. W. Seton-Watson, for example, argued on the eve of the First World War that trialism could be accomplished, and he even recommended it as a first step towards federalization of the Habsburg Monarchy on an ethnic basis. On the other hand, the unification of Croats and Serbs outside the Monarchy could, he felt, only be realized through a general war and a radical redrawing of the European map. Therefore, according to the legendary 'Scotus Viator', Southern Slav unity under the Habsburgs was a better solution: 'The triumph of the Pan-Serb idea would mean the triumph of Eastern over Western, and would be a fatal blow to progress and modern development throughout the Balkans.'[55] Despite the fact that Seton-Watson later became a major advocate of Serbia as the 'Yugoslav Piedmont', his predictions proved accurate. Princip's shots at Sarajevo took away any possibility of a peaceful solution to the Southern Slav Question within the Habsburg Monarchy, and it was Yugoslavia which finally emerged from the ruins of the Great War.

## Notes

1 Ivanka Klemenčič, *Zločin v Sarajevu. Tragična smrt prestolonaslednika Franca Ferdinanda in njegove soproge vojvodinje Hohenberg* (Ljubljana: Katoliška bukvarna, 1914), 50–1.

2 Brigita Mader, *Sfinga z Belvederja in spomeniško varstvo v Istri/Die Sphinx vom Belvedere und die Denkmalpflege in Istrien* (Koper: Historical Society for Southern Primorska, Science and Research Centre of Koper, Regional Museum, 2010).

3 Haus-, Hof- und Staatsarchiv, Vienna, Nachlaß Franz Ferdinand (hereafter HHStA, NFF), II, karton 12: Ottokar Czernin, 'Über die Lösung der ungarischen Frage', May 1911.

4 Georg Franz, *Erzherzog Franz Ferdinand und die Pläne zur Reform der Habsburger Monarchie* (Brünn, Munich, Vienna: Deutsches auslandswissenschaftliches Institut, 1943), 84.

5 Vladimir Dedijer, *Sarajevo 1914* (Ljubljana: Državna založba Slovenije, 1966), 197–9.

6 Hans Ritter von Schlitter, 'Franz Ferdinand, wie er wirklich war', *Neues Wiener Journal*, 9 March 1932.

7 Albert Margutti, *Vom alten Kaiser. Persönliche Erinnerungen an Franz Joseph I. Kaiser von Österreich und apostolischen König von Ungarn* (Leipzig and Vienna: Leonhardt, 1921), 137.

8 Rudolf Sieghart, *Die letzten Jahrzehnte einer Großmacht. Menschen, Völker, Probleme des Habsburger-Reichs* (Berlin: Ullstein, 1932), 240.

9 For more on Bombelles, see Chapter 4 by Iskra Iveljić in this volume.

10 HHStA, NFF, II, karton 10: Bombelles letter to Franz Ferdinand, 25 January 1908.

11 Rudolf Kiszling, *Erzherzog Franz Ferdinand von Österreich-Este. Leben, Pläne und Wirken am Schicksalweg der Donaumonarchie* (Graz and Cologne: Böhlau, 1953), 231.

12 Hrvatski Državni Arhiv Zagreb (Croatian State Archives – hereafter HDA), Rukopisna ostavština Vjekoslava Spinčića (Spinčić MSS), kutija 2, Spinčić diary, 27 February 1912.

13 HDA, Spinčić diary, 6 October 1905.

14 HDA, Spinčić diary, 14 June 1907.

15 Leopold Chlumecky, *Erzherzog Franz Ferdinands Wirken und Wollen* (Berlin: Verlag für Kulturpolitik, 1929), 94.

16 For more on this, see Henryk Batowski, 'Die drei Trialismen', *Österreichische Osthefte* 7 (1965): 265–74.

17 Kiszling, *Erzherzog*, 220–1.

18 Ivanov (Milivoj Dežman), *Južnoslavensko pitanje* (Zagreb: Dionička tiskara, 1918), 71.

19 Joseph Maria Baernreither, *Fragmente eines politischen Tagebuches. Die südslawische Frage und Österreich vor dem Weltkrieg*, ed. Joseph Redlich (Berlin: Verlag für Kulturpolitik, 1928), 235.

20 *Stenographische Sitzungs-Protokolle der Delegation des Reichsrates* (Vienna, 1914), XLIX/2, 19 May 1914, 41–2.

21 'Državnopravno stališče Slovencev in Hrvatov', *Slovenec*, 11 February 1905.

22 According to the dualist agreement of 1867, the 'Delegations' were two parliamentary bodies, nominated respectively by the parliaments in Vienna and Budapest, to discuss annually the areas of defence and foreign policy in the Monarchy. See Éva Somogyi, 'Die Delegation als Verbindungsinstitution zwischen Cis- und Transleithanien', in Helmut Rumpler (ed.), *Die Habsburgermonarchie 1848–1918* VII/1 (Vienna: Akademie der Wissenschaften, 2000), 1107–76.

23 Nikola Zvonimir Bjelovučić, *Trializam i hrvatska država* (Dubrovnik: vlas. nakl., 1911), 8–13.

24 Baernreither, *Fragmente*, 235.

25 Matija Škerbec, *Pregled novodobnega slovenskega katoliškega gibanja*, 2 vols (Cleveland: Samozaložba, 1956–7), I, 158.

26 Jurij Perovšek, 'Ušeničnik in jugoslovanstvo', in Matija Ogrin and Janez Juhant (eds), *Aleš Ušeničnik, čas in ideje. 1868–1952. Zbornik razprav s simpozija SAZU ob 50. obletnici smrti* (Celje and Ljubljana: Mohorjeva družba, 2004), 97–110.

27 Aleš Ušeničnik, 'Slovenci in Hrvati', *Čas* 7 (1913): 431–41.

28 Matjaž Ambrožič (ed.), *Dnevniški zapiski dr. Evgena Lampeta (1898–1917)* (Ljubljana: Arhivsko društvo Slovenije, 2007), 64.

29 Dedijer, *Sarajevo*, 163–4.

30 Arhiv Slovenskega biografskega leksikona, Ljubljana, Mapa Antona Korošca: letter of Engelbert Besednjak to the editorial board of the Slovenian Biographical Lexicon, 9 January 1941.

31 Silvo Kranjec, 'Koroščevo predavanje o postanku Jugoslavije', *Zgodovinski časopis* 16 (1962): 220.

32 Fritz Fellner and Doris Corradini (eds), *Schicksaljahre Österreichs. Die Erinnerungen und Tagebücher Josef Redlichs 1869–1936*, 3 vols (Vienna: Böhlau, 2011), I, 278.

33 Österreichisches Staatsarchiv, Kriegsarchiv, Vienna (War Archives: hereafter KA), Militärkanzlei Franz Ferdinand, E/24/1909: Šusteršič's accompanying text to the memorandum of 25 July 1909, and the letter of gratitude from the heir apparent's military chancellery, 30 July 1909. I am very grateful to Walter Lukan for having forwarded to me these two important documents.

34 Ivan Šušteršič [Šusteršič], *Moj odgovor* (Ljubljana: Samozaložba, 1922), 63–4.

35 Blaž Otrin and Marija Čipić Rehar (eds), *Jegličev dnevnik. Znanstvenokritična izdaja* (Ljubljana: Celjska Mohorjeva družba, 2015), 522.

36 *Groß-Österreich*, 13 October 1912.

37 Ivan Žolger, *Der staatsrechtliche Ausgleich zwischen Oesterreich und Ungarn* (Vienna: Duncker & Humblot, 1911).

38 KA, Nachlaß Alexander Brosch von Aarenau, B 232/20: draft of the Imperial Manifesto of October 1911; Matthias Murko, *Spomini* (Ljubljana: Slovenska matica, 1951), 124–5.

39  Edmund von Horváth, *So starb der Friede. Unbekanntes über die Entstehung des Weltkrieges* (Berlin: Bruecken, 1930), 81.
40  Ibid.
41  HDA, Spinčić diary, 27 February 1912.
42  Heinrich Hanau, *Triaskarte der Habsburger Monarchie*, 1: 1,500.000 (Vienna: Freytag & Berndt, 1909); *Neue Triaskarte der Habsburger Monarchie*, 1: 1,500.000 (Vienna: G. Freytag & Berndt, 1912).
43  For more on this subject, see Janko Pleterski, 'Zveza Vseslovenske ljudske stranke in Hrvatske stranke prava', *Zgodovinski časopis* 39 (1999): 65–73.
44  Kiszling, *Erzherzog*, 234.
45  Richard C. Hall, *The Balkan Wars 1912–1913: Prelude to the First World War* (London and New York: Routledge, 2000).
46  Friedrich Würthle, *Die Spur führt nach Belgrad. Die Hintergründe des Dramas von Sarajevo 1914* (Vienna, Munich and Zurich: Fritz Molden, 1975), 113.
47  *Documents diplomatiques français (1871–1914)*, I–III, eds. Ministère des Affaires Étrangères, Commission de publication des documents relatifs aux origines de la guerre de 1914 (Paris, 1931) III/3, Nr. 74.
48  Michael von Vorner, 'Erzherzog Franz Ferdinand und der Trialismus', *Neues Wiener Journal*, 29 October 1931.
49  Tony Fabijančić, *Bosnia: In the Footsteps of Gavrilo Princip* (Edmonton: The University of Alberta Press, 2010), 62.
50  Christopher Clark, *The Sleepwalkers: How Europe Went to War in 1914* (New York: Harper Collins, 2013), 49.
51  Vojislav Bogićević (ed.), *Sarajevski atentat. Izvorne stenografske bilješke sa glavne rasprave protiv Gavrila Principa i drugova, održane u Sarajevu 1914 g.* (Sarajevo: Državni arhiv NR BiH, 1954), 189–90.
52  Carlo Sforza, *Fifty Years of War and Diplomacy in the Balkans: Pashich and the Union of the Yugoslavs* (New York: Columbia University Press, 1940), 76.
53  Rudolf Wierer, *Der Föderalismus im Donauraum* (Graz and Cologne: Böhlau, 1960), 123.
54  Robert A. Kann, *Das Nationalitätenproblem der Habsburgermonarchie. Geschichte und Ideengehalt der nationalen Bestrebungen vom Vormärz bis zur Auflösung des Reiches*, 2 vols (Graz and Cologne: Amalthea, 1964), II, 261.
55  R. W. Seton-Watson, *The Southern Slav Question and the Habsburg Monarchy* (London: Constable, 1911), 336–7.

# CHAPTER 4

# Noblesse oblige

# The outlook of the Croatian aristocracy on the eve of the First World War*

*Iskra Iveljić*

The world of Franz Ferdinand was that of the Habsburg Monarchy's social elite, so it naturally interacted at times with that of the aristocracy in Croatia-Slavonia. While this in itself makes the latter a valuable case study, supplying new context for the events of Sarajevo in 1914, it especially opens up for us a singular perspective on the thorny Southern Slav Question. It reveals the real diversity of political and national perspectives among (from the outside) a seemingly homogeneous social elite, and underlines why compromise or resolution was so difficult for the key Habsburg decision makers.

For any historian assessing the old elite in a region where the nobility played an important role, it may seem paradoxical to begin with basic issues

---

*This chapter covers the aristocracy of Croatia-Slavonia, that is, the Croatian territory which was administered by the ban (the Croatian royal governor). The Croatian lands were divided up for centuries, not only in their territorial administration but also in their whole social development. Because of this I have not sought to encompass Istria and Dalmatia as well. This research emerged as part of a project funded by the Croatian Science Foundation, Nr 4153, *Croatia and Central Europe: Art and Politics in the Late Modern Period (1780-1945)* led by Dragan Damjanović. I am much indebted to Mark Cornwall for translating and editing this chapter.

about identity and status. Yet these problems are not Croatian but generic, following a recent trend in European historiography that has tried to address the key questions: Who actually belonged to the aristocracy in the modern age, and how did they behave in the face of modernization and national integration? In other words, were those aristocrats of exclusively ancient lineage inflexible and hostile towards modern civic society and emerging nations, or more adaptable than previously imagined?[1] Concerning the nobility of the Habsburg Empire on the eve of the Great War, there is also the question of whether it was unreservedly devoted to the dynasty or whether its loyalty was in fact more complex and multi-layered. While naturally not aspiring to offer definitive answers, we can emphasize from the start an aristocratic affiliation based on various criteria. A lofty title and impressively large estate were simply not sufficient; rather, the true aristocrat had to command a very significant reputation and influence, and above all a corresponding degree of self-stylization. Following the collapse of a feudal society based on estates, aristocratic mindsets were very much shaped by their cultural lifestyle. Nevertheless, we must adjust these criteria to match the specific conditions in different European regions. In Croatia and Slavonia, for example, barons too belonged to the peerage, and alongside other nobles some of them could exercise their right of personal representation in the Croatian Sabor or assembly (as so-called virilists) until the collapse of the Habsburg Monarchy.[2] Furthermore, a clear ascendancy was evident for a new nobility who previously had belonged to the non-noble social stratum. Among the newcomers, notable was the proportion of Serbs who had been ennobled thanks to administrative or military service. Some of them had become a landowning plutocracy with substantial political influence and a proportionate lifestyle, acquiring even baronial titles.

It seems advisable therefore to adopt a broad definition of the Croatian aristocracy on the eve of the First World War.[3] William Godsey has shown how, through being assigned the honorary title of 'court chamberlain', an aristocrat could be incorporated into that most select circle – the court nobility – and how during the era of dualism after 1867 there were 474 such noble families in the Habsburg Monarchy.[4] Interestingly, the criteria for securing the dignity of 'chamberlain' pre-1914 were stricter than in the days of Maria Theresa. Yet that did not mean that this elite circle was inaccessible to new nobility since, with selection operating on a clientele principle, individuals were accepted as chamberlains who did not comply with the formal conditions. However, by the twentieth century the aristocracy could not simply be equated with this court nobility and its self-selecting criteria; it was necessary in every case to define aristocrats according to some external criteria as well. Therefore, for the purposes of this chapter, all nobles will be included as 'aristocrats' who bore at least the title of baron, who had large estates, who exercised substantial influence (especially in the political sphere) and who cultivated an appropriate material lifestyle with regard to their cultural, educational and leisure activities.

## The political world of the aristocrat

On the eve of the Great War, the nobility occupied the major influential posts in the political administration of Croatia-Slavonia – namely, the ban (governor), the county prefects (*veliki župani*), the Croatian minister in the Hungarian government,[5] as well as taking up seats as 'virilists' in the Sabor in Zagreb. At the end of the nineteenth century, they had formed 15 per cent to 30 per cent of the elected Sabor members.[6] In the final pre-war Sabor, in session from 27 December 1913, eighteen of the eighty-eight elected deputies were noblemen, while eight virilists also participated in the work of the assembly. Indeed, including the new ban himself, Baron Ivan Skerlecz, the total number of noblemen in the Sabor was twenty-six, of whom six were barons and five were counts. However, if we examine the Sabor's inner workings, the influence of the nobility is even more striking. Aristocrats chaired half of the Sabor committees (four out of the eight) and formed a third of the important committee that composed the assembly's address to the monarch. Of the forty Sabor delegates chosen to represent Croatia in the lower house of the Hungarian parliament in Budapest (as part of the *Nagodba* – the sub-dualist settlement of 1868), the nobility formed a fifth, but we should also note those Croatian virilists who continued to sit in the Hungarian upper house.[7]

It is indicative of the aristocracy's political culture that the most influential among them rarely spoke in the Sabor in 1913–14: they did not behave like modern parliamentary politicians but like an oligarchy who pulled the strings mainly behind the scenes. The characteristic maxims of their political culture were constitutionalism, law and order, loyalty, respect for authority, hierarchy, an emphasis on principles and corporatism rather than liberal individualism. Implicit in the aristocratic mindset was a superiority to all others, with no limitations on their behaviour; individual freedoms or possibilities were for them and not for commoners. An aristocrat had the right to carve out his own free space of activity, and even to be thoroughly eccentric as long as it did not encroach upon a fellow aristocrat. But when it became a matter of honour, then those barriers fell and duels could still occur. It is remarkable, for instance, how often the conservative aristocrat Baron Pavao Rauch unsuccessfully challenged his political opponents to a duel, the last time when he was ban in May 1908.[8] For Rauch there was a tight link between personal honour and politics: thus, in the face of offensive press articles, he challenged Bogdan Medaković, the leader of the Serb National Independent Party in Croatia (*Srpska narodna samostalna stranka*). Rauch here demonstrated not only the traditional code of honour but also a political naivety and levity, all the more surprising since he really needed to be circumspect towards Serb politicians in view of the imminent high treason trial in Zagreb. To all appearances Rauch was naively confident that he would get the support of Vienna for the duel, something that, however, failed to materialize.[9]

As this suggests, the political culture of the Croatian-Slavonian aristocracy on the eve of war was complex. On the one hand, it was defined very traditionally. On the other, being an aristocrat meant great freedom but also implied adapting to the modern world as part of a strategy of self-preservation. While a significant proportion of aristocrats behaved very conservatively, they knew how to accommodate themselves if it was in their interest. Their rhetoric sometimes was partly at odds with their practice. While they clamoured against any disintegration of authority or traditional values, and criticized the ignorance of the masses, at the same time they took pains to establish economic and political links with the plutocracy. Characteristic here were their relations with the Jews. Although in principle they expressed anti-Semitism in their language, they did not hesitate to cooperate with Jews over business deals, and considered a pronounced and active anti-Semitism as something inappropriate for the upper classes but rather a product of bourgeois nationalism.

Yet the position of the aristocracy was still in a process of considerable flux. The start of the twentieth century was of course marked by a series of crises and conflicts within and without the Habsburg Monarchy: the annexation of Bosnia-Herzegovina and the Balkan Wars made the Southern Slav Question a hotly contested subject. In 1909, the Austrian writer Hermann Bahr wrote in his *Journey to Dalmatia* that while the Monarchy could stay strong in the Balkans only through cooperation with the Southern Slavs, its politicians still did not realize that it had now been transformed from an eastern German empire into a western Slavic empire.[10] Although the Habsburg minister of foreign affairs, Alois Lexa von Aehrenthal, was in fact well aware of this development, his policy of social imperialism – maintaining the Monarchy's Great Power status as an instrument of settling domestic problems – would eventually prove fatal. Indeed, the declaration of war on Serbia in 1914 occurred precisely because a significant part of the Habsburg elite was convinced that it was the only way to preserve the Monarchy's honour and prestige.[11] Through their lens, the Southern Slav Question could only be solved through arms.

At the start of the twentieth century the Croatian political scene was dynamic and variegated, with new parties, public demonstrations, assassination attempts (by members of the nationalist Yugoslav youth movement: *nacionalistička omladina*), and especially peasant and workers' unrest. The situation was exacerbated by divisions among the ruling echelons of the Monarchy, with the empire's dualist structure causing a mass of difficulties in terms of decision making. Even the ruling dynasty was split, for the heir apparent, as Alma Hannig's chapter shows, disagreed on many issues with the monarch. And finally Franz Joseph himself embodied the division for he had to perform and decide differently as Austrian emperor and as Hungarian-Croatian king.[12] So it was not surprising that many aristocrats felt their world was imploding or even in crisis. It is also worth noting that while some major aristocratic families in Croatia-Slavonia had either died out in the male line, left the region or withdrawn from public life (Nugent Westmeath, Sermage, Hilleprand von Prandau, Janković Daruvarski), other non-aristocrats such as Nikola Tomašić, Vladimir Nikolić and Antun Mihalović had recently risen to prominence and proceeded to play leading roles in the state apparatus thanks to their political and economic acumen.

The frequent and fast pace of change in the political constellation meant that politics could not be run on the basis of firm and long-term principles; it could be managed only through constant negotiations and compromises. The multi-centred nature of politics produced constantly fluctuating positions, and since everyone could interact with everybody else, the boundaries between them became ever thinner. Although aristocrats on the whole remained loyal to the sovereign, they were increasingly oriented towards strategies of self-preservation. The economic situation too presented them with a challenge. Symptomatic was the fact that by 1900 one of the largest landowners in Croatia-Slavonia was the ennobled Jewish bourgeois family, Gutmann, which was of Hungarian descent with excellent ties to the Magyar federation of industrialists.[13] Nevertheless, an insecure nobility had a hard time adapting to a market economy, all the more so because the Hungarian government's tariff policy impeded Croatia's industrial development, turning banking and the timber business into the most lucrative parts of the economy as a whole. Therefore nobles who followed a particular political orientation often had strong connections to particular banks or capital providers (e.g. Nikola Tomašić with Hungarian, Count Miroslav Kulmer with Croatian). Croatian-Serbian capital certainly could not compete with Austro-German or Hungarian capital, but it exploited the backing of Czech capital (*Živnostenská banka, Ustřední banka*), which at this time was trying to establish itself in Southern Slav regions for business but also for national-political reasons. When in 1905 a new political grouping, the Croat-Serb Coalition (*Hrvatsko-srpska koalicija*), emerged as a representative of domestic capital, it relied on the Croatian Savings Bank, the Serbian Bank and the Agrarian Bank, all of which were connected to the Ljubljana Credit Bank and the Adriatic Bank in Trieste, both founded to a large extent by Czech capital.

## National stances and the aristocracy

Even though they tried to keep up appearances, the Croatian aristocracy was very much divided on political and national issues. Unlike their Hungarian or Bohemian counterparts, they did not have their own parties;[14] and since the very start of the Croatian national movement in the 1830s, they had been on both sides of the nationalist debate ('Illyrians' as supporters and 'Magyarones' as opponents). Without their own political parties, aristocrats at least on the domestic scene were inclined to a certain cooperation with the bourgeoisie and the new nobility, but until the turn of the century this was restricted because they needed sufficient domestic capital to become reliable economic partners.

While national and political issues were very much intertwined, aristocrats usually found it extremely difficult to define themselves nationally. Their whole way of life meant they had multilayered identities that, seen through the nationalist lens, had to be simplified. Certainly, many still cherished traditional patriotism based on Croatian territory, but most at the same time were also transnational in their economic, political and family connections. Therefore it was possible for them to be vehement opponents of each other in the political arena but behind the scenes to socialize amicably since their families were often related. For example, the conservative and pro-Hungarian Erdödys were related to the pro-Austrian and pro-Croatian Kulmers, Draškovićs and Bombelles. Then there were ties to the Habsburg elite. Surviving correspondence and memoirs reveal strong ties of some aristocrats to Archduke Franz Ferdinand, Aehrenthal or Archduke Leopold Salvator, to a range of influential officers like Moritz von Auffenberg, Maximilian Csicserics (Maksimilian Čičerić) or Eduard Zanantoni, and directly to the monarch himself.[15] One of Aehrenthal's closest aides in the Ballhausplatz was the ennobled Aleksandar Musulin, a Croat diplomat of Serb origin who was exceptionally loyal to the dynasty and personally acquainted with a whole range of Croatian politicians.[16] From the nineteenth century, Croatian aristocrats had taken political positions that were pro-Magyar (the Hellenbachs, the Pejačevićs), pro-Austrian (the Bombelles) or pro-Croatian (the Oršićs, the Jelačićs), yet political orientation was not identical with national identification.[17] Thus during the dualist era in particular, a Croatian national orientation was often combined with a pro-Vienna standpoint since Budapest was considered by many to be the main political foe.

In the decade before 1914, these noblemen supported a variety of political parties: the pro-Hungarian National Party (*Narodna stranka*),[18] the Croat-Serb Coalition,[19] and to a much lesser extent the various parties of (Croatian) state right.[20] With regard to the latter, the parties of Josip Frank and Mile Starčević were attractive to the lesser nobility, at least until Frank's cooperation with the circle around Franz Ferdinand.[21] The disintegration of the Liberal Party in Hungary and therefore of the pro-Hungarian National Party in Croatia, and the rise of the Croat-Serb Coalition that won the 1906 Sabor elections – these events were a heavy blow to aristocrats who were pro-Budapest. They never found a proper party substitute, since the Party of National Progress (*Stranka narodnog napretka*) founded by Ban Nikola Tomašić in 1911 remained a small group. Nevertheless, this inadequacy was compensated for by the activity of high-ranking officials (the ban, the regional prefects, the Croatian minister assigned to the Hungarian government), who were really exponents of Hungarian policy. And since the Croat-Serb Coalition from 1910 supported various compromises with the Magyar regime, some of the pro-Hungarian nobility were prepared to cooperate with it.

Even though the conservative-liberal divide did not follow national and political lines, for there were both liberals and conservatives even in the National Party, the conservative nobility was often anti-Serbian and anti-Yugoslav in its orientation, and was utilized in its power schemes by several political power centres outside Croatia (in Vienna or Budapest, by the army, or the Greater Austrian circle associated with Franz Ferdinand).

A good example as a case study is that of Baron Pavao Rauch, the Croatian ban from 1908 to 1910 (Figure 4.1). Many prominent individuals had warned that Rauch was an unsuitable candidate for the position of ban. On 26 July 1907 General Rade Grba characterized Rauch for the War Ministry in Vienna as a 'Magyarone' of no distinction, a drunkard who lived apart from his wife, a man whose name was detested across Croatia. Grba correctly cautioned that not much was known about Croatia, and that even in Budapest every '*Staatskünstler*' had experimented on her; only these experts felt that Croatia was nurturing a revolutionary ferment that justified their tactics. In fact, according to Grba – who was a Serb – that revolutionary character was exaggerated, the people were loyal to the dynasty, and among them there prevailed the old military sense of allegiance to the monarch. But for this to persist something needed to happen, for after forty years of limited political and economic change, the people wanted more concrete proof of support and progress. Grba finally condemned the abuse circulating against Serb politicians like Bogdan Medaković and Sava Šumanović.[22]

In spite of this warning, Rauch in 1908 still became ban on the basis that he would deflect Croatian political forces from cooperation with Budapest and try to form a political bloc loyal to his regime.[23] Rauch's major task was also to expose Serbs as an anti-dynastic element prone to terrorism, and thus to prepare the stage for the annexation of Bosnia-Herzegovina; this led to the notorious Zagreb high treason trial against fifty-three Serbs, mostly members of the oppositional Serb National Independent Party.[24] It is interesting that in April 1909 Rauch personally visited the historian Heinrich Friedjung in Vienna, urging him to be a witness in the trial, something that Friedjung declined. Friedjung immediately reported to Aehrenthal that he did not get the impression that Rauch was assessing the situation in a way that took account of the well-being of the whole Monarchy; he also expressed his unfavourable impression of the Rauch regime in a letter to the British historian R. W. Seton-Watson.[25]

Rauch fully shared the viewpoint of the prosecution in the Zagreb treason trial of 1909, doubting that there had been any genuine Serbs in Croatia until at least the seventeenth-century migrations. Rather, they were 'Vlachs', who under the influence of the Orthodox priesthood had started defining themselves as Serbs. Thus any group claiming to be Serb or Serbian was suggesting a political allegiance that was per se treasonous since in Croatia there was only one 'political nation' – the Croatian.[26] Not surprisingly,

FIGURE 4.1 *'Baron Pavao Rauch. Ban of the kingdom of Croatia, Slavonia and Dalmatia'*. Official heliogravure by Rudolf Mosinger (Croatian History Museum, Zagreb, Nr 11416).

during Rauch's term of office as ban there were constant problems over the use of the Cyrillic alphabet or the Serbian flag, and his overall policy turned some local petty conflicts into national issues. On this point, it is worth stressing that a good number of the officials whom he appointed were conservative aristocrats. A tighter circle of friends and family then served as a familiar clientele around him, including his nephew Janko Jelačić as prefect (*veliki župan*) in Varaždin county; there were even some individuals who had been on the staff of his father, Ban Levin Rauch (1868–71).[27]

Concerning the agitation and propaganda circulating in these years, the historiography needs to address more carefully the question of how far ordinary local conflicts especially in rural areas could, under the impact of external forces, be interpreted primarily through a national lens.[28] For at this time a whole range of power interests were clashing in Croatia, interweaving the supporters of the Greater Austrian circle, the Vienna and Budapest governments and an array of domestic political parties. Even Croat and Serb political forces were confronted with a complex range of options: the Croats, with pro-Austrian, pro-Hungarian, Greater Croatian, moderate Croatian or Yugoslav options; the Serbs, with a radically nationalist orientation towards Belgrade, or moderate political cooperation with Croats and the Vienna or Budapest power centres. In short, Serbs were increasingly uncertain as to whether Croatia should form a bridge for, or a barrier against, Austro-German penetration into the Balkans.[29]

This tense atmosphere provided ample space for a whole range of political, national, economic and private clashes and intrigues. Anonymous denunciations against Serbs arose even from their fellow-countrymen. For example, in 1908, an anonymous telegram reached Zagreb accusing the Orthodox priest in Brđani near Petrinja of failing to hold a service of thanksgiving on the monarch's birthday (18 August). An investigation found that in the past it had always taken place at the Orthodox festival of the Transfiguration, which usually coincided with Franz Joseph's birthday. In 1908, however, the two had not coincided, so the priest had announced in advance that the service would be held instead on 19 August, to make sure that the church would be full of worshippers. Significantly, the county report for Zagreb noted that the priest was seventy years old and an active supporter of the Serb Radical Party, while the author of the telegram was a hostile teacher and supporter of the Serb Independent Party.[30]

When it came to Great Serbian propaganda in Croatia or the smuggling of arms, the Rauch regime did not at first pose difficulties to individuals or groups arriving from Serbia if there was no reason for suspicion.[31] District and county authorities quite often undertook proper investigations and sent their reports to Zagreb. Despite this, the Croatian government and the ban cannot evade responsibility for some quite tendentious actions. Regularly they relocated or removed from office any adherents of the opposition or any Serbs, regardless of whether they were teachers, civil servants or officials in the local administration. Indeed, in a supplement to one letter of December 1908 sent to Géza Daruváry, the *Sektionschef* of Franz Joseph's *Kabinettskanzlei* in Vienna, Rauch stated clearly how he was against Serbs being strongly represented on the judicial bench, for then the imminent treason trial would not be 'objective' and Croats – especially members of the Frank party – would also be deeply disillusioned.[32]

The Zagreb regime's attitude to the Serb Sokol (gymnastic) organization was also telling. In August 1908, the Croatian government asked local authorities for detailed reports about the Serb Sokol clubs; it wanted data about their location and numbers, about where members lived, their distance from the club's location, and about each Sokol's political activity. The reports submitted were very varied. That from the town of Dvor felt that the local Sokol association had a political agenda for it lacked any gymnastic training or premises; the members came to meetings with Serbian flags and dress. From Vrginmost on the Bosnian border, it was reported that although the club was not conspicuously political, some individuals certainly were; a significant number of those members were very poor and in debt, and the centre of Serbdom in this district was the Vrginmost savings bank. The Zagreb county prefect Aleksandar Vučetić, on the basis of the submitted local data, asked the government to dissolve all Serb Sokol clubs in Kostajnica, and also passed on information about the leaders of the clubs in Korenica and Gračac, asking for their removal. On the other hand, the reports from the Srijem and Senj-Modruš prefects were more moderate and formulaic, supplying just facts with no evaluation.[33] What seemed clear to the Rauch regime was that the Sokol clubs were promoting not just gymnastics but a nationalist agenda as well. It was therefore keen to monitor them in order to staunch Serb nationalism, but that same type of vigilance was not exercised upon the Croat Sokol clubs.

The high treason trial of 1909 placed a great strain on Croat-Serb relations in Croatia. The message which the trial conveyed to Serbs (notably the Serb Independent Party which was part of the Croat-Serb Coalition) was that they should abandon their alliance with Croat parties, display total loyalty or suffer persecution. Part of Rauch's agenda then was to break up the Coalition, enticing its moderate Croat parties into a new coalition with the Frank party in order to create a new and sizeable Croatian bloc. However, the scheme was a total fiasco, not just because Rauch had failed to win a single seat in the Sabor elections of early 1908, but because he was trapped in perpetual conflicts with Budapest and Vienna. Despite his previous pro-Hungarian stance, as ban, Rauch inclined more to Vienna than to Budapest, complaining to the Habsburg monarch and to Aehrenthal about Budapest's lack of cooperation.[34] He regularly corresponded with Daruváry, skirting around Budapest, and was in open conflict with Géza Josipović, the Croatian minister in the Hungarian government, trying to replace him with one of the conservative aristocrats from his own circle.[35]

Rauch therefore had been given a stick but without any carrot. His hopes that he might win over the general public through a programme of economic improvement were also an illusion, since the Hungarian government promptly prevented any major reforms.[36] Ordinary people were of course very interested in raising their living standards, in building waterworks, railways, schools, hospitals and factories. But the Viennese and Budapest centres gave him no help in this regard beyond aiding his appointment to power in Croatia. That was not just a problem for Rauch and Croatia. All the programmes, whether of the circles around Aehrenthal or Franz Ferdinand, were not geared towards any concrete results which would convince national politicians, disgruntled with the way politics was operating, that they could realize their interests within the Monarchy. All the envisaged key changes suggested an uncertain future, especially those of the heir apparent who clashed with Aehrenthal and offered no really concrete solution. Franz Ferdinand, who was neither a federalist nor a trialist, tried with different plans to lure dissatisfied Romanians, Slovaks and Croats, but it was all a fig leaf for a programme intended to strengthen the powers of the Austrian centre. His idea of a basic revision of the Austro-Hungarian Settlement of 1867 to the detriment of the Magyars did not imply any substantial change to the position of the non-Magyar peoples; rather, it would simply offer them equality in inequality.[37]

Hard-line aristocratic conservatives like Rauch favoured a dynastic and 'strong arm' policy for Croatia (even pressing for a military governor), and they fiercely opposed the Croat-Serb Coalition.[38] Rauch's successor as ban, Nikola Tomašić (1910–12), a supporter of the former ban and Hungarian prime minister Károly Khuen-Héderváry, was keen to reconcile with Serbs in Croatia and cooperate with major land and capital owners, especially in Slavonia; he managed to forge a deal with the Coalition. Yet he ultimately failed for the same reasons as Rauch, even if this time the Hungarian opposition played a part. Although the Coalition took a conservative turn, Tomašić's strategy was disparaged by both conservative aristocrats and the Slavonian group of property owners, who were frustrated at not receiving state subsidies for their entrepreneurship. The following period, when the Croatian constitution was again suspended, was abhorred by all aristocrats who mainly set their hopes on the new ban Baron Ivan Skerlecz (1913–17), a confidant of the Hungarian prime minister István Tisza. In November 1913, conservatives would again be disappointed by the settlement agreed between Tisza and the Croat-Serb Coalition.

Even this brief survey shows that Croatia's political scene was tense and complex, stimulated by foreign and domestic crises. All major Hungarian political parties also lacked any consistent Croatian policy; they overestimated the Southern Slav danger, and because they often failed to fulfil agreements made with Croatian parties, Yugoslav options became more attractive to the latter. When in October 1915 Tisza finally came up with a political solution for the Southern Slav Question, it was conceived as a Magyar imperialist agenda and therefore wholly unacceptable to the major Croat and Serb parties.[39]

In terms of other political options for the nobility, the Croat-Serb Coalition and the Frank party could both be enticing. The former option meant cooperation with the Serb National Independent Party and eventually a compromise with Budapest. The latter option meant a more focused Great Croatian orientation which would include trialism, with the new state unit comprising Croatian and Slovenian territory. Pre-war, the Croat-Serb Coalition had really abandoned the core of its original policy of 1905–6, and begun cooperating with the Hungarian government.[40] While Croat members of the Coalition appeared inconsistent and vacillating, the Serb Independents revealed that for them a (Serb) national policy was more important than any inclusive civic option.[41] The Coalition did become acceptable for some of the more conservative and loyal nobility, so that even some aristocrats were to be found in its ranks. However, a tighter incorporation never occurred because there existed a discrepancy between the Coalition's rhetoric and its practice. In other words, the Coalition in spite of its conservative volte-face maintained at least part of the Yugoslav and oppositional rhetoric from the time of its foundation.

By contrast, the Frank party was backed by a circle around Archduke Franz Ferdinand as well as Slovene clerical politicians, and fixated on uniting Croat-Slovene territory on the basis of Croat state right in a new trialist reconstruction of the Monarchy. This attracted the interest of some aristocrats, although they never expressed a party affiliation.[42] For example, following the collapse of the regime's National Party (*Narodna stranka*), Dioniz Hellenbach showed an interest in the Frank party, while in 1906 the army officer Moritz Auffenberg (later minister of war) got to know Josip Frank via his friend Count Josip Drašković.

According to Auffenberg, Drašković was more moderate than Frank himself, for whom trialism had an expressly Great Croatian stamp. But Drašković in a series of letters still clearly expressed his Croat national viewpoint.[43] Thus he was especially enthusiastic about the annexation of Bosnia-Herzegovina, believing that dualism would now collapse and that through trialism a federal empire would be created. He also firmly believed in a Habsburg mission in the Balkans, stating that for at least another century the entire peninsula would be under the direct control of the Monarchy; it would have to advance up to the Aegean as it was drawn fully into the currents of world trade. Thus the Habsburgs would secure in Constantinople the role that the Hohenzollerns played in Munich or Stuttgart. Drašković felt that Croatia was the Monarchy's only viable bridge into the Balkans, for neither Germans nor Magyars would be welcomed in this region. To start with, Bosnia-Herzegovina, Croatia and Dalmatia had to be united in a trialist unit, without any Magyar or German influence. As for Serbia, it could either be pulled closer into the Monarchy's orbit or be crushed at the price of a European war.

Drašković from conversations with Vladimir Nikolić also presumptuously concluded that such a policy would even be approved by some Croatian and Bosnian Serbs.[44] But typically for an aristocrat, Drašković did not directly engage at a party level but lobbied behind the scenes. For instance, in 1908 he told the veteran politician Izidor Kršnjavi in confidence that he, Drašković, would endorse Frank only so long as he represented 'pure trialism' and not the unification of Croat lands under the Hungarian crown.[45] In May 1908,

Auffenberg would propose to Aehrenthal that via Josip Drašković he should buy up the Zagreb newspaper *Agramer Tagblatt*.[46]

In the early twentieth century, therefore, the Croatian aristocracy assumed different viewpoints on a range of national and political issues, mostly inclining towards imperial loyalty and various forms of 'Croatianhood' (usually traditional, rarely radical) with a minority taking a moderate pro-Yugoslav path, often as a strategy of survival. Conservatives and liberals were to be found in all groups, yet among the former, imperial loyalty and Croatianhood were more common characteristics.

## Liberals and conservatives among the aristocracy

The aristocracy in Croatia then is a good example of entangled history, where various layers of identity were superimposed, producing hybrid forms of identification. It is very difficult to categorize individuals' opinions and viewpoints or to characterize with any precision how they identified themselves. If we turn to consider those nobles with a more liberal standpoint, they had usually risen to prominence only in the late eighteenth or nineteenth centuries (for instance the Vranyczany family).[47] As a meritocracy they favoured political and economic cooperation with the middle classes, and some were also keen on South Slav cooperation (the Turkovićs).[48]

Some of these nobles also identified as Orthodox and Serb (Vladimir Nikolić Podrinski, or Baron Josif Rajačić). They had advanced through careers in the military or civil service, or were wealthy businessmen. Many of the Serb politicians who occupied important posts, like Sabor president, deputy-ban, county prefects or departmental heads of government, were noblemen. This Serb ennobled elite was well acculturated, yet its truly aristocratic layer was rather thin. As a rule it tended to a pro-Hungarian orientation, something to which the tactics of Ban Khuen-Héderváry (1883–1903) had greatly contributed, for he had simulated Croat-Serb antagonism through his political and economic schemes. Khuen's departure in 1903 and the Hungarian crisis of 1903–6 had left open the option of cooperation with the Croats. The mediator of this policy was the Serb Independent Party which became part of the Coalition; usually it was keen on Yugoslavism but at the same time was quite loyal to the Habsburgs. A different tactic was employed by the Serb National Radical Party (*Srpska narodna radikalna stranka*) which envisaged the Serbian Church Congregation (*Crkveno-narodni sabor*) as the most important body of Serb autonomy. Disinclined to cooperate with Croat parties in Zagreb, it was oriented more towards Belgrade but in political practice also favoured cooperation with Budapest.

We can illustrate how aristocrats manoeuvred within this fluid political culture with a number of further specific examples. One of the most prominent Serb noblemen was Vladimir Nikolić Podrinski, endowed in 1914 with the title of a Hungarian baron. Although his family had accumulated wealth as merchants, they bought up landed property and owned a large estate in the elite suburbs of Zagreb. After making a political career as a pro-Hungarian politician (vice-ban in 1906–7), Nikolić became a non-party member of the Croat-Serb Coalition, and as a wealthy capital owner he was connected with the First Croatian Savings Bank (the most important Croatian bank). Yet though a domestic capitalist and a Serb who inclined to Serb-Croat cooperation, Nikolić was also a Habsburg-loyal politician who maintained strong connections especially to the Vienna power centre. He was highly ambitious, and asked Aehrenthal in 1909 whether he might become either ban or vice-ban.[49] According to General Maximilian Csicserics who in 1907–8 mediated between military circles and Croatian politicians like Frank, Nikolić was sufficiently ambitious that he would abandon the Coalition if he became ban.[50] Nikolić also had a wider network of social contacts through such individuals as Generaladjutant Eduard von Paar, former chief of the general staff Friedrich Beck-Rzikowski and Archduke Leopold Salvator.[51] He was particularly close to the latter, and in 1919 his daughter would marry the archduke's son. Nikolić's wife, Baroness Ella Scotti, was a Catholic aristocrat and similarly well connected for her father was a senior officer in the Habsburg army.

A second example is the last ban of Croatia, Antun Mihalović, who came from a Serb Orthodox family which in 1763 had converted to Catholicism. The Mihalovićs had risen through military careers, acquired estates in Slavonia and were already ennobled in 1716. Traditionally they were pro-Hungarian in orientation. Like Nikolić, Mihalović changed his political stance and in 1913 entered the Sabor as a member of the Croat-Serb Coalition. He became ban in 1917 and, thanks to his Yugoslav orientation, was acceptable as such even when the National Council of Slovenes, Croats and Serbs (*Narodno vijeće Slovenaca, Hrvata i Srba*) was formed in 1918.[52] Although he resigned in January 1919, he was still active in the interwar period as a member of the Yugoslav Senate.[53]

By contrast, a 'middle of the road' orientation is best exemplified by aristocrats like the Pejačevićs. This wealthy Slavonian aristocratic family was pro-Hungarian, yet the 'cavalier ban' Teodor Pejačević (1903–7) eventually cooperated with the Croat-Serb Coalition, a move which his conservative peers would hold against him. Nevertheless, he remained an important figure in the Croatian power structure and in 1913–17 was the Croatian minister in the Hungarian government.

For an example of an aristocrat strongly connected to both domestic capital and the Croat-Serb Coalition, there is Count Miroslav Kulmer (the younger). He was descended from a family of military officers from Carinthia, which had long been pro-Austrian and rather conservative. At the beginning of his political career Kulmer followed this path, supporting the short-lived 'Centre Party' (*Centrum*) of the counts Josip and Ivan Drašković. In 1906, however, he struck up a somewhat different tune by joining the Coalition as a non-party member. Meanwhile, he ran his estate in an exemplary manner, modernizing it, investing his capital in domestic banks and industry; he was president of the First Croatian Savings Bank and the Croatian-Slavonian Agricultural Society (*Hrvatsko-slavonsko gospodarsko društvo*).

Kulmer is thus an aristocrat who transformed himself into a capitalist and entrepreneur. As such he was supported by a significant section of Jewish capital owners when he ran for the Sabor in 1906. He worked closely with Nikolić (one even spoke of a Nikolić-Kulmer faction in the Coalition), since both of them promoted the interests of domestic capital and Croat-Serb cooperation yet were basically Habsburg loyalists with excellent connections in Vienna. Indeed, Kulmer like Nikolić had high ambitions. Nikolić, as noted, had been a vice-ban and aspired to the top position as well; Kulmer had similar aspirations: especially in 1912–13 there was much talk of him becoming the new ban.[54] Both of them therefore were enterprising imperial politicians, and were also able to develop sophisticated strategies of survival under modern conditions. Because they had important common political and economic interests they could successfully cooperate with each other, while differing essentially in their national and religious viewpoints. Although Nikolić belonged to the ennobled and acculturated Serb elite sympathetic towards the Croats, he was much more sensitive to the Serb problem than Kulmer, who when presiding over the first Croatian Catholic Congress in 1900 had clearly articulated his Croat and Catholic identity.[55] After the war this did not prevent Kulmer becoming persona grata with the new (Yugoslav) regime; he joined the Democratic Party and acquired the nickname 'citizen count' or 'peasant count'. By 1930 he had become vice-governor of the National Bank of the Kingdom of Yugoslavia, but then in 1942 in the wartime Ustaša state he accepted an invitation to join the Croatian state Sabor.[56] This reveals an erratic career, but also shows Kulmer periodically trying to adapt to various political fluctuations.

Before 1914, the polar opposites of Kulmer therefore were utterly conservative aristocrats like Baron Pavao Rauch or Count Stjepan Erdödy. The latter is worth highlighting in view of the rich archival sources we possess. He belonged to a Croatian branch of renowned Hungarian lineage and continued to possess a large estate which was not modernized. As a prominent pro-Hungarian aristocrat, Erdödy was furious because of the dissolution of the (pro-Hungarian) National Party; he favoured strong-arm absolutist rule in Croatia, and was both anti-Serbian and anti-Yugoslav. How thin the dividing lines actually were is revealed by the fact that his own cousins, the Draškovićs and the Kulmers, did not fully share his arch-conservative views. His hunting diary, written in German, presents the image of an isolated and frustrated bachelor who feels that his world is falling apart. Writing in a very aristocratic style, he continually devotes space in this work not just to his own leisure pursuits but to decisive contemporary political events.⁵⁷ He particularly blames 'rotten' politicians like Nikola Tomašić, who have ruined the National Party, or those politicians willing to cooperate with Serbs who are encouraging peasants and common people to raise their heads. Referring to the Croat-Serb Coalition, he blames it for all the difficulties he encounters in running his estate.⁵⁸

During a car trip in July 1910 to Serb localities in Croatia like Vrginmost, Topusko and Glina, Erdödy noted that the people there were primitive, all armed with knives or clubs, and prone to drinking and fighting. He was antagonistic even against women whom he found unattractive.⁵⁹ The previous year he had paid a visit to Bosnia and gave a more favourable description than on his visit to Serb-inhabited parts of Croatia. Yet, he was

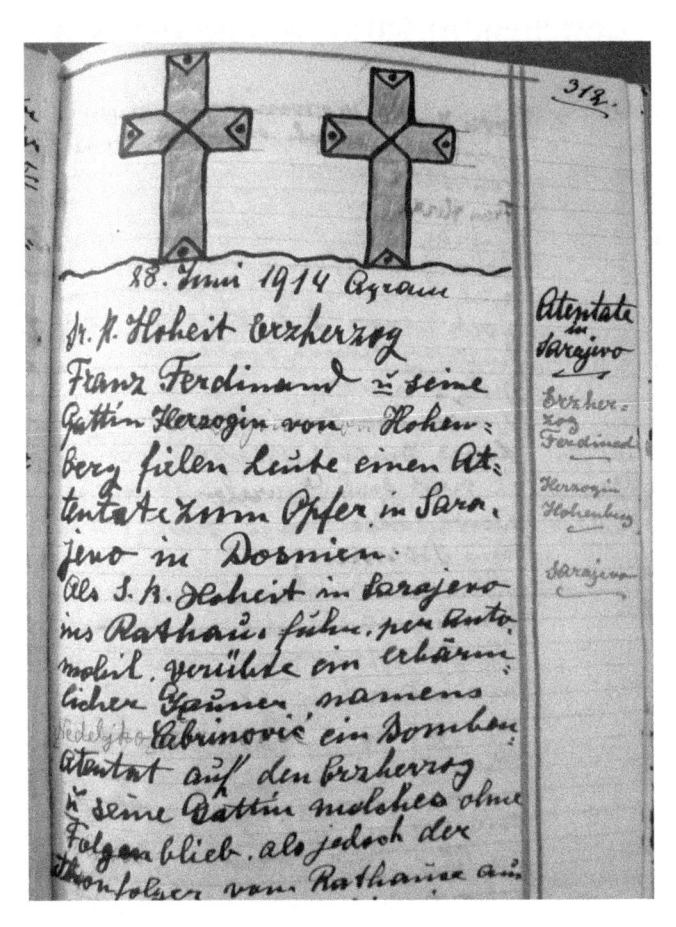

**FIGURE 4.2** *Hunting diary of Stjepan Erdödy: noting for 28 June 1914 the assassination of Franz Ferdinand, 'a man of high intelligence and energy' (Croatian State Archives, Zagreb, fond Nr 712, diary vol. 7).*

still furious because the peaceful natives of Bosnia would be exposed to the vicious influence of 'parliamentarism' when the Bosnian parliament was opened.[60] For him, absolutism was the solution both for Bosnia-Herzegovina and for Croatia: he was even ready to accept a military regime since it was the only way to ensure order and stability. Thus, even before the Great War, he was rather pessimistic about the Monarchy's future, and after the Sarajevo assassination he was quick to point a finger at Belgrade and its 'domestic' allies, adding sadly that 'we have too many enemies and too few friends' (Figure 4.2).[61] Such pessimistic observations and the dramatic turn of events did not thwart his everyday hunting – his main obsession – nor in fact his sense of humour.

## Conclusion: Sarajevo and beyond

The Sarajevo assassination produced across Croatia general outrage and vehement expressions of anti-Serb feeling that often ended in violence. Many aristocrats, especially after the Balkan Wars, had been worried that the very existence of the Monarchy was jeopardized by the Balkan states' ambitions, the most dangerous being Serbia aided by Russia. They saw the assassination as fully part of this scheme, yet we should note that at least some of them were outraged by the anti-Serb incidents. Even Stjepan Erdödy, for example, paid a visit to the demolished Serb shops in Zagreb and criticized the violence, as well as the abrupt and illegal eviction of Serb members from the Zagreb Casino (an elite and mostly pro-regime reading society). Because of this, he not only resigned as the Casino's president but in September 1914 decided to leave the organization.[62]

Many aristocrats too were convinced that the war would not last long, yet at the same time this presumption was paired with a real fear that the Monarchy's existence was at stake. Therefore, they viewed the war as a question of imperial survival. Traditionally, as we have suggested, most nobles were loyal to the Monarchy and the Habsburgs, and either sceptical about the Yugoslav idea or openly opposed it. This did not fundamentally change during the Great War, even though there were some examples to the contrary.[63] However, some aristocrats at least tried to develop strategies in the unfavourable wartime conditions in order to survive should the empire collapse. For most of them, that meant not putting all their eggs in one basket. Besides their basic loyalty to the sovereign, they remained open to a range of political, social and economic options, to cooperate with the middle classes, with Serbs and eventually even with the new Yugoslav regime in Belgrade.[64] In this unstable environment, nobles without estates had to adapt, while landowning aristocrats were usually resolute in their struggle for property. The strategies of nobles for surviving or adapting have been underestimated by historians or at least inadequately researched. Some Austrian aristocrats, like the Windisch-Grätz, who still had estates in the new Yugoslav state after 1918, hoped that taking Yugoslav citizenship would guarantee a better treatment for themselves.[65] They relied on the new state having a king, ignoring the fact that this monarchy had a completely different character and history from the Habsburgs. This Yugoslav monarchy – just like the kingdom of Serbia after 1882 – lacked its own nobility, and viewed the Habsburg aristocracy as an unwelcome and hostile element.

An extreme example of this divided loyalty was Count Josip Bombelles, true *homo triplex*. He was descended from a distinguished aristocratic family from Portugal, which had even supplied Franz Joseph's *Ajo* (private educator). Josip's father Marko was pro-Austrian in his political and economic orientation, belonged to the board of directors of the *K.K. Allgemeine österreichische Boden-Credit Anstalt* in Vienna, and was a hunting companion of Franz Ferdinand who occasionally visited the Bombelles' famous hunting grounds near Varaždin. The two discussed politics, Marko sharing the archduke's hatred of the Hungarian and Serbian political elites, and warning him that Croatian loyalty had its limits.[66] At the same time, Marko was a liaison between the archduke, his circle and Croatian politicians. According to his own testimony, Marko in 1910 urged upon Franz Ferdinand a plan whereby loyal elements of the Coalition should gain power supported by prominent army officers.[67] Yet Josip, the son of this most loyal count (as Vladimir, son of Josip Frank termed him in a letter to Auffenberg), was described in one post-war official report about the Croatian nobility as an enthusiastic Yugoslav who during the war had said he would rather crush stones than fight in the Habsburg army.[68] His loyalty and treason were in fact dangerously interwoven, for in the interwar period he emerged as a triple agent who met a tragic end in an Ustaša jail.[69]

To sum up, Croatian aristocrats of different political and national orientations were in a quandary on the eve of the Great War. They could hardly compete with middle-class entrepreneurs since they had not received the relevant state subsidies to invest in industry. During the dualist era, the nobles who were pro-Austria were forced either to come to terms with Budapest or to oppose the Hungarians. The nobility with a more pronounced Croatian orientation was trapped between Vienna, Budapest and the Greater Croatian or Yugoslav options. The Serb nobility meanwhile manoeuvred between Vienna, Budapest, Zagreb and Belgrade. Those aristocrats who were open to any form of 'Yugoslavism' were treading on thin ice between loyalty and treason, for their allegiance was questioned from both sides, the Yugoslav and the Habsburg.

By 1914, the aristocracy had developed various stances towards national and political programmes, ranging from traditional imperial loyalty, radical and moderate 'Croatianhood' to varieties of Yugoslavism. Predominantly the aristocracy was loyal to the Habsburg dynasty, but at the same time well aware that the general political, economic and national context was shifting and jeopardizing their elite position. Therefore some of them stepped out of their traditional furrow, engaging either in more radical Croatian options that implied the empire's restructuring or even embarking upon a pro-Yugoslav path. Yet, as long as the Monarchy existed, even those on the latter course sought to combine this strategy of survival with imperial loyalty.

In the long run all Croatian aristocrats would fare badly. Even if at first the new Yugoslav regime favoured those who had some Yugoslav reputation, in the process of interwar land reform the Habsburg nobility would generally be treated as opponents, the new Yugoslav state introducing a distinctively anti-aristocratic ideology. Miroslav Kulmer would suffer heavy material losses because of the regime's policies towards Croatian economic bodies like the First Croatian Savings Bank and the Croatian-Slavonian Agrarian Society. In 1925, as an honourable aristocrat, he felt obliged personally to pay off the debts of the society, revealing thereby the true meaning of noblesse oblige.

# Notes

1 Although Arno Mayer qualified the thesis that the old elite was completely unadaptable (*The Persistence of the Old Regime: Europe to the Great War*, New York: Pantheon, 1981), only in the last decades have some excellent historians focused on the nobility. A few examples are David Cannadine, *The Decline and Fall of the British Aristocracy* (New Haven: Yale University Press, 1990); Dominic Lieven, *The Aristocracy in Europe 1815-1914* (New York: Columbia University Press, 1992); Eckart Conze and Monika Wienfort (eds), *Adel und Moderne. Deutschland im europäischen Vergleich im 19. und 20. Jahrhundert* (Vienna: Böhlau, 2004); Eagle Glassheim, *Noble Nationalists: The Transformation of the Bohemian Aristocracy* (Cambridge, MA: Harvard University Press, 2005); Jörn Leonhard and Christian Wieland (eds), *What Makes the Nobility Noble? Comparative Perspectives from the Sixteenth to the Twentieth Century* (Göttingen: Vandenhoeck & Ruprecht, 2011).

2 In 1891 the Sabor listed twenty-five noble families whose adult males had an automatic right to representation in the assembly as 'virilists'. This included older barons but not those newer barons who had secured their peerages on the basis of meritocracy.

3 I would disagree with J. Trygve Has-Ellison, who has argued that in Austria-Hungary we can define as aristocrats only those families identified by William Godsey as having secured the honorary title of chamberlain, thereby eligible to being received at the Habsburg court: J. Trygve Has-Ellison, 'Review of Ellis Wasson, *Aristocracy and the Modern World*', H-German, H-Net Reviews (May 2007): www.h-net.org/reviews/showrev.php?id=13171.

4 William D. Godsey, 'Quarterings and Kinship: The Social Composition of the Habsburg Aristocracy in the Dualist Era', *The Journal of Modern History* 71 (1999): 95–104. Of the cited families, about twenty held property in the Croatian lands.

5   This office had been introduced by the Hungarian-Croatian *Nagodba* of 1868, the minister's function being to act as liaison between the Croatian ban and government, and the authorities in Budapest and Vienna.

6   Among the eighty-eight deputies in the Croatian Sabor of 1892–7, twenty-two were nobles; in 1897–1902, the number was twenty-five; in 1902–6, twenty-seven and in 1906–7, thirteen. These figures do not include 'virilists'. See Mirjana Gross, 'O položaju plemstva u strukturi elite u sjevernoj Hrvatskoj potkraj 19. i na početku 20. stoljeća', *Historijski zbornik* 31–32 (1978–79): 132, 138. English version in Ivo Banac and Paul Bushkovitch (eds), *The Nobility in Russia and Eastern Europe* (New Haven: Yale University Press, 1983). With virilists the number was higher, and varied from forty-six in 1892 (40 per cent of Sabor members) to thirty-five in 1913 (32 per cent). See S. Daniel Lalić, *Der Hochadel Kroatien-Slawoniens. Zwischen Verlust, Verteidigung und Neuerwerb gesellschaftlicher Elitenpositionen (1868-1918)* (Berlin: De Gruyter Oldenbourg, 2017), 74–5.

7   *Stenografiski zapisnici sabora kraljevine Hrvatske, Slavonije i Dalmacije 1913.-1918.*, vol. 1 (Zagreb: Kraljevska zemaljska tiskara, 1914), 13.

8   *Das Aktenmaterial über die 'ritterliche Affaire' des Baron Paul Rauch* (Zagreb: C. Albrecht (Maravić i Dečak), 1908); Veridicus (Pavao Rauch), *Hrvatska u godini 1907. i 1908* (Zagreb: Kraljevska zemaljska tiskara, 1908), 10–12.

9   In a letter to Géza Daruváry, *Sektionschef* of the emperor's *Kabinettskanzlei* in Vienna, Rauch concluded that the matter could only be settled unilaterally, and because of the press onslaught he asked that Franz Joseph's approval of him should be made known. His proposal was rejected. Hrvatski Državni Arhiv Zagreb (Croatian State Archives – hereafter HDA) Mikrofilmovi iz inozemstva (microfilms from abroad), D-1284, fol. 23–4. This is microfilmed material from the Haus-, Hof- und Staatsarchiv in Vienna: Kabinettsarchiv, Geheimakten, 'Kroatische politische Angelegenheiten', karton 26.

10  'Denn nur mit starken Südslawen können wir auf dem Balkan stark sein. In ihrer Kraft ist unsere Zukunft. Aber unsere Staatskünstler wissen noch immer nicht, daß wir aus einem deutschen Ostreich ein slawisches Westreich geworden sind': Hermann Bahr, *Dalmatinische Reise* (Berlin: S. Fischer, 1909), 76.

11  Steven Beller, *Francis Joseph* (London and New York: Longman, 1996), 190. The key maxims of Franz Joseph's manifesto of 29 July 1914, *An meine Völker*, were honour, reputation and the Monarchy's Great Power status (*Ehre, Ansehen, Machtstellung*).

12  Ibid., 190.

13  Following the sale of the estate of Prince Schaumburg-Lippe at the beginning of the century, the largest private properties were (with 64,411 jutara; 1 jutro (German – *Joch*) = 0.575 hectares) those of the Princes Thurn and Taxis, who did not reside in Croatia. The Gutmann estate amounted to 60,910 jutara. The Gutmanns had been ennobled in 1869 as 'de Gelse', and in 1904 became barons de Belišće. In 1884 they appeared in Slavonia, and in time bought estates on which they organized an industry processing timber, with its own railway and industrial colony. See Zdenka Šimončić-Bobetko, *Agrarna reforma i kolonizacija u Hrvatskoj*, 2 vols (Zagreb: Hrvatski institut za povijest, 1997),

I, 27; Hrvoje Volner, 'Drvna industrija Slavonije s posebnim osvrtom na obitelj Gutmann do kraja 1918. godine', *Historijski zbornik* 65:2 (2012): 456, 464.

14  The exception in 1885–7 was the *Centrum* (Centre Party) of counts Ivan and Josip Drašković, whose aim was to preserve Croatian autonomy inside Hungary but with the support of Vienna. This was similar to the *Mittelpartei* in the Austrian half of the Monarchy, especially in Moravia. See Jiři Mališ, 'The Moravian Diet, and Political Elites in Moravia 1848-1918', in Judit Pál and Vlad Popovici (eds), *Elites and Politics in Central and Eastern Europe (1848-1918)* (Frankfurt am Main: Peter Lang, 2014), 101–27.

15  Rauch via Daruváry regularly reported to the monarch, who received him in audience several times, and also to Aehrenthal. Nikola Tomašić privately corresponded with Khuen-Héderváry. Archduke Leopold Salvator had been stationed in Zagreb for the first time in 1894 and maintained a range of political connections. General Moritz von Auffenberg, a confidant of Franz Ferdinand and minister of war in 1911–12, knew the Croatian environment well for in April 1905 he had been posted to Zagreb. He kept up links with a number of politicians, especially Frankists, but also aristocratic families.

16  From 1903 Musulin was in the oriental department of the Ballhausplatz (Foreign Ministry). Aehrenthal considered him a very competent Balkans expert, and in the summer of 1909 in the Bauer hotel in Bad Ischl briefed him on plans for the annexation of Bosnia-Herzegovina, charging him with the composition of two diplomatic notes. Musulin was descended from an ennobled officer family from the old Military Frontier, married the granddaughter of the Bohemian textile magnate Rudolph Isbar and in 1912 was made a baron. See Alexander Freiherr von Musulin, *Das Haus am Ballhausplatz* (Munich: Verlag für Kulturpolitik, 1924), 166; William D. Godsey, *Aristocratic Redoubt: The Austro-Hungarian Foreign Office on the Eve of the First World War* (West Lafayette: Purdue University Press, 1999), 61.

17  Quite often there were different stances taken within the same family, or they changed over the course of time. For example, the Jelačić Bužimskis were Croatian oriented but their Varaždin branch was pro-Hungarian.

18  The National Party of the 1860s was the liberal and Yugoslav-oriented grouping of Bishop Strossmayer and his circle. In 1880, his supporters founded the Independent National Party (*Neodvisna narodna stranka*), while Ban Khuen-Héderváry transformed the remains of the party into a force backing his regime.

19  The Croat-Serb Coalition stood by the basic policies of the so-called New Course of 1905. In foreign policy, they opposed German expansion to the East, were Yugoslav oriented and tried to exploit the contemporary crisis of dualism in the interests of Croatia. They reached an agreement with the then Magyar opposition – the Party of Independence of Ferenc Kossuth. The most important members of the Coalition were the Croatian Party of Right (formed from a combination of the main Party of Right and the Independent National Party), the Progressive Party and the Serb National Independent Party.

20  In its origins a Greater Croatian party. By the end of the nineteenth century it had split into the pro-Austrian and anti-Serb Pure Party of Right (*Čista stranka prava*) under the leadership of Josip Frank, and the (majority) Party of Right

that merged with the Independent National Party and finally ended up in the Croat-Serb Coalition. In 1908, a more moderate party – the Starčević Party of Right (*Starčevićeva stranka prava*) led by Mile Starčević – seceded from Frank's party.

21  One exception was Baron Juraj Rukavina, but he belonged to the military nobility. Another exception was a petty nobleman and writer Ksaver Šandor Đalski, a member of the most liberal party of the Coalition – the Progressive Party (*Napredna stranka*).

22  Solomon Wank, Christine M. Grafinger, Franz Adlgasser, Fritz Fellner (eds), *Aus dem Nachlaß Aehrenthal. Briefe und Dokumente zur österreichisch-ungarischen Innen- und Aussenpolitik 1885-1912*, 2 vols (Graz: Böhlau, 1994), II, 528–33.

23  In a letter to Aehrenthal of 9 May 1908, Auffenberg considered such a policy futile for he felt the Serbs would steadily push towards a Yugoslav option: ibid., 588.

24  For analysis of this development, see Mark Cornwall, 'Loyalty and Treason in Late Habsburg Croatia: A Violent Political Discourse before the First World War', in Jana Osterkamp and Martin Schulze Wessel (eds), *Exploring Loyalty* (Göttingen: Vandenhoeck & Ruprecht, 2017), 97–120.

25  Wank, *Aus dem Nachlaß Aehrenthal*, 673; letter of Friedjung to R. W. Seton-Watson, 9 October 1909, in *R. W. Seton-Watson and the Yugoslavs. Correspondence 1906-1941*, 2 vols (London and Zagreb: British Academy/University of Zagreb, 1976), I, 49.

26  See his argument in a letter to the Croatian minister in Budapest, Géza Josipović, 22 May 1909: HDA, Kraljevski ministar hrvatsko-slavonsko-dalmatinski u Budimpešti, Predsjedništvo (the Royal Croatian-Slavonian-Dalmatian minister in Budapest, Presidency), Nr 149/1909, kutija 26.

27  Pavao Rauch's vice-ban Nikola Crnković had been an aide to Levin Rauch; the Zagreb county prefect Aleksandar Vučetić had been Pavao's former private teacher and the nephew of Levin's close friend Stjepan Vučetić.

28  As an example of this approach, see Pieter M. Judson, *Guardians of the Nation: Activists on the Language Frontiers of Imperial Austria* (Cambridge, MA: Harvard University Press, 2006).

29  Gordana Krivokapić-Jović sees the main centre of national conflicts as the small provincial towns, while villages were little affected: Gordana Krivokapić-Jović, 'Položaj Srba u Habsburškoj monarhiji i izbijanje Prvoga svetskog rata', in *Dijalog povjesničara-istoričara* 7 (Zagreb, 2003), 213–27.

30  HDA, Predsjedništvo Zemaljske vlade (PZV: Presidency of the Croatian Government), 6–14, Nr 2594, kutija 748.

31  For example, approval was given for an excursion of the Women's Teacher Training School from Belgrade through Croatia to Bosnia-Herzegovina and Dalmatia (HDA, PZV 6-14, Nr 2213, kutija 748); and local authorities were invited to help the well-known Serbian scholar Jovan Cvijić when he investigated hydraulic engineering on the Gacka River near Otočac (idem, Nr 3284).

32 HDA, Mikrofilmovi iz inozemstva, D-1284, 'Erläuterung zu den Voranklagen über die Ernennung der Oberrichter'.
33 HDA, PZV, 6-14, Nr 3326, kutija 748.
34 In a letter to Aehrenthal of 27 September 1909, he stressed how he did not have good relations with the Hungarian government which had failed to give him support for a unionist party in Croatia: Wank, *Aus dem Nachlaß*, II, 719.
35 On 5 May 1909, writing to Aehrenthal, he recommended Rudolf and Stjepan Erdödy, his nephew Janko Jelačić or Aladar Janković, and in a letter of 3 July 1909 Thomas Erdödy: ibid., 677, 695.
36 Cf. one overly positive assessment of Rauch's period in office: Mira Kolar, 'The Activities of Vice-Roy Pavao Rauch in Croatia', *Review of Croatian History* 1/1 (2005): 133–57.
37 Solomon Wank, 'The Archduke and Aehrenthal: The Origins of a Hatred', *Austrian History Yearbook* 33 (2002): 102. The author of a new biography of Franz Ferdinand employs the phrase 'the trialist myth'. See Alma Hannig, *Franz Ferdinand. Die Biografie* (Vienna, 2013), 99, and her chapter in this volume.
38 Before becoming ban, Rauch had argued for a military regime in Croatia.
39 It foresaw the incorporation of Dalmatia and Bosnia-Herzegovina into Hungary: Mark Cornwall, 'The Habsburg Elite and the Southern Slav Question 1914-1918', in Lothar Höbelt and T. G. Otte (eds), *A Living Anachronism? European Diplomacy and the Habsburg Monarchy* (Vienna: Böhlau, 2010), 250–1.
40 Günter Schödl, *Kroatische Nationalpolitik und 'Jugoslavenstvo'* (Munich: Oldenbourg, 1990); Nicholas Miller, *Between Nation and State: Serbian Politics in Croatia Before the First World War* (Pittsburgh: University of Pittsburgh Press, 1997), 161.
41 According to Miller, it marked the failure of the civic, constitutional model of participation, and was a modern analogue of the privileges granted in 1690, showing that the Habsburg habit of political patronage had not been abandoned: ibid., 179.
42 According to recent research, Frank supported also a federal restructuring of the empire where Croatia would secure special status as one of the federal units: Stjepan Matković and Marko Trogrlić, *Iz korespondencije Josipa Franka s Bečom: 1907.-1910.* (Zagreb, Split: Hrvatski institut za povijest, 2014), 20–1.
43 Moritz Auffenberg-Komarów, *Aus Österreichs Höhe und Niedergang. Eine Lebensschilderung* (Munich: Drei Masken Verlag, 1921), 106; Günther Kronenbitter, *'Krieg im Frieden'. Die Führung der k.u.k. Armee und die Großmachtpolitik Österreich-Ungarns 1906-1914* (Munich: Oldenbourg, 2003), 65, 160. Frank established relations with Drašković when the latter started the *Centrum* party. It is not insignificant that when Drašković had to sell his estate at Bisag because of financial difficulties, Frank was his legal representative: Stjepan Matković, *Čista stranka prava 1895–1903* (Zagreb: Hrvatski institut za povijest, 2001), 300.
44 Letter to Auffenberg, 23 October 1908. A note at the end of this letter shows that two weeks later it was seen by Aehrenthal who did not agree with it: Trogrlić and Matković, *Iz korespondencije*, 164–9.

45 Iso Kršnjavi, *Zapisci*, 2 vols (Zagreb: Mladost, 1986), II, 547.
46 Wank, *Aus dem Nachlaß*, 594–5. This newspaper had been started by Ivan Drašković with his brother Josip. In a letter to Aehrenthal (from Carlsbad in July 1908), Josip Drašković recalled his own recent visit to the Ballhausplatz where the idea had been mooted that Franz Joseph should buy up the Slavonian estate of Prince Schaumburg-Lippe (in the end Ivan Drašković bought part of it) and that an archduke would again have a permanent base in Croatia; he also mentioned that he had secured the *Agramer Tagblatt* for the Foreign Ministry. He further noted the struggle against Hungary: that only a stronger domestic policy there could ensure a good foreign policy, and that the Monarchy's current position was stymied by the common ministries being helpless eunuchs: Trogrlić and Matković, *Iz korespondencije*, 97.
47 The Vranyczanys were successful entrepreneurs who at the beginning of the nineteenth century had become barons. They supported the Illyrian movement and were of a pro-Croatian and pro-Austrian orientation. They bought up landed estates and owned or built representative urban palaces in Zagreb.
48 The Turkovićs were the Croatian counterparts of the Gutmanns. They were entrepreneurs who had purchased landed property with excellent vineyards (Kutjevo), becoming barons in 1911. They were also Yugoslav oriented and supported the Coalition.
49 Miller, *Between Nation and State*, 142.
50 Mirjana Gross, 'Hrvatska uoči aneksije Bosne i Hercegovine', in *Istorija XX veka* (1962), III, 198–9.
51 See note 15.
52 On 30 May 1918, Mihalović opposed both the Hungarian and Austrian premiers in arguing for a trialist solution of the Southern Slav Question: Andrej Rahten, *Savezništva i diobe. Razvoj slovensko-hrvatskih političkih odnosa u Habsburškoj monarhiji 1848–1918* (Zagreb: Golden Marketing, 2008), 228.
53 As a confidant of Vlatko Maček, leader of the Croatian Peasant Party (*Hrvatska seljačka stranka*), he was consulted by the Court Minister Milan Antić at the time of the Czechoslovak crisis in 1939. Antić was Mihalović's son-in-law. See Ljubo Boban, *Maček i politika Hrvatske seljačke stranke 1928-1941*, 2 vols (Zagreb: Liber, 1974), II, 30.
54 In a letter of January 1913 to R. W. Seton-Watson, Vatroslav Jagić, a professor of Slavic studies at Vienna University, was not optimistic that Kulmer would become ban, and characterized him as more of a gentleman ('Ehrenmann') than a politician. In the same letter Jagić wrote of Croatia as a Hungarian colony: *R. W. Seton-Watson and the Yugoslavs*, I, 131–2.
55 Stjepan Korenić, *Prvi hrvatski katolički sastanak u Zagrebu 1900* (Zagreb: C. Albrecht, 1900), 331.
56 On Kulmer, see Mirjana Gross, 'O položaju', 136; *Hrvatski biografski leksikon*, VIII (Zagreb, 2013), 361–2.
57 A good example of his outlook are the diary notes he made about some newly purchased hunting dogs, whose 'wedding' he portrayed by drawing their

tails tied together with a wedding ring. For him the hunt for otters, which he could never exterminate, was as important as any political events: HDA, Fond Erdödy, Lovački dnevnik (Hunting diary) Stjepana Erdödyja, vol. 4, entry for 5 July 1907.

58 He connected the most minor incidents to the politics of the Coalition. Thus, when two rustics attacked Miroslav Kulmer and his wife near Jaska, after their automobile had broken down, Erdödy considered this as the fruit of liberalism and hoped that Kulmer, sympathetic to these new ideas, would see that all that glittered was not gold: ibid., vol. 2, entry for 24 June 1906.

59 Ibid., vol. 5, entries for 28 June–18 July 1910.

60 Ibid., vol. 4, entries for 24 June–1 July 1909.

61 Ibid., vol. 7, entry for 1 April 1914.

62 Ibid., vol. 7, entries for 26 July and 2 September 1914.

63 As the only aristocrat to write his war memoirs, Count Juraj Oršić (*Na konju i u rovu*, Belgrade 1917; reprint, Strmec Samoborski: Fortuna, 2014) shows his preoccupation with honour. His memoirs are not even overtly politicized; rather, the war is understood as a battlefield on which traditional aristocratic virtues like honour, courage, horsemanship and comradeship are to be displayed. See Filip Hameršak, *Tamna strana Marsa* (Zagreb: Fortuna, 2013), 269. An alternative career trajectory is that of Lieutenant Oskar Jelačić Bužimski, who was captured in 1915 in Galicia, and ended up in Odessa. Although there exist contradictory accounts about his behaviour in Russia, including his own testimony about joining the Bolsheviks, it is clear that he married a Russian and joined the First Serbian Volunteer division. It appears that he left the division due to Bolshevism. After two official post-war investigations, he became an officer in the Yugoslav army. He retired in 1929 with the rank of major. See Branka Molnar (ed.), *Izvori za povijest obitelji Jelačić u Državnome arhivu u Zagrebu* (Zagreb: Državni arhiv u Zagrebu, 2012), 5.

64 A striking example is the minor noble Janko Bedeković who before the First World War as a police inspector distinguished himself with his anti-Serb stance, and following the war became head of the Zagreb police, carrying out notoriously repressive measures.

65 For example, the Weriand lineage of the Windisch-Grätz family. See Marija Wakounig and Hannes Stekl, *Windisch-Graetz. Ein Fürstenhaus im 19. und 20. Jahrhundert* (Vienna: Böhlau, 1992).

66 Rahten, *Savezništva i diobe*, 155.

67 Letter of Josip Frank's son Vladimir to Auffenberg, 22 January 1910. Frank thought that Nikolić was the man behind this scheme: Trogrlić and Matković, *Iz korespondencije*, 349–57.

68 This official report about the nobility of Croatia-Slavonia was sent to Belgrade in 1921 (HDA, PZV, 6-14, Nr 18075/1921, kutija 1166). It was composed from data supplied by local authorities and was not complete or necessarily reliable. Twenty-four families were mentioned in it, of which about ten were characterized as pro-Austrian and seven as pro-Hungarian, while some were said to be wavering between a variety of options. Those designated as

pro-Yugoslav were all the Kulmers, Josip Rorauer, Josip Kiepach, Zdenko and Dragan Turković, Teodor Pejačević, and F. (probably Ferdinandina, Josip's half-sister) and Josip Bombelles. Concerning Ambroz Vranyczany, Aladar Janković and Manfred Clary-Aldringen, it was stressed that at least they were nurturing their children 'in a national spirit'. While a good proportion of the nobility were perceived as loyal, the report described as enemies: Rudolf and Stjepan Erdödy, Pavao Rauch, and Josip, Andrija and Ladislav Janković.

69  In March 1939, he introduced himself to the Italian foreign minister Galeazzo Ciano (whom he knew from hunting expeditions with Prince Paul!) as the envoy of Vladko Maček, while at the same time he was working both for the Ustaša and for the Yugoslav general staff and Prince Paul. After the Ustaša discovered this, they tried to assassinate him, and after they came to power, he finished up in prison in Nova Gradiška. The Ustaša general Slavko Kvaternik thought he was a British agent. See Boban, *Maček i politika,* II, 87, 130; Mario Jareb, *Ustaško-domobranski pokret od nastanka do travnja 1941. godine* (Zagreb: Školska knjiga, 2006), 515.

## CHAPTER 5

# Bosnian-Croatian-Serbian-Serbo-Croatian

# Friction over language terminology in pre-war Bosnia-Herzegovina*

*Tamara Scheer*

In July 1914 with the outbreak of war, thousands of Bosnia-Herzegovina's male inhabitants were called to arms. According to later Habsburg army statistics these soldiers – the so-called Bosniaks – had consisted of Croats, Serbs and Serbo-Croats.[1] The military statistics were based on the personnel forms of individual soldiers where the main language they spoke was taken to be their nationality. In turn, Habsburg official reports tended to stereotype the behaviour of citizens according to their nationality. They referred, for example, to 'treacherous Serbs' and 'hostile Croats and Muslims'.[2] When it came to soldiers from Bosnia-Herzegovina, these generalizing terms not

---

*The research for this chapter was funded by the Austrian Science Foundation (project no. T-602, and the subsequent V-555). I thank the Austrian Office for Science, Education and Culture (Kamala Šertović) and the Austrian Embassy (Ambassador Martin Pammer), both in Sarajevo, for their generous support for the necessary archival research in Bosnia-Herzegovina. Thanks also to Nancy M. Wingfield and Gordana Ilić Marković for their comments on the draft, as well as Sandra Biletić of the Bosnian-Herzegovinian Archive for her endless support.

only were chosen on the basis of the language mentioned in their personnel forms but also took their religious faith into account. The historian Edin Hajdarpasic argues that after 1878 'the Habsburg administration' in Bosnia-Herzegovina used religion as the primary category of difference, while 'language appeared less relevant as a census rubric because most of the population spoke a variant of the same South Slavic dialect'.[3]

Is Hajdarpasic right that in Bosnia-Herzegovina only 'a variant of the same South Slav dialect' – therefore one language – was used? In fact, although most Habsburg bureaucrats were quite aware that Bosnia-Herzegovina was more or less a monolingual part of the Monarchy, they also knew very well that the terminology used for each language was a political signal that could have serious consequences. As the official statistics indicate, at least more than one term was in use in the army. This chapter therefore asks how the terms for the local idiom in Bosnia were introduced and used: Why, when and by whom? As we will see, it was a confusing situation. Several terms were employed at the same time, and sometimes even military offices were in conflict over their use. In fact, 'the' Habsburg administration, as labelled by Hajdarpasic, never actually existed when it came to army bureaucratic practices in Bosnia-Herzegovina. Since the Monarchy imposed an integrated, but complicated, joint civil–military governance there, it meant that there was always more than one institution involved and they often followed contradictory language policies. Moreover, unlike in other parts of the empire, many local army officials in Bosnia followed the policy of the Provincial (civilian) Government in Sarajevo, which meant that they often resisted the general army regulations as set out by the War Ministry in Vienna. For them the official civilian policy made much more sense – namely, one which presupposed the creation of a distinct Bosnian identity and which used the term 'Bosnian' for the local language in order to (in the words of Robin Okey) 'tame Balkan nationalism'.[4]

Yet apart from the military and civil institutions, there was also a third group of local agents engaged in language politics: those citizens in the province involved in a growing number of civil organizations. As Robin Okey shows in his chapter, they increasingly interfered in the Habsburg administration by directly addressing petitions to the army and civilian authorities, and through press propaganda. Usually, these efforts were divided along religious lines with Orthodox civilians calling themselves 'Serbs' and Catholics calling themselves 'Croats'. The Serb newspaper *Zastava*, for example, complained that the term 'Bosnian' was being used for their language instead of 'Serbian'.

The language question in Bosnia-Herzegovina was always strongly connected, although not exclusively, to the Monarchy's Southern Slav Question. All over the empire, not only nationalists but also bureaucrats supported nation-building or understood the constitution of nationalities on the basis of their language.[5] In the modernizing world of a complex multilingual school system, with local and state elections and periodic censuses, the regimental languages became another factor complicating the question of ethnic or national belonging.[6] Pieter Judson has recently commented that 'institutional multilingualism had the effect of strengthening both nationalist and imperial patriotic tendencies at the same time'.[7] Indeed, political discussions during the Great War would show that this process was still ongoing after 1914. Yet, although local citizens in Bosnia were increasingly interfering in Habsburg bureaucratic decisions, in the end it was not the language question that destabilized Austro-Hungarian rule. Rather, it was the unstoppable zeitgeist of nationalism that had appeared not only across the Habsburg Monarchy but also as a European-wide phenomenon.

## Bosnia-Herzegovina under Habsburg rule

At the Berlin Congress in 1878 Austria-Hungary was given the right to occupy the Ottoman provinces of Bosnia and Herzegovina. This mandate of the European Great Powers was preceded by riots that had swept thousands of Christian refugees from this territory into Austrian Dalmatia. Austria-Hungary recognized the need permanently to pacify the entire region, but that was just one aspect of the occupation. In an age of colonies Austria-Hungary was the only European Great Power left with none. When the Austro-Hungarian delegation under Foreign Minister Count Gyula Andrássy went to Berlin, its aim was to take over these provinces and establish its own administration there.[8] Already in the autumn of the same year, Habsburg troops entered Bosnia-Herzegovina. No resistance was expected, as the Ottoman Empire had previously declared itself willing to withdraw its military forces. In fact, however, some troops remained, and together with parts of the Muslim population they organized an armed resistance that faced the Habsburg troops when they invaded.[9]

Although there was no longer an administration in Bosnia-Herzegovina controlled by Constantinople, these provinces formally remained part of the Ottoman Empire; only with the annexation of 1908 did they become part of the Monarchy. Nevertheless, they were never united with one of the two halves (Austria or Hungary), forming instead a quasi-third unit which was administered by the Common Ministry of Finance in Vienna.[10] Initially, the military was the sole authority responsible for the administration, but in time it was the Common Finance Ministry that became increasingly decisive as it was directly responsible for the Provincial Government (*Landesregierung*) based in Sarajevo.[11] The ministry was headed and influenced almost exclusively by bureaucrats from Hungary who propagated not only Hungary's traditional or historic mission in the Balkans but followed a political goal of creating a uniform Bosnian identity with its own language called 'Bosnian'.[12] In particular the Common Minister of Finance Benjámin von Kállay (1882–1903) controlled bureaucratic practices and local politics for many decades, becoming a very experienced counterpoint to the War Ministry in Vienna. And in Johann Freiherr von Appel, who was XV Corps commander in Sarajevo and head of the Provincial Government throughout his term of office, the civilian Kállay secured a very important supporter for his political programme.[13]

In addition to the introduction of bureaucratic practices from either the Austria or Hungarian administrative systems, for instance, the police, schools and local autonomous municipalities, in 1881 general military conscription was introduced into Bosnia (as in the rest of Austria-Hungary from 1867–8).[14] The local population reacted with an armed uprising.[15] Although this was quickly suppressed, and relative calm returned, sporadic regional unrest and riots did continue up to 1914.[16] After the uprising, Bosnian-Herzegovinian infantry regiments were established for the common Habsburg army with recruiting centres in Sarajevo, Banjaluka, Mostar and Tuzla. While each regiment reflected the ethnic mixture of its surrounding territory, these Bosnian natives, in particular the soldiers of Muslim faith, enriched an already multi-ethnic, multilingual and multi-confessional Habsburg army.[17]

Having in mind the fierce resistance in Herzegovina during the first military conscription, the Habsburg military leaders expected soldiers of the newly created infantry regiments to be unreliable. Therefore the Bosniaks were often stationed outside their home territory, mainly in the vicinity of Graz, Vienna or Budapest. On the other hand, dispatching soldiers outside their home territory was not unusual: all regiments had one or more companies in another part of the Monarchy.[18] Likewise, it was not unusual that soldiers were not trained by officers of the same ethnicity. Habsburg officers from all over the Monarchy spent time in Bosnian-Herzegovinian garrisons at some time in their career or were even assigned directly to one of the Bosniak regiments.[19] Nevertheless, decades passed before the so-called *Bosnische Landeskinder* or Bosnian subjects became officers and had an opportunity to shape language policy rather than just be the target of it. When reading newspapers, parliamentary debates, diaries and administrative documents from pre-1914, it becomes obvious that the Habsburg common army was an integral part of daily life in Bosnia-Herzegovina. The army's treatment of its diverse soldiers in terms of language use and ethnic affiliation was also regularly discussed in public.[20]

In the decades after 1878, the steadily growing military and civilian presence in Bosnia-Herzegovina had a dramatic impact on the composition of the population. In addition, the entire occupation zone was characterized by a strong Muslim emigration even if according to official figures this declined steadily. The Hungarian press in particular repeatedly criticized Kállay's policy of uniformity, asserting that 'Mohammedans [Muslims] emigrate in large numbers because they are not allowed to live in their own way'.[21] In 1890, Bosnia-Herzegovina had a population of 1.1 million, but five years later another 400,000. [22] In 1910, there were already 1.9 million inhabitants, including 50,000 Austrian and 61,000 Hungarian citizens, as well as another 6,500 so-called foreigners. According to this census, 'the three main denominations' lived in all parts of the country, but Sarajevo had a surplus of Muslims (about 46 per cent), compared to Serbian Orthodox at 32 per cent and Roman Catholics at 18 per cent.[23] The newcomers from Austria and Hungary were themselves not a homogeneous group; they had diverse social, religious and ethnic origins. Since individual companies of regiments from all parts of the Habsburg Monarchy were always sent to the occupation area for a few years, their officers and soldiers were a representative cross section of the entire Habsburg Monarchy.[24] At the same time, each year some 5,000 Bosnian-Herzegovinian male citizens were residing outside the provinces in Austria and Hungary for military service.[25] The 1910 statistical data referred to 3,200 active military Bosniaks stationed in Austria, 1,100 in Hungary and only 5,104 in their home region.[26] Therefore, by 1914, thousands of male Bosnian-Herzegovinian subjects had experienced the Habsburg army as soldiers.

Although conditions in Bosnia were generally calm, Habsburg military intelligence reports portrayed a steady rise in nationalist agitation stemming from Serbia and affecting the Orthodox population. Yet for the Habsburg public as well as for the ordinary occupation officer, soldier or bureaucrat, this propaganda activity remained hidden for a long time; or at least before the Sarajevo assassination it was not usually viewed as having a serious impact on the broad masses of Bosnia's Serb population. In his memoirs published after the First World War, Moritz Auffenberg-Komarów, commander of the XV Corps based in Sarajevo, wrote of Franz Joseph's visit to Bosanski Brod in May 1910:

> The welcome reception, meticulously planned, was broken to our horror by the Emperor himself, who criss-crossed the dense crowd. But neither here nor elsewhere did the slightest incident occur. This was proof ... that Greater Serbian agitation had not yet reached the point that would trigger the earth-shattering event four years later. Festively-dressed podiums were set up along the whole route, all in a row, with the mayor and the priests at the start, waving black-yellow and national flags.[27]

In the wake of the Young Turk revolution, Austria-Hungary in 1908 finally annexed Bosnia-Herzegovina. Although the constitutional integration resulted in international protests, especially from the Ottoman Empire, it had little impact on the overall security situation. In response, a state statute was passed in 1910, and a state legislature (Landtag or Sabor) was set up with seventy-two elected parliamentary deputies. Many of the officers who were scattered around Bosnian garrisons picked up a negative impression there about the nationality conflicts, but when writing about life in the provinces still did not mention anything negative about the new parliament. As one noted, 'the friendly attitude of the Bosnian-Herzegovinian Sabor towards the army and especially its representatives was perceptible during a reception organized in the officers' club [*Kasino*] where all deputies participated and the most cordial mood prevailed. A rare case in the old Monarchy!'²⁸ The Muslim population was increasingly described as loyal and 'military-friendly', the Catholics were almost never mentioned, and the Serbs were increasingly portrayed as being reserved or 'generally unreliable'.²⁹ The autobiographical testimonies scarcely reported violent incidents, yet their overall verdict, was still mainly negative: 'Those whom we should have been leading to culture and order often had only a feeling of hatred and contempt for us and disregarded us as *Švabas*.'³⁰ The term '*Švaba*' was the one most commonly used by the local population for Austro-Hungarian citizens regardless of their nationality, simply because they were most often heard speaking in German.³¹ Even during the partial mobilization on the occasion of the Balkan Wars (1912–13), Auffenberg still felt that the Serb population was not necessarily hostile, but 'completely reserved, and inclined to passive resistance'.³²

Nevertheless, although the occupied and later annexed territory was administered differently from the rest of the Monarchy and the mixture of population added a new religious group, the regiments recruited there were organized in the same way as the rest of the common army units and the same language system was applied. But there was one particular anomaly: the thorny issue over what exactly to call the local language.

## The Habsburg army language: System and practice

In 1868, after the introduction of universal military service across the Habsburg Empire, a much higher percentage of men had joined the army regardless of their social class, language, ethnic background or religion. The army after the Compromise with Hungary (1867) remained the only institution common to all parts of the empire and organized uniformly. In 1868, it duly underwent a reform, for the Austrian and Hungarian constitutions of 1867 had created, out of Habsburg subjects, state citizens with civil rights and duties. Besides the introduction of universal conscription, the Habsburg army leadership now adopted a key principle enshrined in the Austrian constitution. Article 19 guaranteed all peoples (*Volksstämme*, later exclusively called nationalities) the right to use their first language when making contact with public institutions such as schools, courts and the army. But it distinguished between those designated as official languages and others (omitted) which were viewed as mere dialects such as Friuli or Yiddish.³³

In the common Habsburg army there were subsequently three 'levels' of language practice. The language of command consisted of about eighty phrases in German that every soldier had to learn; the language of service (*Dienstsprache*) was also German and used for internal correspondence between army institutions. These two were mainly of political importance. The third type of language was the regimental language, also called soldiers' language as it referred to the language normally spoken by the recruits. It was a system that took into account the constitutional right of every man to employ his native language during military training. When soldiers were called up for military service, they were asked, before swearing an oath, for their language and writing skills. Following the common practice of decennial census-taking in the Austrian half of the Monarchy, they were not asked for their ethnic affiliation or native language. Nevertheless, official army statistics as well as comments in the press and administrative documents always interpreted language skills as equivalent to ethnic affiliation or 'nationality'. There were no 'German-speakers' or 'Czech-speakers' but only 'Czechs' or 'Germans'. The historian Rok Stergar has noted that the public was very much aware of this process.[34] Yet there were some restrictions on the general constitutional right. Only if a regiment consisted of more than 20 per cent of one language group could that language receive the official status of a regimental language.[35] There was also only one set of (eleven) officially recognized languages: German, Hungarian, Czech, Slovak, Slovene, Italian, Ruthenian (Ukrainian), Polish, Romanian, Serbian and Croatian. As far as regiments from Bosnia-Herzegovina were concerned, for these men the only possible languages that could be inscribed on their personnel forms were 'Croatian' and 'Serbian'.[36]

The most suitable source for analysing local army practice when it comes to the language use of soldiers is their personnel forms (called *Qualifikationslisten* for officers and *Grundbuchblätter* for the rank and file). However, with a few exceptions, neither the forms of Bosniak soldiers, nor of those born in Bosnia-Herzegovina who made it to the rank of officer, have been preserved systematically in the archives. So a quantitative analysis of the army's local practice in assigning certain languages, and therefore ethnic affiliation, is impossible. Nevertheless, some official forms relating to both rank and file and officers have been preserved, enough to get an insight into local bureaucratic practices over many years, and the ministry's responses that followed. The following examples illustrate this, revealing the arbitrary way in which 'nationality' could be assigned.

Scherif (Šerif) Kosmić was born shortly after Austria-Hungary invaded Bosnia-Herzegovina, in 1881 in a village near Jajce. He grew up in the first years of the occupation regime when the Bosnian administration was almost totally dominated by the Habsburg military. As the son of a Muslim landowner, he attended the military residential school for boys in Sarajevo (*k.u.k. Militärknabenpensionat*), then decided to become an officer and graduated with good grades from the infantry officer school in Graz. In 1901, he started his military career. He served in several garrisons such as Znojmo in Moravia before returning to Bosnia-Herzegovina (to Trebinje and

Mostar).³⁷ During the First World War he worked for the sensitive intelligence branch of the Habsburg occupation regime in Serbia, which meant that his superiors assessed him as especially loyal and reliable.³⁸ Beside Kosmić's outstanding career in the common army, it had been his language skills and how they were defined in his *Qualifikationslist* which were of major importance. As with his fellow officers, his language skills were assessed almost every year on a personnel form. In 1904, his superior estimated that he had a good knowledge of German and Hungarian as well as of the '*bosnische Landessprache*' or Bosnian language. But it appears that the use of the term 'Bosnian' was then queried, for it was struck out by somebody and replaced by the term 'Serbian'. This correction was not followed by any comment or justification. Since official statistics only recognized 'Serbian' or 'Croatian', Kosmić would not have been easily classifiable. The Muslim Kosmić therefore ended up in the annually published army statistics as a Serb. Kosmić's case therefore opens up several questions. Why did army institutions use the term 'Bosnian' when it was not an official regimental language in the Habsburg army? Why was it so important to delete 'Bosnian' on an internal military form when it was in no way a public document? And did the usage of 'Bosnian' and its subsequent deletion actually only occur because Kosmić was of the Muslim faith?

If Muslims like Kosmić ended up as Serbs in the annual statistics, what about Catholic and Orthodox officers serving in Bosniak regiments? How were their language skills noted down and then interpreted? Take, for example, the Roman Catholic officer Marcus Gjebić-Marušić who was born near Travnik. In 1899, his military superiors wrote on his personnel form that he knew both 'Croatian and Serbian' in speaking and writing, a sign that he was competent in the (Serb) Cyrillic alphabet. In the years that followed, his language skills continued to be called 'Croatian and Serbian' by his superiors. What these language skills can tell us about ethnic affiliation is more problematic. Unfortunately, we do not know how his case was interpreted in the official statistics, but it seems that for many years such a question did not arise since the statistics knew only one common category: entitled 'Serbs and Croats'.³⁹

Gjebić-Marušić's fellow officer Stjepan Sukić, born in 1883 in Bihać, was also of Roman Catholic faith. His personnel file of 1905 showed that he could speak and write German perfectly but also the Bosnian-Herzegovinian language (*bosnisch-herzegowinische Landessprache*) which was mentioned as the official regimental language on his form. However, in 1906, 'Croatian' was put down instead of 'Bosnian-Herzegovinian', although he was still serving in the same regiment.⁴⁰

All these examples concern officers who were born in Bosnia-Herzegovina, but there were also of course officers serving in Bosniak regiments who had been born elsewhere in the Monarchy. For example, Bruno Brelić, a Roman Catholic born in Split in Austrian Dalmatia in 1880, was noted in 1905 as knowing perfectly the regimental language of 'Bosnian-Herzegovinian' (*bosnisch-herzegowinische Landessprache*), but there was no indication given of his presumed native language of 'Croatian'. 'Croatian' had been mentioned on his personnel form in earlier years before he was transferred to a Bosniak regiment, but this was now simply replaced by 'Bosnian-Herzegovinian'.[41]

While all this reveals the arbitrary army practices on officers' forms, the following examples shed light on the ethnic designation of the rank and file. Nikola Gjurgjević was of Orthodox faith, born in Bosanski Brod in 1878, and assessed as speaking 'Bosnian'.[42] His case shows that the term 'Bosnian' was often used simply for a man hailing from the local territory or serving in a Bosniak regiment, and had nothing to do with the soldier's religious or ethnic affiliation. 'Bosnian' was also used on personnel forms when the man concerned was neither from the region itself nor even serving in a Bosniak regiment. This was, for example, the case with Pietro Tisot, born in the Hungarian town of Arad in 1874. When he was enlisted in Tyrol, the languages noted down in his personnel files were 'Italian, Bosnian and a bit of German'. The unacceptable term 'Bosnian' seems to have been in use all over the Monarchy, although legally it was forbidden. It appears that the soldier was simply asked about his language proficiency and whatever terms he used were noted down.[43]

According to the usual practice, we might assume that due to his religion Nikola Gjurgjević was converted into a 'Serb' in the annually published army statistics. But even the army yearbook altered its designations at certain times – sometimes not subscribing to the official ruling of the War Ministry in Vienna. In the 1885 Yearbook, for example, two separate categories show up: one for Croats and one for Serbs (including Slavonians and Dalmatians).[44] In the 1911 Yearbook, however, statistics for local languages were set out in two columns: the first column was for 'Croatian, Serbian, Serbo-Croatian'; the second for 'Croatian (Serbian, Serbo-Croatian)'. There was no explanation given as to why this new classification occurred, but 'Serbo-Croatian' was clearly a designation for Muslim.[45]

What then can we deduce from this? The use of language terms by local military officials in the *Qualifikationslisten* clearly varied and often did not follow the official War Ministry rules. It resulted from daily practices in the military offices spread across Bosnia-Herzegovina and beyond. The above-mentioned examples suggest that language designation was often casual and unintentional: it cannot always be interpreted as due to some political viewpoint. Rather, the respective NCOs or officers in the local administration were deciding case by case, or simply preferred one language term over another. In the Bosniak regiments too, language designation was probably decided on an ad hoc basis, taking into account the official regimental language and the religion of the individual. In fact, the recurring orders from the War Ministry to local military offices also indicate that there was a huge gap between what was expected (the official army rules) and what was actually practised.

Indeed, 'Bosnian', although often mentioned on the personnel forms, was never recognized as an official language, nor as an ethnic (*Nationalität*) category in the army statistics – in contrast to 'Serbo-Croat' or 'Serbo-Croatian'. If this designation was happening at a grassroots level in the region itself, did this signify that local army offices were supporting Kállay's efforts in constructing a Bosnian nation?[46] Or was it simply a result of the common conviction among Habsburg army officers that natives in Bosnia-Herzegovina mainly spoke the same language, termed 'Serbo-Croatian' in administrative sources according to the scholarly debates of the period?[47] The military were certainly well aware that this practice of exclusively using 'Serbian', 'Croatian' or 'Serbo-Croatian' tended to marginalize Muslims whom they increasingly saw as reliable soldiers. What then was the reaction of the War Ministry, which had its own rules in line with the monarch's decision? As we will see, when it came to the army's language rules and practices Bosnia-Herzegovina was a unique case, as the locally based army institutions followed their own interests.

## Conflicting interests between the civilian administration, the War Ministry and local army bodies

As we have noted, the army personnel's language knowledge and their ethnic affiliation were only one aspect of how the Habsburg authorities managed Bosnia-Herzegovina. There was also a conscious programme to create a Bosnian identity among an ethnically and religiously (but seemingly not linguistically) diverse population.[48] Most army officers were convinced that the bulk of Bosnia's indigenous inhabitants spoke one and the same language even if its actual name was disputed.[49] This is traceable in all administrative documents, letters, memoirs and diaries which regularly asserted that the 'inhabitants of Bosnia and Herzegovina speak one and the same language'.[50]

Nevertheless, already in the 1880s, it emerged that the local army authorities supported the idea of a Bosnian language (*bosnische Landessprache*) instead of using 'Croatian' or 'Serbian'. In 1888, the Provincial Governor Appel suggested to the Common Finance Ministry that the journal for a newly established museum in Sarajevo (Landesmuseum) should be published in the 'Bosnian language' by using both scripts, Latin and Cyrillic.[51] Although Kállay's plans for forging a Bosnian identity by calling the language Bosnian or *Landessprache* had already started in the 1880s, there is no indication in archival sources that the War Ministry or the civilian authorities disputed the local language question until the turn of the century. On 3 February 1899, the War Ministry wrote to the Common Finance Ministry, recalling that the civil administration in Bosnia-Herzegovina differed from the army in the terms it used for the languages present there. Thus the War Ministry was officially recognizing or claiming that any discussion about language use also affected the army. Kállay as common finance minister answered that the term 'provincial language' (*Landessprache*) was usually used in their official documents, deliberately avoiding the use of 'Croatian', 'Serbian' or 'Serbo-Croatian' since one of the ethnic groups always challenged those terms.[52] However, Kállay explained, although the term 'Bosnian' or *Landessprache* was privileged, the civilian administration did also 'accept' the use of other terms such as 'Croatian', 'Serbian' or 'Serbo-Croatian' language. He did not explain further under what circumstances this might occur.[53]

The War Ministry also did not engage further with Kállay's argument but decided that in all army documents only the terms 'Croatian' and 'Serbian' should be used. After all, this had been the official regulation laid down since the army reform of 1868 not only for Bosniak soldiers but for all soldiers and officers deployed in one of those regiments.[54] While Kállay was aiming to achieve uniformity by using 'Bosnian' or *Landessprache*, the army bureaucrats in the War Ministry were focused on achieving their own uniformity, subsequently telling Kállay to ban the use of terms such as 'Bosnian', *Landessprache*, 'Serbo-Croatian' or 'South Slav' (*Südslawisch*).[55] In the end, however, the question was left unresolved. For soon after its blunt order of February 1899, the War Ministry had also informed Kállay that the language term used should be decided on a case-by-case basis, and that it should always be done '*unauffällig*' (without attracting public attention).[56] Certainly, this confusion of signals was one reason why uniformity on language policy in Bosnia-Herzegovina was never achieved at all: local civilian and military officials continued to use a variety of different terms.

In fact, deciding on an ad hoc basis instead of following any clear rules was the pattern for the regimental language system everywhere in the Monarchy. In most cases it caused confusion among military officials as well as among the public; it therefore did not prevent public debate and criticism but only fostered it. Emperor Franz Joseph too in similar instances often said that he would not decide, for a solution was needed on a case-by-case basis at the regional level – from the army's point of view this mainly meant at the corps level.[57] This would have meant in Bosnia-Herzegovina that the corps commander in Sarajevo had to decide. István Deák has summarized the monarch's general perspective, that he was 'the final arbitrator ... who successfully drowned all controversies in a sea of paper'.[58]

A debate over language terminology occurred not only for Bosniak regiments but also for other military institutions in Bosnia-Herzegovina such as the military residential boys' school in Sarajevo (*k.u.k. Militärknabenpensionat*). In 1903, it was the Provincial Government that insisted on the use of the term 'Bosnian-Herzegovinian language' (*bosnisch-herzegowinische Landessprache*) for pupils of all religious faiths and demanded a change in the language terms used in student reports. The War Ministry once again refused this, noting that the language designated for each pupil could not be named after a region but had to correspond to a particular nation(ality) ('Die Sprache nicht nach dem Lande, in welcher sie gesprochen wird, sondern nach der Nation, welche sie spricht, zu benennen'). When in a subsequent communication the Common Ministry of Finance gently suggested that its own views should prevail since it paid for most of the school's budget, the War Ministry again objected, ordering the exclusive use of either 'Croatian' or 'Serbian'.[59] Again the War Ministry seems to have been a driving force in keeping to the rules and thereby marginalizing the provinces' Muslims, although as we have seen the local army authorities were frequently prepared to use the term 'Bosnian'.

The military–civilian discussion of 1899 about language terminology in Bosniak regiments was also revived in 1902. Appel then reported to the War Ministry that Muslim soldiers were regularly complaining about 'Serbian' and 'Croatian' as the only two options for their language competence. The army language practice was quite clear to the soldiers for they were all given military identity cards (*Militärpässe*) where their language skills were noted. Many Muslim soldiers were aware of the statistical practice of interpreting language skills as nationality and therefore complained about 'becoming' Serbs or Croats while doing their military service.[60] As a supporter of the term 'Bosnian', Appel again requested that the War Ministry should finally allow the use of 'Bosnian-Herzegovinian language' for anyone originating from the occupied lands (distinguishing only along religious but not language lines); he argued against the case-by-case decision of 1899.[61] However, interestingly, he also opposed the use of the term 'provincial language' (*Landessprache*) which was being regularly used by the civil administration, for when soldiers were transferred to a regiment outside Bosnia-Herzegovina, he argued, no one would understand what that term meant.

This discussion shows that there was not only a dispute between the War Ministry and the Common Finance Ministry but also a dispute among the military authorities: between the locally based Appel who wanted to stop any marginalization of the Muslims (in line with Kállay's vision) and the War Ministry in Vienna. However, the War Ministry stuck to its decision that 'the language should be designated not according to the region ... but only according to the nationality which speaks it'.[62] This therefore totally ignored Kállay's attempts to create a Bosnian nation with a Bosnian language as well as Appel's suggestion.

In general, for all language rules in the common army and the civil government in Bosnia-Herzegovina, it was the empire's Common Ministerial Council (*Gemeinsamer Ministerrat*) that had the last word. Since the 1867 Compromise had caused the partition of many formerly centralized state responsibilities, there was only this one platform left where the Austrian and Hungarian highest authorities met regularly.[63] At these meetings, the representatives (including the common finance minister) regularly clashed over army issues including the common army's language rulings. However, it was quite typical for any decisions to be postponed until the next meeting.⁶⁴ Even after the language dispute over Bosnian was supposedly solved, with the War Ministry making it very clear what was expected from subordinate military officials, the term 'Bosnian-Herzegovinian language' or 'Bosnian' continued to be used on military personnel forms. In Scherif Kosmić's case, it was noted down in 1904 that as a Muslim he spoke 'Bosnian'; but that term was also used in 1905 in the case of the Catholic officer Stjepan Sukić.

As for using the term 'Serbo-Croatian', it can be traced back to the 1880s in officers' personnel forms, regardless of their ethnic, national or religious background. But, it seems, it was not until 1907 that the term was used more widely, often as a postscript that it was the official regimental language in Bosniak regiments.⁶⁵ This was a time, four years after Benjámin Kállay's death, when the Bosnian Provincial Government was starting to propagate 'Serbo-Croatian' as the official language.⁶⁶ For the War Ministry, this term also corresponded much better to its general argument as it still avoided the use of the region's name. According to the linguist Gordana Ilić Marković, a couple of years before the outbreak of the war the term 'Serbo-Croatian' increasingly replaced the terms 'Serbian' and 'Croatian' and became exclusively used throughout the Monarchy in administration and education.⁶⁷ The last census in Bosnia-Herzegovina in 1910 asked for the mother tongue, and specifically if it was 'Serbo-Croatian' or another language. The result given was that 96.2 per cent of the population spoke Serbo-Croatian, revealing that Croatian and Serbian were not counted separately. This statistic did not reveal a 'nationality', but only speakers of Serbo-Croatian.⁶⁸ Again, local civilian and local military practice went hand in hand: a statistical assessment of 1912, published for the Bosnian-Herzegovinian XV Corps Command, recognized only 'Serbo-Croats' as living in Bosnia-Herzegovina.⁶⁹

Following the annexation in 1908, and the creation of a provincial parliament in Sarajevo, the discourse surrounding language terminology was enriched by local political parties. It is clear that they too took up the term 'Serbo-Croatian'. But as the historians Dževad Juzbašić and Zijad Šehić have suggested, the subsequent political discussion circled more around the equality of the local language vis-à-vis German than about what to call the local language. The political discussion did reveal that a majority favoured the term 'Serbo-Croatian'. According to the programme of the local Serb parliamentary club of 1913, 'Under the principle of complete tolerance for all confessions, we take the standpoint that Croats and Serbs are one people, which leads us to the conclusion that in Bosnia-Herzegovina Serbs, Croats and Muslims have the same blood and speak the official language of Serbo-Croatian.'⁷⁰

With the outbreak of the First World War this political discussion ended as the Sabor was not allowed to meet. But in 1918, the War Ministry's statistics again suggested a new way to name and categorize the Bosniaks, by differentiating in army regiments between 'Croats', 'Serbs' and 'Serbo-

Croats'. This meant that the people of Bosnia-Herzegovina were no longer categorized as one group – either as Bosnians or as Serbo-Croats – but that by implication Muslims secured their own category called 'Serbo-Croats'.[71]

## Conclusion

This chapter has shown that 'the' Habsburg administration never existed in pre-war Bosnia-Herzegovina. There was more than one institution working there, and they often followed contradictory language policies. One practice that lasted for decades was to designate all local subjects under one term – 'Bosnian', later replaced by 'Serbo-Croatian'. At exactly the same time there were officially only two options allowed in the army – 'Serbian' and 'Croatian' – thereby in principle marginalizing any soldiers of Muslim faith. This overall lack of uniformity took place not despite Kállay's mission to create a common identity but rather because of it. For Kállay's efforts had simply added new terminology and made the language practices even more complicated. The use of the controversial term 'Bosnian' even swept across Bosnia-Herzegovina's borders as military personnel in other parts of the Monarchy started to use it.

The army's language practices reveal the sheer complexity for the authorities of defining the Southern Slav Question in Bosnia-Herzegovina. Besides the variety of terms used, we have seen how different perspectives and practices were applied at the same time: from Vienna, Budapest, the War Ministry, the military based in the region or the soldiers themselves. Over the years, opinion from the grassroots, especially from local citizens, also became stronger. Although this debate over language in general imitated the rest of the Monarchy, in Bosnia-Herzegovina – unlike elsewhere – local military officials often followed the policy of the civil government (the Common Finance Ministry/Provisional Government) and resisted general army regulations (the War Ministry). To the local army institutions the categorization into Serbs and Croats simply did not reflect the regional realities, and they also wanted to support every effort to avoid the marginalization of Muslim soldiers. This reveals then the fluidity of national identity compared to the national stereotyping that appeared so strongly in 1914; but in the same way we see a flexible and healthy Habsburg approach towards modernization and the 'taming' of national projects in Bosnia-Herzegovina.

Although the regimental languages were discussed at length among the Habsburg imperial elites, the soldiers of each faith were well aware of the bureaucratic system and how their language was being interpreted as an ethnic affiliation. For a long time the Habsburg military assessed these conflicts in Bosnia-Herzegovina as being rather alien and therefore not a threat to the empire's future; before 1910 there was no indigenous political party system or assembly in Sarajevo. But even the few years between 1910 and the outbreak of war reveal that subjects were becoming more active and influential in shaping their own political future. Many delegates to the Sabor had served in Bosniak regiments, and many more locals had become professional or reserve officers. Although similar to any discussion about the loyalties and identities of all other Habsburg nationalities, the case of Bosnia-Herzegovina was sui generis.

Only during the Great War did a third option really appear: using 'Croatian' for Catholic soldiers, 'Serbian' for Orthodox and 'Serbo-Croatian' for Muslims. Probably it was the wartime success and proven loyalty of Muslim soldiers that caused the War Ministry to retreat from its pre-war agenda and think of grouping them under a special term which was distinct from the other two major ethnic groups. By using the term 'Serbo-Croats' instead of Kállay's 'Bosnian', the military simply took into account the official desire of Muslim politicians in the immediate pre-war years.

The naming of the language spoken in Bosnia-Herzegovina is still under debate, and very often reminds us of Habsburg times. Language use was and is very much interpreted as ethnic affiliation or national belonging, and still there are efforts to create a common identity. The example of present-day Bosnia-Herzegovina shows in stark form that the naming of the local language is still on the political agenda. Usually, when withdrawing money from cash-point machines, customers are asked to choose the language first and in Bosnia-Herzegovina there are two options: English or '*lokalni*' (local language). Also in the public and political discourse over national identity and language use, it becomes obvious that it strongly resembles what the Habsburg authorities were debating before 1914. When travelling through Bosnia-Herzegovina today one finds the public inscriptions in three languages, and the health warnings on cigarette packets are similarly given as 'Pušenje ubinja, Pušenje ubinja, Пушењеубиња (*Pušenje ubinja*)'. It is not necessary to understand a South Slav language to recognize that there is no difference except in the use of the Cyrillic alphabet.

## Notes

1 Österreichisches Staatsarchiv, Kriegsarchiv, Vienna (War Archives: hereafter KA), Militärkanzlei Seiner Majestät (MKSM), karton 1372 Zl.30-1-2, 1918: 'Farbtabellen sprachliche Zusammensetzung Heeresinfanterieregimenter'.

2 This practice was not unique, but appeared all over the Monarchy. It becomes most obvious in the monthly situational reports sent from the Corps Commands to the War Ministry (see, for example, the IX Corps Command records in the Vojenský Historický Archív Prague (Military History Archives: hereafter VHA)). It also became very clear in Habsburg war propaganda. See Mark Cornwall, *The Undermining of Austria-Hungary: The Battle for Hearts and Minds* (New York: Palgrave Macmillan, 2018), chapter 2.

3   Edin Hajdarpasic, *Whose Bosnia? Nationalism and Political Imagination in the Balkans, 1840-1914* (Ithaca, NY: Cornell University Press, 2015), 8.

4   Robin Okey, *Taming Balkan Nationalism: The Habsburg 'Civilizing Mission' in Bosnia, 1878-1914* (Oxford: Oxford University Press, 2007).

5   Rok Stergar and Tamara Scheer, 'Ethnic Boxes: The Unintended Consequences of Habsburg Bureaucratic Classification', *Nationalities Papers* 46:4 (2018): 575–91.

6   See, for example, Pieter M. Judson, *Guardians of the Nation: Activists on the Language Frontiers of Imperial Austria* (Cambridge, MA: Harvard University Press, 2006).

7   Pieter M. Judson, *The Habsburg Empire: A New History* (Cambridge, MA: Harvard University Press, 2016), 368.

8   See Horst Haselsteiner, *Bosnien-Hercegovina. Orientkrise und Südslavische Frage* (Vienna: Böhlau, 1996); Tamara Scheer, *'Minimale Kosten, absolut kein Blut!' Österreich-Ungarns Präsenz im Sandžak von Novipazar (1879-1908)* (Frankfurt: Peter Lang, 2013), 54.

9   On the fierce resistance encountered, see most recently, Clemens Ruthner, 'Besetzungen. Die Invasoren und Insurgenten des Okkupationsfeldzugs 1878 im kulturellen Gedächtnis', in Clemens Ruthner and Tamara Scheer (eds), *Bosnien-Herzegowina und Österreich-Ungarn. Annäherungen an eine Kolonie* (Tübingen: Francke, 2018), 123–46.

10  Joseph Maria Baerenreither, *Bosnische Eindrücke. Eine politische Studie* (Vienna: Hölder, 1908), 51ff.

11  For the general administration, see Karl Gabriel, *Der Aufbau der Verwaltung in Bosnien-Herzegowina 1878 unter FZM Wilhelm Herzog von Württemberg und dessen Biographie* (PhD diss., Vienna 2002); Walter Rojik, *Die Errichtung der öffentlichen Verwaltung in Bosnien-Herzegowina durch Österreich-Ungarn nach der Okkupation im Jahre 1878* (PhD diss., Vienna, 1980).

12  See Benjámin von Kállay, 'Ungarn an den Grenzen des Orients und des Occidents', *Ungarische Revue* 3 (1883): 428–89. Also Magyar Országos Levéltár, Budapest (Hungarian State Archives: hereafter MOL), Bécsi levéltárokból kiszolgáltatott iratok (BLKI), I 67, Thallóczy Lajos közöspénzügyminisztériumiosztály fönök hagyatéka, karton 2. For background to Kállay's thinking, see Ian D. Armour, *Apple of Discord: The 'Hungarian Factor' in Austro-Serbian Relations, 1867-1881* (West Lafayette: Purdue University Press, 2014).

13  Appel served in Bosnia-Herzegovina from 1882 until 1903 as head of the Provincial Government, and – as contemporaries assessed him – was well aware of local ethnic disputes. See Scheer, *'Minimale Kosten, absolut kein Blut!'*, 100.

14  On state building, see Hajdarpasic, *Whose Bosnia?*, 136. For a contemporary perspective, see Baerenreither, *Bosnische Eindrücke*.

15  Markus Koller, 'Bosnien und die Herzegowina im Spannungsfeld von "Europa" und "Außereuropa" – Der Aufstand in der Herzegowina, Südbosnien und Süddalmatien (1881–1882)', in Hans-Christian Maner (ed.), *Grenzregionen*

*der Habsburgermonarchie im 18. und 19. Jahrhundert. Ihre Bedeutung und Funktion aus der Perspektive Wiens* (Münster: LIT Verlag, 2005), 197–216; Mehmet Hacisalihoğlu, 'Muslim and Orthodox Resistance against the Berlin Peace Treaty in the Balkans', in HakanYavuz and Peter Sluglett (eds), *War and Diplomacy: The Russo-Turkish War of 1877-1878 and the Treaty of Berlin* (Salt Lake City: University of Utah Press, 2011), 125–43. For an eyewitness report, see KA, Nachlässe (NL), B/862, Nr. 1, Stillfried, 'Erinnerungen aus meinem Leben. III: Der Aufstand in Bosnien (1881/1882)', 26–8.

16  Hajdarpasic, *Whose Bosnia?*, 153.

17  On the organization of the Bosniak regiments see Zijad Šehić, *U smrt za cara i domovinu! Bosanci i Hercegovci u vojnoj organizaciji Habsburške monarhije 1878-1918* (Sarajevo: Sarajevo Publishing, 2007); Christoph Neumayer and Erwin A. Schmidl (eds), *Des Kaisers Bosniaken. Die bosnisch-herzegowinischen Truppen in der k. u. k. Armee. Geschichte und Uniformierung von 1878 bis 1918* (Vienna: Militaria, 2008).

18  Tamara Scheer, 'Die k.u.k. Regimentssprachen: Eine Institutionalisierung der Sprachenvielfalt in der Habsburgermonarchie (1867/8-1914)', in Klaas-Hinrich Ehlers, Marek Nekala, Martina Niedhammer and Hermann Scheuniger (eds), *Sprache, Gesellschaft und Nation in Ostmitteleuropa. Institutionalisierung und Alltagspraxis* (Göttingen: Vandenhoeck & Ruprecht, 2014), 75–92.

19  See, as one example, Pero Blašković, *Mit den Bosniaken im Weltkrieg. Auszug aus Pero Blašković 'Sa Bosnjacima u svejtskom ratu'* (Vienna: Landesverteidigungsakademie, 2011). Blašković published his memoirs in Belgrade in 1939 where he was a retired general of the Yugoslav army. Before 1918 he was a professional officer in the Habsburg army.

20  For an example of a Muslim newspaper published in Sarajevo, see *Musavat*, 3 June 1911, 2–3.

21  MOL, BLKI, I/67, Thallóczy Lajos közös pénzügy-minisztériumi osztály fönök hagyatéka, karton 1, Beilage: *Budapester Abendblatt*, 20 February 1902.

22  N.N., 'Bosnien und Hercegovina', in *Agramer Zeitung*, 18 June 1906, 1.

23  Karl Czapp, *Das Wehrgesetz für Bosnien und die Hercegovina von 1912* (Vienna: Streffleur, 1912), 18.

24  Šehić, *U smrt za cara*; Neumayer and Schmidl, *Des Kaisers Bosniaken*.

25  Czapp, *Das Wehrgesetz*, 18.

26  Ibid.

27  Moritz von Auffenberg-Komarów, *Aus Österreichs Höhe und Niedergang. Eine Lebensschilderung* (Munich: Drei Masken Verlag, 1921), 133.

28  Ibid., 143.

29  KA, NL, B/600:I, Anton Lehár, Geschichten erzählt, vol. 2, 24.

30  Ibid., 22.

31  Stijn Vervaet, 'Serbischer Okzidentalismus? Anti-westliche Rhetorik in Bosnien-Herzegowina während der österreichisch-ungarischen Besatzung', in Ruthner and Scheer, *Bosnien-Herzegowina und Österreich*-Ungarn, 395. See also,

Zoran Konstantinović, '"Nemac" und "Švaba" in der serbischen Literatur', in Gabriella Schubert and Wolfgang Dahmen (eds), *Bilder vom Eigenen und Fremden aus dem Donau-Balkan-Raum* (Munich: Südosteuropa-Gesellschaft, 2003), 169–78.

32 Auffenberg, *Aus Österreichs Höhe und Niedergang*, 123.

33 'Staatsgrundgesetz vom 21. Dezember 1867 über die allgemeinen Rechte der Staatsbürger für die im Reichsrate vertretenen Königreiche und Länder', in *Reichsgesetzblatt* (1867), Nr. 142. As an example of memoirs dealing with the personal experience in ethnically mixed regions: KA, NL, B/58, Nr. 4, August von Urbański, 'Das Tornisterkind', unpublished manuscript (n.d.), 95.

34 Rok Stergar, 'Fragen des Militärwesens in der slowenischen Politik, 1867-1914', *Österreichische Osthefte* 46/3 (2004): 391–422. This was seemingly also the case for the Bohemian regiments: VHA, Kmenový list, (year/box no.): 1874/315, 1880/69, 1884/427, 1885/397, 1901/274.

35 István Deák, *Beyond Nationalism: A Social and Political History of the Habsburg Officer Corps, 1848-1918* (New York: Oxford University Press, 1990), 122. When the Great War erupted, only a handful of regiments had only one regimental language.

36 KA, MKSM, 87-2/1, Offiziers-/Soldatenstand 1894, 'Der nebenstehende Grundbuchstand enthält nach Sprachen'.

37 KA, Qualifikationslisten, Scherif Kosmić, born 18 August 1881.

38 Hadtörténelmi Levéltár, Budapest (Military History Archives: hereafter HIL), Manuskripte, Nr. 309, Carnegie Report of Hugo Kerchnawe, dated 1922: 'Beilage: Organisation der Nachrichtenabteilung des Militärgeneralgouvernements Serbien', 20 September 1917.

39 KA, Qualifikationslisten, Marcus Gjebić-Marušić, born 15 February 1866.

40 KA, Qualifikationslisten, Stjepan Sukić, born 19 August 1883.

41 KA, Qualifikationslisten, Bruno Brelić, born 4 May 1880.

42 Arhiv Bosne i Hercegovine Sarajevo (Archive of Bosnia and Herzegovina: hereafter ABH), Zemaljska Vlada za Bosnu i Hercegovinu (Provincial Government of Bosnia-Herzegovina: ZVS), 32–105, 1907, bh. Infantry Regiment No. 3 to the Landesregierung in Sarajevo, 13 February 1907.

43 Tiroler Landesarchiv (Innsbruck), Grundbuchblätter, Südtirol, Pietro Tisot, born 1874.

44 *Militärstatistisches Jahrbuch* (Vienna, 1885), 154.

45 *Militärstatistisches Jahrbuch* (Vienna, 1911), 200ff.

46 Dževad Juzbašić, 'Die Sprachenpolitik der österreichisch-ungarischen Verwaltung und die nationalen Verhältnisse in Bosnien-Herzegowina, 1878–1918', *Südost-Forschungen* 61/62 (2002–3): 235–72. See also Imre Ress, 'Versuch einer Nationenbildung um die Jahrhundertwende. Benjámin Kállays Konzeption der bosnischen Nation', in Endre Kiss and Justin Stagl (eds), *Nation und Nationenbildung in Österreich-Ungarn, 1848–1938: Prinzipien und Methoden* (Vienna: LIT, 2006), 66ff.

47 KA, Reichkriegsministerium (War Ministry: hereafter KM), 2. Abteilung, 31-3/2, 1899, Gem. Finanzministerium (Nr. 1245) to KM, 7 February 1899.
48 Ress, 'Versuch einer Nationenbildung', 59–72. See also Robin Okey, 'A Trio of Hungarian Balkanists: Béni Kállay, István Burián and Lajos Thallóczy in the Age of High Nationalism', *The Slavonic and East European Review* 80/2 (April 2002): 234–66.
49 KA, KM, 2. Abt., 31-3/2, 1899, Gem. Finanzministerium (Nr. 1245) to KM, 7 February 1899.
50 ABH, Zajedničko ministarstvo financija (Common Ministry of Finance: hereafter CMF), b. 10724, ZVS to KM, 31 August 1903.
51 ABH, CMF, b. 8779, Appel to CMF, 16 November 1888.
52 ABH, CMF, Odjeljenje za Bosnu i Hercegovinu, b. 1245, 1899.
53 KA, KM, 2.Abt., 31-3/2, 1899, CMF to KM, Nr. 1245, 7 February 1899.
54 KA, KM, Präs, 10-39/1, 1903, 'KM Entscheidung', 5 August 1903.
55 KA, KM, 2. Abt., 31-3/2, 1899, 'Entwurf eines Erlasses', 2. Abt., 18 February 1899. See also: ABH, CMF, b. 9672, KM to CMF, 5 August 1903.
56 KA, KM, 2.Abt., 31-3/2, CMF to KM, 7 February 1899. See also: KA, KM, 2. Abt., 31-3/2, 1899, Notiz am Rückblatt, 4 March 1899.
57 As one example of such an order: KA, MKSM, 2. Abt., 31-32, Note of the KM, 4 March 1899.
58 Deák, *Beyond Nationalism*, 60.
59 KA, KM, Präs, 10-39/1, 1903. See the following documents: XV Corps Command to KM, 7 June 1903, Note of the KM Presidium, 23 July 1903, Proposal of the 6th department of the KM, 3 July 1903, as well as KM decision, 5 August 1903.
60 ABH, CMF, b. 16659, Appel to KM, 4 December 1902.
61 Ibid.; KA, KM, Abt. 2, 12-13, XV Corps Command to KM, 4 December 1902.
62 KA, KM, Präs, 10-39/1, Stellungnahme des Präsidialbüros/Reichskriegsministerium, 23 July 1903.
63 Éva Somogyi, *Der gemeinsame Ministerrat der österreichisch-ungarischen Monarchie 1867-1906* (Vienna: Böhlau, 1996), 92–5.
64 Dževad Juzbašić and Zijad Šehić (eds), *Persönliche Vormerkungen von General Oskar Potiorek über die innerpolitische Lage in Bosnien und der Herzegowina* (Sarajevo: Akademija nauka i umjetnosti Bosne i Hercegovine, 2015), 55.
65 This term also appears in the officers' *Qualifikationslisten* of the 1880s, but its status as regimental language was not mentioned.
66 Milorad Ekmečić, 'Impact of the Balkan Wars on Society in Bosnia and Herzegovina', in Béla Király and Dimitrije Djordjević (eds), *East Central European Society and the Balkan Wars (War and Society in East Central Europe XVIII)* (New York: Columbia University Press, 1987), 268–9.
67 Gordana Ilić Marković, 'Creating a Name for a Pluricentric Language: From Serbian to Serbo-Croatian, Bosnian/Croatian/Serbian', in Rudolf Muhr (ed.),

*Pluricentric Languages and Non-Dominant Varieties Worldwide, Part 1* (Frankfurt am Main: Peter Lang, 2016), 443.
68  Rudolf Kleeberg, *Die Nationalitätenstatistik, ihre Ziele, Methoden und Ergebnisse* (Waidhofen a.d. Thaya: Thomas & Hubert, 1915), 170–1.
69  KA, Militär- und Territorialkommanden, XV Corps Command, Korpskommandobefehl Nr. 17, 5 March 1912.
70  Juzbašić and Šehić (eds), *Persönliche Vormerkungen*, 63–77.
71  KA, MKSM, karton 1372 Zl.30-1-2, 1918: 'Farbtabellen sprachliche Zusammensetzung Heeresinfanterieregimenter'.

# CHAPTER 6

## *Mlada Bosna*

## The educational and cultural context

### Robin Okey

The assassination of Archduke Franz Ferdinand on Vidovdan 1914 is one of the iconic moments in twentieth-century history. The core conspirators, the youthful writers who debated Bosnia's situation in the pre-war years, and the outer circle of some 130 young people whom the Austrians put on trial, will be taken here to constitute the movement – not formally organized but known to history as Young Bosnia (*Mlada Bosna*). Yet for most students of history the assassination has remained only a moment, the 'occasion' of the First World War, from which countless schoolchildren have made their first acquaintance with the elegant distinction between occasion and cause in historical events. As historiography on the causes of the war developed, so even the issues between Austria-Hungary and Serbia, the Balkan question itself, often shrank to the margins of debates on imperialism, the operation of alliance systems, the Fischer thesis of the primacy of domestic policy in an age of challenged elites and so forth. In 2012, Christopher Clark then usefully redirected attention to the role of coincidence beneath the imposing structures of historical theory.[1]

Of course, Sarajevo 1914 never ceased to be important in the Southern Slav lands themselves, and between the wars it played a substantial role in German rejection of the 'war guilt' clause of the Treaty of Versailles. Much press reminiscence in these years, often by surviving Young Bosnians, presupposed themes of national heroism, but controversy about the role of the Serbian government induced reserve on the part of the new Yugoslav authorities. Unlike the Czechoslovaks they did not participate in the ceremonies marking the repatriation of the remains of Young Bosnians who had died in Terezín jail.[2] One of their strongest would-be foreign champions, R. W. Seton-Watson, wrote a book on the 'crime' of Sarajevo, which, while exculpating Belgrade, described the assassins as 'raw and hare-brained youths' whose 'abnormal state of health rendered them apt pupils in terrorism'.[3] Not till the communist period was the place of *Mlada Bosna* as a revolutionary liberation movement officially secure. Vladimir Dedijer's work of 1966 built on belated full-length publications by Young Bosnian participants, setting up a model which held firm till the break-up of Yugoslavia in the 1990s.[4] Now the wheel has turned once more and Gavrilo Princip is again a terrorist in his native Bosnia.[5]

This chapter, however, is not intended to reprise the 'terrorist or revolutionary' approach in its traditional form but to set it in a wider context. Sarajevo 1914 clearly fits a theme of revolutionary student youth, who did not figure in 1789, but appeared in 1848 and then notoriously in Tsarist Russia from the 'movement to the people' onwards. Yet by the early twentieth century the *Narodnik* theme of students acting against a background of sociocultural alienation was developing increasingly ethnonationalist overtones, in situations like revolutionary opposition to the partition of Bengal in 1905, the movements in China, Egypt and Korea in 1919 and then on through the century: Cyprus in the 1950s, Algeria in the 1960s, to the Islamic radicalization of our own day.

This is where Young Bosnia can potentially be placed, in contexts of varied reaction to Western metropoles' pressures on other communities. The approach adopted here, then, entails seeing a colonial aspect to the Austrian occupation. True, occupied Bosnia was not a classic colony in a faraway continent but bordered on territories in the Monarchy speaking its language. It was mainly to nip South Slav nationalism in the bud that it had been occupied, and this nationalism claimed a European pedigree quite unlike the current Islamist rejection of Western ideas. Yet the mixed nature of Bosnia's experience makes it no less interesting for comparison with today's globalizing world, where cultural conflict is played out not just in zones of Western intervention but in Western societies where immigrants from these zones have settled. Recent interventions in the Muslim world show similarities to the Habsburg experience in terms of the confidence, at least initially, in the transformative power of Western culture in societies deemed backward. As to ideological motivation, it depends how important specific ideologies are in the development of youthful terrorism. Underlying the following discussion of Bosnia therefore are two questions of potentially wider relevance. Why do we see Western policymakers repeatedly confident that education in a Western spirit will align other populations, or important cohorts among them, with their goals and values? And what is the balance between psychological and ideological factors in the development of youthful terrorism when occupation of foreign territories occurs?

That Austro-Hungarian Bosnia was part of the East, that its occupation was to be justified in terms of the contemporary trope of 'cultural mission', was not doubted at the time in the Monarchy or elsewhere. Recent objections that 'cultural mission' is a misnomer because it exaggerates the Monarchy's reform intentions miss more than the propagandist point of the phrase.[6] It was a mark of the self-confidence of the imperial age to believe that 'vast … improvement' in non-Western lands could be effected 'by the introduction of little more than the ordinary methods and principles of civilized government', as Alfred Milner put it.[7] 'What we have accomplished in Egypt, what in less measure the French have achieved in Tunis, that has Austria-Hungary performed in these wild Turkish provinces,' wrote the British historian William Miller in his *Travels and Politics in the Near East* in 1898.[8] The quite radical liberal G. P. Gooch echoed Miller's comparison of the Common Finance Minister Benjámin Kállay with Lord Cromer in Egypt.[9] Bosnia's Muslim population was a particular focus for Habsburg travel writers and artists' portrayal of the exotic, but the orientalism of Serbs was no less a tenet of Kállay's political philosophy.[10] Trends in recent historiography criticize the absolute civilizational divide which Balkan Christian nationalists sought to establish between Christian and Muslim and seek to recall the pervasive legacy of Ottoman rule.[11] They are borne out by photographs of befezzed committee members of the Croatian National Association, around 1910, in *Napredak*, the leading calendar of the most Western oriented of Bosnia's confessions. In 1912, the then common finance minister Leon Biliński stated openly that he saw Bosnia as a colony.[12]

## The Austro-Hungarian educational mission

Kállay, the pivotal figure in Habsburg governance in Bosnia from 1882 to 1903, knew he had a developmental as well as a national problem to deal with. It was exacerbated by his administration's obligation, in line with colonial practice, to pay for itself without recourse to the metropole. He set out his educational framework along three lines within which Young Bosnia ultimately developed. First, alongside industrial development to maximize income, the modern schools needed to be few but of good quality, to impress the natives and provide lower cadres for the type of administration long recruited elsewhere; in 1879 only some 5,800 children were receiving a European-style primary education in a population of 1.3 million.[13] Reflecting these priorities, three quarters of the school budgets went on post-primary schooling in 1889, though there was still only one state Gymnasium in Bosnia.[14] By 1914, there were five full and two half (or four as opposed to eight class) state secondary schools, a technical academy and a number of teacher training colleges and state-funded seminaries.

Second, scholarships were relatively generous. In all, grants awarded for secondary and higher education rose three and a half times in the 1890s.[15] There were at first no school fees and textbooks came free. Positive discrimination was applied to Muslims in an effort to build up a Western-educated intelligentsia in a suspicious community whose elite were rarely literate in their own language. Thus grants for the Sarajevo Gymnasium were increased substantially in 1895 to allow for almost all the twenty-five Muslim applicants to receive them – a breakthrough figure – without unduly damaging the prospects of others.[16]

Third, the implicit paternalism had its hard side. When the scholarship system proved wasteful, because few university students from Bosnia made it through to graduation, Kállay founded a special Bosnian Institute in Vienna to house them with a strict regimen, which provoked uproar. The prescribed lecture and examination schedules, set meal times and bans on smoking, visiting cafes or joining associations and assemblies, led to denunciations of a 'prison for Mamelukes' in the South Slav and socialist press; and twenty-six of the thirty-four initial entrants were expelled after police were called to end a barricaded sit-in.[17] There was also an extensive spying system that included student informers in both Bosnia and Vienna. The system was tailored to assuage Kállay's fear, in a recurrent phrase, of the so-called half-educated proletariat, particularly dangerous among jurists and students of the humanities. In the 1900s, the Bosnian Institute regularly offered more grants to trainee vets than to students at the Philosophy Faculty of Vienna University.

Overall, by 1918 these policies had produced just under 1,500 pupils who had completed a state secondary schooling in Bosnia, plus some 300 in private Catholic Gymnasiums, in a population which was 88 per cent illiterate in 1910.[18] The percentage of non-elite students was higher than in other parts of the Monarchy, but was still preponderantly urban. Nonetheless, about 40 per cent of secondary-school pupils by 1914 were living away from home, largely indicative of a peasant background.[19]

In 1904, in a wide-ranging report on education that amounted to an assessment of the Kállay era, the historian and leading official of the Common Finance Ministry Lajos Thallóczy deemed it a success to have 'enticed' these student cohorts into opposing distrust and inertia. But he elaborated on themes often voiced elsewhere: the sheer backwardness of a 'primitive population', underfed and prey to disease in unhygienic accommodation, and the vulnerability of Bosnia's secondary-school graduates on first exposure to the 'hyper-national bubble' in Zagreb University. Then there was the highly politicized South Slav world of petitions, demonstrations and journalistic politics in the endlessly variegated press; above all, there was a psychological alienation between native Bosnians and immigrant officials. 'This young generation', wrote Thallóczy, 'by nature highly primitive in their attitude to life and, despite book-learning, uneducated since they lack the moral support of a long-standing ... cultural tradition – this generation forgot their fathers' suffering [under the Turks] and began to see in the order introduced by us an obstacle to their own advancement.'[20] Still in 1905 native Bosnians made up only 27.5 per cent of officials, mostly in the lowest levels. But immigration brought not only officials. More important than a few dozen peasant settler communities was the competition of businessmen from the Monarchy that undermined the position of Muslim and Orthodox artisans. During the years of occupation, the Catholic population rose from 18 per cent to 22 per cent, and from 3 per cent to 33 per cent in Sarajevo. Of the nineteen secondary-school professors in 1899, seventeen were incoming Catholics for native Catholics did not benefit.[21] Ironically dubbed *kulturtregeri*, from the German *Kulturträger* (bearers of culture) or *kuferaši* ('bag carriers'/ economic migrants), the incomers aroused festering resentment.

Thallóczy hoped that this alienation would ease as a core of 'soberer' youth formed who could deal with the 'realities of the situation'. This sobering was to be the task of the school, as 'a moral compass for the functioning of the whole organism'.[22] But in practice, Central European educational traditions combined an aloofness on the part of the school master with notions of academic freedom that rejected tutelage. The Sarajevo Gymnasium could hardly exercise the desired control over pupils when it did not have a list of their addresses, as revealed in 1894. Thallóczy fumed over one of its teachers' conferences where the confiscation of boys' newspapers was opposed on grounds of personal liberty.[23]

The most illuminating case of government and academics at cross purposes actually concerned Dalmatia, one of the most turbulent South Slav Habsburg regions outside Bosnia before 1914. Governor Nicola Nardelli in 1907 strongly complained ₁about a situation where Dalmatian law students attended their place of study (e.g. Graz University) only to take examinations, but otherwise passed their time at home on odd jobs and political agitation. 'It is manifest that in this way a numerous intellectual proletariat of unruly *politikers* is created which is ... a veritable cancer for public life'; the students, 'inured to indiscipline and demagogy', eventually entered the administration as a concession to the 'stomach question', where their disloyalty and incompetence wreaked havoc. According to Nardelli, regular notification of student attendance should be systematized and the university authorities called upon to play their part. After repeated requests the University of Graz a year later responded. It reported that of the twenty-eight students whose names were mentioned, nearly all had completed their studies, had died, had their absence approved because of illness (tuberculosis was rife in Dalmatia as in Bosnia), had returned belatedly because of the distance or had never registered at the university. In general the university felt that student discipline should be a matter for itself alone; it would not fail to seek help from other authorities if needed, but under the circumstances this was not the case.[24]

The nature of the Central European university system, whereby examinations could be taken when the student chose and staff-student contact was strictly limited, fed these problems. Disciplinary sanctions at secondary-school level were also ineffective; a pupil excluded from one institution simply transferred to another, and if excluded from all Bosnian institutions, they went to the Monarchy proper or to Serbia.[25] Of course, these processes were laborious. Gavrilo Princip once walked the route to Belgrade. Switches of institution from one town to another, and intermissions in study, were also frequent for non-political reasons, financial and medical particularly. A significant source of stress in pupil–teacher relations was suspicion of sectarian bias in marking assessments, something that inflamed the sensitivity of Bosnian youth to slights and honour. Two of the biggest cases of disruption, in Doljna Tuzla Gymnasium in 1906–7 and in Mostar Gymnasium in May 1914, developed from complaints over assessments; both climaxed with a Serb student assaulting the headmaster, in the second case accusing him of having 'insulted Serbdom'.[26]

Here the overrepresentation of Catholics among teachers played a fateful role. It is ironic that the teachers who responded most actively to regime calls to be closer to their pupils were also those most suspected of indoctrinating them politically. A particularly germane issue too was the allegiance of Muslim secondary-school students. Entering a new Western world, Bosnian Muslim schoolboys could be taken up by the national ardour gripping their Christian comrades, for whom it was linked with the European modernity of their dreams. But as the great bulk of Muslims had not yet developed their own 'national idea' – indeed found its associations alien – Western-educated Muslim youth, feeling the pressure to 'nationalize' themselves, had no choice but to adopt Serb or Croat affiliations. Their choices were often arbitrary and superficial, but the process unleashed fierce competition among Christian pedagogues to enlist them on their side. Student hostels, and teachers as hostel wardens, were to the fore in national contestation.[27] Contributing to the envenoming of relations was that partisan newspapers, both local and in the wider Southern Slav world, were available to aggrieved youngsters to spread every item of tittle-tattle.

## The character of *Mlada Bosna*

It is against this testing and often psychologically draining educational background that the evolution of Young Bosnia should be seen. It is unsurprising that officials like Thallóczy tended to reduce discontent to psychological factors in a common dismissive sense, to imply they lacked real substance, reposing essentially in the presumption of immaturity. Yet the psychology of personal interaction, or lack of it, should always be given due weight as part of the human condition, reflecting in fact the whole experience of a situation in its social, cultural and political aspects.

For all its undoubted immaturity, *Mlada Bosna* was an intellectually multifaceted phenomenon that reflected many aspects of an unusually fecund climacteric. Broadly, it drew on four main contributory streams: (1) the progressive movement reaching Bosnia via Bohemia and Croatia; (2) the inheritance of native Balkan traditions of resistance, as later stressed by the historian Vladimir Dedijer; (3) the revolutionary currents of socialism, Russian populism and anarchism, to which one might add an interest in radical philosophers like Nietzsche and Schopenhauer; and finally (4) the Yugoslav idea, which proved flexible enough to provide an umbrella for all these tendencies in the year before the Sarajevo assassinations. But along with these we should remember the wide-ranging literary interests of many Young Bosnians at a time when modern electronic media did not exist and organized sport was yet to make its mark. The first use of the term *Mlada Bosna*, by Borivoje Jeftić in the Serb literary magazine *Bosanska vila* in 1913, denoted a literary movement.[28] Princip and the would-be Bosnian Croat assassin Luka Jukić wrote poems when in prison.

Progressivism represented a deepening of the rationalist current in modern thought as the national liberal era yielded on the left to notions of fuller democracy. It had a natural appeal for young Czech radicals organized as the *Omladina* (Youth) movement in the Bohemian lands in the early 1890s. Those students who sought refuge from the conservative regime of Khuen-Hédérváry in Croatia in the Czech university in Prague came under the influence there of Tomáš Masaryk and his doctrine of pragmatic reform by small deeds. That spirit began to percolate into the Balkans, where South Slav conferences debated the relationship between social reform and national aspirations.[29] The several societies founded by Bosnian Serb schoolboys early in the new century reflected the science-oriented earnestness of progressive organizations in the lectures they arranged among themselves, in which the prominence of sexual education and health as topics reflected practical concerns where young death was so common and, no doubt, sexual curiosity was natural in a strict patriarchal society.[30]

The greater freedom in Bosnia after Kállay's death in 1903 led to the burgeoning of temperance, gymnastic and agricultural societies, as well as reading rooms and literacy courses for peasants offered by students on vacation. In youth literary circles too the idea that the modernization of Bosnian society was a prerequisite of any political progress animated debate. The seventeen-year-old Vladimir Gaćinović, already reading Thomas Buckle, accused Bosnian writers of a fixation with the conservative values of their backward society. Gaćinović saw in the satirist Petar Kočić (1877–1916), who had been expelled both from Sarajevo Gymnasium and from Vienna University, the archetypal mutinous first-generation student who would be able to produce a 'synthesis' of the dark life of a suffering people.[31] In turn, the twenty-two-year-old Dimitrije Mitrinović called for a Serbian literature of universal relevance, such as the Scandinavians had achieved.[32] Young Bosnian writers, oriented both to Serbian and Croatian literature, urged the convergence of the two. Ivo Andrić, the later Nobel Prize winner for literature, and a Bosnian Croat, was the president of the Serbo-Croat Progressive Student Club formed in Sarajevo in 1911.

However, by this time some Bosnian Serbs had already begun to move in more radical directions than any progressive reformist agenda implied. The Austro-Hungarian annexation of Bosnia in 1908, welcomed by most Croats, aroused bitter opposition among many Serbs. Many Bosnian Serb students in Vienna formed a secret society pledged to help Serbia in the expected war with the Monarchy. Others fled to Serbia, including Gaćinović and Bogdan Žerajić, who in 1910 made a failed attempt on the life of the Bosnian Provincial Governor and then committed suicide. Gaćinović's pamphlet, *Death of a Hero*, published anonymously by the Serbian irredentist journal *Piedmont*, placed Žerajić's act in the lineage of other blows against oppression by French, Italian and Russian revolutionaries but also in a Serbian tradition 'rich in suffering, conspiracies and revolts'.[33] This is the Kosovo theme of tyrannicide to which Vladimir Dedijer has drawn attention, linked to the age-old resistance to alien rule.[34] Gaćinović emphasized Žerajić's roots in the harsh, impoverished terrain of eastern Herzegovina; he himself and Princip came from that same broad Dinaric region. The historic Herzegovinian revolt of 1875 had begun near Žerajić's home village, and Princip as a child was told tales of the uprising that followed in Bosnia. The Young Bosnians avidly consumed the stories of tyrannicide from elsewhere, particularly from Mazzini's Italy, but an emotional depth was added by their own tradition. In Gaćinović's hymn to revolution, the leading character of Kočić's short stories, David Štrbac, epitomized the unreconciled, unconquerable spirit of Bosnian peasant defiance. Princip in turn would lay flowers on the grave of Žerajić, whose last words had been: 'I leave it to Serbdom to avenge me.' During their sojourn in Serbia, Gaćinović, Žerajić and Princip all became members of the Serbian secret society *Narodna Odbrana* (People's Defence), but Gaćinović was also recruited into *Ujedinjenje ili Smrt* (Union or Death).[35]

The radicalism of this aspect of Serbian tradition had further consequences. Specifically, it had an appeal for certain young Muslims in revolt against the conservatism of their own community in a period of omnipresent social change. In the 1890s 'nationalization' of Westernized Muslims had generally worked in favour of Croatdom, through personal contact, the prospect of a Zagreb education and an overriding sense that Serbs were the historic enemies of Islam. But a counter tendency grew, propelled by the fact that the Serbs had a state, a militant tradition and were more uncompromisingly opposed to the Austrian occupiers than most Croats. Hence the presence of a number of Muslims in the inner circles of *Mlada Bosna*. Mustafa Golubović, for example, had taken his *matura* in Belgrade and gained a Serbian scholarship to study in Switzerland where he made the acquaintance of Gaćinović. Muhamed Mehmedbašić (a Serbophile cabinet-maker in close touch with student leaders) was recruited first for an aborted attempt on the life of Governor Oskar Potiorek, and then became the only one of the

Sarajevo assassins to escape. Ultimately, he entered the service of Colonel Apis, who described him as an archetypal Russian revolutionary.[36]

Indeed, Serbian radicalism inclined Young Bosnia towards a third strand in its make-up, the Russian revolutionary tradition. Anarchist influences were strong. Gaćinović had arrived in Switzerland as a Bakuninist, with social revolutionary sympathies. Kropotkin was favourite reading, as was Chernyshevsky. Nedeljko Čabrinović, the first to fire on Franz Ferdinand in Sarajevo, had been beaten by his father, a police spy, for reading Chernyshevsky's *What Is to Be Done?*[37] Marxism was less common but not absent: Gaćinović was influenced by it after coming into contact with Trotsky in Switzerland. The attraction of intellectuals in backward countries towards the most radical philosophies available, now so familiar, was already clear. Indeed, in the 1870s the influential Svetozar Marković had been the first Serbian Marxist, his peasant-oriented socialism subsequently watered down after his death by the ruling radical current of Serbian politics.[38] The beginnings of industrialization in Bosnia under Austrian rule then brought a socialist movement into being which held a general strike in Sarajevo in 1906, receiving sympathy from radicals like Petar Kočić. Čabrinović was an active trade unionist, and another socialist was Danilo Ilić, a graduate from the Sarajevo teacher's training college, who as a Young Bosnian was to be executed for his part in the Sarajevo plot. Of course, these idealists' reading habits were various. Curiosity was truly omnivorous among educated youth catapulted from Balkan patriarchalism to a climacteric of modern ideological contestation. While Nietzsche and Schopenhauer competed in the heady mix of ideas, we should not overlook influences from the heavily classical education of the Gymnasium. Official investigations after the assassination showed frequent student underlinings of Horace's famous line, 'Dulce et decorum est pro patria mori' ('It is sweet and fitting to die for one's country').

For all the profusion of tendencies, during the last pre-war phase a certain coming together in a common movement on Yugoslav lines is unmistakable. In February 1912, many Serbs stayed aloof from the large demonstrations by Sarajevo students, held in sympathy with Zagreb students protesting against the suspension of the Croatian constitution. But Yugoslav feeling was boosted by the evolution of external events combined with convergences in domestic standpoints. The policies of the Monarchy's central power structures disillusioned Croatian students, while Serbia's successes in the Balkan Wars of 1912–13 evoked a fervent response among many Habsburg South Slavs. This in turn led the authorities in Dalmatia and Bosnia to curtail civil liberties, provoking further antagonism. The progressive movement had also always had a marked Yugoslav aspect. After the demonstrations of early 1912, the enthusiastic reception given to Croatian students in Belgrade led to attempts to draw up a common programme, whose final form affirmed the 'unification of the Serbo-Croat nation' on a basis of 'intellectual agitation for the philosophy of Serbo-Croat nationalism and the political doctrine of radical democracy'.[39] Further moves gathered pace from 1913 to establish a united youth organization to embody these ideas. To achieve this, from March to May 1914, conferences were held in Zagreb and Prague to celebrate the centenary of the birth of the iconic poet Njegoš, prince bishop of Montenegro.

Cooperation between reformist and revolutionary currents was eased as the self-consciously science-oriented pragmatism at the heart of the progressive project took a harder edge, and notions of social Darwinism and race nationalism gained ground. The Serb-Croat progressive youth duly redubbed itself nationalist. Difficulties rooted in notions of reform through small deeds in a backward milieu drove would-be activists onto a more extreme path. While Gaćinović in 1908 had written of 'noble and propitious small deeds', Dimitrije Mitrinović early in 1914 derided deeds 'invisibly small and aimlessly done' which could not satisfy 'the most essential demand of national being, national honour'. Notably, the article containing these words was published in a Zagreb journal and was entitled 'For Yugoslavia'.[40]

It was symptomatic that the artist most associated with the Kosovo tradition, through his epic statues of muscular heroes, was actually the Dalmatian Croat Ivan Meštrović. This merging of traditions in a common cause was aided by an unprecedented interest taken in Croatia by Serbian writers, led by the influential Belgrade literary critic Jovan Skerlić. In 1913, 150 copies of his pamphlet on Serbo-Croat nationalism were sold by Sarajevo booksellers, largely to secondary-school students.[41] 'Yugoslavism' was also obviously congenial to Western-minded young Muslims because it obviated the need to choose between Serb and Croat. And it accorded with socialist notions of brotherhood: South Slav socialists in the Monarchy called their political organ the Yugoslav Social Democratic Party. Serbs once sceptical of working with Croats were no doubt reconciled by the assumption that they would dominate a united South Slav state. As one such former student sceptic, Vukašin Babunović, commented in 1914, 'I am for this idea [Yugoslavism], but rather for political unification, for such a unification as I as a Serb understand it.'[42] It is fairly clear that among Serbs and also many young Croats and Muslims, the cause of revolutionary Yugoslavism was winning out in the immediate backdrop to the Sarajevo assassination. Princip when on trial in October 1914 would vigorously affirm his Yugoslavism, tracing the Yugoslav movement back to the repression in Croatia, literary-cultural collaboration and the nationalist programme among secondary-school students in Croatia, Dalmatia and Bosnia, as well as to the Balkan Wars.[43]

The background to Young Bosnia then was very complex. European radicalism, the restless politics of the Southern Slav world and literary cross-currents interacted on a situation shaped by foreign occupation, backwardness and the strange atmosphere of the new educational system. Of many resulting tensions the most striking is that between immaturity and ambition. That Young Bosnians were immature is hardly surprising. After the Sarajevo murders, the average age of the ninety-four people put on trial in three of the four major trials was just over seventeen years, ten months.⁴⁴ Most of the activists were secondary school, not university, students. The idealistic appeal of anarchist visions of a society without injustice, or Chernyshevsky's *What Is to Be Done?*, was reflected in the reading matter later found by investigators – for soulful youth, Schopenhauer on honour or women was a best seller. For those on trial, the reason given for their revolutionary commitment was usually the repression of the Monarchy's Slavs. When pressed, the grievances they brought up were hardly commensurate with the violent response – for example, the Bosnian 'exceptional measures' that had briefly suspended some civil rights during the Balkan Wars, or the non-acceptance of Zagreb degrees by other Austro-Hungarian universities.⁴⁵ None of the conspirators were clear about how the assassination of Franz Ferdinand would bring about revolutionary change.⁴⁶

Yet for all the immaturity in 1914, the ferment of enquiry and discussion among Bosnian educated youth is striking. Princip's later comments to his prison doctor – that his friends believed that Kropotkin's view of social revolution could only be realized after national liberation had been achieved in Europe and considered that their primary task – were not shallow; nor was Danilo Ilić's critique, from a left-wing nationalist standpoint, of the Bosnian social democrats' negative stance on the national question.⁴⁷ Young Bosnia also threw up a number of serious thinkers in Dimitrije Mitrinović and Vladimir Gaćinović. Gaćinović's *Death of a Hero*, bombastic as it was, offered a penetrating account of the anomie of unprivileged young members of a poor society in the throes of social transition. Mitrinović made an impressive attempt to adapt a Serbian nationalism based on introverted romantic organicism to the democratizing, positivist age, using particularly Herbert Spencer's ideas of evolutionary individuation (Spencer was still cutting edge in East-Central Europe). Mitrinović wanted to ground his nationalism in an integrated philosophy of politics, ethics and aesthetics, and was not afraid to diverge in places from Jovan Skerlić, his Belgrade model.⁴⁸ Indeed, Young Bosnia's thinkers – another was the aesthetic philosopher Miloš Vidaković who typically died very young – were intensely engaged with intellectual and literary developments both in Belgrade and in Zagreb. Their activity went some way to giving the city of Sarajevo a potential mediating role between those centres, in a conscious mission of advancing the cause of Yugoslavism.⁴⁹

## The Bosnian cauldron in wider context

How far then did the Austro-Hungarian authorities grasp these complexities? Perhaps naturally, they perceived most strongly the passionate excesses of youth. The temperamental divide between Habsburg administrators and South Slav activists is nicely caught in the case of Petar Kočić, whose turbulent student past has already been mentioned. For Habsburg officials, he was 'the well-known agitator', 'the proselytising subversive', 'the fanatical revolutionary', 'the *spiritus rector* of disaffection', 'the boundlessly excitable demagogue'. For Kočić, they were the *kulturtregeri*, 'the carpet-baggers', 'the dirty, dark individuals who since the occupation slink about our land'.[50] Yet we should avoid seeing confrontation only through the ethnic stereotypes that came easily to contemporaries. One starchy comment on disaffected inmates of the Bosnian Institute – that 'in this section of youth one could seek in vain for modesty, gratitude, duty, a sense of decency, indeed, they really seem to exert themselves everywhere to prove the reverse of these qualities' – stemmed in fact from a rare Bosnian Serb official.[51] The aloof bureaucratic teachers whom Bosnians disliked were often Czechs or Slovenes. What counted was the situational response of natives to any kind of alien authority. Here the sheer diversity of foreign officials in Bosnia no doubt increased the natives' sense of being second-class citizens in their own land.

Indeed, the school administration in the last pre-war years reveals diversity turning into confused fragmentation, as personnel of different origins were subject to increasingly complex pressures that strained the limited resources. This prevented education playing the stabilizing role that Thallóczy had assigned it in 1905. As the number of native Bosnian teachers including Serbs increased, confessional tensions broke out within the teaching corps which made Gymnasium staff meetings increasingly discordant. Some masters, for example, opposed disciplining pupils of their own ethnicity, provoking uproar when this was leaked to the press. Attempts to deal with disruptive staff by transferring them to other schools could simply shift disruption elsewhere; they also brought problems familiar to modern observers of reshuffles of divided cabinets. Managerial skills and personnel availability were taxed to the limit in juggling the need to keep unruly staff (mainly Serb) in check, while promoting other Serbs in the interest of confessional balance and the more relaxed Serb policies of Kállay's successors. Indeed, non-Serbs might accuse a new Serb headmaster of pushing a nationalist agenda.[52]

The constitutional era launched in 1910 with a Bosnian assembly (Sabor) exacerbated these difficulties. Governor Potiorek's tough talk on school discipline was belied by concessions in individual cases to keep Serb politicians on board and maintain a workable Sabor majority.[53] The administration's culture department poured out school regulations, at once conciliatory and pettifogging. In the very month of the assassination, the liberalism of pedagogues breathes through the report of the secondary-school inspector Tugomir Alaupović on Mostar Gymnasium's nationalist upheavals: 'Every friend of healthy national development rejoices when youth is nationally minded, when it has ideals and dreams, for these are the most beautiful prerogatives of youth.'[54] However, Princip's deed led to recriminations between Potiorek and Biliński (common finance minister) over negligence, and a draconian turn to the hard line followed. During the war, not just students, but Alaupović himself was put on trial for alleged misconduct (eventually acquitted) in his previous post as Director of Tuzla Gymnasium. Nevertheless, the Habsburg administration before 1914 had not lacked vigilance. In 1912, over 200 student interrogations had been held after student propaganda was discovered in the countryside. But the consistent aim was to uncover the links between them and their presumed instigators among the older generation of politicians and schoolmasters. The one report from 1912 which argued, correctly, that nationalist youth was autonomous and not under the control of older nationalists whom they distrusted was quietly filed away.[55]

This therefore was a government adrift, or is that too harsh a judgement? Any assessment of Austro-Hungarian educational policy must weigh up more than the final terrorist episode and allow for comparison with other imperial contexts. The regime's expectations of native acculturation to Austrian norms were not wholly unfounded. Two high officials in Bosnia's cultural administration, Teodor Zurunić and Božidar Čerović, were Serbs who had themselves been recipients of Bosnian government scholarships. The three leading cultural workers in their respective confessions, the Serb Vladimir Ćorović, the Muslim Safvet Bašagić and the Croat Tugomir Alaupović, were also state employees. Later annual reports on the Bosnian Institute in Vienna were increasingly enthusiastic about the diligence and discipline of the student inmates, though this no doubt owed something to the bent of those selected, earning them the description of 'Mamelukes' in the nationalist press. Indeed, the three key figures mentioned earlier all experienced tensions in their relations with the authorities.

Indeed, other European powers arguably took less pains over education and experienced similar problems. In occupied Egypt, education enjoyed only 1 per cent of the government budget in 1896 because of Lord Cromer's determination to allow only strictly controlled development.[56] Yet a row of assassinations between 1910 and 1915 was sparked there by the murder of the pro-British Egyptian prime minister by a twenty-three-year-old pharmacology graduate, who planned to write a book entitled *La Constitution d'un Gouvernement Musulman*. The disorientation of educated youth in a traditional, patriarchal society under Western impact, so vividly conveyed by Gaćinović, was reproduced still more strongly in the first generation of Western-educated Egyptians. The response too among students was similar: to form a new identity, a novel social group engaged in a lifestyle of demonstrations and political agitation.[57] In India, whose uncontrolled educational development Cromer had reacted against, the British at the turn of the century had also faced the growth of secret student societies in Maharashtra and Bengal, inspired by a doctrine of revolutionary violence. Again, as in Bosnia and the Egyptian assassin's grandiose project, modern ideas under foreign rule produced a ferment of ideas and a dialectic of attraction (modernity) and repulsion (foreign rule). Bengal embraced language-based nationalism, Maharashtra a newly militant Hinduism that was promoted by modern means of organization. Student responses to Western Christianity in China showed a related dialectic.[58] And in the 1950s the first person to be executed in the EOKA struggle against British rule in Cyprus was the product of a prestigious British school there who had excelled at cricket.

The difficulties of legitimizing rule over others by assumptions of modernity were also not limited to Europeans. A wave of schoolboy strikes against the Japanese occupation of interwar Korea stirred the British consul general in Seoul to regret, with some fellow-feeling for the Japanese, that 'the Corean' saw only 'despoil[iation] of his birth right' in the 'inevitable' progress modern Japanese rule was bringing.[59] Of course, only a small minority of the subalterns of empire responded with ethno-national terrorism, but managing populations other than one's own proved harder than anticipated. Indeed, would-be modernizers consistently underestimated the difficulties and this in some ways is more striking than the difficulties themselves. The lack of grasp shown in the Bosnian school administration's last years is curiously mirrored in present-day British confusion about Muslim education in Birmingham and the grooming of youth by radicals, down to the detail that Muslims are suspected, like Bosnian Serbs, of infiltrating the teaching body and headships. Actually, parts of Britain and other Western countries today reflect the generalization in a globalizing world of culturally mixed situations with a colonial reference and close links between metropole and periphery – just as existed in Habsburg Bosnia.

It may be charged that this last analogy is unhistorical. How can one imply comparison between pre-1914 Bosnian terrorism, which sprang from an aspirant rationalist ideology of national self-determination, and a twenty-first-century movement of religious fundamentalism? Certainly, *Mlada Bosna* was specific to its time and region. It drew on Balkan social conditions and traditions of tyrannicide, together with a close connection between literature and politics in the nationalist movements of the Balkans and to an extent of East-Central Europe as a whole. This was a regional reflection of the age of European national liberalism and romanticism, in which linguistic revivalism and the (re)creation of national literatures were intertwined with emerging nationalism. By the close of the nineteenth century such themes were being replaced by more pragmatic, sociologically oriented concerns which, however, were so impregnated by the legacy of the preceding formative era that they effectively amounted to new ways of achieving, or upgrading, old goals. The writings of Dimitrije Mitrinović illustrate this. And the violence of *Mlada Bosna* was restrained by this context. By the time of Vidovdan 1914, both Gaćinović and Danilo Ilić had come to doubt the utility of assassination.[60] Čabrinović also told his interrogators that his aim through terrorism was to replace the present state of affairs by a 'liberal system'.[61] Between this and the ruthless extremism of modern terrorism lay the development across the twentieth century of a universal narrative of resistance to alien government, with the doctrine of anti-imperialism at its core.

Before 1914 elements of such a narrative were not wholly absent. The Serb radical journal *Prosvjeta*, edited by Kočić, explained Bosnia's economic difficulties in 1908 in terms of its 'colonial' position as a 'market outlet' (*Absatz Gebiet*) designed for exploitation by foreign capital.[62] This was drawn from Marxist analysis, well known in the Central European milieu to which Habsburg Bosnia belonged. But Lenin and the Bolsheviks' success in 1917 contributed the vehemence of an all-encompassing ideology which linked social exploitation to a call for national emancipation from imperialism. The diagnosis and the vehemence could be and have been appropriated by movements which disagreed with Leninism's Marxist solution. By contrast, the coarsening of twentieth-century revolutionary violence was absent in Gavrilo Princip's circle. Despite their socially disadvantaged background, education made them an elite imbued with a sense of moral obligation to the suffering 'people'. This is by no means absent in middle-class Muslim terrorists today, but hardly present among those youths enthused by violent videos who have remained trapped and sometimes criminalized in poorly educated urban communities – or for that matter in murderous South Slav militants of the Second World War and the 1990s.

## Conclusion

Do these comments undermine the claim for *Mlada Bosna*'s relevance to the wider context of revolutionary youth movements? Not really. After four centuries of absorption in an Islamic empire Bosnians generally, and not just the Muslims, were regarded by their occupiers in many ways like other non-European populations of the age. Resulting resentments took on some of the colour of grievance that dogged imperial ventures in other parts of the world, and have subsisted beyond the end of formal empire. This gave the Bosnian case the mixed character stressed in this account. Yet beyond this, a binary mode of thought which in the imperialist age played up a civilizational divide between Europeans and non-Europeans, West and East, Christian and non-Christian had its roots deep inside Europe itself. 'Modernity' and its would-be hegemonic model originated in *Western* Europe and can be seen in pre-1914 British attitudes to Celtic Catholic Ireland. Frederick II of Prussia thought German an uncouth language; Austrian modernization started in the bid to emulate Prussia; Metternich quipped that Asia started on the Landstrasse leading south from Vienna. Kállay too believed that Hungary stood between East and West, with the Balkans on the wrong side of the border. The alleged civilizational dividing line has been continually shifting, while the binary psychologies of superiority/inferiority and arrogance/resentment remain constant, though differently applied.

The process of expansion of Western hegemony is a single one, however, to which the Balkans somehow continue to be hinged in the popular imagination. The process has offered opportunities but inevitably caused tensions through imbalances of power, naturally increased by cultural differences, as in the Middle East, where religious divides have a long historical hinterland. When populations feel in the grip of external power, political, economic or cultural, and believe their futures are dictated by others, then the situation seen by *Mlada Bosna* will be reproduced and comparison is meaningful, regardless of the ideological form protest may take. In culturally alienated communities, the psychological factor is itself very powerful, particularly for impulsive teenagers. At that age the cause which is needed to supply a sense of purpose readily appears and action can be purpose in itself. Stendhal's celebrated novel *The Charterhouse of Parma* depicts a sixteen-year-old Italian who, on news of Napoleon's escape from Elba, decides virtually instantaneously to leave home and country and enlist in his cause. It is praised for its psychological veracity.

Of course, a strong ideological support is usually necessary for the highly intelligent; nationalism and religion are both such forces, though the intelligence rarely extends to a clear view of what the terrorist act will achieve. In general, student activism may be most prominent in the first throes of confrontation with 'modernity', with educated youth as the cutting edge of social response.[63] Again, the concern for what Guido van Hengel has called the 'macro' perspective of ideological motivation can be weighed too heavily at the expense of the 'micro' reality of different individual lives. The 'Arrival City' to which the peasant moved, in a process which has continued till today in successive parts of the world, was not uniformly bleak. It could be a dynamic, exciting place where some individuals did succeed – like Princip's elder brother Jovo, becoming a self-made businessman and urging Gavrilo onto the educational path. But the younger Princip, like the majority, was not one of them. The young man who wrote laconically from Belgrade that he had 'flunked' an exam and who was rejected for Serb military service probably experienced some sense of personal failure which sharpened his alienation.[64] This is not to deny Princip's own ideological drive but to locate it generationally; his was a rather inchoate aspiration for a better future, reflecting his sense of living on the threshold of something new.[65]

If the reference to current Western-Islamic relations in this chapter is not absurd, neither is this chapter a submission to Samuel Huntingdon's view that civilizational conflict hangs over any hope for a humane, peaceful world. The argument here has been deliberately framed in terms of power relations and ideas subjectively conceived, and not in terms of reified cultural entities. The leitmotiv is not that Young Bosnian terrorists represented the ultimate truth about Bosnian opinion or the Austrian administration, or that relations between the Western model and non-Western societies must inevitably involve disastrous confrontation. Its sympathies are with the rational pluralist values of the liberal West which hopefully will win out more widely. But it raises questions in the early twenty-first century about the crasser forms of American-led globalization, lacking sensitivity to the considerable problems of cultural and political negotiation that globalization requires, and oblivious to the lessons of past empires.

There is something chilling in Lajos Thallóczy's phrase, quoted earlier, about a 'soberer' youth emerging who would reckon with the 'realities of the situation'. Those who lay claim to universal values, as occupiers of other lands are prone to do, usually have their own axe to grind; Thallóczy was a strong Magyar nationalist. The sheer convenience of the claim to be operating on behalf of progress is part answer to the question posed earlier as to why Western societies repeatedly advance it. It cloaks dealings with weaker societies with the most powerful form of legitimation. Nor is it merely cynical. It gives power wielders a sense of reassurance and entitlement similar to religious faith. The fact is that we do not know what the future will value. As the anniversary of the Great War passes, it is appropriate to note that the march to the left, which began with 1789 and of which Young Bosnia was part, is now clearly over. We do not know what ideological form the resistance of subalterns to hegemonic power will take, but we should be in no doubt that the psychological realities of hegemony and resistance will recur.

## Notes

1 Christopher Clark, *The Sleepwalkers: How Europe Went to War in 1914* (London: Allen Lane, 2012).

2 Nikola. Đ. Trišić (ed.), *Sarajevski atentat u svijetlu bibliografskih podataka* (Sarajevo: 'Veselin Masleša', 1964), 145, citing *Nova Evropa* 11 (1925), 26 June.

3 R. W. Seton-Watson, *Sarajevo: A Study in the Origins of the Great War* (London: Hutchinson, 1925), 79, 141.

4 Vladimir Dedijer, *The Road to Sarajevo* (New York: Simon and Schuster, 1966).

5 For shifting evaluations highlighting successive anniversary commemorations in Bosnia, see *Prilozi/Contributions* 43 (Sarajevo, 2014): 1–144, edited by Husnija Kamberović. This is an English version of 2014 conference papers printed in *Prilozi Instituta za istoriju Sarajevo*. Robert J. Donia, however, notes the increasing tendency for Princip to be seen more widely as a global celebrity rather than in ideological terms (57–78).

6 See the review of Robin Okey, *Taming Balkan Nationalism: The Habsburg 'Civilizing Mission' in Bosnia, 1878-1914* (Oxford, 2007), in *Historische Zeitschrift*, 288/2 (April 2009): 490.

7 Alfred Milner, *England in Egypt*. 2nd edn (London: E. Arnold, 1892), 357.

8 William Miller, *Travels and Politics in the Near East* (New York: Frederick A. Stokes, 1898), 128.

9   Frank Eyck, *G.P. Gooch: A Study in History and Politics* (London: Macmillan, 1982), 269–70. The Common Ministry of Finance, created by the Austro-Hungarian Compromise of 1867, had from 1878 overall responsibility for the administration of Bosnia-Herzegovina.
10  Benjámin von Kállay, 'Ungarn an den Grenzen des Orients und des Occidents', *Ungarische Revue* 3 (1883): 428–89. Kállay distinguished between Western civic tradition and an East dominated by anarchic individualism and corresponding despotism. Serbs were easterners in this paradigm.
11  Edin Hajdarpasic, 'Out of the Ruins of the Ottoman Empire: Some Reflections on the Ottoman Legacy in South-Eastern Europe', *Middle Eastern Studies* 44 (2008): 715–34.
12  *Srpska riječ*, 14 March 1912.
13  Vojislav Bogićević, *Istorija razvitka osnovnih škola u Bosni i Hercegovini od 1463-1918* (Sarajevo: Zavod za izdavanje udžbenika BiH, 1965), 18.
14  The National Archives, London, Foreign Office [FO] 7/1153, Freeman to Salisbury, 11 February 1889.
15  Calculated from Ljuboje Dlustuš, 'Školske prilike u Bosni i Hercegovini od okupacije do danas', *Školski vjesnik* 1 (1894): 538; Arhiv Bosne i Hercegovine (Archive of Bosnia and Herzegovina, Sarajevo: hereafter ABH), Zajedničko ministarstvo financija (Common Ministry of Finance: hereafter CMF), BH 6893/1899: Provincial Government (PG) to CMF, 27 June 1899.
16  ABH, CMF, BH 11512: PG to CMF, 4 October 1895; CMF to PG, 23 October 1895.
17  See a high official's account: Otto Paul, *Bericht über die Tätigkeit des Instituts für bosnisch-herzegowinische Hochschüler in Wien in den zehn Jahren seines Bestandes (1899-1900-1908-1909)* (Vienna: A. Holzhausen, 1910).
18  Srećko M. Džaja, *Bosnien-Herzegowina in der österreichisch-ungarischen Epoche (1878-1918). Die Intelligenz zwischen Tradition und Ideologie* (Munich: R. Oldenbourg, 1994), 173, 184, 185. A stimulating recent study speaks of an 'annual' intake of 2,300 students in Bosnian-Herzegovinian Gymnasia by the 1910s, when 'total' intake is surely intended: Edin Hajdarpasic, *Whose Bosnia? Nationalism and Political Imagination in the Balkans, 1840-1918* (Ithaca, NY: Cornell University Press, 2015), 135.
19  ABH, CMF, BH 4234/1909: PG to CMF, 24 March 1909.
20  ABH, CMF, Pr BH 1282/1904: Thallóczy's report on Bosnian education, 2 December 1904.
21  Džaja, *Bosnien-Herzegowina*, 123, 187.
22  ABH, CMF, Pr BH 1282/1904: Thallóczy's report on Bosnian education, 2 December 1904.
23  Országos Széchenyi Könyvtár (Széchenyi National Library, Budapest), 2549/7: Thallóczy diary, 19 September 1907.
24  Haus-, Hof- und Staatsarchiv, Vienna, Administrativ-Archiv, 1651, Ministerium des Inneren, 5197/1907: Nicola Nardelli to Minister of Culture, 25 May 1907; ibid., 8863/1908: Graz University Rector's report, 30 April 1908.

25  For the details of the grades, see Đorđe Pejanović, *Srednje i stručne škole u Bosni i Hercegovini od početka do 1941* (Sarajevo: Svjetlost, 1953), 74.
26  ABH, CMF, Pr BH 1508/1907 (Doljna Tuzla); Pr BH 705/1914: PG to CMF, 15 June 1914 (Mostar).
27  For example, ABH, CMF, Zemaljska vlada, 1019 res./1909: Mostar Gymnasium director Dragan Kudlich to PG, 20 December 1908; ABH, CMF, BH 4121/1912: PG to CMF, 18 March 1912.
28  For *Mlada Bosna* as a literary movement, see Predrag Palavestra, *Književnost Mlade Bosne*, 2 vols (Sarajevo: Svjetlost, 1965).
29  Luka Đaković, *Napredni Omladinski pokret antiaustrougarske orijentacije u jugoslavenskim zemljama prije Prvog svjetskog rata* (unpublished MSS, Istorijski institut u Sarajevu, 1984).
30  See Vojislav Bogićević (ed.), *Mlada Bosna. Pisma i prilozi* (Sarajevo: Svjetlost, 1954), 21–31, 370–1.
31  Vladimir Gaćinović, in Gaćinović, *Ogledi i pisma*, ed. Todor Kruševac (Sarajevo: Svjetlost, 1956), 23–37 (quotation, 29). Kočić played a prominent part in the Memorandum of Bosnian Serb students in Vienna in 1901, the first major statement of youthful discontent.
32  Dimitrije Mitrinović, 'Narodno tlo i modernstvo', in Palavestra (ed.), *Književnost Mlade Bosne*, II, 41–9.
33  Printed in Gaćinović, *Ogledi i pisma*, 117–32 (quotation, 127).
34  Vladimir Dedijer, *Sarajevo 1914* (Sarajevo and Belgrade: Prosveta, 1966), 387–424. A Serbo-Croat translation, with added material, of the original English text published in the same year. See note 4.
35  For extra details of Young Bosnia's political development, particularly its official and unofficial relationship with Serbia, see a new polemical account: John Zametica, *Folly and Malice: The Habsburg Monarchy, the Balkans and the Start of World War I* (London: Shepheard-Walwyn, 2017).
36  Trišić (ed.), *Sarajevski atentat*, 211; Dedijer, *Sarajevo 1914*, (Serb-Croat edn) 669.
37  Dedijer, *Sarajevo 1914* (Serbo-Croat edn), 314.
38  For an English-language analysis of Svetozar Marković, see Woodford D. McClellan, *Svetozar Marković and the Origins of Balkan Socialism* (Princeton: Princeton University Press, 1964).
39  Programme printed in Dragoslav Ljubibratić, *Gavrilo Princip* (Belgrade: Nolit, 1959), 102–5.
40  Gaćinović, *Ogledi i pisma*, 303; Palavestra, *Književnost Mlade Bosne*, I, 95–6, citing Mitrinović, 'Za Jugoslaviju', *Vihor* 1 (1914): 81–3.
41  Palavestra, *Književnost Mlade Bosne*, I, 201.
42  Bogićević (ed.), *Mlada Bosna*, 112: Vukašin Babunović to Petar Božić, 26 February 1914.
43  Dedijer, *Sarajevo 1914* (Serbo-Croat edn), 558–9.
44  Calculated from Đaković, *Napredni Omladinski pokret*, 230–4, 252–5, 267–71.
45  Dedijer, *Sarajevo 1914* (Serbo-Croat edn), 553–5.

46  Ibid., 509–10.
47  Ljubibratić, *Princip*, 286–7; Danilo Ilić, 'Naš nacionalizam', in Palavestra, *Književnost Mlade Bosne*, II, 24–6.
48  Palavestra, *Književnost Mlade Bosne*, I, 185–6.
49  Ibid., 101–9.
50  *Petar Kočić, Dokumentarna građa*, ed. Todor Kruševac (Sarajevo: Muzej književnosti Bosne i Hercegovine, 1967), 95, 105, 167, 174, 219, 264.
51  ABH, CMF, Kabinettbriefe 13/1903: Teodor Zurunić to Kállay, 13 February 1903.
52  For example, see the Muslim newspaper *Novi Vakat*, 25 December 1913, on the case of Bihać Gymnasium.
53  For the pattern of Sabor politics, see Dževad Juzbašić, *Nacionalno-politički odnosi u bosanskohercegovačkom saboru i jezičko pitanje 1910-1914* (Sarajevo: Akademija nauka i umjetnosti Bosne i Heregovine, 1999).
54  ABH, CMF, Pr BH 705/1914.
55  ABH, CMF, Pr BH 1272, with Government Commissioner Collas's report of 2 August 1912.
56  Haggai Erlich, *Students and University in Twentieth-Century Egyptian Politics* (London: Routledge, 1989), 22.
57  Ibid., 51–2, 234; for the assassin, see Elie Kedourie (ed.), *Nationalism in Asia and Africa* (London: Weidenfeld and Nicolson, 1970), 392–7.
58  Ka-Che Yip, *Religion, Nationalism and Chinese Students: The Anti-Christian Movement of 1922-1927* (Bellingham, WA: Western Washington University, 1980).
59  Annual Report on Corea during 1929 (Consul General Oswald White, Seoul), electronically reproduced from Foreign Office files, FO 262/1751, in the National Archives. Printed copy in Warwick University Library.
60  Dedijer, *Sarajevo 1914* (Serbo-Croat edn), 509–10.
61  Ibid., 536.
62  *Prosvjeta* 2 (1908): 36, 189.
63  The role of student protest in Russia appears to have declined from 1860, as students became a smaller proportion of the educated population: Samuel D. Kassow, *Students, Professors and the State in Tsarist Russia* (Berkeley: University of California Press, 1989).
64  Guido van Hengel, '"Up in Flames" – Gavrilo Princip and the City', in *Prilozi/Contributions* (note 5), 79–88. *Arrival City*, referenced by van Hengel, is the title of a book by Doug Saunders (London: Penguin, 2011) on the theme of rural-urban migration.
65  Hajdarpasic, *Whose Bosnia?* (149–50, 153), from a somewhat different standpoint, likewise emphasizes the forward-facing, generational aspect of *Mlada Bosna*, contrasting it with the atavistic motifs of a folk tradition of tyrannicide stressed by Dedijer. Both aspects were no doubt present in Princip.

## PART II
# International blaze

# CHAPTER 7

# Why did nobody control Apis?
# Serbian military intelligence and the Sarajevo assassination

*Danilo Šarenac*

In 1928, a group of citizens erected a commemorative plaque on a street corner in Sarajevo where Gavrilo Princip had killed the Habsburg heir and his wife in June 1914. From the start it was clear that this project stood out from the hundreds of other commemorations taking place across the Southern Slav kingdom. For years the authorities of the Kingdom of Serbs, Croats and Slovenes had resisted pressure exerted by Princip's admirers to honour the assassin in public. In the end, the Yugoslav authorities backed down and gave approval for a commemorative plaque on the spot where the attack had taken place. However, the inscription was officially unveiled only on 2 February 1930, two years after its initial construction.[1] No officials of the Yugoslav or local Bosnian administration came to the site to witness the ceremony. Apart from the families of the 'Young Bosnians' and some Sarajevo residents, only senior representatives of the Serbian Orthodox clergy were present.[2]

Even the day before the official inauguration, foreign correspondents were reporting to their editors that 'the assassin who caused the Great War' had now secured a monument in Sarajevo. One of those who criticized the initiative was the great friend of the Southern Slavs, R. W. Seton-Watson.[3] It was just the scenario that the Yugoslav authorities had hoped to avoid. Kosta Kumanudi, the acting foreign minister, instantly advised Yugoslav envoys abroad to stress that this tribute to Princip was strictly private in character; moreover, the plaque had not been positioned on any government building but on a private house.⁴

What caused Belgrade's reluctance to commemorate and talk about the Sarajevo assassination? Officially, the Great War was seen as an event producing positive consequences, allowing completion of the 'the centuries-old struggle' for national liberation and unification of the Southern Slavs.⁵ In this interpretation the Sarajevo assassination presented one of the crucial stepping stones. However, it also of course marked the start of catastrophic events for Europe. The kingdom of Serbia was almost completely destroyed in 1915, and the year ended with the occupation of the country and exile for the elite, the army and part of the population. Moreover, the assassination of Franz Ferdinand always enabled the Southern Slav state to be linked to a 'war guilt' narrative. This implied serious political but also physiological consequences. Despite the efforts of the Serbian and then Yugoslav authorities to distance themselves from the assassination and the rampant war guilt debates, several aspects of this event remained inextricably linked with Serbia.

After all, the decision to kill the archduke was most probably made in the Serbian capital. This could have been a simple coincidence, as Belgrade was the place where the Young Bosnians (*Mlada Bosna*) received their information about the archduke's planned visit to Sarajevo. There were nonetheless more serious and undisputed links between the rebellious Habsburg citizens and the Serbian state. For it was in Belgrade that the assassins acquired their guns as well as an elementary knowledge of how to use them properly. Finally, the Young Bosnians completely relied on the logistical help of Serbian border officers and members of Serbian military intelligence in order to enter Austria-Hungary. This support continued after the assassins crossed the state border and proceeded towards Sarajevo. The name of Dragutin Dimitrijević-Apis, at the time head of Serbian military intelligence, appears in all variants of the 1914 narratives.

How was it possible that the men who were officials and employees of the Serbian state escaped any control by the Serbian regime? Was the kingdom of Serbia, as Christopher Clark has controversially suggested, really a 'rogue state'?⁶ In order to answer these questions no new sources are available. But a more detailed analysis of the domestic Serbian social-political context can help us understand better the role of official and unofficial Belgrade in the Sarajevo plot. For Serbia was not an ungovernable state. Rather, since the 1903 coup d'état and the murder of the last Obrenović king, the state had lost control over some of the most sensitive sections of its military. Furthermore, already by the turn of the century politics had become part of the officers' mindset. By the spring of 1914, civil–military relations in Serbia had to be renegotiated due to the changes brought about by the two Balkan Wars. In August 1913 Colonel Dimitrijević-Apis became the chief of Serbian military intelligence. This meant that Serbia's formal and informal spy networks were now to be united in his hands, something that further exacerbated the position of the Serbian government. The accumulated tensions between Nikola Pašić's government and a section of the officer corps brought Serbia to the verge of civil war. This presented a favourable environment for a third party to act, whether that was the Regent Aleksandar Karadjordjević, or some radicalized Bosnian youths. The domestic civil–military conflicts have been partially explored by historians, yet due to their complexity much remains unresearched and unclear.[7]

## The 'golden age' and its troubles

After the Belgrade coup, which took place on the night of 10 June 1903, the subsequent eleven years became known as the 'golden age' of Serbian democracy.[8] Indeed, Serbia did become a parliamentary democracy with a liberal, so-called Belgian constitution. The franchise was widened, enabling almost all males to participate in parliamentary and local elections. The MPs, educated at German, French or Swiss universities, debated whether the British or French model of parliamentary government was most appropriate for Serbian political conditions. In 1911, Serbia had as many as 124 newspapers appearing regularly.[9] Other segments of public life also contributed to a growing national self-confidence.

In its pre-1912 borders the population numbered 2.9 million, of whom 84 per cent were peasants. In terms of ethnicity they were almost exclusively Serbs (over 95 per cent). The villagers owned the land they farmed, creating an impression of a 'small peasant's paradise' and therefore attracting migrants, notably Serbs from Bosnia and Herzegovina as well from the Ottoman Empire. As one migrant from Habsburg Bosnia put it, 'In Serbia you could breathe more easily.'[10] Apart from the possibility of gaining a plot of land, political liberties also played a role. After arriving in Belgrade the Young Bosnian students were amazed that they could freely shout 'Down with Austria!' Serbian agriculture remained the overwhelmingly dominant sector in the economy, but businessmen and small manufacturers were increasing every year. As for an army career, certainly it was attractive, but it is debatable whether it was really what Clark has called 'the biggest show in town'.[11]

Serbia in short was experiencing an era of rapid innovation and modernization. Peasants and small businesses were increasingly investing their savings in, for example, Siemens and Halske turbines, after learning that electricity was the latest technological breakthrough.[12] A generation of outstanding scientists and intellectuals was also active in pre-war Serbia. Most of them were affiliated with the newly established Belgrade University (1905). For instance, Milutin Milanković, a mathematician and astronomer, was writing about climate change, while the geographer Jovan Cvijić became famous due to his studies about the Balkan peninsula. There were many others and the name of literary critic Jovan Skerlić should be emphasized. He was one of the most eloquent advocates of Southern Slav unification and the idol of *Mlada Bosna*.

In the late 1980s, as communist Yugoslavia was disintegrating, the picture of pre-1914 parliamentary and social life in Serbia would be much embellished and romanticized. Yet contrary to this 'golden age' image, new research has pointed out the major shortcomings in economic and political life.[13] The economy lacked capital sufficient for investments, and Serbian peasants, though free, often remained on the borderline of poverty. They expressed almost no interest for industrial goods, so the absence of a local market presented additional difficulty for the growth of Serbia's young industries. Illiteracy rates in the countryside also remained as high as 77 per cent, and poor health conditions were producing high mortality rates.

In political terms, the prevalence of unofficial power centres created major instability. These circles were publicly termed the 'irresponsible elements' or the 'unconstitutional factors'. Such euphemisms mainly targeted those civilians or officers who had participated in the 1903 coup which toppled the Obrenović regime. The regicides of 1903 had immediately elected a civilian government that summoned the National Assembly (Skupština) and subsequently the Senate.[14] The conspirators' aim was to show the Serbian public that they were defending the parliamentary system and that their actions had solely been directed against the late royal couple. However, it became evident on that very day that they did not envisage becoming simple bystanders in Serbian political life. In addition, political life in the kingdom was marked by some general flaws: unfair elections, parliamentary obstruction and violent political rhetoric were commonplace in the political arena, accompanied by aggressive electoral campaigns. The People's Radical Party, which became the dominant political force in the country after 1903, showed little consideration towards the opposition in parliament. If necessary, laws and even the constitution were breached: everything was allowed if such measures favoured the Radicals.[15]

In the post-1903 period, the prime concern of the regicides was to secure their immunity from prosecution, for they had breached their officers' oath by participating in a plot against the lawful king and then murder of the royal Obrenović couple. Dozens of other people had been killed during the coup, including several government ministers. The second priority was to make sure that all participants in the conspiracy were rewarded. This was done by promoting their military careers. These men now began to interfere in the process of decision making at a government level, wishing to act as a corrective in the spheres of both domestic and foreign policy. As one contemporary observed, 'Their influence in the state was ubiquitous, but especially in matters of national and military politics.'[16] The conflict of the military conspirators with the People's Radical Party led by Pašić was immediate, for the new Serbian prime minister tried to strip them of their political influence. But the notion that these officers could be confined within constitutional boundaries was wishful thinking; Pašić's success in 1903 was only partial as he managed to pension off very few of them.

Although the Skupština soon granted an amnesty to the regicides, supporters of the Obrenović dynasty and some other members of the Serbian elite were not prepared to accept the contemporary situation and cheer the conspirators as saviours of Serbia. Two counter-plots were organized, but without any palpable results. In 1905, a 'Society for the Legal Solution of the Conspirator's Question' was formed. Thus, there was a section of Serbia's elite that was not willing to ignore the legal and moral conundrum that the officers had defenestrated the Serbian king and queen, and the 1903 murders continued to be heavily criticized in the Serbian press. However, the 1903 conspirators held firm and put pressure on the government. And even though the above-mentioned society for a legal investigation into the regicide was soon banned, squabbling between the former conspirators and their opponents became a feature of everyday political culture; journalists and opposition deputies, even ministers, were threatened in public or even assaulted in broad daylight on the streets of Belgrade.[17]

In the light of this, the position of King Petar Karadjordjević was an especially difficult one. Until 1906 his court was a key central stronghold of the 1903 conspirators, and the king, though he 'harboured democratic sentiments', felt indebted to those who had brought him to the throne.[18] Various army officers visited him on an almost daily basis, seeking support for their ideas and trying to block any attempt to strip them of political influence. Some even contemplated another change of monarch as they thought that the king's mental powers, as well as his gratitude, did not match the efforts they had invested in helping his accession.[19]

These officers – the so-called irresponsible elements – exerted their influence in a very specific manner. They were not an organization, but more of a network, holding the most senior positions in the army and directing or controlling the careers of more junior officers. Thus, the military hierarchy was used as a shield. They cherished close personal relationships – friendship and mutual support – rather than written rules or any clear ideology. The first important setback, however, for those behind the 1903 coup came in 1906 when the five senior conspirators were pensioned off: this was a condition demanded by Great Britain in order to re-establish diplomatic relations with Serbia. (Contacts between the two countries had been severed after the regicide.) The five officers retired only after long internal negotiation and after the government had agreed to increase considerably their future pensions: it all looked more like promotion than punishment.[20] If this meant that the former plotters had lost their foothold at court, they nevertheless transferred their informal headquarters to the Ministry of War. There, they stayed until January of 1914 when dramatic developments began to unfold.

We should also note that the Serbian officers had their own internal quarrels and dilemmas. These were mostly caused by generational differences, but were also due to conflicting assessments of European politics. Some expressed pro-Austrian tendencies while others favoured France or Russia. Indeed, there were official signs from Vienna that those involved in the 1903 coup might continue to enjoy their amnesty if they would only support Austro-Hungarian interests in Serbia; this became quite clear on several occasions in 1905 and later on in 1906, during the first year of the Customs War (1906–11) between Austria and Serbia.[21] In general the officers were perplexed too when confronted with the realities of Serbian political life. By forming complicated and unusual alliances in the Skupština, Nikola Pašić was often able to outmanoeuvre, confuse and divide the former conspirators. As a result, in short, the 1903 conspirators found it difficult to formulate a clear stance on the numerous domestic and foreign political questions of the day.

After the older conspirators had left the scene, the way was open for those who had been only junior officers in 1903. After 1906 these became the main protectors of the coup's legacy, with Major Dragutin T. Dimitrijević as their unofficial leader. In 1903 he had been one of the most energetic participants, but had not actually belonged to the leadership; his name was not even mentioned in the British documentation which had led to re-establishing diplomatic relations between the two countries.[22] It is not that surprising that many contemporaries saw Apis as a 'congenial' rather than a 'hateful' conspirator.[23] He was constantly surrounded by many friends whom he always helped, and his influence tended to be unofficial, based on a network of clients and comrades. When asked during his trial in Salonika in 1917 about his meetings with members of his secret society 'Unification or Death' (*Ujedinjenje ili Smrt* – better known as the 'Black Hand'), he confirmed that he had met them regularly but not as members of an organization, simply as friends (Figure 7.1).[24]

Apis became one of the symbols of Serbia's 'Golden Age', but he also personified many of the issues that were problematic during this era, embodying several stereotypes about the Balkans. Rumours increasingly circulated that he was somehow linked to all 'mysterious secret organizations' or 'bloodthirsty conspiracies' in Serbia. In reality he was not so powerful. The only post in the Serbian army that gave him official influence was as head of Serbian military intelligence, and he secured that only in August 1913. Rather it was his informal network that provided him with the real means to interfere in all aspects of political and military life. His approval was essential for the appointment of all ministers of war from 1906 to 1914. So his influence was not as straightforward as might appear at first glance, and – as we will see – the crisis of May 1914 showed this very well.

In his military career Apis had studied in Germany and held positions in several Serbian army divisions; by 1906 he was a lieutenant colonel working in the Serbian general staff. Like other senior representatives of the 'unconstitutional elements' he was a resolute, strong-willed man, but poor at expressing his ideas. Slobodan Jovanović, the famous Serbian professor of law and contemporary of Apis, duly noted that Dimitrijević was a man

FIGURE 7.1 *Dragutin T. Dimitrijević ('Apis') (Serbian National Library, Belgrade).*

'without compass or control'.²⁵ Having such an individual as head of military intelligence, one of the most sensitive positions in the armed forces, was especially dangerous as Serbia's relations with Austria-Hungary were fast deteriorating.

## From one crisis to another

On 29 July 1914 the Regent Aleksandar Karadjordjević (substituting for King Petar) announced his proclamation of war. The text began: 'The troubles of our kingdom and our people with Austria-Hungary did not begin yesterday.'²⁶ Indeed the two states had clashed on almost all important questions over the previous fifteen years, creating an impression among the Serbian and Austro-Hungarian publics that war was inevitable due to conflicting ambitions and growing antagonisms. Mistakenly, historians have often suggested that the main watershed in this process was the moment when a more energetic Serbian dynasty came to the throne in 1903 and when the 'intensely nationalist Radicals' took over the government.²⁷ In fact, already after King Milan Obrenović had left the country in 1889, Vienna had lost any solid foundation in Serbia, as the new young king Aleksandar had aspirations to pursue a more vigorous national policy at home and abroad. On several occasions he had boosted hopes of commencing national wars, saying that 'after all, his father King Milan had liberated half of Serbia'.²⁸ In 1903, after Aleksandar's murder, Austria-Hungary, together with Russia, was the first state to recognize the dynastic change in Serbia. This was primarily out of fear that Serbia might become a republic, but it was also clear that the unstable last Obrenović had not been at all popular in Vienna.

Prior to the Sarajevo crisis of 1914 there were several key moments that then marked the deterioration of bilateral relations: with each new crisis the complex problems were exacerbated. Serbia's desire to emancipate itself from the Habsburg grip was demonstrated quite vividly during the so-called Cannon question (*Topovsko pitanje*). After 1903 this was the first large state purchase by the new regime, the idea being to modernize the Serbian artillery (a process already initiated by King Aleksandar). The 'Cannon question' lasted from 1904 until the end of 1906 and developed into a major domestic as well as foreign crisis. For the arms race now arrived in the Balkans and the agents of German 'Krupp', French 'Schneider-Creusot' and Austro-Hungarian 'Škoda' competed to sign a contract with the Serbian state. The 300 rapid firing pieces presented a solid order for any of these factories and especially for Škoda as it was experiencing serious financial troubles at the time. From the start it was clear that the Serbian elite did not wish to buy guns from Vienna; distancing Serbia from the Habsburgs was seen as a priority, while buying weapons implied long-term collaboration to ensure further ammunition and spare parts.

The 'Cannon question' proceeded to topple several Serbian governments, public accusations of bribery were common and strong anti-Austrian voices were heard for months in the Serbian press. In January 1906, just when the old Belgrade-Vienna trade agreement was expiring, the Austro-Hungarian authorities decided to close the state border. This was done under the false pretext that a disease was detected among animals imported from Serbia. At that point up to 90 per cent of Serbian exports went into the Habsburg Monarchy, mostly live animals and fresh meat. Serbia also imported most of its foreign assets (60 per cent), such as petroleum, machines or luxury goods, from Austria-Hungary. By closing the frontier Vienna exerted immense pressure on the Serbian government in the 'Cannon question'. However, Serbia responded with reciprocal measures and all trade came to a halt. So alongside the 'Cannon question', there now began a customs war, more colloquially known as the 'Pig War' in view of Serbia's main export to Austria-Hungary.[29]

The Serbian government finally chose the French-Belgian consortium for financing the cannon deal and contracts were signed in November 1906. However, the 'Pig War' lasted until 1911 and passed through various phases. Just when Austro-Serbian talks about some new trade agreement were about to resume, and political tensions were relaxing, a devastating new crisis unfolded. In the late afternoon of 5 October 1908, the official news reached Belgrade that Austria-Hungary had annexed Bosnia and Herzegovina. Spontaneous demonstrations erupted in Belgrade, involving up to a quarter of the inhabitants. The crowds, twenty-thousand strong, shouted slogans that vividly expressed their pent up hatred: 'Death to Austria!' or 'Death to usurpers!' Others alluded to the possibility of open conflict, crying the name of the border river: 'Towards the Drina!' These events lasted for days in various Serbian towns. While the government, in encouraging the popular protests, soon lost control over the events, a group of citizens decided to try to channel the public anger and spontaneously created on 9 October a society that should recruit volunteers for a potential war with Austria-Hungary. The name of this organization was *Narodna Odbrana* ('People's Defence'). Although on 18 March 1909 the Serbian government was forced to accept reality and the act of annexation itself, *Narodna Odbrana* continued to function as a revolutionary nationalist society, preparing for a potential war with the Habsburg Monarchy.[30] Even if private in character, its president was a retired general of the Serbian army named Božidar Janković.

A few years later in 1911, another society was formed with similar aims. In order to strengthen the work of Serbian irregulars (*četniks*) in Ottoman-ruled Macedonia and Kosovo, and inspired to some degree by the 'Young Turk' movement, several businessmen and officers decided to form a new organization titled *Ujedinjenje ili Smrt* (Unification or Death). The aims of this included liberation of the entire Serb people from 'foreign rule'. Colonel Dragutin Dimitrijević-Apis was one of the first to be called upon to join. Although at the start the organization maintained its secrecy, its existence was soon widely known about; its secret initiation ritual, directly influenced by Masonic rites, as one of its founders was a freemason, created an aura of mystery. But it soon lost its exclusivity as people entered en masse into the 'Black Hand' (*Crna Ruka*) to call it by its colloquial name. For aspiring members it was sufficient to note the names of the most distinguished members as well as the society's general goals; candidates would simply embrace the 'Black Hand' without asking too many questions.[31]

By 1911, when a new Serbian trade agreement had finally been signed with Austria-Hungary, the economic relationship had changed. Serbia had found other markets and was only exporting 11 per cent of its goods to the Monarchy. With the eruption of the First Balkan War in October 1912, the two states were again on the verge of a full-scale war on a par with the annexation crisis of 1909. Successes in the two Balkan Wars meant a huge increase of Serbian prestige among the South Slavs of the Balkans. By doubling its size and acquiring 1.5 million new subjects, Serbia could, as the Habsburg military attaché in Belgrade observed, also double its army size over the next ten years. The issue of a pending Austro-Serbian conflict increasingly became a topic of discussion in Habsburg and Serbian official circles.

Indeed, when in March 1913 the Albanian town of Scutari (Shkodër) fell into the hands of the Montenegrin and Serbian armies, Božidar Janković, the president of *Narodna Odbrana*, made a controversial speech in Prizren (Kosovo). The general allegedly said that Serbs would only be entirely free when the Serbian army had entered Bosnia-Herzegovina. This provoked yet another diplomatic spat with Austria-Hungary, and Janković was asked by

Pašić to clarify what he had said. The general replied, he had suggested that those liberated by the Serbian army in 1912–13 should now join forces with their liberators and free the remaining Serbs who were still living under foreign oppression. The final sentence in this reply made quite clear the overall tone of the offensive speech: 'I did not mention Bosnia and Herzegovina or any other Serbian land specifically.'[32]

With the end of the Second Balkan War, the Serbian army resumed operations in the newly created state of Albania. As Lothar Höbelt explains in his chapter, this was seen as unacceptable by Vienna who sent an ultimatum to Belgrade demanding an immediate withdrawal of Serbian troops. On 6 October 1913, the Orient Express resumed its journeys across the Balkans, thereby signalling that all major violence in the region had ended. On the same day, Serbian troops officially left Albania in order to respect the deadline delivered in the Habsburg ultimatum.

## The network of Serbian military intelligence

Colonel Dragutin Dimitrijević had not participated in the wars of 1912–13 as he had spent those months in bed: during a daring liaison operation in Albania in the autumn of 1912 he had caught Malta fever. In August 1913, however, he arrived in his new office at Serbian military headquarters in Belgrade's Kalemegdan fortress. He was now in position to intermix his private with the official Serbian military intelligence network. At his trial in Salonika, in May 1917, he would claim that at the moment he took on his new job 'he found almost no organization in Bosnia'.[33] Nevertheless, through bits and pieces of the surviving sources it is possible to prove that Serbian military intelligence was already very active in Bosnia-Herzegovina by the time Dimitrijević joined its ranks.

For by 1914 military intelligence was a very solid segment of the Serbian army. In the late 1890s, while preparing war plans against the Ottoman Empire, serious shortcomings had been detected in the domain of intelligence, so in 1897 as part of a systematic reform of the army a special 'External Department' of the chief of staff was formed. The official purpose of this department was to spy on potential enemies (with only three officers at first employed there).[34] In fact, more attention was devoted to securing first-hand information, especially maps of the Turkish border regions; in this respect the Serbian civilian officials working in the embassy and consulates in the Ottoman Empire received regular instructions from the army.[35]

The increased interest of the Serbian general staff in Austro-Hungarian forces in southern Hungary and especially in Bosnia-Herzegovina dated to 1908. Of special interest was the situation in the borderland between Bosnia and the Sandžak of Novi Pazar. Basil de Strandman, first secretary of the Russian legation in Belgrade from 1911 to 1915, noted in 1911 that

Serbian agents were sending through material about the Habsburg military preparations near the Sandžak.[36] In addition, Strandman wrote that the Russian military attaché in Vienna had formed a special network of Russian agents in Bosnia-Herzegovina, recruited from local Serbs. The attaché was dissatisfied with the quality of information he was receiving, not only from Sarajevo but also from Vienna, so wanted to have his own men on the ground.[37] Strandman unfortunately did not say anything about the potential coordination of these steps with Serbian military officials.

An important moment in making the Serbian military intelligence service more effective took place in January 1911 when the Serbian general staff proposed to attach one additional officer to the existing border posts. This officer was to be focused solely on intelligence gathering. The new border officers were to be sent to towns along the Habsburg and the Ottoman frontiers, and for greater efficiency, the borders would be divided into sectors. Šabac, Loznica and Užice were the places where officers had to monitor activity on the Austro-Hungarian border, while the mountain of Javor and the towns of Raška and Vranje were the key observation points designated on the Ottoman frontier.[38]

When Minister of Finance Stojan Protić declined to support the institution of these new border officers, he found himself immediately under pressure from members of the Black Hand. Eventually, the 'Border Officers Decree' was accepted by the government and Protić had to change his views. All six new posts ultimately were occupied by officers who were distinguished members of *Crna Ruka*.[39] In this way, not only did the Serbian chief of staff secure a very valuable tool for monitoring its potential enemies, but Apis and his group took yet another step towards controlling key positions within the Serbian army. The Black Hand could now read and manipulate highly sensitive military data, while at the same time the border officers enabled Apis to have a say in Serbia's foreign policy.

While during the Balkan Wars the entire Serbian army was operating in Macedonia and Albania, relations with the Habsburg Monarchy became very tense. The Serbian High Command feared that the Austro-Hungarian army might attack northern or western parts of Serbia. Consequently, the movements of Habsburg troops were closely monitored and the slightest shift had to be reported. A number of reports made by Serbian border officers poured in to the Serbian High Command now relocated in Skoplje. Thanks to these surviving reports, as well as other documentation, it is possible to reconstruct most of the activities of the border (intelligence) officers. For example, in late November 1912 a report arrived stating that 'the Serbian agent, judge Petar Nikolić' had provided information about the transfer of Austro-Hungarian troops from Banjaluka to the Serbian border.[40] The president of the Mitrovica municipality in Srem (in Croatia) was also named as one of the people providing useful information to Serbian intelligence.[41] In April 1913 the Šabac border officer Major Dimitrije Pavlović sent to Skoplje a general report concerning the situation in Bosnia-Herzegovina.

The major stressed that emergency measures had been implemented in this region by local Austro-Hungarian officials and that Bosnia was practically 'in a state of war'.[42]

One document seized by the Austro-Hungarian army in August 1914, in the border town of Loznica, shows well that the Serbian border officers cultivated very close contact with members of the radicalized Bosnian youth. The Serbian border officer Major Kosta Todorović had kept a confidential diary about his routine at the border and made the mistake of leaving it in his office when war erupted. Entries dating back to July 1912 revealed 'meetings with Bosnian and Herzegovinian youths'. The two meetings had taken place in Serbia, in the small town of Mali Zvornik just near the Drina River on 12 and 21 July 1912. One of those who attended was the famous Bosnian activist, Vladimir Gaćinović, but agents from the towns of Kupres and Mostar were also present. Moreover, Gaćinović and another Bosnian with the last name 'Živanović' had undertaken shooting training with a Serbian M99 rifle as well as with a revolver. The two sides exchanged advice and ideas about further activities: it was noted that one of the topics discussed was the development of the youth and intelligence network in the Bosnian town of Tuzla.[43]

Apart from the official network of Serbian border officers, another intelligence structure was operating more or less independently. Namely, in 1912–13, representatives of the *Narodna Odbrana* were 'sending their own men into Bosnia for information'.[44] The data gathered was subsequently transferred to border officers or directly forwarded to the army high command in Belgrade. For example, in February 1913 the executive board of *Narodna Odbrana* at Šabac forwarded information relevant to the military situation in Tuzla to the Serbian army.[45]

It is clear then that border officers practised reconnaissance on behalf of the Serbian general staff. Each officer apparently was responsible for creating his own network of informants. All data was then filtered and sent to Belgrade. Officers were also well acquainted with all potential border crossings. However, apart from military issues the officers were involved too in propaganda activities – actions colloquially known as 'national work'. This implied regular communication and assistance to Serbian organizations in Austria-Hungary and the Ottoman Empire.

But were there any 'proper agents' of Serbian military intelligence operating in Bosnia? One name stands out: Rade Malobabić. Apis later explained how this man was presented to him in the autumn of 1913 after he took over military intelligence.[46] It seems that Apis was trying to find individuals who could reach further into the Monarchy with the potential to access more delicate Austro-Hungarian military data, and Malobabić was recommended by majors Milan Vasić and Dimitrije Pavlović.[47] The two majors had collaborated with Malobabić in the days before the Balkan Wars, and both testified to him being a very capable man who had managed to provide essential information about the movements of the Habsburg military during the recent conflict.[48] The famous Serb lawyer from Zagreb, Srdjan Budisavljević who happened to be in Belgrade at the time, was also asked his opinion of Malobabić.[49]

Apparently Apis desired men who could be more than mere 'confidants' and who could access more sensitive Habsburg military data. According to Apis, Malobabić's task was 'to develop the intelligence network in the areas which interest us'; soon he would talk of Malobabić as 'his right hand'.[50] So Apis's claim that there was a non-existent spy network in Bosnia in 1913 should be seen in this context – his frustration caused by a lack of high-profile agents. Malobabić in fact was already well known to the Austro-Hungarian authorities as he had been arrested and prosecuted in the notorious Zagreb treason trial of 1909.[51] Since he worked as an insurance agent, he was able to travel freely through Croatia and Bosnia as well as other parts of the empire. From 1911 he was also working for *Narodna Odbrana*, travelling to Serbia two or three times a year: he collaborated closely with the border officer in Šabac, Dimitrije Pavlović, and also developed close ties to Serbian army officers like Milan Vasić and Milan Pribićević.[52] These two were very important for the functioning of the Serbian intelligence network. Vasić was the secretary of *Narodna Odbrana*,[53] while Pribićević was closely linked into the organization and had a good network of contacts with Austria-Hungary.[54] In the end, in late 1913, Malobabić agreed to collaborate with Apis only for the duration of five years as he wanted to retire afterwards.

It is possible that other operatives of Serbian military intelligence were employed on steamboats, in railway companies, or as travelling salesmen. Milan Ciganović, for example, was actually working for the Serbian railways, having emigrated from Bosnia. At his trial Apis also hinted that two women were involved in transporting messages from Serbia into the empire but did not provide any details. Certainly the border officers as well as members of *Narodna Odbrana* were receiving information not only from their agents but also from some Bosnian civilians. While relatives of Serbs who had previously migrated from Bosnia were exploited, deserters from the Habsburg army were seen as another valuable source of information. Strandman noted in his diary that data about the concentration of Austro-Hungarian troops was leaking from Serb officers in the Habsburg army.[55] It becomes clear then that by 1913 Serbian military intelligence was quite actively engaged in Bosnia-Herzegovina and that its operations had certain firm bases. The network – composed of confidants, volunteers, Bosnian radical youths and a few more capable agents – seems very loose but it was probably fairly effective in providing good information about the military developments in the provinces. *Narodna Odbrana*'s resources should be included in the picture as well, even if this organization was viewed, as we will see, as a liability by the Serbian military.

With the end of the Balkan Wars, there was no longer any need for border officers to the south as the Ottomans were no longer a neighbour. As part of the domestic power struggle between the government and the Black Hand,

Pašić now desired to use the momentum and remove too the special officers on the Habsburg frontier, in other words to strip *Crna Ruka* of this important intelligence tool.[56] But although the government officially decided on their dissolution, the intelligence centres on the Drina and Sava Rivers continued to operate.[57] Apis now saw the situation as favourable for focusing all resources on the Habsburg Empire.[58]

## The critical months: Spring 1914

The wartime unity of the government and the army did not last long after the Balkan Wars, for the old issue about the control of the armed forces and their excursions into politics resurfaced. First, spending was a problem. The two wars had exhausted the state finances and new loans were needed in order to repair weaponry and renew the ammunition supplies. Even Marcel Krupp, a representative of the German arms manufacturer, visited Belgrade in May in order to negotiate a contract for repairing numerous pieces of Ottoman artillery, now spoils of war.[59] A special new tax also had to be introduced in order to give financial support to war invalids.

However, the army leaders wanted to make the most of the new reserves of population. In order to incorporate new recruits from the 'new territories' in the south into the Serbian army, money had to be found for new barracks, weapons and other supplies. Most Serbian units from the pre-1912 territory were also still relocated in the south for security reasons: this also cost money. When the government did not want to accept any abrupt increase in the military budget, the dissatisfied Minister of War, General Miloš Božanović, resigned.[60] Showing solidarity with him and his plans for expansion, not a single Serbian general accepted the opportunity to become the new minister of war. This was no longer a conflict just with the Black Hand, or those military men who openly interfered with the government's work, but with the entire officer corps. In the end, in January 1914, one colonel – Dušan Stefanović – agreed to become minister of war, but he was the first such appointment not approved by Dimitrijević-Apis.

Besides the budget issue, controversy arose over the status of the 'new territories' and other areas conquered in the Balkan Wars. Would the local inhabitants secure equal rights and obligations with those Serbian subjects who had been living in the pre-1912 borders? The response of the political elite was negative, but it was unclear whether the provisional administration would be ruled by military or civilian authorities. Soon after the wars, civil and military authorities in Macedonia had clashed over who had precedence.

On 6 December 1913 when the birthday of the Russian Tsar Nicholas II was celebrated throughout Serbia, an incident took place in the town of Bitola (Monastir) in southern Macedonia. There, the local divisional commander verbally clashed with the civil representative over who should be the first to officially respond to the speech of the local Russian consul. Similar incidents took place all over the new territories during various ceremonies or festivities. Behind these symbolic incidents a basic question loomed: Should the army fully obey the civil authorities? It was exacerbated by the fact that the behaviour of civil authorities in the south was becoming more problematic by the day. The press was full of reports about the serious misconduct of civil servants who had been appointed by Belgrade and sent into the new territories. The military protested against such misdemeanours, finding it insulting to have to follow instructions from such an administration.

This topic was discussed in the Skupština as well. The socialist deputy, Dragiša Lapčević, explained that the supremacy of civilian government over the armed forces was 'vital for Serbia': the army must not be 'a state within the state', officers 'cannot be above the government'. However, the main opposition party, the Independent Radicals, expressed sympathy with the military, explaining that their honour had been affronted by government behaviour in the south of the country. This was problematic as various officer groups were now gaining political legitimacy. To settle this question the Minister of Interior, Stojan Protić, in April 1914 issued 'The Priority Act', a document that clearly resolved the debate in favour of the civil authorities. Though the act focused on the new territories, it was clear that Protić, the main political ideologue of the Radical Party, had in mind full legal supremacy of the civil authorities across the entire country. Immediately, heavy resistance sprang up. General Popović, pensioned off following British demands in 1906, had been re-engaged during the Balkan Wars, and by 1914 he was the commanding officer in the new territories. When Popović sent an insulting open letter to the minister of interior, he was replaced, but his successor General Petar Bojović continued to fire off such missives.

General Radomir Putnik, the ageing chief of the general staff, sympathized with the officers' cause and therefore tried to act as an intermediary. For this purpose on several occasions in 1914 he had to rush home from the Austrian spa at Gleichenberg where he was recuperating. Another mediator used was the literary critic Jovan Skerlić. But rumours about a potential military coup continued to spread. In his diary Minister Stefanović noted details he had received from informers about secret military meetings, and the civil–military struggle was increasingly entangled in a whole set of public scandals. For example, General Popović immediately after his removal, had been named as president of the 'Officer's Society for Mutual Help', an organization founded by the minister of war but run by the officers. In 1914 it was widely believed that the society's financial resources were being used to finance the activities of the Black Hand. Since the president of the society's board was Putnik himself (a hero of the Balkan Wars), it was clear that the dissatisfied men enjoyed the full support of the Serbian military hierarchy. Nonetheless, Protić responded to this open challenge by dispatching police into the Officer's Society. There a thoroughly corrupt administration was uncovered.

King Petar was endeavouring to bring both sides to a compromise, but in June 1914 he finally surrendered power to his son, Aleksandar.[61] In May, Apis had also entered the struggle with a radical proposal, asking his friends to expel all civilian authorities from the new territories. But a strange thing then occurred: the officers estimated that this was excessive and rejected his suggestion. It was the first time that Apis had lost the support of his friends and admirers.[62] The extreme militant wing of the protest movement was now abandoned by most officers as the military leadership, including Putnik, had no real desire to bring down the government and install military rule. It seems that they were mainly concerned to keep their strong influence over matters relevant to the army and foreign policy.

## The Bosnian boys in Belgrade

On 16 May 1914 Jovan Skerlić died in Belgrade and one student was chosen to carry the wreath submitted by various youth groups. This was a young man who just three days later reported his arrival to the Belgrade police station: Gavrilo Princip. Since he had problems with the Habsburg authorities in Bosnia, he had come to Serbia to finish his seventh grade in one of Belgrade's secondary schools. That year Belgrade was hosting several hundred pupils or students from Bosnia-Herzegovina, many of whom were already opponents of Habsburg rule and contemplated violence as a way of challenging it. The usual biography of this type of Bosnian émigré had included clashes with teachers over political questions, expulsion from school or even banishment from Bosnia-Herzegovina.[63]

As Robin Okey's chapter shows, 'Young Bosnia' never existed as an organization. It was more a loose group of youths who held similar views on two essential questions. First, they all hated Austria-Hungary, and second, they wanted to be active participants in history. Otherwise, they could hardly agree among themselves on political or social questions. Some embraced Slav solidarity; others favoured Serbian identity. A third group prioritized anarchism or socialism before anything else; their precious books by Peter Kropotkin or Nikolai Chernyshevsky were the last ones that they sold during their poverty-stricken lives in Bosnia or Serbia.[64] In recent discussions about the Sarajevo assassination, *Mlada Bosna* has too easily been branded as a terrorist organization. They were certainly terrorists the moment they embraced violence, but only terrorists by the standards of 1914; making allusions or even comparisons to Al Qaida or other modern-day terrorist organizations is highly problematic. It is true that *Narodna Odbrana*, as well as the Serbian army, organized training camps in Serbia during the years 1908–12 when many Bosnian volunteers passed courses in guerrilla warfare, but can we really call these 'terrorist camps'? All Young

Bosnians had contacts to other youths in Habsburg regions such as Dalmatia and Croatia where individuals also dreamt about some anti-Habsburg revolution, but was this really a network of 'terrorist cells'? Was the ambush on the archduke's motor column so similar to late twentieth-century suicide attacks, or was it, as Vladimir Dedijer wrote in 1966, more in the Balkan 'hajduk' tradition?[65] It is completely erroneous too to describe the Young Bosnians as exclusive 'Serbian nationalists'.[66] In view of the bloody wars that finally destroyed Yugoslavia, it is hard to imagine that the Yugoslav project ever had such intense advocates as the Bosnian revolutionaries; indeed, Gavrilo Princip at his trial declared himself to be a 'Yugoslav' and rejected any national chauvinism in Bosnia.[67]

In May 1914, Princip, Trifko Grabež and Nedeljko Čabrinović were all in Belgrade. At their trial in October they would give conflicting accounts of how they conceived the idea of going to Sarajevo and assassinating the archduke, but they all mentioned reading in the press that Franz Ferdinand would be visiting the city in June. That information had been released in March, but Apis knew about it already in September 1913 thanks to the work of Rade Malobabić. In order to secure weapons for the attack the three men decided to contact their acquaintances in Belgrade pubs that they visited. And they insisted later that the assassination had strictly been their own idea. Certainly they, as well as their friends in Bosnia, were capable ideologically of framing the planned murder as part of a revolutionary anti-Austrian agenda. In this light, it is highly unlikely that they were just 'puppets' of their 'shadowy backers from Serbia'.[68] According to the trial proceedings, the young men had approached former volunteers from the Second Balkan War, Djulaga Bukovac and Milan Ciganović. Both were Bosnian Serbs who frequented local pubs in Belgrade and were unemployed after the Balkan Wars. However, as we have suggested, Ciganović most probably was working for Serbian military intelligence. The two men promised the would-be assassins that they would secure weapons.[69] As Grabež said at his trial in October 1914, 'Četniks had a lot of bombs which were left over from the Balkan War, and it was easy to get them.'[70]

Even so, anyone wanting to acquire more than one bomb had to ask for help elsewhere. Ciganović was in close contact with Vojislav Tankosić, a major in the Serbian army and a notorious figure among Serbian irregulars. Tankosić was known as a brave but hot tempered individual who had 'started' the First Balkan War. Though war had been declared on 17 October 1912, hostilities had already begun two days before. Early on 15 October, a Serbian auxiliary unit composed of četniks and led by the then captain Tankosić had attacked two Ottoman border posts. Tankosić had specific orders not to engage in combat but discreetly to enter Turkish territory. Instead, his unit attacked the border posts head-on and suffered heavy casualties. The logic behind his disobedience was that he feared the Serbian government might decide at the last moment not to declare war on the Ottomans.[71]

In May 1914 Tankosić at first declined any possibility of providing weapons to Princip and his friends. However, after persistent demands he asked advice from Apis. What seems to have happened late in May was that Apis gave free rein to Tankosić even though he knew the purpose of the weapons. Furthermore, Tankosić was asked by Apis to show to the Bosnians the basic principles of targeting.[72] In a recently published monograph, John Zametica has tried to challenge this interpretation, arguing that Apis had almost nothing to do with the Sarajevo plot. Zametica stresses the possibility that Tankosić was most likely working on his own. From this perspective, Apis's role was limited to that of a bystander who tried but failed to stop the assassination.[73] It is true that all evidence linking Apis to the conspiracy is loose and circumstantial. Nevertheless, it is hard to imagine that Apis, who was powerful enough to approve the appointment of so many Serbian ministers of war, was not able to control one Serbian major – indeed, an officer who was one of his closest friends and associates. To exclude Apis from the Sarajevo assassination plan, as does Zametica, would mean seriously to ignore the entire Serbian pre-1914 context.

On 28 May, Ciganović met the students in one of Belgrade's parks and handed over guns and bombs. With Ciganović's recommendation to the border officer, and specific instruction to keep away from the Serbian police, the plotters proceeded to the military border personnel who smuggled them across the border.[74] Apis did not notify his co-members in the Black Hand nor the *Narodna Odbrana* about his blessing for the operation. When they found out, they were appalled and urged him to cancel the whole mission, which he allegedly tried to do but failed.

Several documents from early June 1914 show that Serbian customs officials and military personnel on the Serbian-Austrian border were on the verge of a full-scale conflict. Throughout the spring Pašić had been sending messages to the *Narodna Odbrana* leadership not to take any independent action across the Drina River. On 4 June the new prefect of the Podrinje region on the Bosnian border wrote to Protić, revealing that he had uncovered a plot to smuggle bombs and other weapons across the border into Bosnia. Protić in response on 12 June insisted that such smuggling must be stopped. Two days later the same prefect reported a heavy suitcase being carried by border officials into the forward-most border observation post; he suspected that a weapons transfer was being planned for that very night, something all the more stunning as it was being prepared in broad daylight. Then there was the suspicious behaviour of Rade Malobabić, whom the prefect accused of being an 'Austrian spy'. This time, Protić pressured the minister of war, asking for an explanation. The military chain of commanded was set in motion, Stefanović urging Putnik to explain what was happening on the border.[75] In this light, the warning given to Princip by Ciganović to keep away from the Serbian police becomes more understandable.

What is interesting is that Putnik himself did not know what was happening on the border, and therefore asked his main intelligence officer,

Dimitrijević-Apis, to explain himself. This is how one of Apis's rare surviving reports was created. Apis defended the weapons smuggling, claiming that they were being used to protect the couriers who were working for military intelligence. He also complained about the difficulties posed to his secret work by the civilian authorities, and noted too his unease about *Narodna Odbrana*, saying that at times this private organization's actions were creating difficulties for intelligence work of the Serbian army. The minister of war was not satisfied with Apis's answer and an official military investigation was opened.[76] By then, however, the three Bosnian lads were already far away in Bosnia as they had left Belgrade on 28 May.[77]

## Conclusion

In June 2015 the Serbian authorities unveiled a monument to Gavrilo Princip in Belgrade. At first sight it would suggest that any uneasiness about the Sarajevo assassination had vanished. In fact, the commemorative events of 2013–14 had shown the exact opposite. Most Serbian historians and politicians took an extremely defensive position in the face of foreign academics discussing the Sarajevo assassination and the July crisis, accusing them of having a contemporary political agenda.[78] Even if some of the foreign histories such as those of Christopher Clark or Margaret MacMillan were prone to generalizations, with an anachronistic take on how the Yugoslav wars might skew interpretations of 1914, fresh thinking about the subject can only be welcomed.[79] Implicitly this means making critical and dispassionate judgements about both the civilian and military authorities in Serbia in 1914.

During his trial, Gavrilo Princip was asked how it was possible that Serbian military officials had been able to act on their own (as all the accused claimed) without the knowledge of their civilian superiors. The judge also asked: 'Do you think we could find among our (Habsburg) army officers anyone who would do something like that?' Princip responded: 'Our army is one thing, and the Serbian army is something completely different.'[80] Indirectly, Princip was making a point about the entire context of Serbian society in the pre-war years. The fact that Apis and his associates were in such influential positions by the summer of 1914, with all state resources available to them, was not a coincidence but reflected the nature of Serbian political culture. They could not hold these positions without the support of Radomir Putnik, the chief of the Serbian general staff.

In early 1914 the Serbian government had made serious efforts to control the Black Hand. It was also clear that Putnik did not approve all of the actions of Apis and his likeminded officers. Nevertheless, the duality of power had simply lasted for too long. For about a decade the 'unconstitutional elements' had enjoyed the more or less open support of Serbia's political and military leadership. And all major political players in Serbia believed in the nationalist concept of a Serbian *Risorgimento*. After all, the Black Hand organization called their newspaper the *Pijemont* (Piedmont), signalling that they were the most ardent exponents of the national cause. As long as this national consensus about foreign policy was valid, other more problematic aspects of the officers' behaviour had been tolerated. Yet after 1913, when much of the unification project had been achieved, the paths between the Black Hand and the civilian authorities began to diverge sharply. The break came too late. When Princip and his friends in May 1914 asked for guns in Belgrade, the timing was simply perfect. The border (intelligence) officers were still in place and were following the instructions of Apis and his closest collaborators. Already a month later it was more difficult to smuggle men across the frontier for the vigilance of the civilian authorities was mounting by the day.

The Sarajevo assassination can therefore be seen as one episode in the domestic power struggle between the Serbian government and the military. It is possible to speculate that the 'welcome arrangements for the Archduke' – as Apis allegedly termed the assassination plot – were specifically calculated to harm the government of Nikola Pašić by creating yet another 'difficulty with the Austrians'. By adding his support to a group of young men aged sixteen to twenty who had never before shot at any live target, Dimitrijević was setting the stage for a diplomatic scandal rather than trying to provoke a Serbian-Austrian war. Meanwhile, the experienced irregulars, who actually presented a much greater threat to any Habsburg officials, were being kept unemployed in Belgrade. This shows that the power struggle of the 'unconstitutional elements' with the government was far from over. New elections requested by Pašić's government were scheduled for August 1914: he wanted to further dismantle the officers' network to ensure fresh legitimacy for his regime with a new monarch on the Serbian throne. However, the Austro-Hungarian ultimatum of 23 July interrupted the electioneering. Once more, and for the last time, General Putnik was forced to hurry back from the Gleichenberg spa to the Serbian capital.

## Notes

1 A.K., 'Otkrivanje spomen-ploče Gavrilu Principu', *Politika*, 3 February 1930, 1–2. The next day (3 February) marked the anniversary of the execution of Danilo Ilić, Miško Jovanović and Veljko Čubrilović, the members of *Mlada Bosna* sentenced to death in October 1914.

2 In this text I use the term 'Young Bosnia' for the various revolutionary youth groups existing in Bosnia-Herzegovina prior to the First World War, as this term has generally been accepted in the literature. However, the term was never used by those who committed or were involved in the Sarajevo assassination.

3  R. W. Seton-Watson openly criticized this initiative in the British press. However, the historian Harold Temperley defended the act in an open letter sent to the *Manchester Guardian*. This polemic was closely followed in the Yugoslav press. See 'Jedan engleski naučnik o otkrivanju spomen-ploče Principu', *Vreme*, 13 February 1930, 1.

4  Kosta Kumanudi sent the telegram with these instructions on 30 January 1930 before the ceremony in Sarajevo had taken place; it was sent to the Yugoslav legation in Athens: Arhiv Jugoslavije, Belgrade (Archive of Yugoslavia: hereafter AJ), F-379/9.

5  *Veliki rat Srbije za oslobođenje i ujedinjenje Srba, Hrvata i Slovenaca*, I (Belgrade: Glavni đeneralštab, 1924), 6; Vladimir Ćorović, *Istorija srpskog naroda*, III (Banjaluka and Belgrade: Glas srpski, Ars Libri, 1997), 442.

6  Christopher Clark, *The Sleepwalkers: How Europe Went to War in 1914* (London: Allen Lane, 2012), 452.

7  Dušan Bataković, 'Storm over Serbia: The Rivalry between Civilian and Military Authorities (1911-1914)', *Balcanica*, XLIV (2013): 307–56; Vojislav J. Vučković, 'Unutrašnje krize Srbije i Prvi svetski rat', *Istorijski časopis* 14–15 (1965): 173–229; Radovan M. Drašković, *Pretorijanske težnje u Srbiji. Apis i Crna ruka* (Belgrade: Žagor, 2006).

8  In Serbian historiography, the 1903 coup has been referred to as the 'May Coup' due to the usage of the Julian calendar at the time when the royal couple was killed.

9  Dragoslav Janković, *Srbija i jugoslovensko pitanje 1914–1915* (Belgrade: ISI, Export Press, 1973), 26; Andrej Mitrović, *Srbija u Prvom svetskom ratu* (Belgrade: Stubovi kulture, 2004), 74–5. For more about Serbia in this period, see Dimitrije Djordjević, 'Serbian Society, 1903–1914', in Béla K. Király and Dimitrije Djordjević (eds), *East Central European Society in the Balkan Wars* (Boulder and New York: Columbia University Press, 1987), 227–39.

10  Vojislav Šikoparija, *Sećanja srpskog oficira*, ed. Kosta Nikolić (Belgrade: Zavod za udžbenike, 2014), 5.

11  Clark, *The Sleepwalkers*, 33.

12  Predrag Marković, Čedomir Antić and Danilo Šarenac, *Korak ispred vremena – 125 godina Simensa u Srbiji* (Belgrade: Siemens, ISI, 2012), 77.

13  Olga Popović-Obradović, *Parlamentarizam u Srbiji 1903–1914* (Belgrade: Službeni list SRJ, 1998); Dubravka Stojanović, *Srbija i demokratija: 1903–1914, Istorijska studija o 'zlatnom dobu' srpske demokratije* (Belgrade: Udruženje za društvenu istoriju, 2003).

14  Dragiša Vasić, *Odabrana dela* (Belgrade: Altera and Trag, 1990), 210–11.

15  Popović-Obradović, *Parlamentarizam u Srbiji*, 196, 315.

16  Mladen J. Žujović, *Eseji o ljudima i događajima 1903–1959* (Vrnjačka Banja: Interklima grafika, 2004), 7.

17  Popović-Obradović, *Parlamentarizam u Srbiji*, 110–18.

18  Ivo Banac, *The National Question in Yugoslavia: Origins, History, Politics* (Ithaca and London: Cornell University Press, 1992), 143.

19  Vasa Kazimirović, *Crna ruka. Ličnosti i događaji u Srbiji od Majskog prevrata 1903 do Solunskog procesa 1917* (Novi Sad: Prometej, 1997), 257.
20  Drašković, *Pretorijanske težnje u Srbiji*, 50–1.
21  Dimitrije Djordjević, *Carinski rat Austro-Ugarske i Srbije 1906–1911* (Belgrade: Istorijski institut, 1962), 215.
22  About the conflicting accounts of Apis's role in the 1903 coup, see: Kazimirović, *Crna ruka*, 104.
23  David MacKenzie, *Apis, The Congenial Conspirator: The Life of Colonel Dragutin T. Dimitrijević* (New York: Columbia University Press, 1989); David MacKenzie, *The 'Black Hand' on Trial: Salonika, 1917* (New York: Columbia University Press, 1995); David MacKenzie, *The Exoneration of the 'Black Hand', 1917–1953* (New York: Columbia University Press, 1998). Only the first volume has been translated into Serbian: Dejvid Mekenzi, *Apis* (Gornji Milanovac: Lio, Eurografik and Života Žika Lazić, 1996).
24  Mekenzi, *Apis*, 194.
25  Branislav Gligorijević, *Kralj Aleksandar Karađorđević*, I (Belgrade: BIGZ, 1994), 56.
26  *Veliki rat Srbije za oslobođenje i ujedinjenje Srba, Hrvata i Slovenaca*, I, 16.
27  Margaret MacMillan, *The War that Ended Peace: The Road to 1914* (New York: Random House, 2013), 415.
28  For the latest biography of Aleksandar Obrenović, see Suzana Rajić, *Aleksandar Obrenović. Vladar na prelazu vekova. Sukobljeni svetovi* (Belgrade: SKZ, 2011).
29  Djordjević, *Carinski rat*, 166–87.
30  Jovan Milićević, 'Javnost Beograda prema aneksiji Bosne i Hercegovine', in Vaša Čubrilović (ed.), *Jugoslovenski narodi pred Prvi svetski rat* (Belgrade: Naučno delo, 1967), 549–73.
31  Kazimirović, *Crna ruka*, 318–438.
32  Vojni Arhiv, Belgrade (Serbian Military Archives: hereafter VAB), P.2, k.50 f.3 d.21/1: telegram sent by the Serbian High Command to the Command of the Third Serbian Army, 19 April 1913.
33  Borivoje Nešković, *Istina o Solunskom procesu* (Belgrade: Narodna knjiga, 1953), 170.
34  Milić Milićević, *Reforma vojske Srbije 1897–1900* (Belgrade: Vojnoizdavački zavod 2002), 42, 137.
35  Ibid., 137.
36  Vasilij N. Strandman, *Balkanske uspomene*, I, 1–2 (Belgrade: Žagor, 2009), 77, 87.
37  Ibid., 94.
38  Drašković, *Pretorijanske težnje u Srbiji*, 146–7.
39  Mekenzi, *Apis*, 110.
40  VAB, P.2, k.13 f.1 d.4/14: Confidential report sent to the Serbian High Command in Skoplje from Belgrade, 8 November 1912.

41  VAB, P.2, k.13 f.1 d.4/45: Confidential report sent to the High Command from Šabac, 16 February 1913.
42  VAB, P.2, k.13 f.1 d.4/49: Report of Major Dimitrije Pavlović about the situation in Bosnia-Herzegovina, 20 April 1913.
43  *Mlada Bosna. Pisma i prilozi*, ed. Vojislav Bogićević (Sarajevo: Svjetlost, 1954), 306–7.
44  VAB, 8 November 1912, P.2, k.13 f.1 d.4/14: Report from the Valjevo garrison to the High Command, 19 November 1912.
45  VAB, P.2, k.13 f.1 d.4/44: Report of the *Narodna Odbrana* (Šabac section) sent to the High Command, 4 February 1913.
46  Nešković, *Istina o Solunskom procesu*, 169.
47  Ibid., 169–70.
48  Mile Bjelajac, *1914–2014. Zašto revizija? Stare i nove kontroverze o uzrocima Prvog svetskog rata* (Belgrade: Odbrana, 2014), 49–53, 56.
49  Mekenzi, *Apis*, 111.
50  Ibid.
51  Ibid.
52  Nešković, *Istina*, 126.
53  'Major Milan Vasić', *Pijemont*, 14 June 1914, 1. Vasić was the secretary of *Narodna Odbrana* from November 1911, and in 1912 he became responsible for coordinating activities of all irregular četnik units. In the First Balkan War he was responsible for providing logistics for these units; he was killed in the Second Balkan War as a battalion commander.
54  Milan Pribićević was an officer in the Austro-Hungarian army until 1904 when he resigned and emigrated to Serbia where he continued his military career. He kept up secret links with many Southern Slav intellectuals within the Habsburg Empire, and was also the brother of three Serbs prominent in Croatia: Svetozar, Adam and Valerijan Pribićević (see Chapter 11 by Mark Cornwall). Among other activities he wrote the document: 'What needs to be known about the Austro-Hungarian army'. See 'Milan Pribićević (1877–1937)', *Opštinske novine*, 55, I (1 January 1937): 169.
55  Strandman, *Balkanske uspomene*, 161.
56  Drašković, *Pretorijanske težnje u Srbiji*, 149; Čedomir Popović, 'Banjalučki proces. Narodna odbrana i bosanski nacionalni revolucionari', *Pravda*, 4 December 1933, 1.
57  Drašković, *Pretorijanske težnje u Srbiji*, 149.
58  Mekenzi, *Apis*, 111.
59  'Turski topovi', *Politika*, 19 April 1914, 2.
60  Dragoljub R. Živojinović, *Kralj Petar I Karađorđević. U otadžbini 1903–1914* (Belgrade: Zavod za udžbenike i nastavna sredstva, 2003), 514.
61  In his statement the king evoked Article 69 of the Serbian constitution which implied that this change was only temporary and caused by illness. However, as Dragoljub Živojinović has noted, all contemporaries understood this event

as the beginning of the reign of Aleksandar Karadjordjević: *Kralj Petar I Karađorđević*, 526–7.
62 Ibid., 521.
63 Vladimir Dedijer, *Sarajevo 1914* (Belgrade: Obradović, 2014), 380–401.
64 Predrag Palavestra, *Književnost Mlade Bosne* (Belgrade: Insitut za književnost i umetnost, 1994), 7–11; Miloš Vojinović, *Političke ideje Mlade Bosne* (Belgrade: Filip Višnjić, 2015).
65 Dedijer, *Sarajevo 1914*, 536.
66 MacMillan, *The War that Ended Peace*, 552; Clark, *The Sleepwalkers*, 56–7.
67 Dedijer, *Sarajevo 1914*, 564–6.
68 Cf. Max Hastings, *Catastrophe: 1914. Europe Goes to War* (London: William Collins, 2014), 28; MacMillan, *The War that Ended Peace*, 546.
69 Dedijer, *Sarajevo 1914*, 478–88.
70 Kosta Krajšumović, 'Sarajevski Vidovdan 1914. Princip i drugovi pred sudom', *Politika*, 29 June 1929, 4.
71 Milić Milićević, *Balkanski ratovi* (Belgrade: Zavod za udžbenike, 2014), 23–4.
72 Mekenzi, *Apis*, 143.
73 John Zametica, *Folly and Malice: The Habsburg Empire, the Balkans and the Start of World War One* (London: Shepheard-Walwyn, 2017), 395–405.
74 Dedijer, *Sarajevo 1914*, 490.
75 Bjelajac, *Zašto revizija*, 55.
76 Ibid., 60.
77 Ibid., 49–53; Mitrović, *Srbija u Prvom svetskom ratu*, 32–5.
78 About the 'political' agenda of the First World War centenary commemorations, see: Mira Radojević, Ljubodrag Dimić, *Srbija u Velikom ratu* (Belgrade: SKZ, Beogradski forum za svet ravnopravnih, 2014), 5–8.
79 See, for example, Clark, *The Sleepwalkers*, xxvi.
80 Krajšumović, 'Sarajevski Vidovdan 1914', 4.

## CHAPTER 8

# Why fight a Third Balkan War? The Habsburg mindset in 1914

*Lothar Höbelt*

It was Joachim Remak who in 1971 first wrote about the First World War as the Third Balkan War. The opening line of his article read: 'Fritz Fischer's decade has ended.'[1] That was perhaps a little premature or too optimistic. Attention for almost another half-century remained focused on Germany and German 'war guilt'. This was always strange from a Viennese perspective, but welcome as long as the blame-game continued in academic circles, for Austrians have often loved to indulge in 'self-infantilization' (*Selbstinfantilisierung*). They claimed to have been subjected in the final Habsburg years to a vassal status by Germany, something that would have been a surprise to German diplomats used to the tantrums or monologues of wartime Habsburg foreign ministers (Ottokar Czernin and István Burián respectively).[2] However, after 1968, German historians seemed to be happy to bid for every share of guilt that was available.

If we revert to the origins of the war guilt debate, it becomes a little clearer why the Balkan angle was soon forgotten, since assessing war guilt is a rather anachronistic approach. From Frederick the Great and Napoleon Bonaparte to Otto von Bismarck, all statesmen seemed to be proud of the way they had started wars at the right moment, let alone the sultans and emperors of old who claimed divine inspiration. Something of that carefree attitude continued into the twentieth century: Serbia complained about Austrian aggression in 1914 but had displayed no inhibitions when attacking Turkey in 1912. It was only after the disastrous impact of the Great War that the business of fighting wars ceased to command automatic respect. The American diplomat and historian George Kennan, who coined the term 'seminal catastrophe' for the First World War, was rightly struck by the 'the light-heartedness with which people [in the late nineteenth century] contemplated this prospect' of war, regarded 'solely as a possible instrument of national policy, advantageous or deleterious only insofar as it was successful or unsuccessful'. Kennan's dictum certainly applied to Austrian statesmen: 'It was not understood that the anguish of modern war could weaken even the ostensibly victorious society.'[3] This 'blind spot' was closely linked to the 'short war illusion', which in turn was based on an assumption that seemed to be amply supported by all the European evidence accumulated over the previous decades.[4] Emperor Franz Joseph regarded himself as a '*Pechvogel*' (unlucky person) because of his largely negative wartime experiences; but even the defeats he had suffered in the wars of 1859 or 1866 had been the results of extremely brief periods of fighting lasting little more than a few weeks.

The First World War, however, not only cost millions of casualties but turned the cosy and conservative *fin de siècle* world upside down. Nobody was really satisfied with its results. The Central Powers and Russia had lost the war; Italy talked about a *vittoria mutilata*; Britain had acquired a 'mandate' to lord it over a lot of troublesome deserts, but the City of London had lost its predominant position to Wall Street; the United States felt they had been tricked into hostilities; even France had regained Alsace-Lorraine but in the Russian alliance had lost the cornerstone of its former security arrangements. If anybody had reason to be fairly content for the time being, it was the Czechoslovak foreign minister Edvard Beneš or the Serbian Karadjordjević dynasty. Small wonder that people started questioning who or what was responsible for the catastrophe.

The war guilt debate also provides another insight into why there was no real enthusiasm about pinning the blame on Austria-Hungary (or on Russia). After all, the so-called war guilt clause had been inserted into the Versailles treaty not to please the muck-raking intellectuals, but to provide the legal foundations for reparations. 'The allies were not in fact demanding any admission of culpability, [but] the term stuck and turned a financial transaction into an emotive moral issue.'[5] French politicians could promise their voters with a certain air of plausibility: 'L'Allemagne payera tous.' They would have been laughed out of court if they had claimed: 'L'Autriche payera tous.' And the mood might have turned ugly if they had alluded to the huge sums France was forced to write off because of the Russian Revolution. In fact, one of the more intelligent compromise solutions advanced in 1917 was to let Germany conquer the East, in return for paying off the Russian debts to the Western powers.[6]

The Habsburgs did, in fact, start the Great War. But it is an exaggeration to discuss the Habsburgs in the plural. Austria-Hungary was a dynastic state, but it was not run as a family business. Emperor Franz Joseph was a notoriously lonely character who did not share secrets of state with his relatives. When the Germans, in early 1915, asked his Bavarian son-in-law to lobby Franz Joseph about his policy towards Italy, the prince admitted: 'I have known the Emperor for forty years but he has never spoken to me about politics.'[7] In fact, the heir apparent Franz Ferdinand as the inspector general of the armed forces had been the only archduke to muscle his way into the inner circle of decision makers. But during the July crisis of 1914, of course, Franz Ferdinand was no longer alive.[8] For once, constitutional form and practice were one and the same. Foreign policy issues were decided by the monarch and his foreign secretary, Count Leopold Berchtold. Formally, of course, the two prime ministers, of Hungary and what was not yet (until 1915) called 'Austria', also had the right to be consulted. But whereas Count István Tisza almost wielded a power of veto, no statesman from the Austrian half of the Monarchy could hope to rival Tisza's position. While Tisza relied on a majority of both houses of the Hungarian parliament, Austrian prime ministers were simply civil servants charged with managing the Vienna parliament. As it happened, Count Karl Stürgkh as prime minister did support the declaration of war in 1914, but he could not have prevented it even if he had wanted to. Berchtold in turn was influenced by a group of hawkish junior diplomats in the Ballhausplatz, but in the end it was he and the emperor who took the final decision.

Nationalism has often been blamed for the outbreak of the war. Yet those people in the Monarchy most intimately involved in the decision for war were all conservatives as far removed from the nationalist strand in politics as possible. Berchtold, for example, was the son of the founder of the Moravian Centre Party – a largely aristocratic grouping whose one guiding thought was to stay above the Czech-German fray in their homeland where they had successfully negotiated the Moravian Compromise in 1905. Berchtold once said that he wished conservative parties everywhere the widest possible measure of success; if in his homeland filial piety made him support the Centre Party, he did so in the belief that he was serving the conservative cause indirectly.[9] He often spoke French in his professional life, wrote his diary in German and towards the end of his life moved to Hungary (where his son was drafted into the army one war later). In 1939, when Nazi Germany's army occupied Moravia, the former foreign secretary when asked to put out the flags on Hitler's birthday did not object but dutifully hoisted in front of his castle all three flags, German, Czech and Hungarian.[10]

Count Alexander Hoyos, the diplomat who went to Berlin in July 1914 to collect the so-called blank cheque, was a Calvinist born into the cadet-branch of an Austro-Spanish family by a British mother. His pessimistic nature often let him think that he was indeed the little man who had started the Great War.[11] If anything, his family connections might look like a hostage to fortune to a Marxist interpretation of imperialism. His brother George was managing director of the family firm Whitehead (on his mother's side) that had long been pioneers of torpedo production. By 1914, however, the majority shareholders were British, and a war against Serbia or Russia was not particularly conducive to naval outlays. Yet in Austro-Hungarian terms, what Berchtold and Hoyos had in common was that they transcended the divide between the two 'halves of the empire', Austria and Hungary. While Berchtold held dual citizenship, Hoyos owned a castle in Upper Austria and his 'firm' happened to be based in Fiume (Rijeka) which was part of Hungary. A multinational empire could hardly ask for leaders that were further 'beyond nationalism', to paraphrase István Deák's book title about the Habsburg officer corps.

To lay another ghost to rest that occasionally raises its head, there is little evidence that Austria-Hungary went to war for reasons of domestic policy, 'to stop the rot' from spreading in its southern provinces.[12] The Monarchy had seen crises far worse around the turn of the century – for example, in 1897 the Badeni riots in Vienna, or in 1905–6 the deadlock after the victory at the polls of the Hungarian Independence Party. True, many Southern Slavs in 1912 had been very enthusiastic about the victories of the Balkan League. But in 1913, Slovenian leaders like Ivan Šušteršič actually asked Berchtold to support Bulgaria; and Leon Biliński – the common finance minister in overall charge of administering Bosnia – financed a pro-governmental party of Serbs run by Danilo Dimović that won a series of by-elections to the Bosnian Sabor.[13] A few diplomats who knew little of events on the ground might indulge in alarmist notions.[14] A few politicians might indulge in wishful thinking that a successful war would increase the prestige of the governing elite. (Indeed, it might be argued that Count Stürgkh had already profited from the Balkan crises domestically in 1912–13.) But there was no revolutionary situation, just as on the other hand there was no sign of fundamental devotion and loyalty to the empire. Political leaders in Bosnia, as elsewhere, simply hedged their bets, to be prepared for every possible outcome. Certainly high-school graduates with a philosophical turn of mind and suicidal notions were totally unrepresentative of Bosnia's largely rural and uneducated population.

## Lessons of the Balkan Wars

For the statesmen who actually started the war, the Balkan dimension was obviously crucial. In fact, the decision of Franz Joseph and Berchtold cannot be understood without reference to the two Balkan Wars. If the archduke had been assassinated in 1907 or 1908, it is very unlikely that the outrage would have resulted in a world war. The trouble was that in 1914 Austrians opted for war because they felt that they could no longer afford the kind of peace they had 'enjoyed' in 1912–13.[15] It was the frustrations of success, the emptiness of their diplomatic victories, combined with the escalating cost of the recurrent mobilizations that persuaded Berchtold and Franz

Joseph that next time had to be different. In the year between October 1912 and October 1913 Austria-Hungary had issued several ultimatums to her Balkan neighbours. On the face of it, they had achieved their purpose. As a result, Serbia and Montenegro had to be content with slightly less territory than they had originally occupied. In terms of power politics, those gains or losses were a *quantité negligeable*.

Austria-Hungary, however, had run up huge debts during that year. Indeed, already in 1912 Berchtold had quoted a speech by Sir Edward Grey when he told Count Mensdorff, his ambassador in London, how to explain his reaction to the British: 'Bleeding to death in peace time is worse than war.'[16] The Monarchy had strengthened its frontier defences as soon as war broke out in the Balkans; it had felt constrained to counter Russian troop concentrations in Poland; it had partly mobilized its army to force King Nikita of Montenegro to comply with the Great Powers' ultimatum over Scutari.[17] It did so once again in late 1913 to force Serbia to respect the Albanian frontiers. Altogether, those Balkan crises had cost the Austrians more than the whole dreadnought squadron they had ordered to impress the Italians.[18]

Yet it is wholly misleading to blame the military for the Austrian decision to go to war, or to label the Austro-Hungarian chief of staff, Franz Conrad von Hötzendorf, the 'architect of the apocalypse'.[19] Conrad had unsuccessfully argued for war no less than twenty-four times over the previous years.[20] Why should the politicians or the emperor suddenly listen to him when he did so once more? Franz Joseph was not amused when his advisers spoke out of turn. What was different from the earlier crises in 1912–13 was not the input of the military, but the advice tendered by financial experts who mused that paradoxically it might even be easier to finance a full-blown war because in that case they could do away with orthodox finance, abolish the Bank Act and start printing money.[21]

Austria-Hungary therefore faced a dilemma familiar to many a great power. The Monarchy found it difficult to counter Serbian moves on a tit-for-tat basis. Serbia had practically bankrupted itself in the Balkan Wars, but at least doubled its territory (and the French were willing to bail out Belgrade). Austria-Hungary had almost bankrupted itself for the sake of an independent Albanian state that threatened to fall apart as soon as the first sign of trouble appeared on the horizon (and nobody was willing to bail out the Austrians). Of course, Serbia in itself was not a real threat to the Monarchy. But to contain Serbia threatened to claim a disproportionate share of Austro-Hungarian resources, thus severely limiting its ability to stand up to a confrontation with any other great power – for example, Russia.

As a result in October 1913, Franz Joseph, never eager for war, arrived at a new conclusion: next time the Monarchy would either have to stand aloof from Balkan squabbles or become fully involved. 'He hardly thought it was possible to have a third mobilization and remain inactive.'[22] Or, as

David Stevenson has aptly put it, 'The middle road of armed diplomacy was reaching a dead end.'[23] Another crisis over a few mountain hamlets in Albania or Macedonia might have provoked the first reaction of ignoring Serbia; but the murder of the heir apparent simply seemed a provocation that was too blatant for Vienna to turn the other cheek. Bureaucracies usually follow precedents and rely on 'business as usual'. But by 1914 that was the one option that had been ruled out from the start. The Habsburg elite did not look forward to another crisis; they were not looking for a suitable pretext to fight a war, but if another crisis arose, they would fight rather than go through the motions of all the pointless 1912–13 manoeuvres again. Austria-Hungary would make war because it believed it could no longer afford an armed and uncertain peace. It would fight a Third Balkan War because the other options had apparently been exhausted.[24]

## The failure of Habsburg strategy in the Balkans

If the Habsburg elite had been so eager for war, they should certainly have fought earlier. Why did they fail to do that? The answer to that question sheds some light on their willingness to do so in 1914. In 1914, they were wrong when they thought the war was going to be short; in 1912, they were wrong when they thought the Balkan War against the Ottoman Empire was going to be a long one. They would play a game of wait and see, or as Franz Ferdinand put it, they would watch from the front row as those bastards tore each other to pieces.[25] As it turned out, in 1912 the show was over in no time at all, and even worse, the wrong people had been massacred.

The Monarchy had clearly wanted the Ottomans to win, or at least fight the others to a draw. Yet, they reacted apprehensively when rumours started to arrive that Turkey had asked the Romanians to join her in fighting the Balkan League (and Bulgaria, in particular).[26] Romania, after all, was an ally of the Central Powers, even if not a very reliable one. Romania did not want to go it alone in support of Turkey. The Austro-Hungarian minister in Bucharest reported that the Romanians were expecting a *'mot d'ordre'* from Vienna.[27] With hindsight, Austria should have rejoiced at such an Ottoman-Romanian combination confronting the unruly Balkan League. However, Vienna did what it could to stop the Romanians from making a move. This perfect example of 'restraining alliances' led to both King Carol and Romanian prime minister Ion Brătianu angrily telling the Austrians later that they had missed the bus: they should have fought a war in 1912; now they could no longer rely on Romanian cooperation.[28]

The lightning victory of the Balkan League in 1912 changed Vienna's slogans from 'no change without the consent of the Great Powers' to 'the Balkans for the Balkan nations'. After all, Serbs only made up a tiny share of the population of Turkey in Europe. Once ethnic criteria were used to allot territory, Serbia could expect only minimal gains from the Balkan Wars as there were few Serbs living in the Turkish territory that was to be partitioned. In turn, for Austria, it was crucial to create an independent Albanian state. An independent Albania would not only serve to cut off Serbia from an outlet on the Adriatic Sea. By directing Serbian expansion to the south-east rather than south-west, it would also set Serbia on a collision course with Bulgaria. In May 1913, Berchtold was feted when King Nikita of Montenegro finally gave way over the town of Scutari which the Great Powers had allotted to Albania. But the real action happened behind the scenes, in the tug of war between Austria-Hungary, Romania and Bulgaria.

Here Berchtold encouraged the Bulgarians to be insistent over Salonika and Macedonia. For a few days, just before and after the start of the Second Balkan War, he was even willing to assist them militarily if necessary. He first hinted at the possibility of Austrian military support on 24 June 1913, but the Bulgarians wanted to have that promise in writing. Berchtold's offer, however, was conditional on Bulgaria bribing Romania into neutrality.[29] This brief interlude of Austrian war-like intentions in mid-1913 has usually been ignored by historians. It shows Berchtold in a very different frame of mind from October 1912 when he abhorred any idea of being dragged into a Balkan war. Admittedly, what Berchtold was offering the Bulgarians in June 1913 was a sort of contingency guarantee only. If Bulgaria was willing to buy off and pacify Austria's ally Romania, he was willing to underwrite their war against Serbia; in other words, he promised to rush to their defence if anything untoward happened. The beauty of that arrangement was that if Romania stayed neutral, Bulgaria was supposed to be able to defeat Serbia single-handedly. Or as the Russians warned the Serbian prime minister Nikola Pašić, the Bulgarians would simply destroy Serbia.[30] Thus, it seemed unlikely that Austria-Hungary would actually have to honour its guarantee to ensure the desired outcome.

It is well known that Bulgaria did not see fit to bribe the Romanians into neutrality. Berchtold himself realized far too late that Romanian appetites would not be sated by securing the fortress of Silistria alone.[31] But nor had Bulgaria taken his last-minute warnings all that seriously. Apparently, the Bulgarians assumed that Austria-Hungary would simply have to side with them whatever happened. That at least was the view taken by their king (or tsar), 'Foxy Ferdinand', who admitted that he had given the order to attack the Serbs, but added furiously: 'On m'a trompé. ... Comment est-ce que possible que Vienne ne saisit pas cette occasion pour en finir avec les Serbes?'[32] On 3 July, Berchtold had still noted in his diary that in case of Great Serbian victories, Austrian intervention was inevitable. But when he sent a telegram to Berlin the next day, he had abandoned the idea; he only used the threat of Austrian intervention – and the danger of an escalation – to persuade the Germans to put pressure on the Romanians to deter them from entering the war.[33]

Characteristically, Ferdinand blamed Kaiser Wilhelm for Austrian inactivity. Franz Ferdinand would have been closer to the mark. The heir apparent detested the Bulgarian tsar and warned Berchtold that he would not countenance any action in favour of Bulgaria. Even within his own department, Berchtold faced opposition from the men on the spot: predictably so from Prince Karl Fürstenberg, the Austrian minister in Bucharest, who complained that the empire's pro-Bulgarian policy was bound to antagonize the Romanians; but also from Count Adam Tarnowski, the Polish grandee who represented the Monarchy in Sofia. Tarnowski held that Austria-Hungary should not encourage Bulgarian visions of grandeur; after all, Bulgaria was still run by a Russophile government. Therefore Austria should welcome Bulgaria's difficulties and only intervene at the last possible moment – the way it had saved Serbia in 1885.[34] To make matters worse, not even the proverbially hawkish Conrad saw eye to eye with Berchtold on the Bulgarian issue in 1913. The very week Berchtold was considering joining Bulgaria, Conrad drafted a memorandum suggesting Austria-Hungary should actually offer to support Serbia, in return for an alliance and a customs union, perhaps turning Serbia into a satellite state with a position similar to that of Bavaria within Germany.[35]

Thus, on 4 July 1913, after his talk with Franz Ferdinand, and faced with Bulgarian intransigence vis-à-vis Romania, Berchtold sadly concluded: 'Quos Deus perdere vult' ('Those whom God wishes to destroy will be afflicted with blindness'). This episode had been important as it closed an alternative to war against Serbia – in other words, to have someone else pull the chestnuts out of the fire for them. It also raises an interesting hypothetical question. With a Russophile government in Sofia, would Russia really have objected to an Austrian move in Bulgaria's favour? As it happened, of course, the Second Balkan War produced the worst possible result for the Habsburg Monarchy. Serbia had won, and Austria had antagonized Romania without winning over Bulgaria. Austria-Hungary continued to try and persuade Germany of the merits of a Bulgarian alliance. But after the experiences of the Second Balkan War, Bulgarians would rightly be weary of trusting Austrian promises. Next time around the Austrians would have to do the dirty work themselves.

## The location of a Third Balkan War

The result of the Second Balkan War goes some way towards answering a puzzling question. Why did a Great Power like Austria-Hungary, even if it counted as the least of the Great Powers after Italy, feel threatened by a midget like Serbia which might be an irritant but could certainly not aspire to be a serious rival?[36] After all, even after its recent acquisitions, Serbia was barely a tenth the size of the Habsburg Monarchy, with less than five million inhabitants facing more than fifty million. These statistics point to a certain degree of paranoia in Vienna's ruling circles. However, there are some mitigating factors to be taken into account. To start with, in military terms, Serbia 'punched above its weight', and to some extent, it might be said that Serbia reaped the benefits of backwardness. Serbia drafted every able-bodied young man into the army and, in case of war, did not have to make an allowance for industrial infrastructure requirements. Thus, Belgrade boasted a peace-time army of 22 regiments and 100,000 men (as opposed to Austria-Hungary's 100 regiments and 440,000 soldiers), and a wartime strength of roughly 11 divisions (versus about 50 under the Habsburg colours). So with less than 10 per cent of the population of Austria-Hungary, Serbia's armies equalled more than 20 per cent of the Austro-Hungarian forces.[37]

For the Habsburg elite, however, the real nightmare was that Serbia would not be on its own, but would act as the spearhead of a new League of aggressive Balkan states.[38] German debates about pre-war alliances often referred to the 'encirclement' of Germany that simply happened to be placed between France and Russia. Geopolitically minded authors in Austria-Hungary, too, liked to complain about the empire's 'long, dry borders'. However, when they used the term 'encirclement' in early 1914, Austrian diplomats were not referring to their own plight but to the pressures facing Bulgaria.[39] True, Tarnowski had always held that a Bulgaria nursing its grievances might be the ideal partner for Austria-Hungary. His colleagues, above all Count Ottokar Czernin, the newly appointed Habsburg minister to Bucharest, saw things in a very different and much less optimistic light. Surrounded by potential enemies, Bulgaria might have to take the easy way out and might be reconciled with its recent foes. Thus, in case of conflict, Austria-Hungary might have to face the bleak perspective of a united and hostile South-Eastern Europe.

Alternatively, the Third Balkan War might start elsewhere. Even after the Treaty of Bucharest had ended the Second Balkan War in August 1913, there was still some unfinished business left over from the first war concerning the fate of the Aegean islands. The war that many people expected to erupt sometime during 1914 was not an Austro-Serbian war, but a naval duel between the Ottoman Empire and Greece, as soon as one of them secured the dreadnoughts they had ordered abroad. Britain's position in such a conflict was an ambivalent one, to say the least. Turkey counted as a potential German ally, but the Turks had ordered their battleships in Britain. In Germany, the Kaiser, who actually spent part of spring 1914 in Corfu, was equally facing a dilemma between his brother-in-law, King Constantine of Greece and his Oriental dreams. Of all the European powers, it was Austria-Hungary that could easily afford to regard an Aegean confrontation as a spectator sport; indeed, some in Vienna were quite keen on the prospect.[40]

Once again, Berlin and Vienna did not see eye to eye as far as Balkan affairs were concerned. Berchtold wrung his hands in horror over German attempts to mediate in the Aegean dispute. Doing so, he argued, Berlin would unwittingly be working in the best interests of France and Russia, as any Aegean détente could only be a first step towards the encirclement of Bulgaria. Unfortunately, the Germans did not seem to realize 'the fateful repercussions' (*verhängnisvolle Tragweite*) of their policy.[41] Even the rapprochement between Bulgaria and Romania that Berchtold had prayed for in 1913 no longer seemed an unmixed blessing; the only Balkan alliance Berchtold wholeheartedly approved of would be the one between Bulgaria and Turkey. However, the Ottoman Empire, too, seemed to be hedging its bets, with Talaat Pasha visiting the Russian Tsar in Livadia. The Turks, of course, were playing for time – they wanted to wait until the delivery of both their dreadnoughts gave them naval superiority.[42]

The timing of Archduke Franz Ferdinand's visit to Sarajevo on 28 June or Vidovdan, the anniversary of the Battle of Kosovo Polje in 1389, has often been regarded as a provocation. However, *Mlada Bosna* does not seem to have been overly concerned with the symbolism of the date. With hindsight, it seems Gavrilo Princip and his colleagues were willing to strike at any senior Habsburg official who might appear at any time. If anything, the timing of Franz Ferdinand's visit was significant in a different way. The two battleships for the Turkish navy were almost on their way when the July crisis struck and prompted the British Admiralty to sequester them for their own purposes.[43] Their arrival in the Aegean might have acted as a catalyst. Thus, if the Bosnian manoeuvres, like the Bohemian ones the year before, had been scheduled in the autumn, a Third Balkan War might have broken out somewhere else in the meantime.

## Conclusion

In 1912 the Habsburg elite had shied away from playing the Romanian card, and in 1913 they had flirted with the Bulgarian option but had hedged their bets. In 1914 there was no trump card up their sleeve – they either had to raise their bid or abandon the game. Franz Joseph and Berchtold might have ignored a third Albanian crisis, but the assassination of the heir apparent was a bid they were bound to double. The Habsburg Monarchy certainly suffered from Great Power arrogance. In the opinion of the decision makers in Vienna, Serbia should simply behave like a child that knew its place and not interfere in the games of the Big Five. Switzerland would be ideal as a role model, or maybe even Sweden that had sensibly learnt to live with the loss of Finland.

The trouble was that Austria-Hungary was the main loser when the Concert of Europe, established by the Congress of Vienna in 1815, began to lose control of international events. With respect to Serbia, Vienna unfortunately was in a fairly unique position. Other members of the European Concert might have colonial troubles to handle, but none had to deal with headaches caused by such a troublesome small neighbour. And perhaps even worse, Austria-Hungary was actually not arrogant enough: Franz Ferdinand himself had warned Berchtold that the Monarchy must not itself behave like a Balkan state.[44] But in fact Austria-Hungary was a Balkan state, its Great Power position at least partly dependent on its position in the Balkans, even if its war aims later on oscillated between Poland and *Mitteleuropa*.[45]

If Germany did exert some influence on Vienna's decision for war, it did so indirectly. In 1912–13 Berlin had made it clear that they were not going to fight for the sake of places that their voters could not even find on a map. That was precisely why the German chief of staff Helmuth von Moltke had objected when his Italian colleague Alberto Pollio had argued for a preventive war in 1914.[46] Given the state of public opinion in Germany, Moltke thought, one simply could not start a war like that: a persuasive reason for war was required. In 1914, the murder of the heir apparent had all the makings of such a persuasive reason. Hoyos's mission to Berlin to collect the famous 'blank cheque' was little more than a courtesy call. Once again, to the annoyance of their allies, the Austrians played their cards close to the chest. They needed no prompting from Berlin to take the key decisions for war in the Balkans.

In July 1914 it was not the discordant voices issuing from Berlin, but the earlier German track record of reneging on the Kaiser's promises of unconditional support that made the Austrians overly keen to use this window of opportunity so that the Germans could not backtrack again. Berlin might try to dissuade Vienna from rattling the German sabre too much, but in the end, the Kaiser simply could not afford to see Austria-Hungary destroyed. Indeed, after their disagreements in the Balkan Wars, Berlin 'felt increasingly conscious of the need to rebuild Austrian confidence in Germany'.[47] Thus, in 1914 there was little the Germans could have done, once Austria-Hungary was determined to go to war rather than repeat the costly military exercises of yesteryear. That was the leverage of the weak at its most potent.[48]

## Notes

1  Joachim Remak, 'The Third Balkan War: Origins Reconsidered', *Journal of Modern History* 43 (1971): 353–66.

2  Medievalists, of course, might disagree about the opprobrium of the term: after all, Burgundy was a vassal of France. However, Franz Joseph himself had once quipped, 'After all, I am a vassal of the Sultan'. See Ludwig Bittner and Hans Übersberger (eds), *Österreich-Ungarns Aussenpolitik von der bosnischen Krise 1908 bis zum Kriegsausbruch 1914. Diplomatische Aktenstücke des österreichisch-ungarischen Ministeriums des Äussern* (hereafter ÖUA), 8 vols (Vienna: Österreichischer Bundesverlag, 1930), VIII, 133.

3   George F. Kennan, *The Decline of Bismarck's European Order: Franco-Russian Relations, 1875-1890* (Princeton: Princeton University Press, 1979), 3, 423.

4   Admittedly, colonial wars or civil wars (from the United States to China's Taiping rebellion) usually lasted much longer.

5   Alexander Watson, *Ring of Steel: Germany and Austria-Hungary at War, 1914-1918* (London: Allen Lane, 2014), 563.

6   Wolfgang Steglich (ed.), *Die Friedensversuche der kriegführenden Mächte im Sommer und Herbst 1917. Quellenkritische Untersuchungen, Akten und Vernehmungsprotokolle* (Stuttgart: Franz Steiner, 1984), 287, 326.

7   Haus-, Hof- und Staatsarchiv Vienna (hereafter HHStA), Berchtold papers, karton 5, diary entry for 14 January 1915.

8   In fact, this is why it has been argued that the important thing about Sarajevo was that Franz Ferdinand was eliminated, not that he was assassinated. See Robert A. Kann, 'Archduke Franz Ferdinand and Count Berchtold during his Term as Foreign Minister, 1912-14', in Stanley B. Winters (ed.), *Dynasty, Politics and Culture. Selected Essays by Robert A. Kann* (Boulder, CO: Columbia University Press, 1991), 148.

9   'Ich begleite die conservativen Parteien aller Länder mit wärmstem Interesse und wünsche ihren Bestrebungen überall den weitgehendsten Erfolg. Wenn ich in Mähren diesmal meine molekülenhafte Unterstützung der vom armen Papa ins Leben gerufenen Mittelpartei weihe, so geschieht es auch nur in der Absicht, der conservativen Sache dadurch indirekt einen Dienst zu erweisen.' (Moravian Provincial Archive, Brno, G 77: Serenyi papers, karton 73, No. 276, 6 December 1901).

10  HHStA, Berchtold diary, entry for 20 April 1939. Hugo Hantsch, in *Leopold Graf Berchtold. Grandseigneur und Staatsmann*, 2 vols (Graz: Verlag Styria, 1963), made extensive use of these diaries. In fact, the pre-war diaries are the result of a 1930s compilation, with many references to published documents. They do, however, rely on an earlier version of notebooks, and provide hints to a number of conversations and meetings not covered elsewhere.

11  Berchtold once commented: 'Alex Hoyos sieht stereotyp schwarz in die Zukunft' (HHStA, diary entry for 13 January 1923).

12  On the question of unspoken assumptions, however, see Mark Cornwall, 'The Habsburg Elite and the Southern Slav Question 1914-1918', in Lothar Höbelt and T. G. Otte (eds), *A Living Anachonism? European Diplomacy and the Habsburg Monarchy. Festschrift für Francis Roy Bridge zum 70. Geburtstag* (Vienna: Böhalu, 2010), 242–5.

13  HHStA, Berchtold diary, entries for 27 July and 8 August 1913. See also Martha Cupic-Amrein, *Die Opposition gegen die österreichisch-ungarische Herrschaft in Bosnien-Herzegovina (1878-1914)* (Bern: Peter Lang, 1987); Robin Okey, *Taming Balkan Nationalism: The Habsburg 'Civilizing Mission' in Bosnia, 1878-1914* (Oxford: Oxford University Press, 2007), 227–9.

14  Authors with little grounding in Habsburg minutiae might be misled by such utterings – for example, Marie-Janine Calic, *Geschichte Jugoslawiens im 20. Jahrhundert* (Munich: C.H. Beck, 2010), 68ff.

15 Lothar Höbelt, 'Austria-Hungary and the Balkan Wars, 1912-13', in Jean-Paul Bled and Jean-Pierre Deschodt (eds), *Les guerres balcaniques 1912-1913* (Paris: Presses universitaires de Paris-Sorbonne, 2014), 131–44.
16 ÖUA, V, 131 (15 December 1912).
17 There are persuasive hints that Nikita combined his military retreat from Scutari with a successful stock-exchange operation. Once he accepted the Austrian ultimatum, with the danger of war receding, share prices would predictably rise – and he was the only person who knew exactly when that would happen; HHStA, Baernreither papers, karton 5, diaries, XI, fol. 88. See Elizabeth Roberts, *Realm of the Black Mountain: A History of Montenegro* (London: Hurst, 2007).
18 Wilhelm Deutschmann, *Die militärischen Maßnahmen in Österreich-Ungarn während der Balkankrieg 1912/13* (PhD diss., Vienna, 1965). However, as Samuel R. Williamson Jr. has pointed out, 'the troop totals remain hard to compute': *Austria-Hungary and the Origins of the First World War* (New York: St Martin's Press, 1991), 238.
19 The title of Lawrence Sondhaus's biography of Conrad: *Franz Conrad von Hötzendorf: Architect of the Apocalypse* (Boston: Humanities Press, 2000). For the role of the military, see the magisterial study by Günther Kronenbitter, *'Krieg im Frieden': Die Führung der k.u.k. Armee und die Großmachtpolitik Österreich-Ungarns 1906-1914* (Munich: Oldenbourg 2003).
20 Jean-Paul Bled, *L'agonie d'une Monarchie. Autriche-Hongrie 1914-1920* (Paris: Tallandier 2014), 33.
21 Anatol Schmied-Kowarzik (ed.), *Die Protokolle des gemeinsamen Ministerrates der österreichisch-ungarischen Monarchie, Vol. VI: 1908-1914* (Budapest: Akadémiai Kiadó, 2011), 586–8: meeting of 2 May 1913.
22 József Galántai, *Die Österreichisch-Ungarische Monarchie und der Weltkrieg* (Budapest: Corvina Kiadó, 1979), 179: quotation based on Burián's diary and his letters to Tisza. For an English version, see József Galántai, 'Austria-Hungary and the War – The October 1913 Crisis, Prelude to July 1914', *Etudes historiques hongroises* 2 (1980): 84.
23 David Stevenson, *Armaments and the Coming of War: Europe, 1904–1914* (Oxford: Clarendon Press, 1996), 275.
24 For the decreasing options, see F. R. Bridge, *The Habsburg Monarchy Among the Great Powers, 1815-1918* (New York: Oxford University Press, 1991), 319–44.
25 Alma Hannig, 'Wir schauen in der Loge zu', *Etudes danubiennes* 27 (2011): 51–66.
26 ÖUA, IV, 638ff (14 October 1912).
27 ÖUA, IV, 744 (1 November 1912).
28 ÖUA, IV, 1003 (King Carol: 25 November 1912); V, 723 (Brătianu, 14 February 1913).
29 ÖUA, VI, 721 (24 June 1913), 730 (28 June), 789 (2 July).
30 Richard C. Hall, *The Balkan Wars 1912-13: Prelude to the First World War* (London: Routledge, 2002), 103.

31 The inadequacy of the Bulgarian concessions seems to have dawned on Berchtold between 25 and 28 May; ÖUA, VI, 521, 544.
32 ÖUA, VI, 944: 18 July 1913.
33 HHStA, Berchtold diary, entry for 3 July 1913; ÖUA, VI, 802.
34 ÖUA, VI, 508 (23 May 1913), 563 (29 May), 578 (1 June).
35 HHStA, Berchtold papers, karton 4, letter from Conrad, 2 July 1913.
36 A point rightly emphasized by Vojislav Pavlović during the Belgrade Conference on the First World War in the spring of 2014.
37 ÖUA, VIII, 97, 158.
38 Montenegro, of course, the proverbial only friend of Russia, could always be expected to join Serbia, not through the Petrović dynasty's love for the Karadjordjević, but precisely because of the rivalry of the two dynastic houses. See Mark Cornwall, 'Between Two Wars: King Nikola of Montenegro and the Great Powers, August 1913 – August 1914', *The South Slav Journal* 9/1-2 (1986): 59–75.
39 ÖUA, VIII, 5 (2 May 1914); 189 (as part of the so-called Matscheko Memorandum: see Bridge, *The Habsburg Monarchy*, 334–5).
40 ÖUA, VIII, 5 (2 May 1914).
41 ÖUA, VIII, 38 (14 May 1914); Kronenbitter,*'Krieg im Frieden'*, 442ff.
42 ÖUA, VIII, 88 (27 May 1914).
43 Mustafa Aksafal, *The Ottoman Road to War in 1914* (Cambridge: Cambridge University Press 2008), 107–11.
44 HHStA, Berchtold papers, karton 4, 4 July 1913 (the letter in which Franz Ferdinand vetoed an intervention in favour of Bulgaria).
45 Lothar Höbelt, 'The Austro-Polish Solution: Mitteleuropa's Siamese Twin', in Jean-Paul Bled and Jean-Pierre Deschodt (eds), *Le crise de Juillet 1914 et l'Europe* (Paris: Editions SPM 2016), 125–36.
46 Kronenbitter, *'Krieg im Frieden'*, 454.
47 R. J. Crampton, *The Hollow Détente: Anglo-German Relations in the Balkans, 1911-1914* (London: Prior 1979), 111.
48 Hoyos had already suggested a similar approach in 1912 when he prepared notes for Franz Ferdinand's trip to Berlin; see Konrad Canis, *Der Weg in den Abgrund. Deutsche Außenpolitik 1902-1914* (Paderborn: Schöningh 2011), 497.

# CHAPTER 9

## 'Six powers appalled by war'

## The July crisis and the limits of crisis management

### T. G. Otte

The year 1918 was a momentous one in the history of the Habsburg Monarchy, as it was for Europe as a whole. After four years of dedicated domestic reforms, concerted military modernization and decided diplomatic manoeuvres, Austria-Hungary was well positioned to meet Russia's challenge in early 1918. St Petersburg's impertinent ultimatum of 1 March, demanding in irreconcilable language the release of pro-Russian *agents provocateurs* in Ruthenia, was rejected out of hand. Diplomatic relations were severed, and on 3 March, the Tsar declared war.

Without the Ballhausplatz's shrewd policy since the Second Balkan War, the conflict that now unfolded might well have escalated into a world war. That it did not owed much to the fortuitous combination of prudent provisions made by Vienna and wider international developments. The Habsburgs' determined courting of Albania, Bulgaria, Romania and Turkey ensured that they were on side, and by reaching out in good time to Sweden, Norway and Japan, the Austro-Russian struggle was contained. With France, Russia's ally, kept in check by Germany and Italy, and with Britain weakened by turmoil in Egypt and India, the war remained confined principally to Eastern Europe.

Operations began with a lightning strike by an Austro-Hungarian flotilla against Sebastopol, crippling the Russian Black Sea fleet. On land, the swift and seamless mobilization of Habsburg forces was followed by their thrust, aided by the Romanian ally, into Bessarabia and Ukraine. The first major encounter, the eight-day battle of Berdichev, which commenced on 1 April, compelled the Russian commander-in-chief, the Grand Duke Nikolai Nikola'evich, to pull his forces back to the fortified Dniepr line. On 30 April, the advancing Austro-Romanian armies, commanded by Archduke Franz Ferdinand, clashed with the enemy on a 265-kilometre-wide front around Kiev. Nine days later, after sustained shelling by the Austrian army's famed 'Kaiser-batteries', the Russian lines were breached. This was the decisive moment in the Austro-Russian war of 1918. Russian troops were in full flight. Kiev, Cherkasy and Kremenchuk were occupied in quick succession. Further south, Russia's Odessa army relinquished its positions along the Bug and withdrew to Ekaterinoslav. There, another gigantic nine-day battle ensued, which caused both sides significant losses of men, ending with a Russian retreat along the line Kharkov-Kursk-Moscow. After a lull in fighting, Allied forces concentrated around Kharkov to resume their advance on Moscow in early July.

The Tsar's government was in an invidious position. Military operations in the central theatre of war were on the verge of collapse; the campaigns in the Caucasus and Scandinavia had ground to a halt; in the Western Balkans, Bulgaria and Albania made short work of Serbia and Montenegro, Russia's regional proxies; and in East Asia, Japan, keen to exploit Russia's weakness, had landed a sizeable force to besiege Vladivostok. As Russian troops flooded back, civil unrest erupted in many parts of the empire, and the Tsar was in danger of losing control of the situation. There was nothing for it but to end hostilities, and on Vienna's terms.

On 19 July, the armistice came into effect. Four days later, the second Congress of Vienna gathered. The subsequent peace treaty of 6 August terminated the monumental struggle between the Habsburg and Romanov empires and their allies. Under its terms Russia lost Poland and Ukraine to Austria-Hungary, Bessarabia to Romania and the Southern Caucasus to Turkey, while Montenegro and Serbia had to cede territory to Albania, Bulgaria and the Monarchy. Finland and the Baltic provinces were established as two independent states. The Russians had to pay an indemnity of eleven billion crowns and enter into permanent commercial treaties with their erstwhile enemies, but received some compensation with the creation of two treaty ports with neutral zones around them, modelled on the arrangements at Tangier, at Rodosto (Tekirdağ) in the Sea of Marmora, and Newchwang at the mouth of the Liao-ho River in Manchuria.

The 1918 peace treaty thus helped to stabilize the European international system. France and Russia, now in the second flight of international politics, had to yield to an informal grouping of status quo powers – Austria-Hungary, Germany and Italy – joined by Great Britain, herself now relieved of the Russian incubus in Asia. As for the Monarchy, the war brought about a fundamental transformation. It was finally reconstituted as *Gross-Habsburg*, a federal Monarchy of six states (Austria, Hungary, Poland, the Ukraine,

Croatia and Bosnia-Herzegovina), each enjoying a liberal degree of autonomy but all joined in the *Reichskongress* which legislated on imperial matters.

Gentle readers who have persevered thus far may rest assured that this is not a self-indulgent 'counter-factual' fantasy. Rather, it is a summary of a pamphlet of some fifty-odd pages, published in March 1914 under the pseudonym of 'Octavius' but clearly originating from within Archduke Franz Ferdinand's entourage.[1] Although illustrative of the thinking in Belvedere circles, its wider significance lies in the fact that it indicates growing anticipation about an impending shift in Great Power politics. The assumption that Europe was on the cusp of major change was not confined to Vienna, but had gained a hold on the chancelleries of all the Great Powers. It reflected the resurgence of Russian power. Russia's rise from the nadir of 1904–5 was swifter and more sustained than had been thought possible. Now, in 1914, it held out the prospect of a major shift in the geopolitical landscape.[2] This established the parameters of international diplomacy during Europe's last summer.

## Crisis in international politics

Before these limits are considered, some preliminary observations on the nature of international crises are necessary. In the first place, historians and scholars of international politics are prone to regard crises as aberrations, abnormalities or accidents, as though the natural condition of international relations was static. This fails to capture their altogether more fluid character. Just as the peaks and troughs of 'boom and bust' are immanent in economic life, so crises form an inherent part of international politics. They have considerable heuristic value for the purposes of historical analysis in that they can help to illuminate the vital essence of international politics.[3]

All of this has implications for the study of the July crisis of 1914. Crises mark moments at which the Great Powers readjust their relations. Their origins and the manner in which they are settled reveal much about the wider international constellation and the relative position of individual powers. At the core of crisis diplomacy in the long nineteenth century was a delicate balance between two contrasting objectives. In general, governments sought to settle matters by means short of war – wars were the aberration not crises. But they were more likely to succeed in their diplomatic manoeuvres if they were able to signal readiness to accept the risk of escalation. The more credibly they conveyed that willingness, the more likely they were to obtain a competitive advantage. The threat of conflict, implicit or explicit, then, was central to contemporary crisis management strategies, and their parameters were set by the tension between these two divergent objectives.

The skewed understanding of the nature of international crises in the long nineteenth century (and perhaps beyond) has had significant ramifications for the scholarly debate about July 1914 in particular. For it has helped to entrench a habit of viewing Europe's last summer through the prism of a concatenation of crises. In this reading of events, each of these left unexploded ordnance in its path – enough, ultimately, to shatter the peace of Europe. Underpinning such interpretations is a barely articulated quasi-teleology that Europe was somehow destined to descend into world war, and that the various international crises before 1914 were little more than a dress rehearsal for Europe's final showdown. This is problematic: historians ought not to lose sight of the openness of all historical situations, and of the specific context of each of the pre-war crises.

It is more productive to examine how and why the events of the summer of 1914 after the murder of Franz Ferdinand differed from previous crises.

## Calculations and risks in the July crisis

While the resurgence of Russia cast a shadow over all the chancelleries of Europe, each of the powers operated on the basis of calculations and perceptions that were specific to it. Of all of them, Austria-Hungary alone was intent on war after Sarajevo. Among the diplomats at the Ballhausplatz who were on duty on 28 June, there was not one 'who did not have the gut reaction ... – the fateful day for the Monarchy has arrived'.[4] The Sarajevo murders were no ordinary act of political violence; there could be no 'business as usual' in their aftermath. The violent death of the heir to the throne was a welcome pretext for eradicating the Serbian peril by force. It was imperative 'to seize the first advantageous opportunity for a destructive strike against the kingdom [Serbia]'.[5] This was the overriding consideration. As the chief of staff, Franz Baron Conrad von Hötzendorf, suggested on 1 July, 'If you have a poisonous adder at your heel, you stamp on its head, and you do not wait for the lethal bite.'[6] And the Habsburg foreign minister, Count Leopold Berchtold, did not wish it to be said of him, 'as of Aehrenthal, that I missed the right moment to wage war'.[7] The fear that the growth of Serb nationalism, if unchecked, would accelerate the centrifugal forces within the empire was a powerful stimulant. But there was also a sense that international mediation during the previous Balkan disturbances – the London ambassadorial conference 'of ghastly memory', as the usually dovish finance minister, Leon Ritter von Biliński, put it – had done little to safeguard the Monarchy's vital interests.[8]

Austro-Hungarian policy suffered by this time from an acute form of 'tunnel vision'. It had atrophied to a form of *Balkanpolitik*. The Monarchy no longer thought and acted like a European Great Power, but rather like a greater regional power where 'settling with Serbia' trumped all other considerations. But there was also a certain blasé belligerence about decision making at Vienna: 'If it goes badly, we will lose Bosnia and a piece of Eastern Galicia!' Count Alexander Hoyos was reported to have said.[9] Yet decision making at Vienna was not devoid of intelligence. It was shaped by a combination of diplomatic, strategic and domestic considerations. The experiences of 1912–13 suggested that Belgrade would yield in the face of a determined Austria-Hungary. Perceptions of Russia reinforced assumptions that a third such encounter would follow the same pattern. That country's latent potential was apparent, but so were its financial and domestic weaknesses.[10] For the foreseeable future, the Austrian ambassador, Count Friedrich Szápáry, prognosticated, St Petersburg would regard 'the internal economic and national strengthening of the [Russian] empire as its most immediate task'.[11]

There was, moreover, a strong sense that a more assertive Austrian policy in the Balkans would serve to counteract Russian schemes in the region, so keeping Bucharest in the Habsburg orbit and coaxing Sofia back into it.[12] In the early summer of 1914, in an intriguing parallel with the ideas outlined by 'Octavius', the Ballhausplatz had prepared a diplomatic move with the object of containing Serbia. Now, after Sarajevo, that same plan was recycled to prepare the ground for war.[13] Beyond the Balkans, and less significant, there were concerns about the state of the alliance with Germany, and of the *Dreibund* (the Triple Alliance with Italy). The former, lamented Szápáry, presented a picture of 'a sad decline', and so weakened the inner coherence of the alliance.[14] Greater Habsburg assertiveness, then, would help to invigorate both German policy and the Triple Alliance.

The credibility of a more robust policy depended on effective military levers, and this consideration, too, shaped Habsburg thinking. Vienna had mobilized its armed forces to underline its resolve during the Austro-Serbian crisis in the autumn of 1912. Limited political success, however, had been bought at considerable financial cost. Close to three quarters of the defence budget went on the increase in the peace-time strength of the armed forces.[15] This was scarcely affordable, even if the sums involved had not been raised on stiff terms on the New York money market.[16] The obvious political risks apart, given the fragile condition of Habsburg finances another mobilization was fraught with considerable danger, unless it was guaranteed to enhance the Monarchy's strategic position in the Balkans.[17]

With the parameters of Habsburg policy thus set, the task of crisis management was more intricate than during previous crises. There were further complications. Before turning to them, it is worth emphasizing the paradox at the heart of Austro-Hungarian policy in July 1914. Habsburg officials were not oblivious to the dangers of escalation, but were content to leave it to their German ally to deal with them. And yet, the notion of Germany's international decline was widely shared among them. Energetic action, though 'not necessarily ... war', reasoned the Margrave Pallavicini, would mean 'cutting the Gordian knot' in the Balkans. It would compel Germany to 'go with us through thick and thin', and secure for Vienna 'a free hand in Oriental affairs.'[18]

Germany's position was thus central to Austro-Hungarian decision making. Without her support, no energetic move against Serbia would have been possible. This, then, raises the issue of the motivations behind the so-called blank cheque of 5–6 July. What is striking about Kaiser Wilhelm II's meeting with the Habsburg ambassador, Count László Szögyény, is that it reflected the strategic confusion in German thinking on the eve of the war. The interview itself was a game of two halves – before lunch and after lunch. Before, the German monarch struck a statesmanlike tone, warning of the risk of 'a serious European complication'. After lunch, he yielded to the visitor's renewed appeal to monarchical solidarity, and promised Germany's loyal and unconditional support.[19]

Wilhelm's assurance was confirmed by the chancellor, Theobald von Bethmann Hollweg.[20] The motives of the two men have been discussed extensively. This is not the place to rehearse all the various arguments. Suffice to say that the established consensus favours the view that Berlin took the 'calculated risk' of a continental war; and that, depending on scholarly preferences, Berlin's aim was either a diplomatic triumph or a preventive war. Although these are powerful arguments, the extant evidence is actually suggestive of a different interpretation. The 'blank cheque' did not exceed Vienna's request; Berlin did not coax a reluctant Austria-Hungary into a Serbian war, as Hoyos opined in 1917.[21] That it did not restrain Habsburg policy reflected the lack of policy coordination rather than political intent. Neither Wilhelm's inner circle nor his ministers had prepared him for the meeting with Szögyény. His promise of unequivocal support was made 'impetuously, almost casually'; moral outrage and a sense of monarchical solidarity had prevailed over cold calculation.[22] Only afterwards did the Kaiser seek assurances from his military leaders that the army was prepared for all eventualities.[23] And yet, for all this mercurial monarch's bellicose rhetoric and propensity to view world politics in terms of an impending racial struggle, there had been no systematic preparation for war; nor had there been any systematic analysis of the emerging crisis.[24] Indeed, when faced with the prospect of war at the end of July, Wilhelm was prepared to change course.[25]

The events of 5–6 July were typical of the Byzantine nature of Wilhelmine politics. The *Kaiserreich* had reached the limits of governability, both in terms of its structure and its internal affairs. Imperial Germany was engulfed in a 'permanent crisis of state'.[26] There were few checks on the powers of the Kaiser, who was the only mediating institution between the military and civilian authorities, an inherently unsatisfactory arrangement even with a less volatile monarch on the throne.[27] Certainly, the chancellor provided no antidote. Highly cultured, intelligent and well meaning, Bethmann was very much the product of Prussia's civil service, through whose ranks he had risen swiftly. He was the prototype of the diligent and efficient technocrat, administering problems without solving them. He mediated between competing forces at Berlin, but he did not lead.[28]

True, Bethmann was wary of the internal and external risks inherent in foreign crises. Committing to Austria-Hungary brought with it the danger of escalation. Meanwhile, setbacks abroad threatened to expedite 'the worrisome descent into parliamentarianism'.[29] He was also pessimistic about the state of Russo-German relations.[30] Erroneous intelligence, provided by a well-placed mole in the Russian embassy in London, about an Anglo-Russian naval convention sowed suspicions of British assurances to the contrary, and reinforced Bethmann's fear that the 'ring of encirclement' would soon be closed.[31] He was not the first, nor the last, politician to misread raw intelligence; and it may well be argued that such misconceptions made more susceptible the arguments in favour of a preventive war. Yet, the chancellor's role during the July crisis was rather marginal. He was absent from the capital, and remained remarkably passive until the last week of July.[32] The most striking aspect about German decision making in 1914 is its compartmentalization. The state secretary of the foreign ministry (Auswärtiges Amt), Gottlieb von Jagow, concealed crucial information from the chancellor, who was the constitutional head of that department. Jagow pursued his own diplomatic strategy during the crisis, and even sabotaged the chancellor's attempt to avert war at the end of July, by issuing what amounted to a second 'blank cheque', effectively rendering all but impossible any international mediation in the Austro-Serbian quarrel.[33] He was no warmonger – he had in fact worked for a rapprochement with Britain – but he was deeply pessimistic about Austria-Hungary's future prospects. For him, Sarajevo presented Vienna with a last chance to save the empire.[34]

All of this has implications for the 'calculated risk' theory. For, if there was any readiness for such a gamble at Berlin, it was on the part of individuals. It was not the result of collective deliberations and decisions. Further, if Germany pursued a strategy of 'bluff', seemingly threatening a continental war in order to secure a diplomatic success, then this would have required close diplomatic coordination with Vienna. Nothing of the kind happened. Decision making in the two capitals ran along parallel but separate tracks. Indeed, the poor craftsmanship of Germany's policy is one of the more remarkable features of the July crisis. Wilhelm II and the civilian leadership had embarked on a course, whose trajectory and consequences they had not considered. An economic and military giant, Germany had a political brain of clay. With the 'blank cheque' Germany abdicated her leadership of the Dual Alliance (*Zweibund*) and inverted Bismarck's dictum about alliances having a horse and a rider. After 5–6 July, the Habsburg horse was in the saddle, and the German rider found himself staggering towards the ditch.[35]

Both Vienna and Berlin were certainly imbued with a strong sense of impending change. Sarajevo was an opportunity for removing the Serb threat. If it were spurned, the process of Austria-Hungary's paralysis would be accelerated, and the Monarchy's international problems would grow yet further. In turn, such a development would devalue the alliance worthiness of Austria-Hungary for Germany. Her own options were thus either isolation or an accommodation with Russia, with the latter as the senior partner. Like other declining powers in the course of history, Austria-Hungary and Germany were thus prone to making catastrophic errors of judgement in 1914.

The sense that international politics were on the cusp of change was not confined to the Ballhausplatz and Wilhelmstrasse alone. At St Petersburg's Chorister Bridge, too, it was appreciated that the tectonic plates were shifting. This was reflected in the heightened sensitivities to developments in the Black Sea region that so preoccupied the Tsar's ministers and advisers at the turn of 1913–14. The discussions of the ministerial council of 21 February 1914 revolved, in essence, around a host of emergency scenarios concerning the Turkish Straits. With the future of the region hanging in the balance, both a total Ottoman collapse and the consolidation of rump Turkey seemed possible.[36] For that reason, Turkey's recent purchase of two British-built dreadnoughts set alarm bells ringing: 'It is obvious what fateful consequences the loss of our controlling position in the Black Sea would have, and there we cannot simply watch the further swift build-up of Ottoman naval forces.'[37] None of this constituted a new departure in policy, let alone the beginnings of a more aggressive phase in Russian policy: it was simply imperative to avoid any complications in the Eastern Mediterranean. Even so, heightened Russian sensitivities in the region limited the scope for international mediation.

The uncertain state of affairs in South-Eastern Europe aside, the Russian foreign minister, Sergei Dmitri'evich Sazonov, and his officials were preoccupied with the cooling of relations with Britain.[38] Neither Austria-Hungary's destruction nor Russia's complete ascendancy in the Balkans was an aim of Russian policy, nor could either further her interests. For now, these lay in developing the country's internal resources; and that required peace. Troubles abroad could not advance this immediate goal, Sazonov advised, and Belgrade should 'exercise extreme caution' after Sarajevo.[39]

Urging restraint was one thing, letting Serbia succumb to Austria quite another. This was more a question of geopolitics than of pan-Slav affinities. Geography made Serbia a vital piece in the international jigsaw, especially so in the event of the complete crumbling of Ottoman power and the further decline of Austria-Hungary. If Serbia were now crushed by her Habsburg neighbour, Russia's position, too, would be diminished with potentially adverse consequences in the event of a Turkish collapse. In an intriguing parallel with the shift of influence within the *Zweibund*, there was here a reversal in the patron–client relationship between St Petersburg and Belgrade, the latter exercising a form of negative power over Russia. This, too, narrowed the room for diplomatic manoeuvre.

Crucially, for all Sazonov's, and the other ministers', desire to consolidate Russia's position, the country was in a much stronger position now than at any point since the double crisis of 1905. The Russian economy was growing annually at an astonishing 3.25 per cent; national income was almost on a par with that of Britain and Germany, and exceeded that of France; and record harvests had replenished treasury reserves.[40] Russia's economy was sufficient once more to support the country's Great Power status, as was underscored by the 'Great Programme'.[41] This did not imply aggressive designs on Russia's part, but it certainly enabled St Petersburg to amplify diplomatic signals with military posturing.

As at Berlin, so at St Petersburg there was a domestic dimension to the proceedings in July 1914. Ministers were alive to the potential of foreign crises to disrupt Russia's internal affairs.[42] The reverse also held true, however – domestic developments complicated foreign policy making. This was not a matter of putative pre-revolutionary pressures, even if Britain's ambassador thought Russian society was 'deeply permeated by revolutionary sentiments'.[43] Nor was it a matter of rowdy pan-Slav or Russian chauvinist protestations in the Duma and without.[44] Indeed, if anything, the imperial regime had regained its composure after the double crisis of 1905. And therein lay the problem. For this was principally a question of governance. In February 1914, the Tsar, encouraged by conservatives at the court, had staged a miniature coup to remove Prime Minister Vladimir Nikola'evich Kokovstov and the last remnants of Stolypin's constitutional reforms. Intended to bolster the monarch's position, the move produced deleterious results. The new government under Ivan Loginovich Goremykin was riven with infighting. Under their superannuated figurehead, the ministers were 'all at sixes and sevens, but they have all been at work ... with their intrigues'.[45] In turn, the manoeuvres of doves and hawks constrained Sazonov's ability to act and so complicated strategic decision making at St Petersburg.

This sense of impending change was shared by politicians and officials in Paris and London. But the reaction here was rather different. During the July crisis itself, French diplomacy remained largely reactive. A number of factors combined to ensure that this would be so, most of them rooted in the precarious position of party politics. If the Third Republic was secure, the current administration under René Viviani, in office since 14 June 1914, was built on flimsy foundations. The prime minister, who was also foreign minister, was yoked together in an uneasy cohabitation with the 'Man of Lorraine', the right-wing President Raymond Poincaré. As the president's diaries make clear, he thought Viviani 'hesitant and pusillanimous' and unsound on foreign policy.[46] Such party and personality clashes aside, France's political elite was consumed by the contemporaneous Caillaux scandal rather than the brewing crisis in the Balkans.[47] Finally, the official visit to St Petersburg by the Poincaré-Viviani duo at the end of July meant that French diplomacy was not fully functional. In the vacuum created by their absence from Paris the private initiatives by France's ambassador at St Petersburg, Maurice Paléologue, acquired greater significance. Unencumbered by restraining instructions from the Quai d'Orsay, the ambassador went far in his assurances of France's commitment to a hard line.[48]

Poincaré himself, however, had reinforced Russian assumptions of a firm French commitment by unilaterally redefining the *casus foederis*. If Russia ever decided to go to war against the *Zweibund*, 'France also will wage war'.[49] Poincaré's assurance of French support came close to constituting a French version of a 'blank cheque', though it was not as unconditional as the German offer to Austria-Hungary; nor did it 'balkanize' the Franco-Russian alliance.[50] The geographical locus of any future crisis was less relevant here than the measures Germany would take and how Russia chose to respond. From now on, France was far less likely to restrain Russia. This also held true of Viviani. Although sceptical of aspects of official policy – a scepticism reinforced by his own profound ignorance of foreign affairs – he was determined not to loosen France's vital relations with St Petersburg, even if it caused him much personal anguish.[51] And to that degree, too, French diplomacy helped to restrict the parameters of European crisis management.

That France could not be relied upon to act in a moderating sense was not lost on British diplomats.[52] But Foreign Secretary Sir Edward Grey was also conscious of a wider shift in the international landscape. As during the two recent Balkan crises, he hoped to preserve the unity of the powers and to maintain the cohesion of the combination with France and Russia. The two objectives were linked. Maintaining the Concert of Europe was the best means of preventing an Austro-Russian quarrel. It was an axiom of all calculations of policy in London that 'the rivalry which exists in an acute form between Russia and Austria' was the chief source of European tensions.[53] Direct mediation between them, however, was considered inopportune, indeed scarcely practicable. A more indirect approach, then, was required. This was in keeping with British notions of relative aloofness from continental affairs. But here, too, there were problems. Without Anglo-German collaboration, seemingly so successful during the Balkan Wars, Austria-Hungary could not be restrained. Yet without continued cooperation with France and Russia, St Petersburg was unlikely to respond to moderating advice. It was for this reason that Grey had sought their cooperation on diverse Balkan questions which were of little intrinsic interest to Britain.[54] The challenge then, as now, was to balance these divergent demands. Grey's ability to do so had been the key to his success so far. While Grey hoped to avoid having to choose between the two, he was nevertheless alive to the inherent tensions within this policy.

Grey understood Germany's more precarious position in international politics, as was underlined by his conversations with the German and Russian ambassadors on 6 and 8 July. These hold the key to a proper understanding of Grey's moves during the July crisis. Britain, he intimated, could not be ignored if the dispute escalated. To prevent this, it was for Germany and Russia to reassure each other of their peaceful intentions. If this was no explicit warning, it was neither necessary nor desirable at this stage. It was a clear indication that Grey wished to continue the recent, seemingly so successful policy of cooperating with Germany in Balkan affairs.[55] This was important to him. He appreciated that the recent shift in Europe's military balance had been to Germany's disadvantage. The more it shifted, 'the more leverage Austria will have over Germany',[56] and the greater would be the risk of escalation.

Against the backdrop of recent experience, this was an entirely sensible policy. There were no indications yet that German policy had changed. Warning Berlin would have been counterproductive. Equally problematic for Britain was the growing realization that it was no longer possible 'to enlist French support in an effort to hold back Russia'.[57] There was the danger now of the two alliances swinging into operation, and this made it more necessary to work with Germany. Any explicit warning addressed to Berlin would merely have pushed Germany to side with Austria-Hungary, thereby moving the crisis beyond the reach of diplomacy. Russian restraint, meanwhile, could only be purchased by conceding to likely Russian demands for an alliance: 'And to that question he [Grey] could not have given an affirmative answer.'[58]

Apart from considerations of European diplomacy, Grey's unwillingness to give that 'affirmative answer' was to no small degree conditioned by the constraints which the disturbed state of British domestic politics placed on him. The minority Asquith government was in office but hardly in power, dependent for its survival on a loose and disparate coalition of Irish Nationalists, Labour MPs and its own capricious radical element. The Ulster crisis, industrial unrest, suffragette militancy and assorted other domestic troubles left the government casting about for ways 'to reenergise [its] own flagging party'.[59] There was little inclination among the Liberals to concern themselves with foreign matters; and until the invasion of Belgium dispelled such delusions, there was a 'very strong feeling that whatever happens amongst the other European powers England must keep herself out of the quarrel'.[60] Under such circumstances, Grey had to tread a thin line between the twin dangers of European complications and splitting the ruling party and so dividing the country at large.

## The failure of mediation and deterrence

Europe's diplomatic elite, then, had to operate within much narrower parameters in July 1914 than during previous crises. This did not rule out a peaceful settlement. Indeed, this was the preferred outcome for most governments, except that at Vienna. Even so, mediation on the basis of some form of localization, such as 'Halt in Belgrade', was now the only possible outcome. Ironically, Grey understood this, even if later historians did not. Grey's initiative, of 26 July, for a four-power conference, a sort of miniature European concert, to mediate between Vienna and Belgrade, suited the plans of the German chancellor.[61] With even a limited campaign against Serbia not imminent for another fortnight, such a scheme was entirely practicable.[62] But it depended on German pressure on Vienna to accept mediation. And this Bethmann refused to apply, unless the Austro-Serb dispute were separated from that with Russia.[63] Bethmann's insistence on localization reduced the diplomatic room for manoeuvre further. Russia, meanwhile, might have accepted the temporary occupation of some points across the Danube and Sava Rivers, provided that Serbia's sovereign rights were not violated in the subsequent settlement.[64]

While the focus of diplomatic efforts remained on mediation of some kind, a number of factors conspired to make this difficult to accomplish. First, given Britain's limited ability to restrain France and Russia, the viability of the conference proposal depended on a suspension of all military activities by all sides. If Habsburg troops entered Serbian territory before a diplomatic framework was agreed, escalation was inevitable. Conversely, if Russian military preparations continued apace, it was understood that diplomatic 'wiggle' room would be further curtailed.[65]

Second, to varying degrees, the key actors pursued deterrence strategies during the crisis, using the spectre of conflict to force their opponents to accept a settlement on their own terms. Military preparations, or the threat thereof, were thus principally a means of increasing leverage so as to extract some advantage from the situation. But if this was the intention, understandings of deterrence were not sufficiently sophisticated for such strategies properly to be implemented. Poincaré and Sazonov had always insisted that 'clarity of intent' was key to the successful containment of the two Germanic powers. But in the case of France this translated into a degree of rigidity that impeded diplomacy. It is interesting to note here that the British ambassador to France – no friend of Germany – complained that Paris was 'not sufficiently *coulant*' to Berlin.[66]

As for Russia, Sazonov's deterrence strategy, with its mixture of offers of mediation and military preparations, was flawed. The balance between the two components was ill judged. Moreover, he kept changing his mind as to what form mediation should take – direct talks with Vienna, or mediation by an international quartet as suggested by the British. His violent language to the German ambassador, followed by amiable exchanges with the Habsburg representative, was liable to confuse matters, especially since both were likely to compare notes – as, indeed, they did. It is little wonder, then, that the two envoys remained convinced until the very end that Russia would not intervene, or that the British Foreign Office came to regard Sazonov as unreliable.[67]

Sazonov's strategy was based on a twin-track approach. On the diplomatic track, Vienna was to extend the time limit of the ultimatum in return for a conciliatory reply by Belgrade. To reinforce the proposal, thirteen army corps were to be prepared for mobilization against Austria-Hungary. There was a general sense at St Petersburg, as Tsar Nicholas II recorded in his diary, that '8 [of the Austrian demands] are unacceptable for an independent state'.[68] The perceived shift in the geopolitical landscape enhanced the significance of the Serbian factor in Russian calculations. If Russia's influence in the Balkans was to be preserved, Serbia could not be allowed to be crushed by Austria-Hungary.

Conversely, the anticipated consequences of this geopolitical transformation left the Wilhelmstrasse more determined to shield Vienna against external pressure. The Austro-Serbian conflict therefore had to be insulated against the wider Habsburg-Romanov struggle for ascendancy in the Balkans. Austria-Hungary had to reassert her influence in the Balkans, lest Germany find herself in complete isolation in the near future.[69] Under such circumstances, the desired increase in leverage did not materialize, and it was at this point, from 31 July to 1 August, that narrow military calculations of railway timetables and mobilization logistics began to dominate thinking in the three Eastern capitals. In the case of Russia, there were two further complications, the first of which reflected the many shortcomings of the imperial regime. Sazonov and the other civilians were detached from the military leadership and its plans. This systemic flaw made coherent decision making all but impossible. It also magnified the professional failings of individuals – Sazonov's changeable stance, or the chief of staff's insufficient grasp of the intricacies of Russia's mobilization schemes. The second complication was intelligence-related, coupled with the general staff's proclivity to its planning on 'worst-case' scenarios. Intelligence gleaned from along and across the Galician frontier suggested that Austria-Hungary was mobilizing more troops than Russian estimates considered necessary for a Serbian campaign, with the strong implication that Vienna's ambitions were not confined merely to chastising its obstreperous small neighbour.[70]

Third, the final factor counteracting attempts to localize the Balkan conflict concerns the *Zweibund* and the argument about the significance of the alliance systems in general. The reversal of roles in the *Zweibund* meant that 'Halt in Belgrade' was never a practicable solution. Without prior diplomatic or military coordination between Berlin and Vienna, the scheme ran into the buffers of Conrad von Hötzendorf's war plans. These envisaged the invasion of Serbia from the West, with the aim of annihilating the Serbian army, cutting across the natural lines of advance rather than moving across the Danube *via* Belgrade.[71] Here, too, then, civilians and the military were dangerously divorced; and, more significantly, two allies were curiously detached.

Two further points follow from this, one relating to the nature of Great Power politics in general, the other touching on the more contingent aspects of international politics. As for the former, however much the powers depended upon their respective allies, there was little systematic coordination of policy between any of them. Talk of the alliance 'system' as one of the contributing factors to the war, then, is somewhat exaggerated.[72] Insofar as the contingent aspects are concerned, the considerable latitude enjoyed by ambassadors and the sometimes tenuous control exercised over them by their own ministers are also vital to a deeper understanding of the July crisis. The personal diplomatic manoeuvres by the German and French ambassadors at Vienna and St Petersburg respectively served to counteract all efforts to find a diplomatic solution.

Similarly, domestic political arrangements mattered. The excruciatingly slow pace of Habsburg decision making meant that Austria-Hungary missed the opportunity for a swift punitive strike. It was left to the leader of a small nation, Ion C. Brătianu, the Romanian premier, to point out the obvious: if she had acted immediately after Sarajevo, she 'would have had the sympathies of Europe on [her] side', and there would have been little risk of escalation.[73] Berchtold himself later reflected that 'the only mistake of which we can accuse ourselves is that we struck *too late*' (emphasis in original).[74]

The compartmentalization of politics in Berlin allowed Jagow to sabotage Bethmann's belated attempts to regain leverage over Austria-Hungary. And in issuing a second 'blank cheque', leaving to the belligerent ambassador at Vienna the decision whether to compel the Ballhausplatz to accept mediation, he also pulled the rug from underneath his own feet when he, too, attempted to reverse policy.[75] The tensions between Poincaré and Viviani added an element of uncertainty to French policy making, while the infighting between hardliners and moderates sowed confusion at St Petersburg and abroad. Sazonov's poor political tradecraft merely added to this. And with the Damocles sword of the minority Liberal government in London fracturing over the issue of British intervention, Grey, too, was constrained.

## Conclusion

'Six Powers are appalled by and fear world war, and yet do not know how to resist it,' wrote Walther Rathenau, the German industrialist and shrewd but perpetually frustrated observer of Wilhelmine politics, in a Berlin newspaper at the end of July 1914.[76] That they did not know reflected the fact that, in sharp contrast to earlier crises, the scope for diplomatic action was much reduced during Europe's last summer. This was rooted primarily in concerns about the stability of alliance partners. The existing alliances reinforced a sense of weakness. The prospect of Habsburg decline handed Vienna a form of negative power over its German ally, so reversing the traditional power balance within the *Zweibund*, while the fear of Russia buckling once more under Austro-German pressure made French policy more rigid than was prudent.

A sense of impending change in international politics was widespread. Attuned to Social Darwinian notions of the rise and fall of nations, it seemed to have fallen to the generation of 1914 to deal with the fallout of the collapse of two empires. Continued Ottoman decay invested Serbia with great strategic significance for both Russia and Austria-Hungary. The anticipated further decline of the Habsburg Empire posed an even more fundamental challenge, one that touched on the core relations in Europe, especially those between Germany and Russia. How to manage the process of the Austro-Hungarian succession was one of the unsolved questions of Great Power politics on the eve of the war. In Austria-Hungary it engendered the audacity of despair. At Berlin it encouraged attempts to bolster Germany's position in the shifting strategic landscape by backing the Habsburg ally. In St Petersburg it hardened the resolve not to allow Serbia to be trampled underfoot. To that extent, a small state like Serbia wielded indirect power to an extent that would have been incomprehensible, indeed intolerable, to Talleyrand or Alexander I at the beginning of the long nineteenth century.

With the parameters established in this manner, the scope for individuals to cause mischief was thus even greater. If Gavrilo Princip's two shots on 28 June 1914 reverberated around the world, they did so only because the strokes of innumerable pens across Europe amplified them during the month that followed.

## Notes

1  'Octavius', *Gross-Habsburg, das Resultat des russisch-österreichischen Krieges 1918* (Cracow: Deutscher, 1914). The catalogue of the Hoover Library, Stanford University, suggests a Captain Gross as the author, which seems doubtful. The notions contained in the pamphlet of a diplomatic offensive in the Balkans and of a federal reconstitution of the Monarchy, and the Darwinian diction in which they are advanced, bear a strong resemblance to some of the ideas advocated by Count Ottokar Czernin and others in Franz Ferdinand's entourage. Despite an open avowal to the contrary, the pamphlet was not the work of merely a patriotic Habsburg-German 'without connections to high political or military circles' (ibid., 5). It is probably thus no coincidence that the putative head of the 'Gross-Habsburg' government in 1918 was a Count Czerno. For Franz Ferdinand's 1911 *'Programm zum Thronwechsel'* and his relations with Czernin, see Jean-Paul Bled, *François-Ferdinand d'Autriche* (Paris: Tallandier, 2012), 240–6; Alma Hannig, *Franz Ferdinand. Die Biografie* (Vienna: Almathea, 2013), 99–103, 144–71; Robert A. Kann, 'Count Ottokar Czernin and Archduke Francis Ferdinand', *Journal of Central European Affairs* 16/2 (1956): 117–45; Robert A. Kann, *Erzherzog Franz Ferdinand. Studien* (Munich: Oldenbourg, 1976).

2  For more on this see T. G. Otte, 'Détente 1914: Sir William Tyrrell's Secret Mission to Germany', *Historical Journal* 56/1 (2013): 175–204; T. G. Otte, 'A "Formidable Factor in European Politics": Views of Russia in 1914', in Jack S. Levy and John A. Vasquez (eds), *The Outbreak of the First World War: Structure, Politics, and Decision-Making* (Cambridge: Cambridge University Press, 2014), 87–114.

3 Glenn Snyder, 'Crisis Bargaining', in Charles F. Hermann (ed.), *International Crises: Insights from Behavioural Research* (New York: Free Press, 1972), 127.

4 Karl Freiherr von Macchio, 'Momentbilder aus der Julikrise', *Berliner Monatshefte* xiv, 10 (1936): 765.

5 Haus-, Hof- und Staatsarchiv Vienna (hereafter HHStA), Politisches Archiv (PA) I/810, Liasse XX 'Attentat auf Erzherzog Franz Ferdinand', Storck to Berchtold (no. 98A, strictly confidential), 30 June 1914; T. G. Otte, *July Crisis: The World's Descent into War, Summer 1914* (Cambridge: Cambridge University Press, 2014), 41–2.

6 Berchtold, 'Die ersten Tage nach dem Attentat vom 28. Juni', unpublished manuscript from Nachlass Berchtold, as quoted in Hugo Hantsch, *Leopold Graf Berchtold. Grandseigneur und Staatsmann*, 2 vols (Graz: Verlag Styria, 1963), II, 558.

7 Heinrich Graf von Lützow, *Im diplomatischen Dienst der k.u.k. Monarchie*, ed. P. Hohenbalken (Munich: Oldenbourg, 1971), 218. The conversation between Lützow and Hojos took place on 13 July.

8 Miklós Komjáthy (ed.), *Protokolle des Gemeinsamen Ministerrates der Österreichisch-Ungarischen Monarchie, 1914-1918* (Budapest: Akadémiai Kiadó, 1966), no. 3: minutes of Common Ministerial Council meeting, 31 July 1914. Biliński was highly skilled at cutting nicotine- and coffee-fuelled deals with South Slav politicians: see his *Wspomnienia i dokumenty, 1846-1922*, 2 vols (Warsaw: Księgarnia F. Hoesicka, 1924–5), I, 238–9. For a nuanced reassessment see Mark Cornwall, 'The Habsburg Elite and the Southern Slav Question, 1914-1918', in Lothar Höbelt and T. G. Otte (eds), *A Living Anachronism: European Diplomacy and the Habsburg Monarchy. Festschrift für Francis Roy Bridge zum 70. Geburtstag* (Vienna: Böhlau, 2010), 239–70.

9 Lützow, *Im diplomatischen Dienst*, 219.

10 For example, HHStA, PA X/139, Ottokar Czernin to Berchtold (no. 40F, confidential), 24 October 1913; PA X/140, Szápáry to Berchtold (no. 23B), 21 May 1914. See also Otte, 'A "Formidable Factor in European Politics"'.

11 HHStA, PA X/140, Szápáry to Berchtold (no. 10B), 22 February 1914.

12 HHStA, PA X/140, Ottokar Czernin to Berchtold (no. 14G), 14 March 1914. Also Barbara Jelavich, 'Romania and the First World War: The Pre-War Crises, 1912-1914', *International History Review* 14/3 (1992): 441–51.

13 HHStA, PA I/1091, Matscheko Memorandum (revised by Hoyos), n.d. (c. 1 July 1914); the printed version is in Ludwig Bittner and Hans Übersberger (eds), *Österreich-Ungarns Aussenpolitik von der Bosnischen Krise 1908 bis zum Kriegsausbruch 1914* (hereafter ÖUA), 8 vols (Vienna: Österreichischer Bundesverlag, 1930), VIII, no. 9918. For further thoughts, see M. B. A. Petersson, 'Das österreichisch-ungarische Memorandum an Deutschland vom 5. Juli 1914', *Scandia* XXX (1964): 138–90.

14 HHStA, PA X/140, Szápáry to Berchtold (no. 21D), 25 May 1914.

15 Wilhelm Deutschmann, 'Die militärischen Massnahmen Österreich-Ungarns während der Balkankriege 1912/13' (PhD diss., Vienna, 1965); Samuel R. Williamson, *Austria-Hungary and the Origins of the First World War* (London:

Macmillan, 1991), 126–32; David Stevenson, *Armaments and the Coming of War: Europe, 1904-1914* (Oxford: Clarendon Press, 1996), 279–85.

16  For the loan, see *The Economist*, 7 December 1912; also Eduard März, *Austrian Banking and Financial Policy: Creditanstalt at a Turning Point* (London: Orion, 1984), 26–35.

17  This latter consideration carried a good deal of weight. A limited campaign, even if successful, it was feared, would produce no lasting solution, just as the 1848 campaign in Italy had not halted Austria's decline there: see HHStA, PA I/811, 'Memorandum des Herrn Molden über die Situation', 6 July 1914; also Solomon Wank, 'Desperate Counsel in Vienna in July 1914: Berthold Molden's Unpublished Memorandum', *Central European History* 36/2 (1993): 281–310.

18  ÖUA VIII, no 10083, Pallavicini to Berchtold (private), 6 July 1914. Pallavicini's views carried some weight at Vienna: see William D. Godsey Jr., *Aristocratic Redoubt: The Austro-Hungarian Foreign Office on the Eve of the First World War* (West Lafayette, IN: Purdue University Press, 1999), 195–6.

19  ÖUA VIII, no. 10058, Szögyény to Berchtold (tel. no. 237), 5 July 1914; Otte, *July Crisis*, 72–8.

20  Karl Kautsky et al. (eds), *Die Deutschen Dokumente zum Kriegsausbruch* (hereafter DD), 4 vols (Berlin: Deutsche Verlagsgesellschaft für Politik und Geschichte, 1919) I, no. 15: Bethmann to Tschirschky (tel. no. 113), 6 July 1914.

21  HHStA, Nachlass Mérey, karton 10, Hoyos to Mérey, 20 July 1917. Representative of the 'preventive war' arguments are Andreas Hillgruber, 'Riezlers Theorie des kalkulierten Risikos und Bethmann Hollwegs politische Konzeption in der Julikrise 1914', in W. J. Schieder (ed.), *Erster Weltkrieg. Ursachen, Entstehung, Kriegsziele* (Cologne: Kiepenheuer & Witsch, 1969), 240–55; and Konrad H. Jarausch, 'The Illusion of Limited War: Chancellor Bethmann Hollweg's Calculated Risk in July 1914', *Central European History* 2/1 (1969): 48–76.

22  Avner Offer, 'Going to War in 1914: A Matter of Honour?', *Politics and Society* 23/2 (1995): 222.

23  Immanuel Geiss (ed.), *Juli 1914. Die europäische Krise und der Ausbruch des Ersten Weltkriegs,* 3rd edn (Munich: Deutscher Taschenbuch-Verlag, 1986), no. 5: Falkenhayn to Moltke (strictly secret), 5 July 1914.

24  John C. G. Röhl, *Wilhelm II*, 3 vols (Munich: C.H. Beck, 1993–2008), III, 1080–86; for the lack of preparations, see Stevenson, *Armaments*, 287–98.

25  The altogether fragmentary extant evidence does not support the rumours that Wilhelm and Franz Ferdinand had plotted war at their last meeting at Konopiště; for a recent attempt to reassert this myth, see John Zametica, *Folly and Malice: The Habsburg Empire, the Balkans and the Start of World War One* (London: Shepheard-Walwyn, 2017), 425–9.

26  Hans-Ulrich Wehler, *Deutsche Gesellschaftsgeschichte*, III, *1849-1914* (Munich: C.H. Beck, 1995), 1000–1; also T. G. Otte, 'War, Revolution and the Uncertain Primacy of Domestic Politics', in Richard N. Rosecrance and Sean E. Miller (eds), *The Next Great War?: The Roots of World War I and the Risk of US-China Conflict* (Cambridge, MA: Harvard University Press, 2015), 104–7.

27  See John Röhl's penetrating analysis of the nature of policy making in the *Kaiserreich*, *The Kaiser and His Court: Wilhelm II and the Government of Germany* (Cambridge: Cambridge University Press, 1996), esp. 107–30.
28  T. G. Otte, 'The Limits of the Possible: Some Reflections on Chancellor Bethmann Hollweg and the July Crisis', https://networks.h-net.org/node/350 08/discussions/55746/ann-h-german-forum-first-world-war-otte-december-2014.
29  The National Archives, London (hereafter TNA), GFM 25/10, Nachlass Eisendecher: Bethmann Hollweg to Eisendecher, 4 June 1911. Bethmann excised the phrase 'under all circumstances' from Tschirschky's instructions: DD, I, no. 15, note 5.
30  TNA, GFM 25/3, Nachlass Pourtalès, Bethmann Hollweg to Pourtalès, 30 July 1912.
31  Grey was not interested in pursuing such a convention: TNA, FO 371/2092, Grey to Buchanan (no. 249, secret), 1 May 1914. For the Siebert source and Berlin's reaction, see Erwin Hölzle, *Der Geheimnisverrat und der Kriegsausbruch 1914* (Göttingen: Musterschmidt, 1973), 10–13; Manfred Rauh, 'Die britisch-russische Marinekonvention und der Ausbruch des Ersten Weltkriegs', *Militärgeschichtliche Mitteilungen* 10/1 (1987): 37–62.
32  Eberhard von Vietsch, *Bethmann Hollweg. Staatsmann zwischen Macht und Ethos* (Boppard: Boldt, 1969), 197.
33  ÖUA VIII, no. 10793, Szögyény to Berchtold (tel. no. 307, strictly secret), 27 July 1914.
34  TNA, GFM 25/16, fos. 97-8, Nachlass Jagow, 'Juli 1914 und Kriegsausbruch', n.d.
35  Otte, *July Crisis*, 100–1.
36  Otto Hoetzsch (ed.), *Die internationalen Beziehungen im Zeitalter des Imperialismus*, *1911-14* (hereafter IBZI), 1st series, 5 vols (Berlin: R. Hobbing, 1931–6), I, no. 295: minutes of special conference, 21 February 1914. (Dates below from Russian sources have been adjusted to the western Gregorian calendar.) For the argument of implicit Russian aggression, see Sean McMeekin, *The Russian Origins of the First World War* (Cambridge, MA: Harvard University Press, 2011), 31–5.
37  IBZI, II, no. 384, Sazonov to Benckendorff (confidential), 8 May 1914.
38  Ibid., IV, no. 56, Sazonov to Benckendorff (tel. no.1310), 2 July 1914. See also S. D. Sazonov, *Fateful Years, 1909-1916* (London: Jonathan Cape, 1928), 128–32.
39  IBZI, IV, no. 112, Sazonov to Hartwig (tel. no.1351), 7 July 1914; also D. C. B. Lieven, 'Bureaucratic Authoritarianism in Late Imperial Russia: The Personality, Career, and Opinions of P.N. Durnovo', *Historical Journal* 26/2 (1983): 391–402.
40  For some statistics, see A. P. Korelin (ed.), *Rossi'a 1913 god. Statistiko-dokumental'nyi Spravochnik* (St. Petersburg: BLITS, 1995), 152–65; also Paul R. Gregory, *Russia's National Income, 1895-1913* (Cambridge: Cambridge University Press, 1982), 153–65.

41 Norman Stone, *The Eastern Front, 1914-1917* (London: Hodder & Stoughton, 1975), 24–36; John W. Steinberg, *All the Tsar's Men: Russia's General Staff and the Fate of Empire, 1898-1914* (Baltimore, MD: Johns Hopkins University Press, 2010), 184–9.

42 HHStA, PA X/139, Czernin to Berchtold (no. 43D), 21 November 1913; David M. McDonald, 'A Lever Without a Fulcrum: Domestic Factors and Russian Foreign Policy', in Hugh Ragsdale (ed.), *Imperial Russian Foreign Policy* (Cambridge: Cambridge University Press, 1993), 268–312.

43 TNA, FO 371/2092/10333, Buchanan to Grey (no. 60), 4 March 1914.

44 For some of this, see Dietrich Geyer, *Russian Imperialism: The Interaction of Domestic and Foreign Policy, 1860-1914* (New Haven: Yale University Press, 1987), 299–300.

45 TNA, FO 371/2090, Pares memorandum, 14 January 1914, enclosed in Boswell to Grey, 20 January 1914. For some comparative observations, see Otte, 'War, Revolution, and the Uncertain Primacy of Domestic Politics', 103–25.

46 Bibliothèque Nationale, Paris, Bnfr 16027, Poincaré papers, Poincaré diary, entries for 29 and 31 July 1914.

47 For the murder trial, see Jean-Claude Allain, *Caillaux*, 2 vols (Paris: Imprimerie Nationale, 1981) II, 403–43; Gerd Krumeich, 'Raymond Poincaré et l'affaire du "Figaro"', *Revue Historique* CCLXIV, 3 (1980): 365–73.

48 Ministère des Affaires Étrangères (ed.), *Documents Diplomatiques Françaises, 1911-1914*, 3rd series, 11 vols (Paris, 1929–36), XI, no. 19 (hereafter DDF (3)): Paléologue to Bienvenu-Martin (tel. no. 281), 24 July 1914; Otte, *July Crisis*, 234–5, 248–50.

49 Friedrich Stieve (ed.), *Der Diplomatische Schriftwechsel Iswolskys*, 4 vols (Berlin: Deutsche Verlagsgesellschaft für Politik und Geschichte, 1924), IV, no. 554: Izvolsky to Sazonov, 7 November 1912. For Poincaré's more circumspect version, see his note to Izvolsky: DDF (3), IV, no. 468, 16 November 1912.

50 Cf. Christopher Clark, *The Sleepwalkers: How Europe Went to War in 1914* (London: Allen Lane, 2012), 293–301, for the 'Balkan inception' argument.

51 DDF (3), X, no. 491, Viviani to Paléologue (tel. no. 318, very confidential), 10 July 1914. For his erratic behaviour during the St Petersburg visit, see Poincaré diary, entry for 22 July 1914.

52 Northamptonshire Record Office, C(A) 45, Cartwright MSS, Cartwright to Nicolson, 11 April 1913; Cambridge University Library, vol. 93, Hardinge MSS, Nicolson to Hardinge (private), 15 January 1914.

53 Bodleian Library Oxford, Rennell Rodd MSS, box 14, Nicolson to Rodd, 30 November 1912. See also T. G. Otte, *The Foreign Office Mind: The Making of British Foreign Policy, 1865-1914* (Cambridge: Cambridge University Press, 2011), 369–75.

54 For instance on the Danube-Adriatic railway project, see TNA, FO 371/1244/4958, Grey minute (n.d.) on Serbian note of 8 February 1911.

55 G. P. Gooch and H. W. V. Temperley (eds), *British Documents on the Origins of the War, 1898-1914* (hereafter BD) 11 vols (London: HM Stationary Office,

1928–38), XI, no. 41, Grey to Rumbold (no. 223, secret), 9 July 1914; DD, I, no. 30, Lichnowsky to Bethmann Hollweg (confidential), 9 July 1914.

56  As summarized in IBZI, IV, no. 146, Benckendorff to Sazonov (private), 9 July 1914.

57  BD, XI, no.101, Buchanan to Grey (tel. no. 166, urgent), 24 July 1914.

58  Temperley MSS (in private possession): Temperley interview with Grey, n.d. (1929).

59  Bodleian Library Oxford, Harcourt MSS, Ms. Harcourt. Dep. 444, Hobhouse to Harcourt, 15 January 1914; H. V. Emy, *Liberals, Radicals, and Social Policy, 1892-1914* (Cambridge: Cambridge University Press, 1973), 189–280.

60  Rowntree to wife, 30 July 1914: Ian Packer (ed.), *The Letters of Arnold Stephenson Rowntree to Mary Kathleen Rowntree, 1910-1918* (Cambridge: Cambridge University Press, 2002), 153. Rowntree was the MP for York, 1910–18.

61  BD, XI, no. 139 (a) and (b), Nicolson to Grey (tel.) and reply, 26 July 1914, Otte, *July Crisis*, 294–302.

62  BD, XI, no. 231, Rodd to Grey (tel. no. 127), 28 July 1914.

63  DD, I, no. 234: Draft instructions for Schoen, Lichnowsky and Pourtalès, 26 July 1914; Otte, *July Crisis*, 308–10 and 348–51.

64  DD, II, no. 421, Pourtalès to Auswärtiges Amt (tel. no. 192), 30 July 1914; IBZI, V, nos. 277 and 278: Sazonov to Sverbe'ev (tel. no. 1554, pts. 1 and 2), 30 July 1914. A facsimile of Sazonov's handwritten draft is in Graf F. Pourtalès, *Meine letzten Verhandlungen in St. Petersburg Ende Juli 1914. Tagebuchaufzeichnungen und Dokumente* (Berlin: Deutsche Verlagsgesellschaft, 1927), 16.

65  DD, I, no. 236, Lichnowsky to Auswärtiges Amt (tel. no. 161), 26 July 1914.

66  British Library, Add. MSS. 63033, Bertie MSS, Bertie to Grey (private), 27 July 1914.

67  ÖUA, VIII, no. 11044, Szápáry to Berchtold (tel. no. 181), 30 July 1914; BD, XI, no. 174: Nicolson minute, n.d. (27 July 1914), on tel. Buchanan to Grey (no. 174), 27 July 1914.

68  Nicholas II diary, 25 July 1914, 'Nikolai Romanov v pervikh dniakh voyni', *Krasny Arkhiv*, LXIV (1934): 133. For a detailed examination, see D. C. B. Lieven, *Russia and the Origins of the First World War* (London: Macmillan, 1983), 141–4.

69  Jagow's fear of the demise of Austria-Hungary is telling. See Bodleian Library Oxford, De Bunsen MSS, box 11, Nicolson to de Bunsen, 30 March 1914; Otte, *July Crisis*, 98–9.

70  Bruce W. Menning, 'Naslediye Agenta No. 25', *Rodina* no. 8 (2014): 32–5, and Bruce W. Menning, 'Russian Military Intelligence, July 1914: What St. Petersburg Perceived and Why It Mattered', *The Historian* 77/2 (2015): 213–68. I am grateful to Professor Menning for letting me see advance copies of these two important articles.

71  Franz Conrad von Hötzendorf, *Aus meiner Dienstzeit*, 5 vols (Vienna: Rikola, 1921–5), IV, 300–4; Günther Kronenbitter, *'Krieg im Frieden': Die Führung*

*der k.u.k. Armee und die Großmachtpolitik Österreich-Ungarns, 1906-1914* (Munich: Oldenbourg, 2003), 504–5.

72  For further thoughts, see Otte, *July Crisis*, 506–10.

73  HHStA, PA I/810, Liasse XX, Czernin to Berchtold (tel. no. 241), 24 July 1914.

74  HHStA, Nachlass Berchtold, karton 5, Berchtold diary, entry for 4 September 1918.

75  In an intriguing parallel with the original 'blank cheque', the only evidence is in the Austrian files: see ÖUA, VIII, no. 10793, Szögyény to Berchtold (tel. no.307, strictly secret), 27 July 1914. For the background, see Otte, *July Crisis*, 330–3 and 371–7.

76  Walther Rathenau, 'Ein Wort zur Lage', *Berliner Tageblatt*, 31 July 1914 (written on 29 July); Shulamit Volkov, *Walther Rathenau: Weimar's Fallen Statesman* (New Haven: Yale University Press, 2012), 119–21.

# CHAPTER 10

# The British elite and the Sarajevo assassinations

## F. R. Bridge

The contrast between the attitudes of the British establishment towards Serbia and Austria-Hungary on the eve of the Sarajevo assassinations can hardly be overstated. Serbia, for example, was almost universally disliked, regarded as a pariah state ever since the brutal murder of King Aleksandar and his wife in 1903. After that, at the instigation of Edward VII, Great Britain – alone of the Great Powers – had demonstratively broken off diplomatic relations with Belgrade. Although after a few years these were grudgingly restored when the new regime renounced its ties with the regicide army officers, the latter were still notoriously active in the nationalist groups agitating for a Greater Serbia that would include Bosnia and the other Southern Slav lands of the Dual Monarchy. Just as Serbia's record of brutality against conquered Bulgarians and Albanians during the Balkan Wars of 1912–13 had alienated even the Balkan Committee in London (the traditional advocates of Slav interests in Great Britain), so Serbia's unassuaged expansionist ambitions were seen by some as a serious threat to European peace. As the British ambassador in Vienna, Sir Fairfax Cartwright, warned Sir Arthur Nicolson, permanent undersecretary at the Foreign Office, in January 1913,

> Servia [sic][1] will someday set Europe by the ears and bring about a universal war on the Continent. ... I cannot tell you how exasperated people are getting here over the continual worry which that little country causes to Austria under encouragement from Russia. It may be compared to a certain extent to the trouble we had to suffer through the hostile attitude formerly assumed against us by the Transvaal Republic under the guiding hand of Germany.[2]

Not surprisingly, the bloody deed of Sarajevo, which even the Russian press admitted had been plotted in Serbia, did nothing for her reputation in London. The *Daily Telegraph*'s roving reporter in Vienna, E. J. Dillon, was emphatic: Serbian 'methods' – conspiracy and assassination – had been 'banned in all civilised states from the first'. While there might as yet be no conclusive evidence that the Serbian government and its agents had been directly involved, there existed already 'proofs of complicity not sufficient for a judge but sufficient for a politician'.[3] Indeed, it was becoming increasingly clear that Great Serbian propaganda was an important element in the Austro-Serbian confrontation; and as the horrifying prospect of a European war arose, it was on Serbia that the British Liberal press concentrated its fire.[4] As early as 17 July even the Conservative *Standard* had called her a nuisance to Europe, while the *Manchester Guardian* of 1 August expressed the despairing wish that Serbia might be towed into the middle of the ocean and sunk. On the same day *The Economist* published a long letter from Vienna from the notoriously well-connected Professor Josef Redlich denouncing 'Serbian imperialism'. It was, according to Redlich, 'the fruit of that bloated diseased nationalism which the Carnegie Commission [on the Balkan Wars] notes is characteristic of the modern Balkan races'; by contrast, 'Austria-Hungary has for centuries stood as an unshakeable focus of European Conservatism, the firm bulwark of Western culture and the friendly rivalry of differing peoples.'[5]

True, 'friendly rivalry' was hardly a term that would have occurred to some cognoscenti in the British establishment, notably the traveller and commentator R. W. Seton-Watson, or Henry Wickham Steed, *Times* correspondent in Vienna from 1902 to 1913, both of whom had recently become increasingly critical of German-Magyar domination over the nine other nationalities of the empire.[6] They had a soulmate at the heart of the Foreign Office in Eyre Crowe, senior clerk in the Western Department, for whom 'Austrian and Hungarian records in the matter of corrupt administration and police brutalities are of the very darkest. ... We have the Agram [Zagreb treason] Trial [of 1909] and Dr Friedjung's forged documents still fresh in our minds.'[7] Indeed, although the acquittal in 1911 of a Croatian MP who had fired a pistol at the Hungarian prime minister in parliament seemed 'beyond comprehension' to some in the Foreign Office, Crowe was completely unfazed. It was, he noted, 'one of the results of a long period of oppression and unconstitutional government [in Croatia]. It arouses the political passions to the extinction of ordinary feelings of right and wrong.'[8]

It must be emphasized, however, that such views found no echo among the vast majority of the British political elite who were less versed in the details of Austro-Hungarian politics, or even in wider Foreign Office circles. Cartwright, for example, replying to a complaint from his colleague in Constantinople that Steed 'took the record for nonsense', was robust in his condemnation:

[Steed] is a fanatic against Turkey and an enthusiast for the Serbs, and he dreams of nothing less than a great uprising of all the Southern Slavs in this Empire and a final burst-up [sic] of Austria-Hungary. I have had plenty of trouble in calming down many of the alarms which he has caused our Foreign Office by his exaggerated representation of things here.[9]

In fact, so far as the Foreign Office was concerned, once the London Conference under Sir Edward Grey's chairmanship had successfully steered Europe through the dangerous crisis of the Balkan Wars of 1912–13, Anglo-Austrian relations seemed better than they had been for several years. When in May 1914 Count Berchtold, in his annual review before the Delegations of the Austrian and Hungarian parliaments, singled out and praised Great Britain's contribution to the resolution of the late Balkan crisis (while significantly ignoring any such contribution by Russia or France), Grey was, according to his private secretary, 'quite exceptionally pleased', commenting that 'it helps and makes one's work pleasanter and easier'. Grey himself told the Austro-Hungarian ambassador: 'It was things of that kind that gave one a little pleasure in public work.'[10]

The Austrians for their part, even if Great Britain and Austria-Hungary were in opposite diplomatic camps, were gratified to note that the British were lending their Triple Entente partners no assistance in their frantic efforts to draw the Balkan states into their orbit. The *Militärische Rundschau* might well bleakly observe that 'in the centre of the hostile naval forces [facing the Monarchy in the Mediterranean] stands the English fleet at Malta'.[11] But the spring of 1914 witnessed an extraordinarily successful visit by this same squadron to Adriatic ports of the Monarchy. Cartwright's successor at the Vienna embassy, Sir Maurice de Bunsen, hastened to inform Berchtold, 'I can truly say that on no occasion of the kind have I ever seen a more agreeable exhibition of good fellowship between a visiting fleet and the authorities and population of the place visited. Admiral Milne tells me that he has been most agreeably struck by the same thought.'[12] In short, as far as the British establishment was concerned, what were after all perhaps rather theoretical diplomatic and military considerations did not seem to threaten the cordiality that characterized Anglo-Austrian relations in the summer of 1914.

At the very pinnacle of British society, the court of King George V, Austria-Hungary also enjoyed a quite exceptional position, thanks to the ties of blood existing between the monarch and the long-serving (1902–14) Austro-Hungarian ambassador in London: from the 1890s Albert Count Mensdorff-Pouilly-Dietrichstein was *persona gratissima* at Windsor, Sandringham and Balmoral. Equally, the Bohemian spas had always been a favourite haunt of Edward VII. (As late as 1929 Mensdorff was amused to receive from King George a letter addressed to him in 'Marienbad, Austria', commenting, 'if the Czechs only knew, what a face they would pull!')[13] In September

1910, Mensdorff thanked King George for the assistance rendered by the Royal Navy to an Austrian vessel in distress. The monarch in turn took the opportunity to emphasize that

> there has never been anything other than good friendship between us. ... Here in England, Austrians have always been received quite differently from other foreigners, and in Austria too the English have always been welcomed as friends. Of all the European states, it was always Austria-Hungary with whom we were on the best terms. Never against each other and so often allies.[14]

In fact, in 1912 the king caused the Foreign Office a good deal of trouble with his persistent, if ultimately vain, attempts to insist on honouring the aged Franz Joseph, in his view the doyen of European monarchs, with the first state visit of the new reign.[15] ('We made too much of the French Republic,' his private secretary truculently informed Whitehall.)[16] In 1914, too, Queen Mary was lamenting to Mensdorff that Paris would have to come first, and that unfortunately sensitivities in St Petersburg meant that their keenly anticipated state visit to Austria-Hungary must be deferred and undertaken simultaneously with one to Russia in 1915.[17] Even so, as she was to assure him in a letter long after the war, it was 'a pleasure to think that I did once see Vienna in all its glory, and had the pleasure of making the acquaintance of your beloved Kaiser, who was always in the eyes of *our* family, Cambridge, Strelitz and Teck, "Der Kaiser" par excellence [emphasis in original]'.[18]

King George's affection also extended, from at least when he visited Vienna as Prince of Wales in 1903 to Archduke Franz Ferdinand. 'You know, I really like the Archduke': they shared a passion for shooting.[19] Franz Ferdinand in turn was especially gratified by (in contrast to Vienna) the refreshingly unstuffy reception accorded to his morganatic wife at the British court. Their last visit to England, in November 1913, was judged a tremendous success; it had included a week at Windsor, where their fellow guests included not only old aristocratic friends such as the Lansdownes, Portlands and various Tory statesmen, but all the leading members of the Cabinet.[20] Indeed, Mensdorff went so far as to claim that the archduke had now quite lost his old Anglophobia of the Boer War years and become a 'convinced friend and admirer of England'.[21]

## The reaction to Sarajevo

Not surprisingly therefore, at the highest level, the reactions of the British elite to the news of Sarajevo reflected their Austrophile sympathies.[22] The very next morning the king came unannounced to the embassy in Belgrave Square to express his condolences to Mensdorff; the ambassador was overwhelmed with letters from court and county society, and from leading members of the political world (see Appendix I). The keynote was essentially one of stunned horror, coupled with an obviously sincere sympathy for the bereaved, particularly for the old and much-tried emperor; as Grey wrote, his life was 'so bound up with the peace of Europe that I dread anything that must try his strength'.[23] For the most part, however, these writers did not dwell on the possible international consequences of the murders. Perhaps this was because they were responding to what was, for them, as acquaintances of the victims, primarily a personal tragedy; perhaps they were simply bewildered by the suddenness of the event. But it was also the case that for the elite, the political future was entirely dominated in these weeks, right until the presentation of the Austro-Hungarian ultimatum to Serbia, by the Irish crisis and the looming prospect of civil war in Ireland.

The reactions of the British political elite were similar, at least on a personal level. Eloquent tributes were paid in parliament. Prime Minister Herbert Asquith's words were, Mensdorff assured him, 'most highly appreciated not only by our Emperor but all over Austria-Hungary, where everybody values the traditional ties of friendship existing between our two countries'.[24] Similarly, it gave Andrew Bonar Law (leader of the Conservative Party) 'a great pleasure ... to think that [Mensdorff regarded] what I said on Tuesday as an adequate expression of the feeling which is universal in this country of deep and friendly sympathy with the Austrian people and their venerable Emperor'.[25] On 3 July, both the social and political elites were well represented at the memorial service for the deceased.[26] Meanwhile, demonstrative displays of sympathy by British diplomats in Vienna and Belgrade were noted with some irritation by their Russian colleagues; in turn, the British minister in Belgrade was sharply critical of the 'very singular' indifference of his French and Russian colleagues over attending memorial services or flying flags at half mast.[27]

As might be expected, of course, in contrast to the social elite, the political and diplomatic elite had rather more to say about the possible repercussions of the assassinations. De Bunsen, the British ambassador in Vienna, suspected quite early that the Austrians might take some punitive action. He warned:

> those who remember the circumstances of the notorious Agram and Dr Friedjung trials in 1908 and 1909, when the efforts of the Austro-Hungarian Government to justify the expected war with Servia by publishing proofs of a widespread irredentist Servian plot so woefully broke down, will hesitate to accept without adequate proofs the wholesale denunciations of the Servian patriotic societies which may now be expected to be made.[28]

The striking feature about the reactions of De Bunsen's Foreign Office masters however, was their sanguine imperturbability. Crowe was perhaps an extreme case. He noted drily, when the consul in Sarajevo in late June confined himself to assessing the cost of damages wrought by anti-Serb rioters in the city, that 'Consul Jones seems to look upon the assassinations with the eye and in the spirit of an insurance agent'.[29] But De Bunsen fared no better with the permanent undersecretary, Sir Arthur Nicolson. The ambassador reported to London that the Ballhausplatz was 'very angry' with Serbia but that his Russian colleague, N.N. Schebeko, thought the indignation confined to a few professors and 'people of sixteen quarterings'. Nicolson, who knew Schebeko personally from his time in Russia and considered him eminently sensible, doubted 'whether Austria will take any action of a serious character and I expect the storm will blow over'.[30]

Certainly, the Foreign Office for almost three weeks seemed to be completely unaware of the momentous shift in Habsburg policy that had followed the assassinations. Namely, Berchtold had decided to abandon his planned appeal to Berlin for support in a diplomatic campaign to strengthen Austrian influence in the Balkans (the so-called Matscheko Memorandum of 24 June). Instead, he favoured the military chastisement of Serbia, both to put an end to Franco-Russian schemes for a new Balkan League and to restore Austria-Hungary's position as the dominant power in the Balkans once and for all.[31] There are several possible explanations for what might at first sight seem astonishing ignorance or insouciance on the part of the British.

In the first place, there was Austria-Hungary's recent record, both during and since the great Balkan crisis of 1912–13, of uttering threats and issuing ultimatums without actually going to war. Thus, in February 1914 a warning from De Bunsen that Vienna was becoming desperate about St Petersburg's attempts to create a new Balkan League, which the leading Austrian liberal paper described as 'a dagger in the hand of Russia pointed straight at the heart of Austria', was simply dismissed out of hand in London as a manoeuvre to whip up votes in parliament for the latest army bill.[32] In the second place, the Habsburg elite was remarkably successful in concealing its intentions until President Poincaré's state visit to Russia had ended and the French decision makers found themselves literally at sea (24 July). This secrecy was influential in preventing London from guessing what was being prepared. Indeed, Mensdorff himself was noting in his diary as late as 15 July: 'I do not know what we are intending to do about Serbia, but we are preparing some demarche. Given the incoherence [*Kopflosigkeit*] and lack of planning prevailing in the Ballhausplatz, I don't have much confidence.'[33]

In the third place, the British were perhaps themselves in something of a state of denial, characterized by a reluctance to confront the terrible implications of the assassinations in terms of a clash between Slav and Teuton. Russian susceptibilities being what they were, it was at any rate politic for the British to steer clear of any debate whatever over the Sarajevo issue, even if it seemed that the Austrians might have a reasonable case. As early as 1912, for example, when Nicolson had admitted that

Russia's attempts to promote a Balkan League 'might possibly eventually lead to serious trouble', he still felt it essential 'for us to keep on the best possible terms with Russia and not to have the appearance of criticising any action which they may think desirable to take'.[34] Thus, when, on 17 July, Mensdorff raised with Grey the subject of Sarajevo, and spoke of outrageous attempts by the Serbian press 'to promote revolutionary movements in territories that form an integral part of the Monarchy, which no state – however peace-loving – can tolerate', Grey agreed, but he did not pursue the subject.[35]

For the most part the reactions of the British press, meanwhile, had been similarly sympathetic, if fairly non-committal.[36] While the anti-German *Morning Post* was almost uniquely sceptical (on one occasion describing the assassinations as the outcome of Habsburg misgovernment in Bosnia), the Liberal papers were united in their condemnation of Serbian terrorism, of the idea of war and above all of Tsarist Russia. Mensdorff, instructed by Berchtold to use his excellent social contacts to influence the British press, had to confess this would be difficult:

> The only way to influence the important journalists is through the information one gives them. The language of our papers with their talk of Serbian provocations and the threads of the conspiracy that undoubtedly lead to Belgrade does not make much of an impression. If once the enquiry confirms that Serbia is guilty of involvement in the Sarajevo murder, then I think that public opinion will be on our side. People here have little time for suspicions [*Vermutungen*] that are not based on documentary evidence.[37]

He nevertheless felt it worthwhile to send Lord Lansdowne some translations from the Belgrade papers. For these were

> full of insults for us. They go so far as to say that the murder of the Archduke was engineered in Austria in order to have a pretext to assimilate the Servian population in Bosnia-Herzegovina. ... It is of the highest importance that the people in Servia should be given to understand that the whole civilised world is unanimous in the condemnation of the horrid murder. ... The desire of Austria-Hungary to maintain peace has been frequently demonstrated ... but we must of course defend our territorial integrity and the State cannot tolerate such a perpetual campaign to incite Austro-Hungarian subjects of Servian nationality to revolt and crime, by continually advocating the realisation of the Great Servian dream, at the expense of territories forming an integral part of the Austro-Hungarian Monarchy. ... There seem to be many elements – of course not in England – who are interested in promoting unrest and international trouble, that I think that it would be most useful if some important personage in this country could enable the public to form a fair estimate of the situation.[38]

Lansdowne was impressed enough to write to Geoffrey Robinson, the editor of the *Times*, who replied 'that he hopes to be able to draw attention to the attitude of the Servians and the dangerous situation which is constantly arising'.³⁹ The upshot was a leader in the *Times* of 16 July, generally recognizing the right of the Austrians to an investigation and 'guarantees against agitation' – but still reminding them that recourse to war had in the past only spelt disaster for the Monarchy.⁴⁰ The *Westminster Gazette* went further, recognizing the Monarchy's right to call Serbia to account but not containing any warning against going to war. This drew a complaint from the Russian embassy in Vienna that a British government newspaper should be encouraging Austria-Hungary to take action against Serbia, but Grey simply denied all connection with the paper.⁴¹

Mensdorff's efforts to influence the *Times* by putting pressure on Steed also rather misfired. When on 17 July he arranged a luncheon for Steed at which the embassy staff and the editor of the *Neues Wiener Tagblatt* bombarded him with a catalogue of charges against Serbia, this only roused the suspicion in Steed's somewhat paranoid mind that Vienna had known about the assassination plot in advance.⁴² To make matters worse, when Mensdorff himself lunched alone with Steed on 21 July and remarked that he had assurances that in the event of war Great Britain would remain neutral, Steed was convinced that Vienna was determined to attack Serbia. He informed the *Times* proprietor Lord Northcliffe of his suspicions with the result that a *Times* leader on 22 July – 'A Danger to Europe'– warned that unless Austria-Hungary could prove that the Serbian authorities were themselves involved in the conspiracies 'to the reasonable satisfaction of European opinion, she would be branded an aggressor and a danger to the general peace'.⁴³ This came only after Steed had wasted time on a visit to the Foreign Office; there his warnings had failed entirely – and to his considerable irritation – to make any impression on Grey's private secretary, Sir William Tyrrell.⁴⁴

Grey himself remained equally non-committal on 23 July when Mensdorff (in an attempt to head off any unwelcome advice) called at the Foreign Office to give him the gist of the note to be presented at Belgrade the following day. Grey simply refused to be drawn over the Austro-Serbian dispute. As he noted, 'If Austria could make war on Serbia and at the same time satisfy Russia, well and good. I could take a holiday tomorrow. But if not, the consequences would be incalculable.'⁴⁵ In turn, if the Monarchy's grievances proved well founded and its demands on Serbia reasonable [*ausführbar*], 'one could hope that Russia would exercise a moderating influence in Belgrade'.⁴⁶ The danger though was of a flare-up of Slav feeling in Russian public opinion; therefore, he regretted the time limit that made it impossible for the powers to bring pressure on Belgrade. When Mensdorff again expatiated on the threats to the Monarchy from Serbian subversion, and the failure of Belgrade for over three weeks to take any action against the conspirators, Grey 'recognised the difficulty of [Vienna's] position'.

But he stressed to Mensdorff the seriousness of the situation: if four Great Powers – Austria-Hungary, Germany, Russia and France – were involved in a war, that would amount to the bankruptcy of Europe. There would be no credit anywhere, industrial centres in uproar, and in most countries, whether victors or vanquished, 'so many existing institutions [would be] swept away'.[47]

Matters looked even more serious to Grey when on 24 July he saw the actual text of the Austro-Hungarian ultimatum: it was 'the most formidable document that has ever been addressed to an independent state'.[48] Berchtold's promise not to annex any Serbian territory was neither here nor there, for, as Grey informed the Cabinet, it was not a question of territory but of an attempt to banish Russian influence from the Balkans.[49] Mensdorff meanwhile confided to his diary: 'Our note as sharp as possible. Clearly intended that Serbia cannot accept the conditions.'[50] Even now, however, he could still draw some comfort from the fact that Grey was not talking in terms of British intervention but hoping against hope that direct Austro-Russian talks might yet save the situation.[51]

Others at the Foreign Office, notably Nicolson (who regarded himself as the chief architect and guardian of the Anglo-Russian Entente), took a very different view, especially after Vienna rejected the Serbian reply, broke off relations with Belgrade on 27 July and then, in their determination to head off any third-party intervention, hastened to declare war the following day. Crowe and Sir George Buchanan, ambassador in St Petersburg, shared Nicolson's outlook. For Crowe, on first reading the terms of the ultimatum it was

> clear that France and Russia are decided to accept the challenge thrown out to them. Whatever we may think of the merits of the Austrian charges against Servia, France and Russia consider that these are pretexts and that the bigger cause of the Triple Alliance versus Triple Entente is definitely engaged.[52]

He thought it would be 'impolitic, not to say dangerous, for England to attempt to controvert this opinion'. Nicolson agreed: 'Our attitude during the crisis will be regarded by Russia as a test, and we must be careful not to alienate her.'[53] From St Petersburg Buchanan telegraphed similarly that

> if it comes to war Russia cannot allow Austria to crush Servia and become [the] predominant power in Balkans. We shall have to choose between giving Russia our active support and renouncing her friendship. If we fail her now we cannot hope to maintain that friendly cooperation with her in Asia that is of such vital importance to us.[54]

Meanwhile in Paris, Sir Francis Bertie took it upon himself to warn the French that 'public opinion in England would not support a war in support of Russia if she, as protector of the Slavs, picked a quarrel with Austria over [the] Austro-Servian difficulty'.[55] But a report in the *Daily Telegraph* of 27 July from Dillon – according to Nicolson 'an intimate friend of Count Berchtold' – made a strong impression in Whitehall. As Nicolson observed, Dillon stated

> Austria's case with a simplicity which is notable. He avows that the Serbian 'question' is merely a pretext for an endeavour, in conjunction with Germany, to re-establish Austria's position in the Balkans and to displace Russia – and it is stated that no intervention or mediation will be allowed. We are witnessing a most cynical and desperate measure and Germany should, for her own reputation, show by her acts that she is not willing to associate herself with it, or in any case will assist in mitigating its effects and limit its scope.[56]

As late as 31 July Mensdorff noted in his diary: 'Nobody wants war ... here no trace of anti-German feeling in the public.' In fact he was beginning to despair. He had to admit that the Monarchy's latest actions had damaged its reputation with the British: they 'understand our position regarding Serbia', but they felt 'we should have been content to accept satisfaction and suspect that we are seeking to annihilate Serbia for good and to expel Russian influence from the Balkans'. This being the case, he concluded that 'short of a miracle there will be general war tomorrow. ... One despairs of humanity. ... It is the result of the alliance system that everybody is dragged into war against his will because of a few Serbian murderers.'[57]

In the event, of course, it was the German ultimatum to and declaration of war on Russia (from 31 July to 1 August) that dashed the hopes that Grey had placed in direct Austro-Russian negotiations, British mediation or German moderating influence in Vienna. Here, 'Serbian murderers' were no longer the issue. Indeed, by her action Germany took from Austria-Hungary's shoulders the mantle of chief warmonger – or so the British decided. In the British government's white paper on the last days of peace, the Monarchy came off remarkably lightly: there had been 'good hopes' of peace until Germany 'banged the door' on negotiations by attacking Russia – a point that was seized on, to the satisfaction of the Austrians, by the whole British press.[58]

## The breaking of diplomatic relations

Looking back in 1925, when Grey sent him a copy of his memoirs in which he regretted not having made his mediation proposal directly to Vienna rather than via Berlin, Mensdorff doubted whether this would have made much difference (even if 'it would have forced those criminal idiots of ours at the time to show their colours, and perhaps something could have been done').[59] The point was that the issue had become no longer one of an Austro-Serbian or even Austro-Russian confrontation. Indeed, Mensdorff had heard this from Grey himself in 1924 on his first post-war visit to England:

> He confirmed to me that none of the [Anglo-French] military agreements had committed England. ... If Germany had not marched into Belgium the Cabinet here would have 'broken up', as the partisans of peace were very strong. From the moment the enemy marched into Belgium everybody was united, government, parliament and country.[60]

Certainly, by 9 August 1914 Mensdorff had admitted that the 'violation of Belgian neutrality has made the Germans and indirectly us, unpopular ... as the aggressors. ... An irony of fate that a conflict that started over Serbian and Balkan questions should now turn into a struggle in Belgium, the old battlefield of Europe, over supremacy in Western Europe.'[61]

It was significant that Austria-Hungary did not declare war on Russia (under German pressure) until 6 August; and that the Western powers did not declare war on the Monarchy for almost two weeks after the start of the war in the East. There were what Grey termed 'very obvious strategic reasons' for the delay.[62] So long as the French Mediterranean fleet was busy convoying troops from North Africa, the British Mediterranean fleet, which had no dreadnoughts, would have had to cope alone in the Adriatic with the Habsburg navy, which included three. In fact, the Foreign Office was already considering war with the Monarchy to be only a matter of time. This was clear from Grey's acquiescence in Franco-Russian proposals to offer Hungarian territory to Romania, and his support for ceding Habsburg territory in the Adriatic to Italy; Grey himself insisted that 'certainly Trieste must be thrown in'.[63]

All this was at a time when Great Britain and Austria-Hungary were still at peace. The British official mindset was unknown to Mensdorff, who lived in a strange diplomatic limbo until he received his passports on 12 August – the most painful moment of his life: 'What a sad irony of history that *I* should be the first Austrian ambassador in history to leave London after a declaration of war [emphasis in original].'[64] Yet even these last experiences are of some interest in illuminating the reactions of the circles he moved in – the cosmopolitan society of court and country house – to the outbreak of modern war. It shows that the contrast between the affection felt in those circles for Austria-Hungary and the realpolitik of the Foreign Office had survived and perhaps had even been sharpened by the July crisis.

On 9 August, for example, Mensdorff was summoned to Buckingham Palace, drove in by a side gate to avoid journalists and photographers, and there he had tea with the king and queen. George V was 'as friendly and kind as ever and said that he hoped that it would not come to war between

England and Austria-Hungary', to which Mensdorff replied that 'unless you send your fleet to bombard our coast in the Adriatic, I don't see how hostilities between us can take place'. At this, the king 'said repeatedly, "I don't think there is any intention of doing so", but it was an anomalous situation: "you being at war with Russia and we with Germany, if we don't come to blows it certainly shows a great drive to maintain our friendship".' Altogether, the king was at pains to stress that 'Great Britain was waging war for the neutrality of Belgium and for the defence of the French coast, not for Serbia or Balkan questions'. To this Mensdorff replied: 'that was precisely why it might be possible to separate the war in the east from that in the west.'[65]

The only suggestion – a very tentative one – of any possible connection between these events and Sarajevo appears in Mensdorff's report of a long conversation with the British journalist Sydney Brooks on 5 August.[66] For the most part this went off well enough. Mensdorff insisted that there was no need for war so long as the British did not attack in the Adriatic, while Brooks assured him 'that there was no feeling at all against the Monarchy here' – although this might change if Italy joined in, and 'the greatest efforts were being made to stir up Italy' against Austria-Hungary. When Mensdorff pointed out that to reduce Austria-Hungary to a second-class power would only make Russia too strong, Brooks agreed. He 'thought that the present war against German predominance would have to be fought against Russia in fifty years or less. But for the moment they were not thinking of the future, but only of the present war. (The fear of Germany is indeed very great and deep rooted.)' However, almost as an afterthought, Brooks said

> there was just one thing that could stir up feeling against us, namely, revelations unfavourable to us about the murder of Archduke Franz Ferdinand. I had absolutely no idea what he meant and he didn't want to say, but in the end I asked him if he meant the silly and infamous slanders in the Belgrade papers, that the murder had been arranged in Vienna in order to provide a pretext to annihilate the noble Serbian nation.

He said this story was being spread about 'and they work it up for all its worth'. This rendered Mensdorff 'speechless', though he managed to protest that 'this was not cricket'. In the end, however, when Mensdorff recovered sufficiently to report the matter to Grey's secretary, it all proved of little significance: 'I could only say that English morality was different from Serbian and I did not expect for a moment that attempts to spread such things here could have any success. [Tyrrell] described it all as "infamous and stupid" but said he knew that busy attempts were being made here to spread such infamous slanders.' Clearly, such tales were not having any effect on the calculations of British decision-making circles in the critical days.

The material in the Mensdorff papers in the Vienna archives relating to events between the final declaration of war on 12 August and the ambassador's departure four days later further illuminates two significant features of the *mentalités* of the British elite. First, its continuing sympathy for Austria-Hungary; second, the genuine dismay with which it greeted the outbreak of war, a far cry indeed from the chauvinist demonstrations in continental capitals – from the German crown prince's 'Auf, zu einem frisch-fröhlichen Krieg' or even from Rupert Brooke. Whereas the departure of ambassadors from Paris, St Petersburg and Berlin had been marred by violently hostile demonstrations – in the case of Berlin, according to Nicolson, 'quite unprecedented in diplomatic history even if one went back several centuries'[67] – there was none of this in Mensdorff's case. On the contrary, both Nicolson and Grey were deeply moved. The latter sent him, along with the formal declaration of war, an 'endlessly friendly letter', and had to struggle with tears at the moment of parting.[68]

Naturally Mensdorff's royal relatives – his 'affectionate cousins and sincere friends, George and Mary' – were even more grief-stricken; and Queen Alexandra on taking leave of him wept and kissed him.[69] He was overwhelmed (see Appendix II) with letters from English country houses – some of them sharply critical of the turn events had taken – and his departure on 16 August was accompanied by extraordinary scenes.[70] The king sent his chamberlain to the station, where Grey's whole secretariat also turned up; there were shouts of 'Three cheers for Count Mensdorff' from the crowd. When the ambassador, his staff and a company of some 240 fellow citizens travelled by ship to Genoa (the North Sea being deemed unsafe), the first British warship they met greeted them with the signal 'The British Navy present their compliments to Your Excellency and hope to see you soon again'. That was 'cricket'.

\* \* \*

# APPENDIX I[71]

## *Letters to Count Mensdorff (June–July 1914)*

*Mary, duchess of Roxburgh*
I must send you a line to express my horror at these brutal murders and to offer my sympathy. I was so shocked at the terrible news. Both the Archduke and the Duchess were so kind to us last year and it seems most cruel that they should have met their end in such a dreadful way. There is only one consolation – I am sure they would have chosen to die together as a more devoted couple I have never met.

# THE BRITISH ELITE AND THE SARAJEVO ASSASSINATIONS

*Sir Gerard Lowther* (former British ambassador at Constantinople)
28 June
My dear Ambassador,
What can words avail? I will not weary you with them. But my heart goes out to you and your great people and above all to your Grand old Emperor over the dastardly act and the awful calamity. Pray accept my very deep sympathy for your Government, yourself and for the many kind friends I have in Austria who poured kindnesses on me when I was there.

*Marquess of Lansdowne*
28 June
My dear Mensdorff,
I cannot tell you how deeply this tragedy has shocked us. It is appalling. I need not assure you of our sympathy. We are perhaps more touched than others because, as you know, His Imperial Highness was good enough to honour us with his friendship. We have never forgotten the visit which he paid to us when we were in India, and on occasions when in subsequent years, he came to this country, he was always more than kind to us all, including my son, who was attached to his suite. Among those who will mourn for the loss which your country has sustained none will do so more sincerely than ...

*Sir Francis Knollys* (King George's private secretary)
A line of sympathy and condolence on the terrible tragedy which took place yesterday. It is too sad and ghastly and everybody's heart must go out to the poor Emperor who has now had another shock and grief added to the long list of misfortunes which have fallen upon him in the course of his life.

I hope they will not give the murderers a prolonged trial as doing so will only give them an opportunity of indulging their vanity.

*Marquess of Crewe* (secretary of state for India)
29 June
My dear Albert,
You must let me send you one word of condolence, which needs no reply, from us both on the appalling act of yesterday. Our pleasant meeting with His Imperial Highness and the Duchess at Windsor last autumn, when they were very kind to us, brings home closely to us the horror of the tragedy. One thinks almost equally of the Emperor, with this fresh calamity in the evening of his life, and of the orphaned children for whom their morning of life is made so dark.

*Sir Edward Grey*
29 June
Dear Count Mensdorff,
I must add to our official expression of feeling a personal line to you to say how deeply I sympathize in the loss that has befallen Austria-Hungary; the

cruel circumstances attending it add to the tragedy. You will know how much we all feel for your Emperor and for the shock and grief that he must suffer: his life is so bound up with the peace of Europe that I dread anything that must try his strength.

It is less than a year since many of us saw the Archduke and his wife enjoying their visit to Windsor and seeming to be so happy here, and this too quickens our sympathy. Every feeling political and personal makes me sympathize with you.

### *Evelyn Byng*
30 June
Dear Count Mensdorff,
I must send you a line to say how shocked I am at the horrible tragedy to the Archduke. Really, your poor gallant old Emperor seems to be 'a man of sorrows and acquainted with grief' to a terrible degree – One only hopes the shock of the crime won't kill him, for a mere child, as his successor is, would certainly not be suited to hold the reins of Empire in times as troubled and with problems as intricate as those which exist throughout Europe in the present day.

### *FML Lord Roberts*
3 July
Dear Count Mensdorff,
I greatly regret that I cannot do myself the honour of being present at the Requiem Mass in Memory of His Imp and R H the late Archduke Francis Ferdinand and Her Highness the Duchess of Hohenberg at Westminster Cathedral this forenoon. I had the privilege of meeting the late Royal Duke at Calcutta, and of spending the weekend with His Royal Highness and Her Highness the Duchess of Hohenberg at Welbeck Abbey quite a short time ago, and I need not say how shocked and grieved I am at the tragic and terribly sudden end they have met with – with all my countrymen I would tender my most sincere and most respectful sympathy to His Imperial Majesty the Emperor of Austria.

### *Lord George Hamilton* (leading Tory politician)
My dear Count Mensdorff,
You must allow me, both on behalf of my wife and myself, to express to you our horror of the foul assassination of the Archduke Franz Ferdinand and His Duchess. It seems only the other day that we were all at Welbeck where both the Arch Duke and the Duchess charmed us all by their kindly and engaging personalities. That a Slav should think he could advance his country's interests by the murder of so kindly and high minded a royalty seems incredible. But the foul deed has been done and we can only express to you, as representing Austria, our deep solicitude and sympathy for you in this shocking tragedy.

*Princess Louise* (Princess Royal and younger sister of King George V)
Monday morning.
Dear Albert, Just seeing the papers and in spite of the extra work which will now be thrown upon you I must send you a few lines, to express my very deep sympathy and intense horror and distress, at this terrible crime which has been committed. The Archduke was so charming and so kind and they both left such a very unusually good impression here last autumn and I know they are beloved in their country it really is very terrible – The poor Emperor! Has he not had sorrow and difficulties enough! It must have been a terrible shock to you dear Albert I fear. What cruel times we are living in.

All my sympathy is with your Emperor and his family. You know that if Lorne [Louise's late husband] were still with us, how great his sympathy and distress would have been.

*Edith Robertson*
6 July
My dear Count Mensdorff,
I must write you a line – rather late I fear – but none the less sincere – to tell you how horrified both Freddie and I were at the horrible murder of your poor Archduke and his wife. It was a crime that made all the world shudder and I am so dreadfully sorry for those 3 poor little children, who seem so especially forlorn and unfortunate in every way.

Besides being dreadfully shocked at the crime, we are very sad that it has deprived us of what would, I know, have been a delightful evening in your house. Hoping to see you soon.

*Douglas Dawson* (Lord Chamberlain's Office)
My dear Albert,
You have my deepest sympathy at the moment of this appalling tragedy. It is too terrible to think of, and in this country it will be universally felt and grieved over, for he had begun to make so many friends here. The King was so overcome when I saw him on Sunday, but you will have seen him twice.

I had the honour of coming here with the Archduke the first visit he ever paid here, and I have watched with pleasure the gradual warming of his feelings for this country, feeling as I did that we had in him a true friend. It is too sad, and I felt I must send you a line, which please don't trouble to answer. The poor Emperor!!

Ever, dear Albert, with deepest sympathy,

Later on, I would be glad to hear how the Emperor is.

*Minnie Paget* (sister-in-law of Ralph Paget, former British minister at Belgrade)
My dear Mensdorff,
What an awful, hideous tragedy. I have thought of nothing else since I read of it. I cannot get it out of my mind. In common with nearly everyone in the

world my heart goes out in sympathy with your Emperor, who seems indeed to be 'spared nothing'. Such horrible wickedness is beyond imagination. And what terrible anxiety it must cause you all.

*Theo Russell* (former counsellor at the British embassy at Vienna)
Dear Count Mensdorff,
There are no words for me to express my deep sympathy to you and your country in this appalling tragedy. It is impossible to realize and it is only by degrees that one takes in the whole horror of the situation. All the world will mourn for your poor country and for the venerable Emperor who has suffered so much. This requires no reply. It is only to show that I am thinking of you and your country, which I love, in the hour of distress and misery.

# APPENDIX II

## Farewell letters to Count Mensdorff on the outbreak of war

*Lord Curzon*
It must be a very sad and tragic moment for you, leaving England where you have made so many friends and have so long represented a Power with which we have so many ties of friendship and attachment. I express the hope that in due time when all these calamities are over we may see you again.

*Claude Hay, MP*
9 August
We used to be such friends in days gone by that I feel I must write to you, although in these your 'big' days I have not seen much of you. All the more reason to tell you of my intense sympathy with you in a situation which must give you unhappiness and of my unbounded admiration for your Emperor. The fools of the press here have never taught the public what are the facts as to Austria's long-sufferance and generosity towards the *Schweinerei* of Servia and now the whole case of Austria is lost in the general war.

Like you I am suffering! Poor Muriel! a son in the Uhlans and every other relation and friends I have either fighting (*Gott sei Dank*) or in trouble & I cannot help them I am doing my quiet share, inter alia making folk know the Austrian case.

If you want a quiet – *mit telephon* 1¼ hours from London, 500 ft above the sea, to be perdu '*mit oder ohne Secretary*' you can come whenever you like to this lovely spot (tucked away in the hills 9 miles from Newbury and 3 from Hungerford) and nobody can know you are here.

***King George V***[72]
12 August 1914
My dear Albert,
It is a great grief to the Queen and myself that you are going to leave England. We have been such intimate friends for so many years that we cannot let you leave without sending you one word of farewell. We trust that when these terrible times have passed and peace once more reigns in Europe that we shall have the pleasure of welcoming you back to England is the earnest prayer of your affecte cousins and sincere friends, George R.I. and Mary.

***Queen Alexandra*** (widow of King Edward VII)
Thursday [13 August]
Dear Mensdorff,
This is *too terrible* you should have to leave England like this. No words can express what one feels after so many happy years here. Anyway let us hope when all these ghastly times are over you will return and make England your home. God bless you, Alexandra.

***Lord Haldane*** (Lord Chancellor)
13 August
My dear Mensdorff,
[It is a] personal sorrow to me to think that we are parting. You are one of ourselves, and we hate the idea of fighting with your country. But we are all swept into the whirlpool. I send this line to say good bye. '*Auf Wiedersehen*' I hope, before long.

***Sir Thomas Sanderson*** (former permanent undersecretary at Foreign Office)
13 August
My dear Count Mensdorff,
We are such old friends and have worked, and laughed, and groaned together over so many problems in the past, that I cannot refrain from writing. ... It will be a great happiness to me if I should live to see the end of this dreadful nightmare, and perhaps to welcome you back to England.

***Sir Francis Knollys***
13 August
As it is, we can only look forward to the day when we shall be able to welcome you back.
  God grant that it may be soon for the present situation is dreadful.
  Goodbye, my dear Mensdorff, and do not forget your English friends.

***Earl of Harewood***
14 August
One line to wish you goodbye. It is lamentable that your nation and ours should be at war, for we owe you no grudge, except for having put the

match to the fire. It will be a fearful war, but I hope it may not last long and that we may find ourselves sitting in the old box at the Opera next year.

*Princess Louise*
14 August
My dear Albert,
How too dreadful this all is. I do so feel for you, who have been ever such a dear true friend of England and our dear relation. Do accept all my sympathy. It is too dreadful to feel you must go after *all* you have done to *try* and help for keeping peace. All that is dear to us is gone ... & now your country has to go against us it is cruel.

May God direct and speedily end this cruel unnatural war that has been forced upon us. Ever yr affcte cousin, Louise.

*Charles Dust*
16 August
My dear Mensdorff,
I hear that you sail tonight and I write a line to wish you goodbye. Our Navy and yours have always been such good friends that I do not dare to think of the position in the Mediterranean.

There is something wrong with the western world for I do not believe that one Englishman in 100,000 is pleased at the idea of fighting against Austria.

I can but wish you good luck, I fear that your life is permanently changed now. Please do not think of answering this.

## Notes

1. The spelling 'Servia' was a common designation for 'Serbia' before 1914.
2. Northamptonshire Record Office, Cartwright MSS, Cartwright to Nicolson, private, 31 January 1913.
3. E. J. Dillon, in *Daily Telegraph*, 13 July, reprinted in *The Economist*, 18 July 1914.
4. D. C. Watt, 'The British Reactions to the Assassination at Sarajevo', *European History Quarterly* 1/3 (1971): 233–47.
5. *The Economist*, 1 August 1914: Josef Redlich letter of 21 July.
6. F. R. Bridge, 'British Official Opinion and the Domestic Situation in the Hapsburg Monarchy', in B. J. C. McKercher and D. J. Moss (eds), *Shadow and Substance in British Foreign Policy 1895-1939* (Edmonton: University of Alberta Press, 1984), 103ff.
7. The National Archives, London (hereafter TNA), Foreign Office files (hereafter FO) 371/827, Howard to Grey, d(ispatch no). 51, 20 June 1910 and minute.
8. FO 371/1298 Grant Duff to Grey, d.46, 18 December 1912, minute by Crowe.

9   Cartwright MSS, Lowther to Cartwright, private, 7 January 1913.
10  FO 371/1899, Grey to Wingfield, d.74, 6 May 1914; Haus-, Hof- und Staatsarchiv Vienna (hereafter HHStA), Politisches Archiv (PA), VIII/151, Mensdorff to Berchtold, d. 21C., 8 May 1914.
11  *Militärische Rundschau*, June 1914; FO 371/1899, De Bunsen to Grey, d.120, 19 June 1914.
12  PA VIII/150, De Bunsen to Berchtold, 17 May 1914.
13  HHStA, Mensdorff MSS, karton 5, Tagebuch (diary), 12 July 1929.
14  PA VIII/145, Mensdorff to Aehrenthal, private, 2 September 1910.
15  F. R. Bridge, *Great Britain and Austria-Hungary 1906-1914: A Diplomatic History* (London: Weidenfeld and Nicolson, 1972), 195-6.
16  FO 800/179, Bertie MSS, Memorandum by Bertie, 17 February 1912.
17  PA VIII/150, Mensdorff to Berchtold, private, 13 February 1914.
18  Mensdorff MSS, karton 5, Queen Mary to Mensdorff, 26 November 1931.
19  PA VIII/139, Mensdorff to Aehrenthal, d.58B, 29 November 1907.
20  PA VIII/149, Mensdorff to Berchtold, private, 21 November 1913.
21  Mensdorff MSS, karton 1, Mensdorff to Lansdowne, draft of letter, 14 July 1914.
22  Cf. F. R. Bridge, 'The British Declaration of War on Austria-Hungary in 1914', *The Slavonic and East European Review* 47 (1969): 401–22.
23  Mensdorff MSS, karton 11, Grey to Mensdorff, 29 June 1914.
24  Ibid., Mensdorff to Asquith, 1 July 1914.
25  Ibid., Bonar Law to Mensdorff, 2 July 1914.
26  Ibid., karton 4, Tagebuch, 5 July 1914.
27  PA I/810, Storck to Berchtold, t(elegram).132, 6 July 1914; Giesl to Berchtold, d.177P, 13 July 1914.
28  FO 371/1899, De Bunsen to Grey, d.129, 29 June 1914.
29  Ibid., Jones to F.O., telegram, 30 June 1914 and minute.
30  Ibid.
31  F. R. Bridge, *From Sadowa to Sarajevo: The Foreign Policy of Austria-Hungary 1866-1914* (London: Routledge & Kegan Paul, 1972), 368–70.
32  FO 371/1899, De Bunsen to Grey, d.32, 13 February 1914 and minutes.
33  Mensdorff MSS, karton 4, Tagebuch, 2 July 1914.
34  G.P. Gooch and H.W.V. Temperley (eds.), *British Documents on the Origins of the War, 1898-1914* (hereafter BD) 11 vols (London: HM Stationary Office, 1928–38), IX/1, no. 570, Nicolson to O'Beirne, private, 21 May 1912.
35  PA I/810, Mensdorff to Berchtold, d.34C, 17 July 1914.
36  Watt, 'The British Reactions', 235.
37  PA I/810, Mensdorff to Berchtold, d.34B secret, 17 July 1914.
38  Mensdorff MSS, karton 9, Mensdorff to Lansdowne (copy), 14 July 1914.

39  Ibid., Lansdowne to Mensdorff, 16 July 1914.
40  Watt, 'The British Reactions', 242ff.
41  Ibid.
42  Ibid.
43  Ibid.
44  Ibid., 245.
45  FO 371/2159, Grey to De Bunsen, d.124, 27 July 1914.
46  PA I/810, Mensdorff to Berchtold, t.107, 23 July 1914.
47  PA I/812, Mensdorff to Berchtold, d.35A, 29 July 1914.
48  Mensdorff MSS, karton 1, Tagebuch, 26 July 1914.
49  TNA, CAB/41/35/21, Asquith to George V, 28 July 1914.
50  Mensdorff MSS, karton 1, Tagebuch, 26 July 1914.
51  Bridge, 'The British Declaration of War', 410–11.
52  FO 371/2158, Buchanan to Grey, d.166, 24 July 1914, minute.
53  Ibid., minute.
54  Ibid., Buchanan to Grey, t.109, 25 July 1914.
55  Ibid., Bertie to Grey t.86, 25 July 1914.
56  FO 371/2159, minute by Nicolson, 27 July 1914.
57  Mensdorff MSS, karton 1, Tagebuch, 31 July 1914.
58  CD 7596, which is in fact a dispatch of 1 September 1914 from De Bunsen to Grey (FO 371/1900); PA VIII/150, Poppauer to Berchtold, 17 September 1914.
59  Mensdorff MSS, karton 5, Tagebuch, 17 December 1925.
60  Ibid., 8 November 1924.
61  Ibid., karton 1, Tagebuch, 9 August 1914.
62  FO 371/ 2163, Buchanan to Grey, t.240, 7 August 1914 and minutes.
63  FO 371/2162, Nicolson to Grey, 6 August 1914 and minute.
64  Mensdorff MSS, karton 1, Tagebuch, 14 August 1914.
65  PA I/823, Mensdorff to Berchtold, d.39, 10 August 1914; Mensdorff MSS, karton 1, Tagebuch, 9 August 1914.
66  PA VIII/823, Mensdorff to Berchtold, d.37B, 6 August 1914.
67  FO 371/2162, Bertie to Grey, t.389, 3 August 1914, minute.
68  Mensdorff MSS, karton 1, Tagebuch, 14 August 1914.
69  Ibid., karton 8, George V to Mensdorff, 12 August 1914; karton 1, Tagebuch, 14 August 1914.
70  Ibid., karton 1, Tagebuch, 21 August 1914.
71  This correspondence is located in: ibid., karton 11.
72  This letter is from ibid., karton 8.

# PART III
# Regional blaze

# CHAPTER 11

# Between Budapest and Belgrade

# The road to pragmatism and treason in 1914 Croatia

*Mark Cornwall*

When the innkeeper Mica Kranjčević of Brlog first heard about the Sarajevo murders on 28 June 1914, she fired off twenty rounds from her rifle to celebrate. That at least was the official version based on eyewitnesses in the Otočac district of south-western Croatia. Kranjčević was a well-known local eccentric and apparently of 'a vicious disposition'. She had once been charged with attempted murder and malicious damage to property, after stabbing two horses in the *zadruga* of Glumac. And in May 1914, when the Habsburg Archduke Franz Salvator passed through on his way to Bosnia, she had strung up twenty Serbian flags around her house and across the street. When warned by a neighbour about the possible consequences, she hoisted one Croatian flag as well, but left the Serbian flags in place. Kranjčević did not deny disturbing the peace on the night of 28 June, but claimed her explosion was timed to celebrate a joyful anniversary: her husband's departure for America the previous year. The authorities, however, took the past and present evidence gathered by the local gendarmerie and behaved typically in the vigilant atmosphere of July 1914. Mica Kranjčević was not only sentenced to a month's imprisonment for flying Serbian flags and illegal possession of fire arms (five weapons were discovered). Her case was also forwarded to the Gospić regional court with a view to further action and a charge of 'anti-dynastic behaviour' that could be akin to treason.[1]

Unfortunately, we do not know the outcome as the Gospić court records have not survived.

This eccentric Croatian Serb's actions in the summer of 1914 might be interpreted in various ways at the time and since, but for the local authorities on 28 June there was only one explanation since all the telegraph offices and rumour mongering that day told of a brutal assassination to which there was only one response. The responsible, official response was recorded in the Croatian urban capital, in Zagreb, in the diary of Archbishop Antun Bauer. On learning of the heir apparent's murder, Bauer noted down: 'Everyone was dumbfounded and disgusted. A darkness came over my eyes: for all of us, rightly or wrongly, had put our trust in him since he was reputed to be generally dissatisfied with how the Monarchy was governed and planning to change it radically.'[2] Ivan Skerlecz, Croatia's ban (governor) for the past seven months fully shared the archbishop's hierarchical loyalty; he advised him to go to the archduke's funeral in order to show public solidarity after such an appalling act, one that had been committed on 'Croatian soil' [sic]. Only four days later, however, the ban's own allegiance was somewhat shaken. In Vienna he attended what he described as the 'third-class funeral' of Franz Ferdinand – a man who in life had shown such energy – organized by Viennese circles who gave Skerlecz himself the cold shoulder. In response, he questioned whether 'a Monarchy led by such people can withstand the enemies who from all sides are stalking it like prey'.[3]

These two dramatic reactions, one from Zagreb and one from the Croatian hinterland, are a useful starting point from which to assess the political culture of Croatia across the year of 1914, both before and after the Sarajevo assassinations. Not only can we probe how conflicting allegiances were evolving there, and how they were reinterpreted by the state authorities when – after June 1914 – the international context radically altered. This chapter also emphasizes the (under-researched) significance of Croatia as a key fulcrum of the Southern Slav Question in the Balkans. Or as Franz Ferdinand once put it, Croatia was 'the heartland of the Balkan turmoil'.[4] For it was there, even more than in Bosnia, that Croat and Serb aspirations for radical change alternatively clashed or fused together. It was there, too, that imperial idealists from the two halves of the Dual Monarchy were at loggerheads.

The Hungarian government for decades had tried to curb Croat nationalism or the myth of Croatia's 'state right', asserting that the devolution granted to Croatia through the Compromise of 1868 (the *Nagodba*) never obscured the fact that it was still really a province of the greater Hungarian kingdom. In turn, this Hungarian 'imperial' approach faced competition from those 'Greater Austrian circles' tied to Franz Ferdinand who interpreted Croatia simply as 'Austrian Croatdom', a region that must be bound more closely into a centralized Habsburg empire.[5] The historiography on this era in Croatia is not small but, just like the contemporary Croatian political culture it discusses, it tends to be fragmented.[6] Often it has reflected the national or nationalist lens through which each historian has approached the same subject, given a new lease of life by the Yugoslav wars of the 1990s. Much, therefore, is open for reassessment: to query the covert or openly nationalist explanations, while at the same time avoiding an overly teleological 'Yugoslav' approach to what was happening in 1914.

As Iskra Iveljić's chapter illustrates with the aristocracy, political allegiances in pre-war Croatia were, thanks to the shifting geopolitical context, exceedingly complex and diverse. Many political actors made opportunistic calculations based not just on the power structures within Croatia but also on Croatia's turbulent relationship with Hungary as well as on the Habsburg Monarchy's foreign dynamic with the kingdom of Serbia. The last two variables shifted dramatically in 1913 and explain the Croatian political scene of 1914. First, as a result of the Balkan Wars, Serbia had doubled the size of its territory. Serbia's victory and expansion aroused wild enthusiasm among many South Slavs of the Monarchy, but pushed the Habsburg elite into believing even more that Serbia and its 'Greater Serbian' dream were an existential threat that must soon be scotched.

Second, by 1914, the new Croatian political scene was not at all to the liking of Franz Ferdinand or those loyalists (dynastic or Croat state-right adherents) whom he loosely patronized in the region. For even if Croatia was being superficially stabilized, that process was being carried out by a very pro-Hungarian ban (Skerlecz), one who had also sealed an agreement with the Croat-Serb Coalition – precisely with those parties whom the archduke always saw as most treacherous.[7] For Franz Ferdinand therefore the regime of Ivan Skerlecz could never be an encouraging development. Parties in the vanguard of South Slav idealism seemed to be gaining ground in Croatia – matching the archduke's own alarm about mounting Serb irredentism elsewhere; at the same time the Skerlecz regime was a real boost for continued Hungarian power. For someone who despised Magyars and Serbs in equal measure, the new situation in Croatia could only be viewed pessimistically.[8]

Indeed, unsettling for many observers was that the most influential and stable element in the Croat-Serb Coalition was the Serb Independent Party led by Svetozar Pribićević. As we will see, this party in 1913 opportunistically took the lead in pushing for a new agreement with Budapest, first in order to secure influence in Croatia, but second – fundamentally – in order to end almost two years of Hungarian dictatorship in the kingdom (the so-called royal commissariat of 1912–13). Few could have missed the irony that only four years earlier (1909) it was prominent figures of the Serb Independent Party who had been tried and found guilty in the notorious Zagreb high treason trial – not least Pribićević's own brothers Adam and Valerijan.[9] Even if that trial backfired on the state and the thirty men convicted had to be released in 1910, the impact on Serb politicians had been salutary, convincing them to proceed gingerly within the Croatian political system.

At the same time, it is clear that that traumatic experience, and a loss of faith in the Habsburg *Rechtsstaat*, was never forgotten. For many educated Serbs, opportunism replaced any strong loyalty to the empire or to some Croatian homeland, since those who had governed Croatia in 1909 had stigmatized Serbs (25 per cent of the population) as outsiders in the state community. It was therefore a volte-face when, in the months before the war, Serb politicians leapfrogged into a position of influence; to some Croat nationalists it suggested a return to the regime of Ban Khuen-Héderváry who before 1903 had allied with Croatia's Serbs.[10] But any such favour this time was to be very short-lived.

The following discussion picks up both the Hungarian and the Serb strands in Croatian society and politics, against the backdrop of a noisy Croat nationalist opposition. I weigh first the often ignored Hungarian relationship which dominated Croatian political discourse for the first half of 1914. What were the main themes of that discourse, and how superficial or solid was the stabilization introduced by the Skerlecz regime after twenty months of unconstitutional rule? What do the conflicting voices and public rituals tell us?

The second part of the chapter turns to consider how Serb loyalty or disloyalty was interpreted both before and after June 1914. While there were ample signs of official vigilance against Serbs before Sarajevo, after the assassinations the simple rhetoric about traitors turned into concrete action, with a repetition en masse of the arrests that had led to the 1909 treason trial. In the wartime atmosphere, former Serb-Habsburg loyalists like Dušan Popović would be suspected of treason, while the Croat 'state-right' or *pravaši* element in politics came into its own. Indeed, with an intensified military focus on anyone who had links to the Serb or Serbian enemy, 'Croatian national interests' – fused increasingly with patriotic and state interests – quickly began to dominate the public discourse. In turn the Hungarian question – so prominent in the first half of 1914 – began to gain less attention; it was just one example of how the wartime insecurities would 'regionalize' the empire. Yet if, for Budapest, Croatia inevitably became less a priority, the Hungarian question – as we will see – never actually disappeared from the mindset of those obsessed with Croatian national interests.

## The Hungarian question in Croatia

While some historians have tried to suggest that the Habsburg Monarchy before 1914 was a model *Rechtsstaat*, the turbulent situation in pre-war Croatia disproves that contention.[11] For six years, 1907–13, Hungary ran Croatia on unconstitutional lines, alienating many Croatians committed to a 'state of law' and blatantly violating the terms of the 1868 *Nagodba*. Typical for feeding national grievances in these years was the so-called railway pragmatic of 1907, a Hungarian law introduced to make Magyar the compulsory language on Croatia's railway network. The British expert, R. W. Seton-Watson, observed that from 1907 'an era of absolutism, sometimes veiled, sometimes open and unashamed' prevailed in Croatia.[12] Things deteriorated even further under Ban Slavko Cuvaj who simply suspended the Sabor (national assembly in Zagreb), increased police vigilance and imposed heavy press censorship. Faced with mounting protests and strikes, Budapest in April 1912 appointed Cuvaj as a 'royal commissioner' with autocratic powers, a post only used once before in 1883. This 'commissariat' was, in Seton-Watson's dramatic language, a dictatorship 'unique in the annals of modern Europe'; an alien Hungarian government imposed its will on Croatian aspirations to liberty and the rule of law.[13]

It might be suggested that, via the commissariat, Hungary was at least successful in dampening Croatian political agitation and then forcing concessions out of certain parties.[14] Hence the loose deal of November 1913 reached between the Hungarian government of Count István Tisza and the Croat-Serb Coalition. Yet the long-term impact of arbitrary rule was very corrosive, making Croatia's political elite ever more sceptical that either Budapest or Vienna would accede to their national or constitutional demands; grievances on those points would be softened or shelved as politicians became adept at following opportunistic paths. The Tisza-Coalition settlement was only possible because both sides were pragmatic, wishing to end the emergency rule of the commissariat as a base for securing particular benefits for themselves.

For Tisza's government, appointed in June 1913, a priority amid the turmoil of the Balkan Wars was to stabilize Croatian discontent.[15] It was something that the monarch Franz Joseph and other critics (including Franz Ferdinand) had long placed at the door of Cuvaj and the royal commissariat. Hungary simply needed a partner among Croatia's political parties to work with a new ban; and, since true (pro-Hungarian) unionists were thin on the ground and Croat nationalists too hostile, only the Croat-Serb Coalition was offering itself as a potential ally. Here the Coalition's tactics are particularly intriguing. Croat and Serb historians have often stressed that a key determinant was Belgrade's advice. The Serbian prime minister, Nikola Pašić, in September 1913 had allegedly advised Svetozar Pribićević to compromise with Hungary, thereby advancing the Coalition again to a governing position in Croatia and helping to stabilize the region. In that way, in the wake of the Balkan Wars, Pašić felt Austria-Hungary would not be able to invent some excuse about Belgrade interfering in Croatia in order to launch an attack on Serbia.[16]

Yet if we accept that Pribićević took soundings from Belgrade, his pro-Serbian agenda was not as carefully calculated as some might suggest in hindsight.[17] The Coalition, with Serbs taking the lead along with Croat legal experts like Alexander Badaj, saw the chance to abolish the commissariat but also to secure a slice of power for itself. To that end it was certainly ready to adopt something of a 'unionist mask' and to downplay Hungary's violations of the *Nagodba*.¹⁸ But it also had a 'Croatian' agenda. It demanded the removal of the hated railway pragmatic, and hoped in time to secure real influence in the new ban's government. Such optimism seemed valid when in the Sabor elections of December 1913 the Coalition parties, coupled with Skerlecz's placemen, managed to secure fifty-nine of the eighty-eight seats. In short, we can see the Coalition leaders pragmatically exploiting the power framework that had emerged from mid-1913. Certainly the secret talks resulted in abundant rumours that the Coalition had made secret promises to Tisza. But it is too easy, indeed misleading, to interpret their behaviour as a front for either a Magyar unionist (Magyarone), Serb nationalist or idealistic Yugoslav agenda – in other words, something supposedly at odds with 'the will of the Croatian nation'.¹⁹

Later of course some Croat historians would condemn the Coalition for that Serbophile or Magyarone 'betrayal' of Croatia, and question the real benefits of the Tisza-Coalition negotiations. Josip Horvat, for example, saw the Coalition as bamboozled into playing Budapest's game, their stance starkly at variance with the radical Yugoslav agenda increasingly espoused by young South Slavs across the region.²⁰ At the time, too, the Coalition's opportunistic accommodation was met with strident challenges from the Croat (nationalist) opposition. The transition under Skerlecz, a loyal Tisza man who was now officially appointed as ban, was bound to be viewed with suspicion by those *pravaši* parties committed to Croatia's state right. Typical was the Sabor speech of Mile Starčević whose party had won eleven seats in the elections. He refused to take part in the introductory ceremony for Skerlecz and sneered at the Coalition:

> We see that the Magyars ... have sent us as the esteemed ban, Mr Skerlecz, their man, their confidant, not to defend Croatian rights but to defend the Magyar national state and Magyar profits, someone who weakly knows the Croat language! I maintain that your friend Count Tisza could not give a stronger slap in the face or inflict a greater outrage than that!²¹

The point about Skerlecz's language skills was true. Although he had lived in Zagreb as an adolescent, for seventeen years he had been working in the higher ranks of the Budapest civil service. He publicly apologized for his weak command of the Croat language, but emphasized his Croatian identity by birth and in his heart – he did not come as a foreigner.²² Certainly, he would not be employing such 'strong-arm' tactics as bans Rauch (1908) or Cuvaj (1911), but it is questionable whether Croatia really required that in 1914 as one Hungarian historian later suggested.²³ Rather, Skerlecz would manoeuvre as a quiet compromiser, the ultimate civil servant and one committed to Tisza's agenda for a Croatia that was peaceful and loyal to its Hungarian 'motherland'. According to Tisza, Skerlecz was a man of 'cold-blooded decisiveness'.²⁴

Reflecting the illusion of a reinvigorated *Nagodba*, Tisza himself on 18 January made an official visit to Zagreb, trudging around in the snowy streets, and apologizing that he could not speak Croatian. It was recognized as a unique event – the first lone visit by a Hungarian prime minister to the city – and the rituals that day were duly organized to reflect sentiments of 'Croatian loyalty and affinity' (Tisza's words) in a common Hungarian state. When Skerlecz's deputy, Mark Aurel Fodroczy, publicly assured Tisza that Zagreb was doing everything possible 'to increase the radiance and power of the [Hungarian] crown of St Stephen', Tisza replied that 'hand in hand, shoulder to shoulder, we are working for our mutual common interests'. At the Sabor he was cheered by Coalition deputies; at the official dinner Skerlecz toasted him with champagne as an extraordinary personality and friend of Croatia. Thus the elite's allegiance to Budapest was being reaffirmed and Tisza, simply by his presence, was suggesting at least some mutual respect.[25]

Yet the public response that day was undoubtedly indifferent or downright hostile. One socialist leader told protesters in Zagreb that a good relationship with Hungary was to be welcomed but only in order to achieve democracy through a radical reform of the franchise; instead, Tisza was simply visiting his old commissar in Hungary's Croatian 'colony'.[26] Many newspapers were equally scathing. According to the *Ilustrovani list*, just one look at Tisza and you knew why he was hated. One of its cartoons entitled 'Hossana Tisza!' showed Tisza entering Zagreb, Christ-like, on a donkey (Figure 11.1). He holds an olive branch and carries new railway signage in Croat, a reference to the abolished 'railway pragmatic'; his path is lined with Croatian police saluting him, and the caption notes that 'great homage is expected from this nation'. Another cartoon implied a dubious and aloof relationship between the prime minister and Croatia. At a time when the French aviator Adolphe Pégoud flew over Zagreb to dramatic acclaim and a warm welcome, Tisza was also caricatured as 'Our Pégoud', flying his aeroplane – called '*Pragmatika*' – aloft in a similar ostentatious gesture. On the ground, Croatian politicians cheer him somewhat ambiguously: 'Long live Tisza – his first dive!' (Figure 11.2).

Any positive effects from Tisza's brief visit were quickly offset anyway. The Coalition leaders might argue optimistically that, with their impressive Sabor majority, they were slowly 'parliamentarizing' Skerlecz's regime. They certainly hoped, as one result of their pragmatism, to gain some extra footing in the government and perhaps even create a fully parliamentary government.[27] Whether or not Tisza had even hinted at that in his talks in late 1913 is unclear but seems unlikely since it would signify a firm degree of trust in the Coalition, as well as marking a radical step towards a further devolution of powers to Croatia. In retrospect this was surely a lost opportunity in the Hungarian-Croatian relationship. There were signs that Skerlecz himself was inclined in this direction, particularly to accept some Coalition members into his governmental team as heads of key departments.

**FIGURE 11.1** *Count István Tisza enters Zagreb ('Hossana Tisza!'*, Ilustrovani list, 17 January 1914, 72).

But Budapest by late April had firmly rejected the idea, and the Coalition then gave it up too.[28]

Indeed, the brief illusion that the *Nagodba* had somehow shifted in favour of Zagreb seemed ever more questionable. Actual Hungarian influence appeared to be increasing rather than retreating. Even the repeal of the controversial railway pragmatic – a key demand of the Coalition in their talks with Tisza – was ambiguous. For although Croat signage now returned to the railways and a knowledge of Magyar was no longer compulsory for all rail employees (in other words, the 'pragmatic' was de jure removed), the everyday reality on the rail network was that Magyar still remained the common language and those who only knew Croat were a minority, employed mainly in manual jobs.[29] Another red rag to those upholding Croatian sovereignty was the realization that the Coalition – possibly as

FIGURE 11.2 *Tisza as the Croatian Pégoud* ('Naš Pégoud', Ilustrovani list, 14 February 1914, 168).

agreed with Skerlecz – did not plan to block the founding of new Magyar schools in Croatia. It naturally led firebrands like the Peasant Party leader Stjepan Radić to exclaim that Hungarian policy had not really changed at all: Croatia in 1914 was being led in a 'neo-Magyarone political direction'.[30]

Yet most controversial in these months was the sudden emergence of a law that suggested – even more than the railway pragmatic – that Budapest saw autonomous Croatia as just one province of the Hungarian state. By early March, the Croatian public was learning in the press of a bill, debated and passed through the Hungarian parliament, which would make it easier for the Hungarian authorities to nationalize territory on the Croatian coast.[31] This regulation of *izvlastba* (expropriation) was not wholly new. Previous Hungarian laws – for example, in 1881 – had laid down the principle of state nationalization of essential infrastructure common across the kingdom of Hungary (railways, rivers, bridges, the telegraph system); and for Zagreb it always invited controversy since the Sabor reserved to itself any matters that they considered in the sphere of 'Croatian autonomy'. The 1914 law was essentially a refinement of 1881, focusing on expropriation of territory on the Croatian coast in areas where it was deemed vital to the common state or 'public good'. Most crucially, it interpreted Croatia as within that common Hungarian state. And it placed all definitions and adjudications about 'the coast' and 'maritime interests' in the hands of the governor of Rijeka (Fiume), that city state which since 1868 had been directly subordinate to the Hungarian government and outside Croatia's control. Whereas until 1914 disputes had often arisen over who had jurisdiction over the Croatian coast, Budapest had now clarified that executive power rested with the governor of Rijeka in his capacity as head of the 'Royal Hungarian Coastal Authority'; he in turn would take directives from the Hungarian minister of commerce in Budapest.

Some legal scholars have assessed the law on *izvlastba* quite positively, since for the first time it set out a clear legal jurisdiction for the maritime coastland.[32] We might also argue that those like Tisza or Skerlecz interpreted it not as a question of some Hungarian imperial expansion to the sea but simply as a regulation of common state interests on 'Hungary's' short coastal territory. Yet for Croat nationalists at the time and some historians later, there could be only one interpretation – namely that *izvlastba* signified creeping Hungarian imperialism and a blatant violation of Croatia's sovereignty and its sacred territory. Even to the eminent historian Mirjana Gross, it was a first step to securing the coastline for Magyar capital.[33] Or as the newspaper *Obzor* noted in March 1914, 'Hungary's maritime authority will be the master of the situation on our Croatian territory'.[34]

For the opposition parties this issue became an ideal rallying cry about the ongoing transgression of Croatian national interests, and they managed to mobilize sections of the population, not least on the coast. For the largest rally, on 15 March at Sušak near Rijeka, some people arrived under the Croatian tricolour, singing, 'it's not a Hungarian but a Croatian sea!' The ex-Coalition leader Frano Supilo proceeded to explain the abusive law to a crowd of 2,000, noting especially its violation of the *Nagodba* (Figure 11.3). He then did not ignore the Croatian nation's 'correct' relationship with Hungary and the dynasty, but stressed that in line with the *Nagodba*, the Croatian minister who served as a liaison in Budapest (Teodor Pejačević – a former ban) should have blocked the *izvlastba* law and discussed it with the king, Franz Joseph. As for the Coalition deputies, some of whom were present and shouted down at the rally, Supilo portrayed them as Magyar lackeys who in abandoning a radical course were betraying their country. The gendarmerie intervened when he called out, 'we do not have a ban but a commissar'.[35]

The large Sušak rally does seem to have quelled coastal anger, but the issue lingered on for months. It was exploited, for example, in the many speeches given to peasants in northern Croatia by Stjepan Radić who

**Skupština protiv izvlastbe morske obale na Sušaku**

FIGURE 11.3 *Frano Supilo speaks to the crowds in Sušak ('Skupština protiv izvlastbe morske obale na Sušaku',* Ilustrovani list, *21 March 1914, 265).*

naturally stressed that the politicians were interested only in the fate of property, not people; Radić also played the national card, asserting that soon there would be a 'united Croatia' in the south of the Monarchy.[36] The *izvlastba* issue therefore reveals well the vibrant and fluid grassroots political culture of Croatia, where in 1914 national or social grievances could easily be exploited by populists like Supilo or Radić. Equally, however, the regime of Ban Skerlecz in alliance with the Croat-Serb Coalition showed it had the power network to stabilize the situation. The Coalition leaders, it seems clear, were taken unawares by the *izvlastba* law, which they had not agreed beforehand with Budapest.[37] In the face of the opposition clamour, their embarrassment on this issue is evident from the fact that at the Sušak rally, one of their leaders Bogoslav Mažuranić (deputy for a coastal constituency) felt forced to claim that the law would need Sabor approval and that that would never happen.[38]

In fact, the law on this state matter only needed to be passed by the Hungarian parliament, and in the Sabor the Coalition deputies sang a different tune, quickly defending *izvlastba* as a subject of 'common interest' where the Croatian voice would still be heard. They also coordinated their approach with Skerlecz himself who sought to dampen the law's significance. In the Sabor he gave his word that *izvlastba* would neither infringe on Croatian autonomy nor harm private property; it was alarmist and party-political to suggest otherwise.[39] In May 1914, in a further sign of compromise, Skerlecz and the Hungarian minister of commerce issued a joint statement, stressing that in any adjudication by the governor of Rijeka about coastal territory, the ban or the local Croatian authorities would also have to be consulted.[40] This did not pacify the opposition, but they could not contest the fact that this controversial law now had Franz Joseph's approval.

In this episode Skerlecz revealed himself as an 'intelligent and energetic' individual who had quickly acclimatized to Croatian conditions and was careful to take his Coalition allies with him.[41] His task had been to stabilize Croatia, and some Hungarian newspapers praised the speedy progress already made. In the tradition of previous bans, he also tried to promote his concept of the *Nagodba* in the provinces, conducting a regional tour from April 1914 to solicit public allegiance and advertise his own patronage. Typical for his inclusive approach, and offering an alternative message to the recent opposition rallies, was his visit in May to the northern town of Varaždin. A set ritual and display took place. As school children lined up clutching little tricolour flags, a band played the imperial anthem followed by the Croatian ('*Lijepa naša domovina*'), and Skerlecz was greeted by the local župan Stjepan Belošević in front of a huge triumphal arch (a standard construction on these occasions). Tactfully, Skerlecz praised the local Coalition mayor, Pero Magdić, who reciprocated with Varaždin's homage to this constitutional ban. He then visited the local Serb Orthodox Church and the synagogue. His speeches were depoliticized with no mention of Hungary, stressing that he came chiefly as the monarch's man in Croatia, out of duty and interest in the locality: 'My warmest wish is that I stay in constant and direct contact with all inhabitants of our homeland.'[42]

Pre-war Croatia therefore evinced as much stability as conflict in the community. Inevitably, historians have looked for the tensions in view of what came later, but there were equally abundant signs of accommodation and pragmatism by those prepared to work with a reinvigorated form of the *Nagodba*. As the Hungarian semi-official newspaper *Pester Lloyd* noted in April 1914, one could perhaps be optimistic about a 'consolidation and development of the newly created conditions' after seven years of abnormal rule.[43] Even so, while Tisza had set the *Nagodba* on a new footing, most of the underlying grievances about insufficient devolution had not disappeared. In particular, it was perhaps a mistake that Budapest did not bind the Coalition more firmly into the system by moving towards something of a parliamentary government; for Tisza such a radical step was anathema and a threat to overall Hungarian sovereignty. Instead, Coalition politicians like Svetozar Pribićević could remain opportunistic, keeping one eye on Belgrade while not submitting wholly to the Croatian political regime.

## Discovering traitors in the community

If political culture in the first half of 1914 had a veneer of normality, it was still an extraordinary situation. Through Skerlecz's alliance with the Croat-Serb Coalition, many individuals who only recently had been associated with the ultimate crime of treason were now suddenly characterized as loyalists, committed to upholding the Hungarian-Croatian *Nagodba*. Prominent defence lawyers from the 1909 treason trial like Srdjan Budisavljević and Dušan Popović were spokesmen for Coalition policy in the Sabor, Popović on record as praising a unionist approach which served both 'king and homeland'. Even more surprising in late April 1914, one of the key 'traitors' of 1909, Valerijan Pribićević, was elected in a Sabor by-election; allegedly both Skerlecz and Tisza had opposed this Coalition candidate.[44] Three months later, all of these prominent Serbs were on the way to being once again stigmatized and investigated as traitors to the state, their past behaviour evaluated in a new light.

As we have seen, the behaviour of Croatia's Serb politicians has usually been interpreted as wholly opportunistic, taking a lead from Belgrade or at least seeking to protect their community in an era of heightened international tensions. It is a short step from this to suggest in hindsight that Croatia's Serbs knew that war was coming, were plotting war in league with Serbia or were warding off a potential Croat genocide.[45] Nicholas Miller has been most convincing in clearing away the wildest speculation, arguing that the Serb Independent Party under Svetozar Pribićević had retreated in 1913–14 into the 'politics of collective defence'.[46] In the Coalition there was still evidence of its Yugoslav commitment – asserting Serbs and Croats as one Southern Slav nation; there were also lingering signs of Pribićević's earlier belief in some civic model for the nation on the territory of Croatia-Slavonia, where all citizens might identify as 'Croatians'. However, the rise of Serbia since 1912 had put both of these concepts in a new geopolitical framework, as well as making Serb lives in Croatia more insecure. Past experience, not least the years of the high treason trial and the commissariat, certainly made many Serbs wary of trusting Hungary or the Habsburgs. Equally it made them pragmatic in working within a power structure dominated by Hungary. Few of course considered themselves to be 'traitors' when they embraced the multiple and overlapping loyalties permitted in peacetime: to their local Serb community, their homeland (Croatia), their (Habsburg) king, as well as to their wider Southern Slav community now headed by Serbia.

Yet past experience also made the Hungarian and other state authorities wary of fully trusting a Coalition force with such prominent Serb leadership. The latter might well mouth their commitment to the *Nagodba*, but as one Hungarian newspaper put it, the Croat-Serb Coalition had no tradition of unionism – respect for Hungarian culture – and was probably pursuing a Yugoslav or Great Serbian agenda.[47] In this light, and mindful of recent

Serb 'traitors' – who after 1909 had never officially been pardoned by the Habsburg regime – the security services in Croatia were constantly alert. Much of their attention before June 1914 was focused on Croat nationalist agitation against Hungary, but the sources also hint at underlying police vigilance of anyone with regular links to Serbia. Particularly monitored was the growing dissemination of 'Great Serbian propaganda' – for instance, the discovery of printed calendars where the family tree of the Habsburg dynasty was missing.[48] Then there were ample incidents of 'treason by word' near the eastern border with Serbia: individuals who were overheard stating publicly that Croatia was a Serb land, who praised the Serbian and belittled the Habsburg army, or who claimed that Orthodox Christians would surrender without a fight in a war with Serbia.[49]

One incident in particular reveals the regime's hyper-anxiety about potential violence. On 20 May 1914, as Skerlecz was leaving the theatre in Zagreb, police arrested a student on suspicion of planning his assassination; nineteen-year-old Jakob Schäfer had a pistol in his pocket and had been acting erratically. From these slivers of evidence, the police quickly moved to imagine a broader 'Yugoslav' or Great Serbian plot by the local *omladina* (radical youths).[50] For while the tight-lipped Schäfer seemed to be a cypher, the investigation found his fellow students singing Serbian national songs and soon uncovered more sinister signs. One of Schäfer's acquaintances, Rudolf Hercigonja, had regularly spoken about Southern Slav unity with Serbia; he hated Skerlecz as Tisza's agent, and had actually proposed murder as a way to educate the public, through the assassination of high officials or even of Archduke Franz Ferdinand. Since the investigating magistrate also discovered that both Hercigonja and Schäfer had recently visited Belgrade, by mid-June a prosecution case was pending but would not inevitably proceed.

Only after the death of Franz Ferdinand was the indictment finalized with the charge of treason and attempted murder sharpened by that event. By the time it reached trial in October 1914, it was Hercigonja who was the main criminal, the youth with the deeper Great Serbian motivation. Although he was clearly a potentially violent idealist, the state now interpreted Hercigonja's pre-war rants in a fresh light; retrospectively he was a 'traitor' who had plotted to cause anarchy in Croatia and provoke a war with Serbia. He and Schäfer received long prison sentences and were not released until the end of the war.[51]

The Sarajevo events therefore fundamentally transformed how state loyalty was interpreted in Croatia – or, more accurately, they accelerated existing security anxieties about Serb treachery. Skerlecz was immediately instructed by Budapest to take the temperature of loyalty or disloyalty across the region. On 11 July, he ordered each of his regional prefects (*veliki župan*) to send in reports about the impact of the assassinations. In response, many župans emphasized the devastating effect. The town of Gračac in the south-west was typical. 'Every citizen gave a visible sign of their deep national grief' with black flags hoisted and bells rung for a week to mark 'the terrible event which struck our esteemed dynasty and Monarchy'; requiems held in all Catholic and Orthodox churches confirmed there a common stance by everyone, 'sincerely devoted and loyal to the supreme throne and state'.[52] Other districts, for example, Varaždin or Bjelovar in the north, gave a formulaic response and stressed their town's reputation for 'traditional dynastic loyalty'.[53] But there were hints of a different story, for instance from Karlovac, where the murders were said to have evoked little response at all; in the first days educated people had certainly shown 'deep compassion', but the rest of the population who did not read newspapers were clearly indifferent.[54]

Most interesting for future stereotyping were those districts where Serb allegiance was either emphatically emphasized or abruptly questioned. The district authority in Vojnić south of Karlovac wrote that the (mainly Serb) inhabitants were descendants of the 'frontiersmen' (*graničari*) who until 1881 had populated the empire's old military border. Just as they stood shoulder to shoulder and always had their dynastic homage inscribed on their hearts, so now, there was no house without a black flag.[55] This was a contrast to places like Otočac and Dvor on the Bosnian frontier where the Serb mindset was seen in a different light. In Otočac (the district of Mica Kranjčević) the authorities clearly differentiated between Catholic behaviour – weeping and cursing the assassins – and the 'Greek Orthodox'. The latter were supposedly apathetic, showed no grief and were tending to absent themselves from public venues; indeed 'on the faces of the intelligentsia one could read some evil intent'.[56] In Dvor, the Serb allegiances were questioned more subtly: it was noted that some were indeed mourning and condemning the atrocity but were doing so because they feared themselves coming under suspicion. The Dvor district administrator reminded Zagreb that the national consciousness of local Serbs was extraordinarily strong, fed by Serb propaganda from both Bosnia and Zagreb: he advised keeping the national leaders under strict observation.[57]

In July 1914 the police and gendarmerie – wholly in line with vigilance across the Southern Slav region[58] – stepped up their interventions against anyone who had Serbian or South Slav nationalist sympathies. The evidence from previous months and years was re-examined, trapping individuals from all levels of society. As the case of Rudolf Hercigonja shows, behaviour which before July might have led to a caution was now, in the light of Sarajevo, interpreted as treason and resulted in a criminal prosecution. What exactly constituted 'treason' became dangerously fluid and was based on the most petty transgressions.[59] For example, the man who, on finding he could not buy a bottle of beer on the day of the archduke's requiem, swore violently against Franz Ferdinand; the train driver who, on learning of the murders, said it was 'one less Austrian dog'; the socialist who was overheard suggesting that all rulers and heir apparents should be massacred.[60]

With the declaration of war in late July, as the local civilian authorities inclined to a narrower interpretation of state allegiance, such incidents mushroomed. The trend was aided by a wave of denunciations as patriotic citizens shopped their neighbours. Some were very personal. A school boy reported how his teacher had congratulated the man who had killed a member of the imperial family.[61] A blacksmith from Mitrovica in eastern Slavonia was betrayed by his wife for speaking against Franz Ferdinand and possessing pictures of the Serbian king.[62] More serious was the junior clerk from Brod in the Posavina region who suddenly denounced his office superior for condemning the Habsburgs and wishing that Croatia would fall under Serbian rule.[63] Many of these cases stemmed from one witness's denunciation; many were retrospective on the basis of treasonable words spoken long before the war.

Yet it was the sudden army incursion into Croatia which helped to accelerate this stereotyping of all Serb Orthodox communities as treacherous. At first, amid the confusion, Skerlecz was quite ready to use these military units to maintain order; on 27 July he declared martial law. This subjected civilians to military jurisdiction for political or war crimes (treason, rebellion and other security offences), giving the Zagreb military command under General Eugen Scheure the power in theory to intervene where he thought necessary. The way was set over the next six months for a major power struggle between Skerlecz and the military, with the latter steadily flexing its muscles and seeking to impose a full military regime. Croatia's status as part of Hungary, however, obstructed this. Already in mid-August Tisza, in the face of arbitrary military encroachments, successfully adjudicated that in Croatia civilian law would predominate and any military detentions would need the assent of the local civilian authority.[64] This assured Skerlecz a strong degree of independence from Scheure. By the end of the year he felt confident enough to seek to abolish martial law for most crimes on the basis that (under Hungary's patronage) he had the overriding jurisdiction in Croatia.

The security files in the Zagreb archives show well how military interventions early in the war exacerbated the persecution of Serb civilians, yet the civilian authorities too played their part. When in September 1914 many Serb civilians in the Zemun/Mitrovica area were found to have colluded with the enemy during Serbia's short military occupation, the Austrian military retribution was severe, and it had a ripple effect westwards. Yet already by early August, on the basis of existing lists of suspects, local civilian authorities had targeted and interned 320 (Croatian) Serbs across Croatia-Slavonia. Skerlecz's subordinates could give him precise figures with a naturally high number in Orthodox areas: Gospić reported eighty-three arrests, Osijek seventy-four and Varaždin only three.[65] The prevailing mood meant that visible signs of Serb Orthodox culture would also soon be banned: Serb flags, roof tiles in Serb colours and the use of Cyrillic except in public announcements.[66] Although we find a few examples of Orthodox communities (like Petrinja) continuing to claim devotion to the Habsburg dynasty, for many Serbs there were only a few ways to assert their allegiance or recover some sense of belonging.[67] One way, by the end of 1914, was to contribute to the fund for war widows and orphans, with the local Orthodox priests often leading their flock by example.[68]

By contrast, Croatians who were not Orthodox Christians could more easily adhere to a range of public rituals to demonstrate their loyalties. Some were spontaneous at a local level. Thus, in the town of Ilok on the eastern border, on hearing of victory over Russia in early September, the mayor organized a festive procession for the population; the council duly repeated its homage to the Habsburg dynasty.[69] A comparable parade in Zagreb even included the singing of Hungarian patriotic songs.[70] In Zagreb the tone of patriotic leadership was clearest. A singular event, reinforcing dynastic loyalty, was the celebration of Franz Joseph's eighty-fourth birthday on 18 August. While Ilica, the main thoroughfare, was lit up and the Rudolf barracks festooned in flowers and flags, about 50,000 people took to the streets with lamps so that the city was truly 'swimming in a sea of light'. As one paper noted, the crowds shouted for their king and the heir apparent against the Serbs and murderers: 'Enthusiasm for the old ruler was indescribable, but equally for the war which he had declared on the enemy.'[71]

This time of heightened emotions was of course highly problematic for members of the Croat-Serb Coalition – the body of politicians allied to Skerlecz and committed to cooperation between Serbs and Croats as a Southern Slav fraternity. They faced, especially in the early months of the war, a barrage of abuse from the *pravaši* opposition parties who in the wake of Sarajevo savaged them as 'traitors and murderers' in the Sabor. Svetozar Pribićević was forced publicly to defend a Coalition vision of 'loyalty and political rectitude', standing firmly by the *Nagodba* and having 'no connection with Serbian policies'.[72] Tisza and Skerlecz soon realized that keeping their loose alliance with the Coalition was the best way to maintain stability, for it would ward off not only the hostile *pravaši* nationalists but also the danger of a military occupation of the region. So a 'military commissariat' was avoided, but Budapest by default was allowing a degree of political discourse that periodically would throw up much (Croat) nationalist criticism of Hungary.

Nor did the support from Budapest mean that the Croat-Serb Coalition was in a safe space, as is clear from the early wartime experience of their prominent deputies. In July 1914 the Coalition members agreed that rather than emigrating during the war, they would try to maintain their power base at home (only a few like the lawyer Hinko Hinković dissented and left the country). Yet because Skerlecz prorogued the Sabor for a year – until July 1915 – many Coalition celebrities were quickly caught up in the swirl of anti-Serbian denunciations and arrests. The Pribićević brothers were naturally marked men despite their theoretical parliamentary immunity. Valerijan Pribićević was locked up without trial for three years, although the state attorney in Zagreb could uncover no concrete evidence against him.[73] His brother Svetozar in mid-1915 would volunteer for the army but Tisza then appears to have intervened and ordered his internment for two years in Budapest (probably to protect him from military prosecution).[74]

The experience of Coalition deputies reveals well how the civilian authorities too, in investigating alleged cases of treason, were politicizing the rule of law. This entrapped both Croats and Serbs. From August 1914 for instance, a three-month judicial investigation took place into the Croat mayor of Varaždin, Pero Magdić, whom Skerlecz had only recently visited and praised. Magdić was certainly a provocative and outspoken character whose relations with the garrison commander of Varaždin were tense. Not surprisingly a series of anonymous denunciations occurred; Magdić was accused of publicly mocking the German army but also indulging in suspiciously pro-Serbian activity before 1914. Zagreb's state attorney – not least because of military complaints about Magdić – felt bound to launch an investigation. It was only closed in October when all the evidence was deemed to be malicious hearsay.[75] Nine months later Magdić would be prominent again in public life when the Sabor reopened and he chaired its sessions.

More serious, since they were Serb deputies, were the charges brought against Dušan Popović and Srdjan Budisavljević. Both had been defence lawyers during the high treason trial of 1909, and were – especially Popović – keen advocates of Serb-Croat cooperation under the *Nagodba*. Their experience in late 1914 shows the tightrope that prominent Serbs now had to walk, but we should emphasize too the actual limits to arbitrary justice in this part of the wartime Habsburg empire due to Hungarian protection. Popović and Budisavljević were first investigated in August and charged with 'disturbing public order'. Witnesses claimed that in late July, when the two Serbs were walking down Zagreb's Ilica Street, they had encountered and mocked a group of well-known *pravaši* politicians, suggesting that the latter's joy about the Habsburg war would soon turn to tears now that Russia had mobilized. Both Serbs were arrested, imprisoned, and an investigation was launched. Again, this was a case that collapsed a few months later, for Tisza and Skerlecz agreed that the 'crime' was too minor to have the deputies' parliamentary immunity set aside. The Hungarian government now reaffirmed the thirty-year-old precedent that MPs might be arrested and lose their immunity only if they were suspected of endangering state security.[76] Popović therefore was freed and allowed to return to his legal practice, whence – remarkably and bravely – he continued to speak out publicly about a future for the Serb people in Austria-Hungary.[77] Although this meant he was consistently branded a 'traitor' by Croat nationalists and the military authorities, he himself managed to walk the tightrope for the rest of the war. He was, in the words of Bogdan Krizman, 'undoubtedly one of the most agile and intelligent leaders of the Coalition'.[78]

Far less successful was Srdjan Budisavljević who, just as the above-mentioned case collapsed, was already being prosecuted on a charge of treason

– in other words endangering state security. This was specifically linked to a common legal interpretation after the Sarajevo assassinations, that spreading 'Great Serbian propaganda' was equivalent to plotting treason against Austria-Hungary.[79] Indeed, the case against Budisavljević followed directly from an investigation in Bosnia-Herzegovina into the Serb Sokol (gymnastics) organization, suspected of being a prime Serbian vehicle for spreading treacherous propaganda. Since Budisavljević in 1910 had been elected head of the Zagreb branch of the Serb Sokol, he was one of several Sokol leaders from Croatia who were fingered and then prosecuted for treason. As in Bosnia, the judicial investigation from November 1914 revolved around interpreting the Sokols as a 'Serbian national army' in waiting, arguing that they were fully a part of Belgrade's 'treasonable enterprise'.[80] When the case finally came to trial in late 1915, Budisavljević had been held in prison for well over a year, stripped of his parliamentary immunity.

Yet even this treason trial is evidence for us that Croatia's legal system – a rule of law – was preserved to some degree in wartime: it largely avoided the kind of military interference or direct control witnessed across so much of Austria and Bosnia.[81] Although Budisavljević had been charged with high treason (a crime carrying the death penalty), he was found guilty instead on the lesser charge of 'disturbing public order'; he was sentenced to only eight months' imprisonment, quickly commuted to six. Such 'leniency' did not of course stop his own radicalization. In 1917, on returning to the Sabor, he refused to support any longer the pragmatic course of the Croat-Serb Coalition.

The trauma that these Coalition deputies suffered certainly shows the potential in wartime Croatia for Serb or 'Yugoslav' behaviour to be interpreted by the civilian authorities in a criminal fashion and prosecuted. It was not the arbitrary military justice experienced by Croatian Serbs living on the border with Serbia; in late 1914 they were subject to full martial law, with many summary executions and the internment of about 24,000 people from the Srijem (Syrmia) county.[82] But the politicization of the law across the rest of Croatia was a reality forcing many Serbs to tread warily. Not surprisingly, when Skerlecz finally reconvened the Sabor in July 1915, Serb members of the Coalition agreed to absent themselves so that they would not be a prime target of abuse by opposition deputies.[83] And while the Serb deputies continued to have some official protection from Hungary, the lesson of 1914 was that fluctuations in the war against Serbia could easily imperil their safety and lead to the indiscriminate persecution so evident in neighbouring Bosnia.

## Conclusion

This chapter has dug deep into Croatian political culture, focusing on 1914 and the predominant Serb and Hungarian questions of the day. While the

Sarajevo assassinations superficially suggest a watershed, just as evident is the continuity of the underlying political discourse. During the war the 'alliance' of the Croat-Serb Coalition with Budapest continued, ensuring that the Croat nationalist opposition could not take charge of the political agenda even if its public voice remained very strong. Thus in July 1915 when the Sabor reconvened, the opposition launched fierce nationalist attacks on the *Nagodba*, Stjepan Radić referring to 'the hell of this union with the Magyars'. Tisza in turn would try to steady the ship with periodic acclamations about the Croatian nation's bravery and its brotherhood with Hungary, but the underlying nationalist demand for radical reform of the *Nagodba* remained.[84]

As for the Coalition, its pragmatism continued through the war years and would eventually pay off. In early 1914 it had vainly hoped for a parliamentary government from Ban Skerlecz. In July 1917, under the more constitutional rule of the new Emperor Karl, it would finally achieve that: for with a Coalition deputy, Antun Mihalović, chosen as the new ban, members of his government were also selected from the Coalition ranks. Yet the decade of almost persistent unconstitutional rule in Croatia – a glaring violation of the Habsburg *Rechtsstaat* – had had a lasting impact on trust in the Austro-Hungarian system of government. Until 1917 in wartime, Serbs of every social status across Croatia faced constant insecurity and potential harassment. Admittedly, most were not subject to military justice, but a politicization of civilian justice took place that often outweighed the protection that came from the Coalition's privileged political status. Most Coalition deputies, thanks to the power reality of 1913–18 in favour of Hungary and against Serbia, were induced to take a conservative and pragmatic approach to Croatia's future. However, when the wind changed at the end of the war, Belgrade effectively toppled Budapest from its control of the region. Breaking out of the territorial confines of Croatia, the broader 'Yugoslav' vision of those like Svetozar Pribićević and Dušan Popović could suddenly become a reality.

Returning to Franz Ferdinand's murder, it is clear that its main impact on Croatia was as a spark or excuse from which widespread Serbophobia was legitimized. 'The Serbs' had supposedly attacked the dynasty and betrayed the state. Yet the persecution that followed was still a short-term phenomenon; the stigmatization of Serbs in the community had certain limits. Equally, any memory of the archduke quickly slipped back into perspective. For all those who briefly mourned his removal as a dynastic figure or even a hope for the future, there were many more who were indifferent or had different loyalties. These included Ban Skerlecz himself. In December 1914, he was asked by the local authority in Mitrovica on the Serbian border whether the town's 'Saint Stephen Square' (commemorating the Hungarian holy crown) might now be renamed in honour of Franz Ferdinand as was common in many wartime towns. Skerlecz refused since this would be a slight to Hungary and 'against our pious duty'. Instead, the new sign should read, 'Square of the King Saint

Stephen', in case anyone thought that Stephen was a Serbian historic figure. As for Archduke Franz Ferdinand, a minor street nearby could bear his name.[85]

## Notes

1. Hrvatski Državni Arhiv, Zagreb (Croatian State Archives: hereafter HDA), 78. Predsjedništvo zemaljske vlade (presidency of the Croatian government: PZV), kutija 867, 4212-4252/1914, 4212-4869/1914.
2. Quoted in Ivan Bulić, *Ivan Skerlecz Lomnički 1913-1917. Kraljevski komesar i hrvatski Ban* (PhD diss., University of Zagreb, 2011), 220.
3. Ibid., 223–4.
4. Mirjana Gross, 'Hrvatska politika velikoaustrijskog kruga oko prijestolonasljenika Franje Ferdinanda', *Časopis za suvremenu povijest* 2/2 (1970): 49.
5. Ibid., 71.
6. Among useful general studies from a variety of angles, see Nicholas Miller, *Between Nation and State: Serbian Politics in Croatia Before the First World War* (Pittsburgh, PA: University of Pittsburgh Press, 1997); Ivan Bulić, 'Politika Hrvatsko-srpske koalicije uoči Prvoga svjetskoga rata 1907.-1913.', *Časopis za suvremenu povijest* 2 (2012): 415–53; Mirjana Gross, *Povijest pravaške ideologije* (Zagreb: Institut za hrvatsku povijest, 1973); Nicholas Novosel, *Regnum Regno: Croatia's War Aims 1914-1917* (PhD diss., Indiana, 1986); and for a Serbian nationalist approach, Vasilije Krestić, *History of the Serbs in Croatia and Slavonia 1848-1914* (Belgrade: Izdavačko-grafički zavod, 1997). The classic works of R. W. Seton-Watson give us a contemporary British perspective: *The Southern Slav Question and the Habsburg Monarchy* (London: Constable, 1911); *Absolutism in Croatia* (London: Constable, 1912).
7. Bulić, 'Politika Hrvatsko-srpske koalicije', 433.
8. See the lucid discussion by Mirjana Gross who suggests that for Franz Ferdinand by 1914 Serb irredenta was even more serious than any danger from the Magyar oligarchy: 'Hrvatska politika velikoaustrijskog kruga', 63–7.
9. See Mark Cornwall, 'Loyalty and Treason in Late Habsburg Croatia: A Violent Political Discourse Before the First World War', in *Exploring Loyalty*, eds Jana Osterkamp and Martin Schulze Wessel (Göttingen: Vandenhoeck & Ruprecht, 2017), 97–120.
10. Bulić, 'Politika Hrvatsko-srpske koalicije', 447.
11. See the claims in John Deak and Jonathan E. Gumz, 'How to Break a State: The Habsburg Monarchy's Internal War, 1914–1918', *American Historical Review* 122/4 (October 2017): 1117, 1125.
12. Seton-Watson, *Absolutism in Croatia*, 6.
13. Ibid., 51. The press censorship was 'the most reactionary which the civilized West has known' (46).
14. Bulić, 'Politika Hrvatsko-srpske koalicije', 422.

15 Gusztáv Gratz, *A dualizmus kora Magyarország története 1867-1918*, 2 vols (Budapest: Magyar szemle társaság, 1934), II, 278. It was also essential to secure an extension of the financial side of the *Nagodba*, regulating the Hungarian-Croatian economic relationship, since that expired at the end of 1913.

16 Adam Pribićević, *Moji život* (Zagreb: Srpsko kulturno društvo, 1999), 38–40. And for interpretations of Belgrade's role, see: Bulić, 'Politika Hrvatsko-srpske koalicije', 427–9; Krestić, *History of the Serbs*, 603–4; Jaroslav Šidak et al., *Povijest hrvatskog naroda g.1860-1914*. (Zagreb: Školska knjiga, 1968), 289.

17 For a measured analysis, see Miller, *Between Nation and State*, chapter 5.

18 Bulić, 'Politika Hrvatsko-srpske koalicije', 426.

19 See, for example, some of Bulić's rather nationalist asides: ibid., 448 fn 110, 452.

20 See Josip Horvat, *Politička povijest Hrvatske*, 2 vols (Zagreb: August Cesarec, 1990), I, 324–7.

21 Bulić, *Ivan Skerlecz*, 158. Starčević equated Skerlecz with his ancestor, the Zagreb župan Nikola Škrlec, who in 1790 had proposed tighter links to Hungary.

22 Ibid., 161.

23 Cf. Gratz, *A dualizmus kora*, II, 325.

24 Iso Kršnjavi, *Zapisci. Iza kulisa hrvatske politike*, ed. Ivan Krtalić, 2 vols (Zagreb: Mladost, 1986), II, 698.

25 'Grof Stjepan Tisza u Zagrebu', *Hrvat*, 19 January 1914, 2. *Hrvat* was the organ of the Starčević party.

26 Ibid., 3. At this time 8.5 per cent of Croatia's population had the vote.

27 For a Coalition view on the benefits of a stable government composed from their Sabor majority, see 'Konflikat ili mir?', *Hrvatski pokret*, 19 April 1914.

28 Mislav Gabelica, 'Zakon o izvlaštenju zemljišta na morskoj obali iz 1914. godine', *Radovi – Zavod za hrvatsku povijest* 46 (2014): 239–61 (here 248, 257–8); Bulić, *Ivan Skerlecz,* 191–6; Miller, *Between Nation and State*, 164. Notable too was Skerlecz's willingness to stand as a candidate in future Sabor elections; thereby the head of the government would be in parliament: see 'Das Landtagsmandat des Banus Skerlecz', *Pester Lloyd*, 23 March 1914, 1–2.

29 Šidak, *Povijest hrvatskog naroda*, 290.

30 Bulić, 'Politika Hrvatsko-srpske koalicije', 443. See also Starčević's Sabor speech against Magyar schools: 'Interpelacija', *Hrvat*, 21 February 1914, 1–3.

31 The following draws heavily on Gabelica's very full article: 'Zakon o izvlaštenju zemljišta'.

32 Goran Vojković and Marija Štambuk-Šunjić, 'Pravni status morske obale od stupanja na snagu Općeg gradjanskog zakonika do 1914', *Zbornik radova Pravnog fakulteta u Splitu* (Split, 2007), 267–82.

33 Šidak, *Povijest hrvatskog naroda*, 291. Also Josip Horvat, *Pobune omladina 1911-1914* (Zagreb: SKD Prosvjeta, 2006), 272: 'It was the most ruthless attempt at Magyarization.'

34 Quoted in Horvat, *Politička povijest Hrvatske*, II, 329.

35 HDA, 78. PZV, kutija 845, 153/1912 (1613/1914), Rojčević, Sušak district authority, to PZV, 16 March 1914 (typed report).
36 See ibid., 153/1912 (1745/1914) for the calmer atmosphere after Sušak; 153/1912 (3030/1914) for Radić's rallies, for example, in the Varaždin district where he called for a united Croatia within the Habsburg Empire. In May 1914, 400 attended one rally in Croatia's borderland; 300 another. For Radić's outlook, see Mark Biondich, *Stjepan Radić, the Croat Peasant Party, and the Politics of Mass Mobilization, 1904-1928* (Toronto: University of Toronto Press, 2000).
37 See Bulić, *Ivan Skerlecz*, 197–8; cf. Gabelica, 'Zakon', 249, who suggests unconvincingly that the Coalition leaders had agreed to the law in return for abolition of the railway pragmatic.
38 HDA, 78. PZV, kutija 845, 153/1912 (1613/1914). Cf. Mažuranić's speech in the Sabor only a week earlier, supporting the *izvlastba* law over maritime interests: *Hrvatski pokret*, 8 March 1914, 4–5.
39 See 'Hrvatski sabor', *Hrvatski pokret*, 26 March 1914, 2–3.
40 Gabelica, 'Zakon', 255–7.
41 'Intelligent and energetic': Kršnjavi, *Zapisci*, II, 695.
42 'Ban u Varaždinu', *Hrvatski pokret*, 13 May 1914, 4; 'Značajna banova izjava', *Hrvatski pokret*, 14 May 1914, 1.
43 'Die Ergebnisse der Tätigkeit des kroatischen Landtags', *Pester Lloyd*, 2 April 1914, 2.
44 Bulić, 'Politika Hrvatsko-srpske koalicije', 437; Gabelica, 'Zakon', 258: Gabelica hypothesizes that this election was in order to give Valerijan Pribićević parliamentary immunity in case of war with Serbia. If so, the Coalition was being overly optimistic.
45 For the last claim, see Krestić, *History of the Serbs*, 605, 611.
46 Miller, *Between Nation and State*, 167; see also his conclusions (174–9) about the Serb politicians abandoning any civic national model for Croatia.
47 *Az Újság*, 13 December 1913, as quoted in Bulić, 'Politika Hrvatsko-srpske koalicije', 443.
48 HDA, 78. PZV, kutija 831, 471/1914: Oberst Zeidler (13KK) to PZV, 10 February 1914.
49 Ibid., kutija 831, 3701/1914; kutija 854, 3445/1914; kutija 831, 2082/1914: police cases from the eastern district of Mitrovica (April and June 1914).
50 For an analysis of *omladina* activity on the eve of war, see Mirjana Gross, 'Nacionalne ideje studentske omladina u Hrvatskoj uoči I svjetskog rata', *Historijski zbornik* 21–2 (1968–69): 75–140.
51 See the main documents of the case: HDA, 78. PZV, kutija 854, 2941/1914. For differing views on Schäfer's 'innocence', see Horvat, *Pobune omladina*, 273–82; Bulić, *Ivan Skerlecz*, 174–8.
52 HDA, 78. PZV, kutija 854, 3899/1914: Veliki župan Gospić to PZV, 15 July 1914, enclosing report from Gračac of 8 July 1914.
53 Ibid., Varaždin report, 24 July; Bjelovar report, 18 July 1914.

54 Ibid., Veliki župan Zagreb to PZV, 25 July 1914: enclosing two reports from Karlovac. A police report in fact contradicted the district authority report by suggesting a 'deep impact'.
55 Ibid., Veliki župan Ogulin to PZV, 25 July 1914, enclosing report from Vojnić, 22 July 1914.
56 Ibid., Veliki župan Gospić to PZV, 24 July 1914, enclosing reports from Otočac, 20 and 28 July 1914. The Gospić prefect, Gjuro Horvat, also noted on 30 July that the Serb soldiers mobilized from his district were dangerously pro-Serbian; he asked that gendarmerie reinforcements be dispatched from Karlovac and they should not be Serb: Ibid., kutija 855, 4656/1914.
57 Ibid., kutija 854, 3899/1914, Dvor district authority to Zagreb župan, 15 July 1914.
58 See, for example, the extra activity now in Slovene territory: Martin Moll, *Kein Burgfrieden. Der deutsch-slowenische Nationalitätenkonflikt in der Steiermark 1900–1918* (Innsbruck: Studien Verlag, 2007).
59 For more on the state manipulation of treason law, see Mark Cornwall, 'Treason in an Era of Regime Change: The Case of the Habsburg Monarchy', *Austrian History Yearbook* 50 (2019): 124–49. By the end of 1914, Croatia's Supreme state attorney would conclude that while crime across Croatia had generally declined since the start of the war, the crime of 'treason' had notably increased, especially in Serb Orthodox areas: HDA, 78. PZV, kutija 854, Državni nadodvjetnik to PZV, 27 December 1914.
60 Ibid., kutija 831, Veliki župan Zemun to PZV, 30 July 1914, enclosing reports about individual incidents.
61 Ibid., Grubišno Polje district authority to Veliki župan Bjelovar, 29 July 1914.
62 Ibid., kutija 854, 3929/1914: Mitrovica police to PZV, 10 July 1914.
63 Ibid., kutija 872, 4351-6490/1914, Zagreb gendarmerie to PZV, 5 September 1914.
64 Bulić, *Ivan Skerlecz*, 241–5. See also HDA, 78. PZV, kutija 875, 4559/1914: Tisza already on 28 July had demanded that the army authorities in Croatia (notably the Zagreb military command) respect the sphere of influence of the civilian authorities; it was for the latter to decide about security measures in their own district.
65 HDA, 78. PZV, kutija 866, 4855/1914, Skerlecz order to župans, 6 August 1914, and their replies. These figures excluded the large number of citizens of the kingdom of Serbia arrested in Croatia by early August (1,344 in total). Lists of the suspect local Serbs (late July 1914) are contained in kutija 867, 4212/1914: for example, twenty-seven suspects in the Gospić district.
66 Ibid., kutija 855, 5292/1914 (flags: 26 August); 856, 9014/1914 (roof tiles: January 1915); 876, 5747/1914 (Cyrillic: 25 August). The Gospić župan had already banned Cyrillic altogether early in the war.
67 See ibid., kutija 855, 5001/1914, podžupan Zagreb to PZV, 8 August 1914, sending report from Petrinja.
68 See ibid., kutija 878, 7380/1914, for details about the contributions from Orthodox communities. While the Zagreb Orthodox community donated 133 crowns from only 35 people, that in Srpska Kapela gave 125 crowns from 101 people.

69 Ibid., kutija 877, 5751/1914, Skerlecz to imperial Kabinettskanzlei (Vienna), 22 October 1914.
70 'Jučerašnje manifestacije', *Hrvatski pokret*, 17 September 1914, 3.
71 *Ilustrovani list*, 22 August 1914, 794–6.
72 Quoted in Novosel, *Regnum Regno*, 50.
73 HDA, 397. Državno nadodvjetništvo Zagreb 1875-1945 (Supreme state attorney: hereafter DNO), kutija 78, K 127/1915, Viktor Aleksander to DNO, 7 May 1915.
74 See Bogdan Krizman, *Hrvatska u Prvom svjetski ratu. Hrvatsko-srpski politički odnosi* (Zagreb: Globus, 1989), 99–102.
75 Documents of this case in HDA, 397. DNO, kutija 74, K 156/1914. A newspaper Magdić had edited, *Naša pravica*, was suspected of being 'not loyal or dynastic'.
76 Hrvatski povijesni muzej, Zagreb (Croatian Historical Museum), Gradja advokatske kancelarije Dušana Popovića (documents from Popović's legal practice), kutija 49, P-74. The 'abused' *pravaši* politicians were Isidor Kršnjavi, Ivo Frank and Aleksander Horvat, none of whom could confirm that the accused had actually mocked them. For the Hungarian cabinet's discussion and resolution on 11 November 1914 about when parliamentary immunity could be lifted, see Emma Iványi (ed.), *Magyar minisztertanácsi jegyzőkönyvek az első világháború korából* (Budapest: Akadémiai kiadó, 1960), 105–7.
77 See Popović's defence speech at the Serb Sokol trial in early 1916: *Sokolski veleizdajnički proces u Zagrebu iz 1915.-1916. godine* (Zagreb: Savez srpskih zemljoradničkih zadruga, 1927), 295–300.
78 Krizman, *Hrvatska u Prvom svjetskom ratu*, 252.
79 This was the interpretation used against those involved in the plot to murder Franz Ferdinand: see Mark Cornwall, 'Traitors and the Meaning of Treason in Austria-Hungary's Great War', *Transactions of the Royal Historical Society* 25 (2015): 125–7.
80 HDA, 397. DNO, kutija 74, K 174/1914, report of Zagreb state attorney (Viktor Aleksander) to DNO, 10 November 1914 (esp. folio 8 about Budisavljević's crimes).
81 As argued recently by Deak and Gumz, 'How to Break a State'. For the Sokol trial see *Sokolski veleizdajnički proces u Zagrebu*.
82 See Jonathan Gumz, *The Resurrection and Collapse of Empire in Habsburg Serbia, 1914-1918* (Cambridge: Cambridge University Press, 2009). For the figure of 24,000, see, HDA, 78. PZV, kutija 877, 6287-9154/1914 (memorandum of 23 December 1914).
83 Novosel, *Regnum Regno*, 98.
84 Ibid., 70–1 and (for Radić's criticism in the Sabor), 105. See also Krizman, *Hrvatska u Prvom svjetskom ratu*, 92–3.
85 HDA, 78. PZV, kutija 844, 8656/1914, Vladin povjernik Mitrovica to župan Imbro Hideghety, 19 November 1914; Skerlecz to Hideghety, 7 December 1914. Other Croatian towns were more successful at petitioning to name streets after Franz Ferdinand: for instance, Osijek in November 1914 (88914/1914) and Ogulin in May 1915 (4450/1914).

# CHAPTER 12

# The outbreak of war in Habsburg Trieste*

## *Borut Klabjan*

Gavrilo Princip 'fired a bullet not only into some archduke but also into the façade of a peaceful and apparently stable world', wrote Vladimir Dedijer, the most notable historian of Sarajevo 1914.[1] Assassinations of emperors and members of royal families were anything but rare in the long nineteenth century: witness the deaths of Italy's king Umberto I or Portugal's king Carlos I. The House of Habsburg was no exception. In 1882 Guglielmo Oberdan, an Italian irredentist, had failed to assassinate Emperor Franz Joseph on his way to Trieste to celebrate the five-hundredth anniversary of the city's devotion to the monarchy; in 1898 the emperor's wife Elisabeth was stabbed to death on the shores of Lake Geneva. Never before, however, did an assassination have such consequences as the killing of Archduke Franz Ferdinand. Amid a vast historiography, much attention has been paid to the vital interests and international entanglements of the European powers, including the 'diplomatic bullying and blundering [that] preceded the Austro-Hungarian declaration of war on Serbia'.[2] Yet reactions to the murders at a local level remain relatively neglected. Such a focus sheds an illuminating grassroots perspective on the eve of the long nineteenth century's eclipse. The following case study of how the Sarajevo murders were received in the important city of Trieste seeks to open up questions about

---

*This chapter is based on a lecture delivered at Northern Illinois University in November 2013. I would like to thank Nancy M. Wingfield for the invitation, the participants for their useful suggestions, and Stefan Wedrac, Pieter Judson and Mark Cornwall for their helpful comments on earlier drafts of this chapter.

ethnic affiliation, nationalism and irredentism, imperial loyalty, and how in the summer of 1914 local society reacted to a hostile political environment. Even if the analysis is restricted in time and space, the aim is not to suggest some 'inevitability' about the state's collapse in 1918 under the weight of a 'nationalities problem'.[3] Rather, a bottom-up analysis of the origins of the Great War at a local level gives us a more nuanced understanding of the Habsburg Monarchy and Europe as a whole at this crucial turning point.

By 1900, the present-day Italian city of Trieste (Triest in German, Trst in Slovene, Croatian and Serbian) was the fourth largest metropolis of Austria-Hungary and its most important port. It was a multinational emporium, the seat of many global companies and an important centre of commercial and financial services. Since its 230,000 inhabitants were ethnically and religiously very mixed and multilingual (alongside Venetian dialect as the lingua franca there were substantial Slovene and German minorities), it had a cosmopolitan culture.[4] However, from the last decades of the century such cosmopolitanism had been gradually replaced by nationalist confrontation, the city becoming a pivotal point of contention between national movements.[5] At one and the same time, it was the major object of Italian irredentists, the southern end of the bridge to the Adriatic (*Brücke an der Adria*) in the eyes of German nationalists, and the centre of a future state for idealistic Yugoslavs.[6] With its history of fractured empires, Central European and Mediterranean melting pots, ethnic struggles and growing nationalism – with its important socialist movement and its influential Jewish community – Habsburg Trieste in 1914 represents an ideal urban case study, with wider relevance for understanding the empire and the ripples of Sarajevo that spread across the continent.

## Assassination and mourning

On 24 June 1914 many Triestines had greeted the heir apparent Franz Ferdinand and his entourage as they arrived in the city before continuing on their way to Dalmatia and Bosnia. Nobody could have imagined that the archduke and his wife Sophie Chotek, duchess of Hohenberg, would return a week later in a funeral procession. Immediately after the Sarajevo assassinations, the newspapers were issued in special editions all over the Monarchy. In Trieste many papers rushed to emphasize the primacy of their own consternation and in the following days produced editions with a special black mourning border. Like the majority of newspapers, the official *L'Osservatore Triestino* (The Triestine Observer) described the course of events in great detail in a special issue.[7] The organ *Il Piccolo*, voice of the local ruling Italian middle and upper class, was similarly meticulous over the news. Already on the day of the murders, on Sunday afternoon, it issued a special edition in neutral tones.[8] If in the past this newspaper had been critical of Habsburg policy, especially in view of Italian nationalist aspirations, in this case it joined in the grief displayed by loyalist papers. In the following days, it described in detail the police investigation, the background to the assassination, the assassins' profiles and anti-Serb rioting across Bosnia and Croatia. It continued with several articles related to the assassination until mid-July when the reporting slowly flowed into a wider narrative about the increasing tensions between Austria-Hungary and Serbia and the generally unstable Balkan situation. The local German daily, the *Triester Zeitung*, and its morning version, the *Triester Tagblatt*, also devoted much attention, describing how members of the local loyalist associations had rushed to hang out black flags at their administrative centres.[9] Similarly, *Edinost* (Unity), the newspaper of the local Slovene bourgeoisie, underlined the 'extreme sorrow prevailing among Slovenes'.[10]

Another side of the coin, however, was clear among the local Italian nationalist bourgeoisie, who considered Franz Ferdinand an enemy because his trialist plans appeared to favour the Southern Slavs and obstruct Italian aspirations. Not surprisingly, the irredentist *L'Indipendente* displayed overt indifference. The day after the assassination it dedicated just one page to the event, and thereafter only summarized news from other (Italian) newspapers.[11] Its tone of writing was also in line with most of the nationalist press in Italy, where the Habsburg Monarchy and its regime were seen as enemies rather than allies in the Triple Alliance. As Christopher Clark has observed, most people in Italy 'regarded the elimination of the late archduke as almost providential'.[12] The socialist *Il Lavoratore* (The Worker), voice of the local Italian working class, also failed to cover the event for weeks, as if the socialists were not affected by the Sarajevo assassination. Like many others, this newspaper and most of the very strong local socialist movement did not comprehend the gravity of the moment, warning its readers simply about the 'very serious situation' between Vienna and Belgrade in late July after the ultimatum to Serbia.[13] In subsequent issues, it followed the sliding of local and European socialism into the war on white, partially censored pages.[14] When general mobilization occurred, censorship was then imposed across the whole Austrian Littoral region. On the one hand many newspapers were banned, and others simply decided not to publish: such was the case with *L'Indipendente*.[15] On the other, *Il Lavoratore* at the start of the war continued as a daily paper and in the following years represented a key reference point for Italian-speakers of the city; even so, like other newspapers it could not avoid the severe interference of the Austrian censors.[16]

In the days after the assassination all city councils and organizations of every type from the entire region gathered at extraordinary meetings to express their condolences to Emperor Franz Joseph. Many commentators stressed the tragedy of the event, the emperor's personal pain and the misery of the entire Monarchy and its dynasty. On 30 June the mayor (*podestà*) of Trieste, Alfonso Valerio, summoned an extraordinary meeting of the city council and invited citizens to take part in the ceremonies.[17] Many officials, cultural, political and educational societies as well as businesses and ordinary people signed a book of condolences, regardless of their political, religious or national affiliation. And news of the murders caused a similar reaction in all parts of the province (the Littoral). In Friuli, on the border with Italy, theatre performances were interrupted, concerts were cancelled and black flags were displayed. The city council of Cormons decided to rename a street in front of the railway station – until then known as Via Stazione – as Via Francesco Ferdinando. The local *podestà* reported that there had been no riots and that the population had shown 'true patriotism' and 'dynastic love'.[18] In general, the reports of local authorities spoke of the 'shocking impression' that the news had made on the people of the Austrian Littoral.[19]

This initial shock was followed by a population transfixed when the bodies of Franz Ferdinand and his wife arrived in Trieste (Figure 12.1). On 30 June, a special train from Sarajevo brought the deceased down to Metković on the Dalmatian coast. They were boarded on the *Viribus Unitis*, and the ship sailed all the way to Trieste, accompanied by other vessels of the Austrian navy. When on 1 July the flotilla under the command of Admiral Anton Haus entered the Gulf of Trieste, it was welcomed by the ringing of all church bells. The next day, everything was ready for the reception. The highest officials of the city and regional authorities were present, as well as Bishop Andrej Karlin, Mayor Valerio, members of the city

**FIGURE 12.1** *The arrival of the bodies in Trieste (Archivio del Civico Museo di Storia Patria, Trieste, Fond Zanetti, 1914 1°973).*

council, representatives of all religious communities, patriotic associations, the chambers of commerce and industry, delegates of the Austrian Lloyd company, the Southern Railway and pupils from the city schools (Figure 12.2). Starting from the pier San Carlo (today Audace) in front of the main city square, the solemn procession passed the Stock Exchange, turned into the Corso, then made its way up to Via Caserma and the adjoining square (today Piazza Oberdan) before ending at the railway station of the Südbahn.[20] The city centre was all adorned with black funeral flags hanging from windows, and many took up position to watch the funeral cortege from their windows and balconies. The Statthalter Konrad Prince Hohenlohe-Schillingsfürst could report to the Austrian prime minister Count Karl von Stürgkh that 'there was not a single house in the whole city without mourning flags and decoration' (Figure 12.3).[21]

No problems occurred during this procession from 8 am to 9.30 am. Before departure at the Südbahn the two coffins were blessed by Bishop Karlin, then, just before 10 am, the convoy left the Trieste railway station and travelled onwards towards Ljubljana, Graz and Vienna. After funeral solemnities in the imperial capital, the coffins were transported to Artstetten to be buried in the family tomb. On 4 July during the funeral in Vienna, a solemn mass had also taken place in the cathedral in Trieste. At this commemoration the whole range of local Habsburg dignitaries was again on display – city and regional authorities (civil and military), representatives of the Stock Exchange, the Southern Railway, the chambers of commerce

**FIGURE 12.2** *The procession on Trieste's main square, today Piazza Unità d'Italia (Archivio Fotografico Civico Museo di guerra per la pace Diego de Henriquez, Trieste, 000462).*

**FIGURE 12.3** *Detail of the procession on the Corso in Trieste (Archivio del Civico Museo di Storia Patria, Trieste, Fond Zanetti, 1914 1°973 II).*

and industry, veteran associations and loyal newspapers like the *Osservatore Triestino* and *Triester Zeitung*. In short, official Trieste was hailing its archduke and his wife for the last time.

## Protest and subversion

Yet the widespread mourning and condolences to the emperor were only one part of the picture. Stefan Zweig, the famous Austrian writer, would explain in his memoirs that Sarajevo did not awaken any compassion: 'Two hours later, signs of genuine mourning were no longer to be seen. The throngs laughed and chattered and as the evening advanced music was resumed at public resorts.'[22] Although Zweig's quotation cannot entirely match the mood in Trieste, it could be seen there that mourning was far from universal. In the days and weeks that followed, the Austrian police treated dozens of cases that speak of various insults related to the emperor's name and opposition to the Habsburg dynasty in general. In a context of tensions and suspicion, every word uttered in an inappropriate place or at the wrong time could cost people dearly. The Good Soldier Švejk, who at the beginning of Jaroslav Hašek's novel talks with his charwoman Mrs Müller about the Sarajevo assassination, would have been quite severely punished if his statement – 'we never ought to have taken Bosnia and Herzegovina from them' – had been made elsewhere at an inappropriate time. This happened to the worker Julius Taučer: he was denounced by a policeman, when, on the evening of 29 June, he entered an inn and shouted that 'they've killed the boss of cops (*birič*)'.²³ He was punished with eight days in prison and a heavy fine.²⁴ The same evening, in a buffet on the other side of the city, an engineer Marcello Polli reacted to the news of Franz Ferdinand's death by cursing his name; he too was arrested.²⁵

Yet it is impossible to speak only of an impulsive reaction by some individuals, as similar cases reoccurred in the following days and weeks. During the funeral procession through the city, Vincenc Rožaj, a baker, was arrested having been caught in front of the cafe *Universo* saying that if 'the Serb who killed the heir to the throne knew that such a parade would be organised for him ... he would certainly kill one more'.²⁶ The worker Jakob Poglaj was sentenced to eighteen months in prison for his statement that 'Franz Joseph is an ass and the late Ferdinand makes two'; he defended himself by saying that he was very drunk. However, according to the police investigation, he was also a 'fanatical member of the social-democratic party'; and on a house search, the discovery of several Slovenian newspapers and letters which 'could be related to the criminal matter' did not help his claim of innocence.²⁷ In another case, Johan Gustinčič could not resort to an intoxication defence either, although it was a well-known fact that he was a 'drunk and an alcoholic'; when Aloisia Kumar reported him to the police for stating that the assassinated archduchess had been 'a slut', she claimed that Gustinčič had been 'only slightly tipsy or hardly at all'.²⁸

Indeed such incidents of disrespectful rhetoric were often accompanied by alcohol. Many people expressed their opposition to the Habsburg dynasty or Monarchy while they were heavily intoxicated, often shouting pro-Serbian, pro-Russian and pro-Italian slogans. At the tavern *Al Dalmata*, Heinrich Cibulka, an electrical engineer originally from Bohemia but working in the port of Pula, was singing Italian songs with other customers. Among them was the Triestine Karel Babuder. After one of the songs Babuder screamed 'Long live Serbia!' and Cibulka reported him to the authorities.²⁹ Similar cases were frequent among soldiers garrisoned in Trieste. On the day of the general mobilization, one month after the assassination, Anton Coslovich, a soldier of the 97th infantry regiment stationed in Trieste, addressed other soldiers in one of the several inns of Trieste in pro-Serbian and anti-Austrian language.³⁰ But comments less tied to political beliefs were also being punished. One Triestine cook, Thomas Ružič, who worked on the ship *Zara*, was heard saying that 'this time Austria will take a beating from Russia'; a court in Šibenik sentenced him to three months' imprisonment.³¹

The police dealt with numerous similar cases, especially those where individuals were shouting slogans that were pro-Serbian or pro-Russian, or that questioned the military capability of the Habsburg Monarchy. It was not necessary for such thoughts to be expressed loudly in public. Even in the intimacy of domestic spaces it was necessary to be wary of denunciations. From November 1913 until the end of July 1914, the twenty-one-year-old

Frančiška Hreščak was working as a maid for a widow, Karlota Mayerweg, who lived in Trieste with her son Rudolf and her daughter Karlota. On 29 July, the day after the Austrian declaration of war on Serbia, Hreščak was fired due to an improper conversation with the daughter in which she had supposedly praised the Serbs. At the police station Hreščak was called upon to defend herself and vainly countered: 'I firmly deny saying anything about the Serbs since I don't know them and I've never been interested in politics.'[32] Similar denunciations even from the workplace – where the denounced knew their denouncers – reveal that an air of suspicion enveloped everyday social encounters in Trieste from the very start of hostilities.

Although these examples suggest that not all inhabitants were simply concerned about the fickle summer weather as one Triestine Italian nationalist journalist wrote in his memoirs, many did believe that the so-called July crisis would be peaceably resolved in the manner of so many others in the past.[33] Therefore, when the declaration of war came, it caused no little surprise among the population of Trieste. After the general mobilization and Austria-Hungary's break of relations with Serbia, Admiral Baron von Koudelka, the commanding officer of the Trieste Naval District, reported to Vienna about the dynastic loyalism and patriotism of the local population.[34] Yet if war euphoria and cries in favour of the Habsburg army were widely present on the streets of Trieste, they very soon began to be intertwined with restraint and reluctance because of hostilities. From the end of July, the city had been flooded with recruits; and journal entries and the daily press reveal how local people were confused and anxious about the exodus of the male population.[35] This all indicates a non-linearity of reactions and choices caused by the declaration of war and by the first, heavy losses of the local 97th regiment on the Galician front.[36] Thus Karel Jurca, a corporal in the Austrian army, who left Trieste with other conscripts at the end of September 1914, wrote in his memoirs: 'We were all adorned with flowers and greenery: outer joy, secret sadness.'[37]

At times in the city over the summer there were reports of scuffles erupting between the new recruits and civilians, but usually insubordination meant inappropriate public statements about the war. On this basis ordinary citizens continued to be denounced and sent to prison. It happened to Franz Bressano, after he started talking to three Bosnian soldiers of the 4th infantry regiment in a brothel in Via del Solitario (today Via D'Azeglio): they denounced him to the authorities since he was being disrespectful to the emperor.[38] Like the cases from Lower Styria analysed by Filip Čuček and Martin Moll, such verbal offences were strictly punished despite the fact that they usually originated in the distress of the moment, caused not by any political conviction but by an escalation of tension during the mobilization and the subsequent declaration of war.[39]

Although the scale of denunciations and imprisonments in Trieste cannot be compared with the high numbers recorded in Lower Styria, it all shows the strict vigilance of the Austrian authorities throughout the country. Suddenly, a military regime was being imposed that immediately curtailed civil rights; it was based on emergency laws that limited political freedom and citizens' rights while increasing the role of the army in the public sphere.[40] As Jonathan Gumz has noted, 'the army aggressively moved to develop its bureaucratic-absolutist program as far as possible within the empire while at the same time upholding a rigid boundary between the army and civil society.'[41] If the arrests in the wake of the assassination were directed against various forms of hate speech and disloyalty towards the emperor, in the following weeks the military authorities began to monitor citizens more systematically.

This 'rapidly produced a mood of vigilance bordering on discrimination against certain nationalities of the empire'.[42] Italian nationalists and irredentists had been strictly watched in the years before the war, some of their organizations had been disbanded, and at the start of hostilities in August 1914 most newspapers in the Italian language were prohibited. Meanwhile, on the state level, Italy and Austria-Hungary had been competing intensively to spread their influence in the Balkans. However, even if Italian nationalists lamented the alleged oppression of Italians in Austria's Adriatic provinces, especially over language rights and the issue of an Italian university in Trieste, both states were still bound by a thirty-year-old political alliance. If Austria reinforced coercive measures against the Monarchy's Italians, it would exacerbate the relationship with an ally that had a crucial role in the balance of any European war.[43]

In summer 1914, a crucial period for the negotiation of international alliances, Vienna and Berlin therefore had no interest in provoking Italy with a political persecution of Italians. It was only after May 1915, when Italy had declared war on the Monarchy, that these became the victims of expulsion and internment. Indeed, until then the main targets of suspicion were not Italian irredentists, but the local 'Yugoslav movement'. Even if Slovene political leaders publicly expressed their loyalty, the military authorities systematically moved to imprison or intern many Slovene and Croatian politicians and other individuals who were considered to be potentially dangerous to the war effort.[44] Walter Lukan writes of more than 900 Slovenes arrested and accused of 'Serbophilia' and 'Panslavism'; and for Trieste alone, Janko Pleterski, using the papers of the governor Alfred von Fries-Skene, has noted how 230 'Yugoslavs' were arrested at the beginning of the war.[45]

Yet this was not a systematic plan of persecution by the army against the mostly loyal Slovene population. Rather, as some historians have recently suggested, the 'military's interventions created a system of distrust that permeated society and government' in general.[46] As a result, the impact of wartime absolutism in the Austrian half of the Monarchy in 1914–17 was even more serious, for it spread a psychosis well beyond the police authorities. Austrian citizens without distinction of gender, class or nationality cooperated closely with the security services to denounce suspicious individuals.⁴⁷ In fact, from the very beginning of the conflict, most allegations and resulting detentions emerged from voluntary denunciations made to the police by ordinary people of all classes and nationalities. Even the Joyce brothers, Stanislaus and his more famous brother James, who spent ten years in Trieste before the war, were victims of such allegations. A letter from 7 August sent to the authorities by a 'Triestine who loves his country' observed that the Joyce brothers were 'pretending to be professors' when in reality they were English spies. The anonymous letter writer proposed that the police carry out a house search.⁴⁸ The policemen who verified this information did not find any irregularities, and there were no legal proceedings against the Joyce brothers. Nevertheless, James Joyce decided to leave Trieste, returning for a short period only after the war.⁴⁹ In the meantime, hundreds of denunciations strictly delimited the Triestine community between 'patriots' and 'traitors'.

As Sheila Fitzpatrick and Robert Gellately have concluded, denouncing and informing take many guises. From the start of hostilities many denunciations were delivered to the police in person or usually via anonymous letters.⁵⁰ The atmosphere of panic, the feeling of danger experienced by many inhabitants, caused irrational interventions against the basic rights of the individual. Even if more research is needed in local archival collections, several examples show that it was not the shortage of material goods that caused this behaviour. Well, before April 1915, when Trieste witnessed violent demonstrations because of the lack of food, the city also experienced a 'culture of denunciation'.⁵¹ Arrests affected many local hard-left members of the Adriatic section of the Austrian socialist party, as well as anti-militarists, republicans and suspected members of the anarchist movement. While already by mid-July the authorities had arrested sixteen anarchists at the coffeehouse *Verdi*, frequently the denunciations were related to imaginary dissidents since the term 'anarchist' was often used as a generic and superficial label for an undefined threat to state security.

Such was the case with the anonymous denunciation of Alessandro Barni, an official of the Lloyd shipyard in Trieste, who had allegedly stated in a city inn that Franz Ferdinand's assassin 'deserves a monument' as he had 'killed two crowned heads at the same time'. In the denunciation, Barni was labelled an 'anarchist, full of debts and capable of doing anything just to make some money'. On investigating the incident, the police found that Barni was neither a political suspect, nor a member of any political organization, nor listed in the official register of anarchists. But even if in this case no legal proceedings were instituted, the investigation resulted in several political suspects being monitored and eventually imprisoned.⁵² Along with those political suspicions, it was very often ethnic affiliation that proved to be the main basis for denunciation. And in Trieste the local population seems to have cooperated closely with the state in this project of surveillance.

## Dynastic loyalty and ethnic confrontation: Slovenes and Italians

The Sarajevo assassinations had caused mass riots against Serbs in many places across the Monarchy. Not only were there revenge attacks in Sarajevo and elsewhere in Bosnia-Herzegovina such as Knin, Tuzla and Livno, but violence also flared up in Croatia. On the day of the funeral procession through Trieste, the Slovene newspaper *Edinost* was published with a bold text. It warned its readers that 'yesterday serious news spread across the city that well-known Italian street lads are planning an anti-Slovene demonstration after the funeral ceremonies, that is to say, they want to organize riots with attacks directed at our people and our property'.[53] Minor brawls and riots subsequently occurred in front of the Serbian consulate, but there were no mass attacks. Even the mighty Church of St Spyridon, symbol of the Serbian Orthodox community of Trieste, was not vandalized as had happened in other parts of the Monarchy.[54] However, this was far from being a sign of greater tolerance in the city. The situation was tense. Feelings of sadness were mixed with anger and suspicion. In Trieste and in the rest of the Littoral many citizens were arrested on suspicion of involvement in the assassination.

A few days after the murders, the news broke that one of the Sarajevo assassins had been Nedeljko Čabrinović – perpetrator of the first and failed bomb attempt – who had been employed as a typesetter at the Slovene printing house of *Edinost* in Trieste. As a result, the director of the printing house was interrogated. Although this in fact had no connection with the assassination, it underlined the sense of distrust among Italians and Germans towards Slavs of the Monarchy and neighbouring states like Serbia. In this sense, for many people, Serbian citizenship itself gave ample cause for denunciation or violence. One local artisan, Francesco Zitnik, contacted the authorities soon after the general mobilization because one of his employees was a citizen of Serbia. Even if there was no justification for proceeding, a police officer duly arrested the 'suspect' on the grounds that he might eventually be 'politically or militarily susceptible'. While some correspondence was found during the house search, the material could not be immediately used as it was written in the Cyrillic script which was unintelligible to the police. Nonetheless, Cyrillic alone aroused suspicions and formed a legitimate basis, in the eyes of the police, for the subsequent arrest of the twenty-one-year-old Serbian Budimir Veljović.[55]

As this shows, in Trieste as in other crown lands, many accusations were based simply on some affiliation to Serbia, in that an individual supposedly supported Serbia or viewed positively the political efforts of South Slavs.[56] The Austrian authorities saw potential enemies in many Slovene, Croat or Serb-speaking citizens as well as any supporters of the Yugoslav idea. However, again, this obsession was not limited to Austrian officialdom.

The following case of Anna Pegan and Ida Spetich illustrates the precarious conditions in the city fabric in terms of gender, class or ethnic relationships. Very often in the period after the Sarajevo assassination but especially with the outbreak of war a month later, the tense environment erupted onto the surface of society. On 31 July, Anna (also Ana) Pegan, born in 1885 in Vipava, a town 50 kilometres to the north, but residing now in Media Street in Trieste, mother of three and four months pregnant at the time, was reported to have made a brusque comment to *Il Piccolo* seller Lucia Stopar, owner of a newsstand on Piazza Borsa. She allegedly told Stopar: 'Why are you crying for Austria? Cry for Serbia instead. Long live Serbia!'[57] Supposedly on the basis of these words, another woman named Ida Spetich then attacked Pegan. When interrogated by the police, Pegan defended herself: 'I admit to purchasing meat at the Spetich butcher shop every day, ... but I have to deny ever getting involved in conversations about politics in the way Ida Spetich claims I did.' Pegan saw other motives for the attack on herself: 'For the past five days, every time I came to buy meat in her shop, Ida Spetich started baiting me with various remarks about the Slovenes (*"sciavi"*).' Apparently, a few days before, Spetich had told Pegan that the '*sciavi*' were to blame for the war, because they had killed 'our' heir apparent.

Pegan's testimony illustrates the state of mind of some elements of the population who stigmatized Triestine Slovenes as culprits or accessories in the Sarajevo assassination and, consequently, as begetters of the war. The word *sciavi* used by Spetich encapsulated both the Serb youths who had killed Franz Ferdinand and the Slovenes living in Trieste. Pegan paid Spetich back in her own coin, retorting that one should then also fight against Italy, since 'an Italian had killed our unfortunate Empress'. Here Pegan was referring to the Italian anarchist Luciano Lucheni who in 1898 had stabbed to death the Empress Elisabeth, to whom in 1912 a monument had been erected in Trieste. The bickering reveals how Imperial deaths were translated into everyday lives and directly affected all levels of the local social microcosm. It is important, however, to emphasize that both participants in this quarrel leaned on their own loyalty to the state – Pegan by invoking the assassination of 'our' Empress Elizabeth, and Spetich by using the assassination of 'our' heir apparent. In her defence, Pegan rejected the accusations, claiming that 'she had been provoked by Spetich' and that the latter's abuse had created a tense situation where Pegan ended up the victim of a physical assault. For apparently, this aggression was not an isolated incident. Pegan continued her explanation by setting the violence in a broader time frame:

> These past days I haven't been given a moment's peace by that part of the Italian public who know me, because I am Slovene. They have been taking every opportunity to provoke me. My guests at the tavern can testify to my beliefs and tell you that I have never declared myself in favour of Serbia.

Pegan therefore saw the reason for the attack on her as the hostile climate developing against Slovenes in Trieste:

> Today's incident is only an expression of the national hatred against the Slovene people that is growing around me day after day – I am no longer safe from actual and verbal attacks. I didn't know what to do anymore because of this agitation, when I saw I was hated just for being a Slovene.

At the close of her testimony, Pegan also explained her encounter with Lucia Stopar, the owner of the *Piccolo* newsstand: 'I would also like to mention that today, when I came out of the butcher's, a woman selling *Il Piccolo* on Piazza Borsa punched me first, giving me a bloody nose.'[58] Regardless of Pegan's statements, from which we learn that it was Stopar rather than Spetich who attacked her (together with other 'harridans'), it is clear how Pegan felt and experienced the prevailing atmosphere in the city in the days following the declaration of war. Spetich denied she had wanted to cause any upheaval for 'national reasons', but did admit it was possible that in an outburst of anger she might have used the word *sciavi*. The newsseller Stopar, who had reported Pegan for her alleged pro-Serbian comment, also admitted she had 'jumped at Pegan' but denied she had punched her. It is uncertain whether Stopar was penalized in any way, but it is clear that the Austrian authorities decided to incarcerate both Pegan, for reportedly cheering on an enemy state (she was transferred to Ljubljana prison), and Spetich who was sentenced to a two-day sentence for her disorderly behaviour.[59]

Even if no mass riots occurred in Trieste, there were thus numerous attacks on individuals who exposed themselves to danger through their open Yugoslav or Slovene allegiance. But these were usually active members of the local Slovene societies. Alojz Kodrič, the treasurer of the *Obrtnijško društvo pri sv. Ani* (Tradesmen's Society at St Anna), had to defend himself because of his alleged Serbophilia. In December 1912 the members of the society had decided to send twenty crowns to the Balkan Red Cross, an organization active on the Serbian side during the Balkan Wars. As was the case in other nationally mixed regions of the Monarchy, nationalist activists took these opportunities to 'finger their local opponents as subversives'.[60] In the eyes of the local Italian nationalists, Kodrič was a hostile element and therefore was denounced to the authorities. Just like Toma Gulas, the protagonist of a short story by Ivo Andrić (Gulas was beaten in the streets and escorted to jail in the midst of anti-Russian acclamations), this scene was repeated for many other individuals who were viewed as active supporters of the Slovene or Yugoslav movements and therefore labelled as traitors to the Monarchy.[61]

As the previous cases reveal, news of the assassination caused inter-ethnic tensions as Italian nationalists used the new context to settle accounts with their Slovene counterparts.[62] *Edinost* duly protested against the attacks and the increasingly frequent abuse of 'Abbasso i sciavi'.[63] The socialist leader Ivan Regent noted in his memoirs that when Austria-Hungary declared war on Serbia, 'ethnic hatred mixed with patriotic feelings reached the lowest level of savagery' among some Triestines; 'the pro-Austrian mood mixed with Italian nationalism produced some very dirty and tasteless results.'[64] Similarly, in his book about the history of Trieste, the Italian nationalist Attilio Tamaro observed that the mourning ceremonies in Trieste were much larger than expected due to 'hatred against the Slavs'.[65] Like Tamaro, many Italian nationalist writers expressed their relief when Trieste's local irredentists were allowed, unpunished, to shout 'Evviva l'Italia' and 'Abbasso i sciavi'. For at that time Italy was still a precious ally for the Central Powers and open expressions of support for Italy were not uncommon. They were not just tolerated but even welcomed by those Austrian (military) officials who saw the war against Serbia as a 'struggle against Slavdom'.[66] In the summer days of 1914, newspaper articles and memoirs speak of brass bands playing both the imperial anthem (*Serbidiola* as it was termed in Italian Triestine dialect) and the Italian *Marcia Reale* in the crowded inns of old-town Trieste.

This political moment linked the ethnic animosity of Italian nationalists against local Slovenes with Austria's war politics against Serbia. In fact, many local Italians accepted with enthusiasm the declaration of war against Serbia due to their anti-Slav feelings.[67] Thus, anti-Slav sentiment seems to have shaped how many of Trieste's inhabitants approached the forthcoming conflict. It found expression in anti-Slovene attitudes and in simple enthusiasm for a war against Serbia and Russia – against the 'infamous race' as the ensign Adolfo Faidiga termed the enemy in his letters from the Balkan front.[68]

## Conclusion

In Trieste even the funeral procession of Franz Ferdinand revealed social and nationalist tensions. Even before the war, ethnic conflicts in the city had been quite common. There had been fights at the Trieste high school between Slovene and Croatian pupils on the one side and Italians on the other, and on May Day 1914 there were skirmishes during the parade of Slovene workers. However, the Sarajevo murders produced a wave of violent clashes that merged a feeling of loyalty to the dynasty with hatred against Trieste's 'Other'. Especially public statements concerning Serbia, which originated often from the Balkan Wars of 1912–13, gave rise to doubts about the loyalty of the local Slovene community and represented the basis for an imagined Slav 'fifth column' in the Monarchy. Just as the slippery term 'Czech' was interchanged with 'Slav', 'Serbophile' or 'Russophile' by German nationalists in Vienna, so the term 'Slav' or even '*sciavo*' was used in Trieste as a synonym of Slovene and as a catchword for anyone who was suspicious or allegedly posed a threat to the community and the empire.[69]

Sarajevo, and the tense atmosphere that followed and ended in war, aroused previously latent symptoms of intolerance in a more aggravated form. Although it would be erroneous to equate this precisely with the authorities' hostility to Serbs in Bosnia or Ruthenes in Galicia, it was not only in Carinthia and Styria, where Slovenes 'rubbed shoulders' against Germans, but also on the south-western edge of the Monarchy that Slovenes encountered hostility.[70] In the Austrian Littoral, Slovenes were mainly confronted with Italians, allies for the moment in the Triple Alliance against Serbia. Even if Italy declared its neutrality at the start of the conflict, many local Italians thought that at some stage it would enter the war on the side of the Central Powers.[71] While many Triestine Italians also became suspect after Italy declared war against Austria-Hungary in May 1915, between the summer of 1914 and the following spring it was local Slovenes who were the main target of repressive measures. Several hundred Slovenes, from political leaders to ordinary citizens, were interned or imprisoned in this first phase of the war.[72]

Earlier, complex and contradictory inter-ethnic animosities emerged even more accentuated than before, and they affected the social fabric as a whole. In the days after the declaration of war, rumours spread around the city, presenting local Slovenes as somehow involved in causing the European conflict. This revealed a mindset among many people who quickly stigmatized local Slovenes (and Slavs in general) as sharing the guilt of the Sarajevo assassins. The result was a mass of verbal and physical attacks on members of the Slovene-speaking community, seen not just by the Austrian authorities as hostile elements.[73] This is not to suggest or conclude that in some way Slovenes 'suffered more'. Rather we see that traditional national perspectives are inadequate to explain the complex phenomena occurring. Under the veneer of supposedly opposing nationalisms, a more detailed analysis of archival material shows that the anti-Slovene position was not an exclusive feature of Italian nationalists and irredentists, but rather a frequent and modifiable form of ethnic intolerance. Frequently, hatred against the external enemy (Serbia and Russia) and the internal opponent (the Slovene from Trieste, the 'Slav') went hand in hand with support for the Monarchy and dynastic loyalty.[74] The increased tensions and forms of popular violence in the summer months of 1914 show that forms of anti-Slovene violence were not a prerogative of Italian nationalists but were rather accompanied by many grassroots agents of Habsburg loyalty. Thus, if the impact of the Sarajevo assassinations revealed several forms of verbal iconoclasm with regard to the Monarchy and its symbols, it did not result in widespread dynastic disloyalty in favour of nationalist demands.

In short, the case of Trieste in the summer of 1914 confirms that it would be misleading simply to reduce the fall of Austria-Hungary to the victory of the national idea, as nationalist post-war narratives tended to do. First, the local Slovenes were not under pressure because of their revolutionary demands for an imagined Yugoslav state but, rather, because of an anti-

Slav resentment among the Austrian authorities, both civil and military, and among parts of the local population. If this picture was not specific to Triestine Slovenes but part of a general rejection of civil society and popular politics by the Austrian military, it is also true that some parts of society experienced this hostility more harshly than others. Second, this violence cannot be linked to Italian irredentist demands, but rather it shows how elements of the local Italian population associated it with feelings of imperial patriotism. This incoherence was disturbing to Italian nationalists and their political project. For rather than pushing for more radical solutions in the direction of an annexation of the city by Italy, Austrian Italians were being reinforced in their imperial loyalty.

The state policies of surveillance and suspicion had catastrophic consequences. With its absolutist attitude, the state was allowing a 'brutalization' of society even before the official start of the war.[75] If in the summer of 1914 socialist, anarchists, anti-militarists, Slovenes and other Slav communities were the main target of these repressive measures from above and increasing violence from below, after the Italian declaration of war in May 1915 several hundred Italians experienced similar situations. In fact, the Pandora's Box opened by the Austrian ruling elite in the summer of 1914 did irreparable damage to civic cohesion that went well beyond the First World War. As elsewhere, the collapse of the Habsburg Empire brought not peace but an escalation in social chaos and a range of new repressive state policies to deal with opponents.

## Notes

1 Vladimir Dedijer, *Sarajevo 1914* (Ljubljana: Državna založba Slovenije, 1966), 26.
2 Lonnie R. Johnson, *Central Europe: Enemies, Neighbors, Friends* (Oxford: Oxford University Press, 2002), 173.
3 See Pieter M. Judson, '"Where Our Commonality Is Necessary …": Rethinking the End of the Habsburg Monarchy', *Austrian History Yearbook* 48 (2017): 1–21.
4 Anna Millo, 'Trieste, 1830–70: From Cosmopolitanism to the Nation', in Laurence Cole (ed.), *Different Paths to the Nation: Regional and National Identities in Central Europe and Italy, 1830–70* (Basingstoke: Palgrave Macmillan, 2007); Dominique K. Reill, *Nationalists Who Feared the Nation: Adriatic Multi-Nationalism in Habsburg Dalmatia, Trieste, and Venice* (Stanford: Stanford University Press, 2012); Jože Pirjevec, *'Trst je naš!' Boj Slovencev za morje (1848–1954)* (Ljubljana: Nova revija, 2007); Moritz Csáky, *Das Gedächtnis der Städte. Kulturelle Verflechtungen – Wien und die urbanen Milieus in Zentraleuropa* (Vienna: Böhlau, 2010), 314–20; Paul Waley, 'Introducing Trieste: A Cosmopolitan City?', *Social & Cultural Geography* 10 (2009): 243–56.

5   Millo, 'Trieste', 60–81.
6   Borut Klabjan, '"Scramble for Adria": Discourses of Appropriation of the Adriatic Space before and after World War I', *Austrian History Yearbook* 42 (2011): 16–32.
7   'Mortale attentato a S. A. I. e R. l'arciduca Francesco Ferdinando e alla consorte S. A. la Duchessa di Hohenberg', *L'Osservatore Triestino*, 29 June 1914, 1.
8   'S. A. I. L'Arciduca Francesco Ferdinando e la consorte duchessa di Hohenberg uccisi in un attentato a Saraievo', *Il Piccolo*, 28 June 1914, 1. Cf. Fabio Todero, *Una violenta bufera. Trieste 1914* (Trieste: IRSML - FVG, 2013), 39–68.
9   'Die Trauer in Triest', *Triester Tagblatt*, 29 June 1914, 2.
10  'Tržaško mesto žaluje', *Edinost*, 29 June 1914, 2.
11  'La tragedia di Sarajevo', *L'Indipendente*, 30 June 1914, 1.
12  Christopher Clark, *The Sleepwalkers: How Europe Went to War in 1914* (London: Allen Lane, 2012), 405.
13  'Il gravissimo conflitto austro-serbo', *Il Lavoratore*, 25 July 1914, 1. Cf. Marina Rossi and Sergio Ranchi, 'Lontano da dove ... Proletari italiani e sloveni del Litorale nei vortici della guerra imperialista', *Qualestoria* XIV/ 1–2 (1986): 102.
14  Marina Cattaruzza, *Socialismo adriatico. La socialdemocrazia di lingua italiana nei territori costieri della Monarchia asburgica: 1888-1915* (Manduria: Piero Lacaita Editore, 1998), 173–4. In his memoirs Ivan Regent – one of the leading personalities of the Trieste Committee of the Yugoslav Social Democratic Party – wrote that 'both, the Italian as well as the Yugoslav Socialist Party in Trieste, were not ideologically and organizationally prepared to act against it in a mass or revolutionary way': Ivan Regent, *Spomini* (Ljubljana: Cankarjeva založba, 1967), 85.
15  Giuliano Gaeta, *Trieste durante la guerra mondiale. Opinione pubblica e giornalismo a Trieste dal 1914 al 1918* (Trieste: Delfino, 1938), 52.
16  Mark Cornwall, *The Undermining of Austria-Hungary: The Battle for Hearts and Minds* (New York: Palgrave Macmillan, 2000), 16–39; Giuseppe Piemontese, *Il movimento operaio a Trieste. Dalle origini alla fine della prima guerra mondiale* (Rome: Editori Riuniti, 1974), 300–304.
17  Archivio generale della città di Trieste, Verbali del Consiglio comunale di Trieste, 1914, 27/1914.
18  Archivio di Stato di Trieste (State Archive of Trieste: hereafter AST), I. R. Luogotenenza del Litorale (1850–1918) (hereafter IRLL), Atti Presidiali (AP), busta [b.] 381, Faszikel [Fasz.] Kondolenzen, Nr 1226/14, 8 July 1914.
19  AST, IRLL (1850–1918), AP, b. 381, Fasz. Kondolenzen, Nr 1409, 2 July 1914.
20  The route was the one that had been taken in 1868 during the mourning procession for Archduke Maximilian, younger brother of Emperor Franz Joseph, who had been executed the year before when emperor of Mexico.
21  AST, IRLL (1850–1918), AP, b. 381, Fasz. Kondukt, Nr 1409/3.

22  Stefan Zweig, *The World of Yesterday* (Lincoln: University of Nebraska Press, 1964), 216.
23  Names in this chapter appear as they are quoted in the archival sources. AST, Direzione di Polizia (hereafter DP), Atti presidiali riservati 1814–1918 (APR), b. 374, Nr 1712.
24  AST, Tribunale provinciale, Atti penali, b. 4704, Nr 2463.
25  AST, DP, APR 1814–1918, b. 374, Nr 1754.
26  AST, DP, APR 1814–1918, b. 374, Nr 1707.
27  AST, DP, APR 1814–1918, b. 374, Nr 1746.
28  AST, DP, APR, 1814–1918, b. 374, Nr. 1751.
29  AST, DP, APR 1814–1918, b. 374, Nr 1775.
30  AST, DP, APR 1814–1918, b. 374, Nr 1786.
31  AST, DP, APR 1814–1918, b. 374, Nr 1792.
32  AST, DP, APR 1814–1918, b. 374, Nr 1872.
33  Silvio Benco, *Gli ultimi anni della dominazione austriaca a Trieste*, 3 vols (Milan: Risorgimento, 1919), I, 17–21.
34  Stefan Wedrac, '"Das Wohl des Staates ist oberstes Gesetz" – Die Nationalitätenpolitik der staatlichen Verwaltung in Triest zu Beginn des Ersten Weltkrieges', in Claudia Reichl-Ham (ed.), *Der Erste Weltkrieg und der Vielvölkerstaat* (Vienna: Heeresgeschichtliches Museum, 2012), 69–82.
35  Haydee Astori and Bruno Astori, *La passione di Trieste. Diario di vita triestina (luglio 1914 – novembre 1918)* (Florence: Bemporad, 1922); Carmela Rossi Timeus, *Attendiamo le navi. Diario di una giovinetta triestina 1914-1918* (Bologna: L. Capelli, 1934).
36  Marina Rossi, *Irredenti giuliani al fronte russo. Storie di ordinaria diserzione, di lunghe prigionie e di sospirati rimpatri (1914-1920)* (Udine: Del Bianco, 1998), 17; Roberto Todero, *Dalla Galizia all'Isonzo, storia e storie dei soldati triestini nella Grande guerra. Italiani, sloveni e croati del k.u.k I. R. Freiherr von Waldstätten nr. 97 dal 1883 al 1918* (Udine: Gaspari, 2006), 36.
37  Karel Jurca, *Vojni dnevnik desetnika* (Trieste: Mladika Trst, 2008), 26. For an analysis of the popular mood, see Mark Cornwall, 'The Spirit of 1914 in Austria-Hungary', *Prispevki za novejšo zgodovino* 55/2 (2015): 7–21.
38  AST, DP, APR 1814–1918, b. 374, Nr 1873 PI. On brothels and prostitution in the late Habsburg Monarchy, see Nancy M. Wingfield, *The World of Prostitution in Late Imperial Austria* (Oxford: Oxford University Press, 2017).
39  Filip Čuček and Martin Moll (eds), *Duhovniki za rešetkami. Poročila škofu o poleti 1914 na Spodnjem Štajerskem aretiranih duhovnikih / Priester hinter Gittern. Die Berichte der im Sommer 1914 in der Untersteiermark verhafteten Geistlichen an ihren Bischof* (Ljubljana: Arhivsko društvo Slovenije, 2006), 7–8; Martin Moll, 'Erste Weltkrieg und politische Justiz in Österreich-Ungarn: Empirische Befunde aus der slowenischen und deutschsprachigen Steiermark', in Oto Luthar and Jurij Perovšek (eds), *Zbornik Janka Pleterskega* (Ljubljana: Založba ZRC, 2003), 253–83. For a thorough analysis of the Styrian case, see Martin Moll, *Kein Burgfrieden. Der deutsch-slowenische*

*Nationalitätenkonflikt in der Steiermark 1900-1918* (Innsbruck: Studien Verlag, 2007).
40  Tamara Scheer, *Zwischen Front und Heimat. Österreich-Ungarns Militärverwaltungen im Ersten Weltkrieg* (Frankfurt and New York: Peter Lang, 2009).
41  Jonathan E. Gumz, *The Resurrection and Collapse of Empire in Habsburg Serbia, 1914 – 1918* (Cambridge: Cambridge University Press, 2009), 15.
42  Cornwall, *The Undermining of Austria-Hungary*, 19.
43  Leo Valiani, *La dissoluzione dell'Austria-Ungheria* (Milan: Il Saggiatore, 1966), 97–126.
44  Petra Svoljšak, '"Zapleni vse česar ne razumeš, utegnilo bi škoditi vojevanju." Delovanje avstrijske cenzure med veliko vojno', in Mateja Režek (ed.), *Cenzurirano. Zgodovina cenzure na Slovenskem od 19. stoletja do danes* (Ljubljana: Nova revija, 2010), 55–65.
45  Walter Lukan, 'Iz črnožolte kletke narodov' v 'zlato svobodo'. *Habsburška monarhija in Slovenci v Prvi svetovni vojni* (Ljubljana: Zveza zgodovinskih društev Slovenije, 2014), 31; Janko Peterski, *Prva odločitev Slovencev za Jugoslavijo. Politika na domačih tleh med vojno 1914-1918* (Ljubljana: Slovenska matica, 1971), 28. See also the documents published by Janko Pleterski, *Politično preganjanje Slovencev v Avstriji 1914-1917. Poročili vojaške in vladne komisije* (Ljubljana: Archivsko društvo Slovenije, 1980).
46  John Deak and Jonathan E. Gumz, 'How to Break a State: The Habsburg Monarchy's Internal War, 1914–1918', *American Historical Review* 122/4 (2017): 1122.
47  Tamara Scheer, 'Denunciation and the Decline of the Habsburg Home Front During the First World War', *European Review of History: Revue européenne d'histoire* 24 (2017): 214–28.
48  AST, DP, APR 1814–1918, b. 374, Nr 1973.
49  John McCourt, *Gli anni di Bloom* (Milan: Mondadori, 2005).
50  Sheila Fitzpatrick and Robert Gellately (eds), *Accusatory Practices: Denunciation in Modern European History, 1789-1989* (Chicago: Chicago University Press, 1997), 2.
51  Maureen Healy, *Vienna and the Fall of the Habsburg Empire: Total War and Everyday Life in World War I* (Cambridge: Cambridge University Press, 2004), 149. On denunciations as part of a shared political culture in Habsburg Austria, see also Tara Zahra, *Kidnapped Souls: National Indifference and the Battle for Children in the Bohemian Lands, 1900–1948* (Ithaca: Cornell University Press, 2008).
52  AST, DP, APR 1814–1918, b. 374, Nr 1711.
53  'Opozarjamo', *Edinost*, 2 July 1914, 3.
54  'Dimonstrazioni', *Il Piccolo*, 26 July 1914, 2; Benco, *Gli ultimi anni*, I, 33–4.
55  AST, DP, APR 1814–1918, b. 374, Nr 1806.
56  Moll, *Kein Burgfrieden*, 472–99.
57  AST, DP, APR, 1814–1918, b. 374, 1826 PI.

58 AST, DP, APR, 1814–1918, b. 374, 5666/1.
59 AST, DP, APR, 1814–1918, b. 374, 5748/4.
60 Pieter M. Judson, *The Habsburg Empire: A New History* (Cambridge, MA: Harvard University Press, 2016), 397.
61 Ivo Andrić, *La storia maledetta. Racconti triestini* (Milan: Mondadori, 2007), 14.
62 In a letter to Scipio Slataper, his friend Elody Oblath (who was the youngest daughter in a mixed Jewish/Hungarian and Italian wealthy Triestine family and future wife of the writer Giani Stuparich) revealed her aversion to the dynasty and the 'Slavs' and asked her mother not to hang a black flag out of the window on the day of the procession: Todero, *Una violenta bufera*, 58–9.
63 'Poniževalci avstrijskega imena', *Edinost*, 2 August 1914, 2. '*Sciavoli*' is an offensive play on words, connecting the terms 'Slav' and 'slave'; it was used by local Italians against Slovenes.
64 Regent, *Spomini*, 84.
65 Attilio Tamaro, *Storia di Trieste* (Rome: Stock, 1924), 571.
66 Alan Kramer, *Dynamic of Destruction: Culture and Mass Killing in the First World War* (Oxford: Oxford University Press, 2007), 75–6.
67 Anna Millo, 'Un porto fra centro e periferia (1861-1918)', in Roberto Finzi, Claudio Magris and Giovanni Miccoli (eds), *Storia d'Italia. Le regioni dall'Unità a oggi. Il Friuli – Venzia Giulia* (Turin: Einaudi, 2002), 228. Alessandro Minutillo, an Italian nationalist publicist, claimed that 'the war against Serbia meant war against the Slavs and it was almost popular here [in Trieste]': Alessandro Minutillo, *Trieste durante l'ultimo periodo di occupazione austriaca* (Rome and Bracciano: C. Strabioli, 1915), 7.
68 Rossi and Ranchi, 'Lontano da dove', 106.
69 Healy, *Vienna and the Fall of the Habsburg Empire*, 153.
70 Cornwall, *The Undermining of Austria-Hungary*, 21.
71 Rossi and Ranchi, 'Lontano da dove', 106.
72 Wedrac, 'Das Wohl des Staates ist oberstes Gesetz', 77–8.
73 Lucio Fabi, 'Una città al fronte. Trieste 1914-1918', *Qualestoria* XI/3 (1983): 6.
74 Judson, *The Habsburg Empire*, 394.
75 The term 'brutalization' refers to the thesis formulated by George Mosse that soldiers brought the experience of the trenches back home after the conflict: *Fallen Soldiers: Reshaping the Memory of the World Wars* (Oxford: Oxford University Press, 1990).

## CHAPTER 13

# The inner enemy in wartime

# The Habsburg state and the Serb citizens of Bosnia-Herzegovina, 1913–18

*Heiner Grunert*

Already a year before the Sarajevo assassination and the start of the war, Habsburg imperial rule was changing. This shift was very apparent in the state's attitude towards the Bosnian Serbs, viewed as the most problematic ethnic group in the youngest province of one of the Monarchy's tensest regions. Responding in 1913 to a supposed existential threat, the decisive political actors surrendered a major principle of the enlightened empire – the political equality of all officially recognized ethno-confessional groups. Although it was in July 1914 that the shift in state policy towards the Serbs became really noticeable, the main principles of imperial policy were already being watered down a year earlier as foreign and security issues began to dominate domestic policy. This chapter explores how the break in the relationship between the state and the Serb community in Bosnia-Herzegovina occurred, as well as the leading protagonists who promoted that rupture. It focuses on the reactions of the military and civil leadership to the perceived threat and how the enemy within, especially in Herzegovina, was defined and managed.

In the autumn of 1912, as Lothar Höbelt shows in his chapter, Vienna perceived the military successes of the Balkan League against the Ottoman

Empire as an enormous threat. From October, troops were strengthened in Bosnia, especially along the borders with Serbia and Montenegro. In November, numerous political circles including that of Archduke Franz Ferdinand were arguing openly for armed engagement with Serbia. The atmosphere in Bosnia therefore was very tense. On the one hand, both the Serbian Orthodox and Catholic constituencies were enthusiastic about the successes of Christian troops; Muslims, however, were frightened by the massive violence against fellow-Muslims and the influx of refugees, especially from Kosovo and Macedonia.[1] From the end of the year, hundreds of Bosnian Serbs had fled to Serbia and Montenegro to fight voluntarily in their ranks. Serb associations in Bosnia, notably the cultural organization *Prosvjeta* (Enlightenment), were collecting donations to support the two Serb armies of Serbia and Montenegro.[2] In Sarajevo, the Provincial Government (*Landesregierung*) urged local administrators to be vigilant and in December suspended the activity of the Bosnian assembly (Sabor/Landtag).[3] In spring 1913 the siege of Scutari by Montenegrin and Serbian troops became a red line for the Habsburg elite who refused to countenance any annexation of the town by one of the two Serb kingdoms. While Serbia withdrew its troops after substantial international pressure, Montenegro was obstinate in continuing the siege. Austria-Hungary openly threatened to begin hostilities against King Nikita of Montenegro.[4]

At this point and after repeated entreaties from Bosnia's *Landeschef* (General Oskar Potiorek), the common finance minister and ex-officio governor of Bosnia, Leon Biliński, agreed to impose a state of emergency. In early May 1913, many civil rights in Bosnia were abolished – freedom of movement, freedom of speech, the right to assembly and the privacy of correspondence. The decrees also dissolved all Serb and socialist organizations. A broad range of societies was targeted: from *Pobratimstvo* (Fraternization), *Trezvenost* (Sobriety) and the national gymnastics club *Srpski Sokoli* (Serb Falcons or Sokols) to professional and cultural associations like the Union of Priests, the Saint-Sava Club and even the Serb amateur theatre in Sarajevo. *Prosvjeta*, consisting of dozens of local clubs all over Bosnia-Herzegovina, was the most important and largest of the organizations affected.[5] By contrast, Muslim, Catholic or Jewish associations were not at all damaged by the regulations. They were clearly not viewed as subversive.[6] At the same time, General Potiorek enforced discriminatory treatment. He started to levy irregular troops from among Catholics and Muslims to form the so-called *Grenz-Schutzkorps* (border-security forces). Serbs were explicitly excluded from these forces.[7] Potiorek at the end of 1912 had hoped but failed to implement these plans due to the Common Ministry of Finance's resistance; he realized them six months later.

Only when Montenegro, in response to international pressure, withdrew its troops from Scutari on 5 May did Vienna cancel its war preparations. The Bosnian Provincial Government now lifted the emergency laws – after only twelve days' validity. Even so, this governmental shift of 1913 had significantly weakened trust and loyalty towards imperial institutions, strengthening anti-Habsburg sentiment in the local Serb communities.[8] Already in 1913 many Serbs had been given a taste of how military rule might affect the empire. In Bosnia this was accompanied by the fact that the army, already in 1912, had strengthened its position within the Bosnian government at the expense of civil servants: Bosnia was again being transformed into the Monarchy's military borderland.[9]

## The assassination and anti-Serb riots

Dangerous times lay ahead for Habsburg Serbs after Franz Ferdinand's assassination. On that day, demonstrations in Sarajevo and Mostar turned into pogrom-like riots against Serbs and their property. Soon, in almost all towns across Bosnia, Serb private houses, schools, libraries, club houses and churches were attacked, looted and often destroyed. Only rarely did security forces intervene. They were surprised and overstrained, but also often unwilling to take action against explicitly Habsburg-loyal, anti-Serb violence.[10] The destruction mostly affected places where Serbs constituted a minority – such as the central and western parts of Herzegovina. In Mostar, Serb shops and the Orthodox Church were demolished, and one Serb was even killed. In the small town of Konjić, protesters wrecked the church, the school and the reading rooms, and threw books and icons onto the streets. In the west-Herzegovinian town of Duvno a mob allegedly numbering 1,000 peasants attacked Serb houses. Shops were plundered and goods, money and credit books stolen; the Serb library was destroyed, the school teacher's flat demolished and the parish house plundered. In the end some tried to burn down the school (Figure 13.1). Similar attacks on Serbs' private, collective and religious property occurred in the towns of Čapljina and Ljubuški as well as at the monastery of Žitomislić.[11] These events revealed the latent tensions in Bosnian society and showed how deeply the assassination had destabilized public order.

In the July crisis, tensions between the civil and the military administration in the Habsburg Empire were resolved largely in favour of the military. This was especially true for Bosnia. From 1878, the commander of the XV Corps in Bosnia was automatically the head of the government and followed directives from the War Ministry in Vienna. But as head of the Bosnian government, he was also subordinated to the empire's Common Ministry of Finance.[12] Immediately after the assassination, the War Ministry assumed increasing responsibilities and power in Bosnia. Already on 2 July, the Minister of War Alexander Krobatin demanded the imposition of emergency rule across Bosnia; all Serb organizations were to be dissolved and all Serb priests, teachers and students strictly monitored.[13] Biliński (common minister of finance) tried to prevent these measures. On 3 July he demanded

**FIGURE 13.1** *Anti-Serb riots and the devastation of Serb property* (Das interessante Blatt, *Vienna, 28/33, 9 July 1914, 7).*

'that the government cannot in any way make the whole loyal and innocent population of Bosnia and Herzegovina responsible for the atrocities carried out by a few individuals or groups'.[14] Biliński was not, as he would claim later, an opponent of war.[15] But concerning the treatment of Serbs he argued in terms of civil rights. Already two days after the assassination, he had reminded Potiorek by telegram of the negative effects the emergency measures of 1913 had already had on the loyalty of Bosnian Serbs:

> I very much regret that last year at the time of the imposition of emergency rule the military administration clearly deemed it unavoidable to dissolve all Serb societies and thereby pushed elements friendly to the government into the hostile camp. Hence I am now of the opinion that in future we should deal with cases arising on an individual basis, and when we uncover any subversive [*staatsfeindlich*] tendencies by organizations, we should intervene vigorously against those particular cases.[16]

Despite this, on 3 July 1914 the War Ministry's planned measures targeting the Bosnian Serb population of Bosnia were introduced.

During the first two weeks of July, security forces therefore imprisoned and searched dozens of homes as part of their investigations into the background of the assassination.[17] Furthermore, by mid-August hundreds of charges of high treason or disturbances to public order had been brought to the civil courts. Serbs were accused of having praised the assassin Gavrilo Princip, of joking about the mourning underway for Franz Ferdinand and his wife; one Serb from Herzegovina even allegedly stated that within four years Serbia would rule Bosnia.[18] Some of the cases did deal with violence and religious insults against Serbs, and in this regard the provincial regime even compensated a handful of selected loyal Serbs who had been injured during the earlier anti-Serb raids. Yet although even Potiorek planned to rebuild damaged Orthodox churches with state funding, these aspects of the rule of law almost completely disappeared with the mobilization of 25 July.[19]

## Hostages and internment

Parallel to the mobilization of Habsburg troops, the civil administration and the judiciary were placed under military control. Civil rights were restricted or completely suspended along the lines evolved by the War Ministry years before.[20] For Bosnia these preparations for war were particularly far-reaching since the whole civil administration was placed under military supervision. Associations had to end their activities and any public assemblies needed prior approval by the authorities.[21] Two days before the declaration of war against Serbia, this meant the beginning of a state of war within the empire. In Bosnia, in concerted actions, the army, gendarmerie and, later, irregular forces arrested and interned several thousand Bosnian Serbs as hostages. Although detailed figures on the Serb civilians arrested as hostages do not exist, different sources suggest similar numbers. In the southern parts of Bosnia-Herzegovina alone, military correspondence recorded more than 1,200 hostages. In March 1915 the Austrian politician Josef Redlich noted about 4,000 Serb hostages from Bosnia, while in the same year Pero Slijepčević, an agent of the Serbian government who hailed from eastern Herzegovina, wrote of about 5,000 Serbs arrested across Bosnia.[22] Similar actions were taking place against Serbs in Croatia-Slavonia, among the Ruthenian, Polish and Jewish populations of Galicia and Bukovina, or – after May 1915 – among Italians in the south-west of the Monarchy. Habsburg forces were automatically targeting ethno-confessional groups in the borderlands on suspicion of collaborating with the enemy.[23]

The purpose of hostages was to create human shields. In case of an uprising or an attack on military targets such as railways, tunnels, bridges or telegraph lines, hostages were immediately executed. For the affected persons and for the public, hostages symbolized the state's degrading impact on a specific national or denominational community. In the first months of the war, Serb hostages were lined up on bridges, near tunnels or railway stations. They were forced to march in front of military transports or spent weeks on military trains in order to protect those assets; they were often maltreated, some even killed. In Herzegovina several hundred Serb hostages died in the first weeks of the war alone.

Soon, prisons, military posts and gendarmerie stations were overcrowded with interned Serbs. Especially in eastern Bosnia and eastern Herzegovina, on the borders of the two arch-enemies, the authorities feared uprisings and acts of sabotage. Teachers and Orthodox priests in particular were arrested. In Bosnia about two-thirds of the Orthodox priests were imprisoned, in Herzegovina even more.[24] Furthermore, in a 20-kilometre-long strip of land along the eastern border, the army arrested almost every adult Serb male who had not fled to Montenegro or Serbia. In Montenegro, three battalions consisting of a thousand Herzegovinian deserters were formed; in Serbia, four divisions of Serb volunteers from abroad sprang up.[25] Although hostage-taking was designed to prevent Serbs fleeing abroad, it clearly had the opposite effect. Therefore, we can view hostage-taking as revealing the Habsburg military administration's lack of imagination on how to handle the real or assumed disloyalty of the population.

Some Serbs were shot or hanged for assumed collaboration with the enemy – accused of sending light signals to Montenegro, sabotaging telegraph lines or fleeing across the state frontiers.[26] In the region of Trebinje in south-eastern Herzegovina, Archpriest Stevan Pravica was the only priest not to end up in jail in the first two years of the war. At liberty, he attended dozens of executions of Orthodox Serbs. After the war he would recall that on 10 August 1914,

> they started to hang people. These awful sights, these atrocious passions are indescribable. All the more so because I had to hear their confessions, to give them their final communion, to lead them to the gallows and read out a requiem for them – and this over three years for 77 men and two women. These are passions that kill life and reason and every nerve of a man. It is easier to be in jail than to perform all this. But whether you want to or not, you have to do it.[27]

For military commanders, the decision whether to impose martial law was influenced by rational considerations as well as by disappointment, paranoia or a desire for revenge. In this regard the empire's Serb subjects were wholly equated with those from the enemy states of Serbia and Montenegro. Often the Habsburg Serbs were discursively dehumanized, with the Serbian Orthodox Church above all considered a breeding ground for treasonable conspiracy. The Habsburg military mostly described Serbs as suspect, brutal and irrational beings. In September 1914 a military commander in Višegrad reported to Sarajevo about the situation in his region, calling Serbs 'bloodthirsty and ruthless enemies' and 'beasts incarnate'.[28] In November, another military commander from Zagreb wrote to the War Ministry:

> *Every SERB inside himself remains a SERB*, and I am convinced that one would more easily succeed in making a cat out of a dog than in turning a SERB into a loyal citizen. ... Always when treacherous activity is revealed, the Serb Orthodox clergy are involved.[29]

A telling example of the treatment of local Serbs was the priest Vidak Parežanin who on 12 August 1914 was sentenced to death by a court martial together with other Serbs from his village. All the convicted came from Lastva, a village directly on the border with Montenegro. They were punished for the escape of their fellow Serbs across the frontier. According to several sources, Parežanin on the gallows shouted, 'Long live Serbia, the Serbian army, the Serb nation, and great Russia!'[30] The government in Sarajevo repeatedly took these ravings of convicted criminals as proof that deep anti-Habsburg feelings reigned in the hearts of most Orthodox priests. Even more bizarrely, Parežanin had formerly been considered a loyal priest who, just before the war, had been designated as a military chaplain.[31]

The case of Parežanin is proof of how effectively at the highest state level a military understanding of the law – including collective guilt and punishment – superseded any civil principles of law. Mileva Parežanin, widow of the executed cleric, demanded a pension from the priest-widows' fund (*Priesterwitwenfonds*) into which her husband had made payments for years. She was left with six underage children, and her house was plundered and destroyed in the first weeks of the war. Although the diocesan church court in Mostar was prepared to grant her a pension, the Provincial Government intervened and annulled that decision, even though the fund was administered by the church. Writing to the Common Ministry of Finance in Vienna, the government in Sarajevo justified its actions on 'both legal and political grounds':

> in these turbulent days ... granting the family of Parežanin a pension which derives from a fund subsidized by the Provincial Government could hardly be justified. Moreover, such a regulation would have a confusing effect on the public. When normal times return it will doubtless be necessary to mitigate some of the unfortunate hardships of the state of war. Then there may well be a possibility of showing mercy to the severely affected and obviously innocent family of Parežanin.[32]

In this way the government postponed until after the war the apparent paradox of showing mercy towards an innocent person.[33] The message of the militarized state towards its domestic enemies was that interned hostages had even more to lose than their own lives.

Apart from taking hostages, the government interned thousands of 'politically suspicious' and 'unreliable' subjects. The legal and political reality was – as with the hostages – that these people were Habsburg citizens, not enemy aliens (*Feindstaatenausländer*), not prisoners of war, nor civilians from occupied territory. Because international laws of war did not address the legal relationship between a state and its citizens, Serbs from Bosnia or Croatia who had been interned by the Habsburg government were not affected by such laws of war.[34] Civil law stood – as usual in times of war – under the primacy of military law, which on the other hand recognized little if any difference between domestic and external enemies. Practically, the internment of the empire's own civilians hardly differed from that of enemy combatants: they went to the same camps.[35]

From early August 1914, Habsburg security forces started to transfer 'politically suspicious' Serbs to special detention camps.[36] First these were transit camps in Bosnia, in Doboj, Bosanski Brod and Žegar near Bihać, in each of which several hundred Serbs were interned.[37] From there internees were soon deported outside the province, predominantly to Hungary where the largest camp for Serbs was the fortress of Arad. By September 1914, around 3,500 Serbs from Bosnia-Herzegovina were imprisoned there. In 1915 their number grew to more than 4,000, with Serbs arriving from Dalmatia and Slavonia and later on from occupied Serbia; more than a thousand prisoners came from Herzegovina. Several thousand people died in these camps due to miserable hygienic conditions, malnutrition, typhus, tuberculosis, cholera and dysentery.[38]

Starting in autumn 1915, many were then sent on from these camps to those in Hungary and Austria – for internment in Nezsider/Neusiedel am See, Nagymegyer, Sopron, Kecskemét, Komárom, Túrony or Thalerhof near Graz.[39] Simultaneously, the military began to gradually release civilian prisoners from Bosnia since the Bosnian Serbs were no longer considered so dangerous after the occupation of Serbia and Montenegro. Priests therefore were allowed to return to their home parishes, where they were sometimes put under house arrest or compelled to do forced labour; others were appointed as military chaplains.[40] Most of the other Serb detainees were drafted into the army, which meant that in the second half of the war, the loyalty expected towards the state from members of the armed forces was considerably lower than it was previously.[41] In response to growing public pressure, and as a sign of policy change under the new Emperor Karl, the detention camps for Habsburg civilians were then closed in spring 1917. It was a sign of the civilian leadership regaining some control of the state.[42]

Back in 1914, the family of the executed priest Vidak Parežanin had been deported. His sixteen-year-old son was sent to Arad for two years, after which he was assigned to the army. Parežanin's widow Mileva, together with her remaining five children, ended up for two years in the camp of Žegar near Bihać.[43] With the exception of the priest Parežanin himself, clearly no family member was ever tried in a court – civil or military. They were simply detained for being suspicious because of their religious denomination, and their family and geographic origin. In comparison to the practice of taking several thousands hostage and the mass internment of civilians, the well-known trials for high treason organized in Banjaluka and other towns (1915–16) appear almost like due process of law.[44]

Although some liberal newspapers reported on the hostage-taking and internment of civilians at the start of the war, the topic seems to have been of no special public interest outside Bosnia.[45] Broader discussions did not start in Vienna before the autumn of 1917, when some Dalmatian deputies of the Austrian Reichsrat reported their experiences and unsuccessfully requested investigations.[46] Although wartime internment and hostage-taking of the empire's own citizens show the principal change in global warfare, it is still quite neglected in the historiography of the First World War.[47]

## Irregular military activity

Until October 1914 the Bosnian frontline had repeatedly shifted dozens of kilometres from east to west. During the alternating conquests, mass atrocities took place on all sides, targeting local civilians mostly depending on their religious affiliation. When incoming troops were celebrated by one denominational group, the opposite side later took revenge upon the allegedly disloyal confessional group. This led to a huge migration of refugees – the Orthodox fled south and east to Montenegro and Serbia, while thousands of Muslims from eastern Bosnia and the Sandžak fled in the opposite direction.[48]

From early on too, the Habsburgs recruited irregular military units in Bosnia from among Muslims and Catholics, forming the so-called *Schutzkorps* (protection corps). The district administrators (*Bezirksvorsteher*) chose the commanders, trained them, distributed weapons and paid the recruits.[49] In Herzegovina these units were responsible for mistreating and killing dozens of Serb civilians. They plundered and destroyed Serb property, resulting in reprisals especially at the end of the war.[50] Memories of the destruction of churches, or even target practice on church icons, burnt themselves deep into the collective memory of the Orthodox community.[51] Such narratives served to define the borders of the ethno-confessional group against the outsider and strengthened inter-denominational loyalty.[52]

After recapturing eastern Bosnia and Herzegovina between August and October 1914, the Habsburg forces also executed hundreds of predominantly Orthodox civilians and destroyed whole villages.[53] In eastern Herzegovina, in the town of Foča alone, the army on its own count executed seventy-one Serbs who had obeyed the recruitment drive of the interim military administration of Montenegro.[54] In this way the coercive measures of various armed forces often overlapped and contradicted each other. Once more it was shown how arbitrarily military commanders imposed penalties for 'disloyalty'. A month earlier, three out of five hostages were killed because they were deemed possible deserters. Two Serb Orthodox priests as well as a well-known Serb merchant were killed on the same night.[55] Foča's district administrator later on regretted the killing of one of the priests, saying his public execution would have had a better impact on the local Serbs. He also complained that forty Serbs sentenced to death were 'mistakenly deported as "politically suspicious individuals"'.[56] Furthermore, the Provincial Government reported euphemistically about punitive measures against civilians in eastern Bosnia following recapture:

> It is probably self-evident that under such circumstances it repeatedly came to the punitive killing of hostages, convictions under martial law, and other military reprisals such as the destruction of whole villages or single farmsteads.[57]

From October 1914 such events in Bosnia were supported by a decree that allowed the confiscation of the property of those who had taken up arms against the state or collaborated with the enemy. The seized assets were to be distributed among those groups of the population who had allegedly been harmed by the expropriated.[58] In this way the state shaped loyalty in two directions: both among the Monarchy's alleged friends and among its enemies.

## State norms and legitimized discrimination

After six months of war, everyday life in Bosnia slowly normalized on two levels: Orthodox Serbs learnt what to expect from different state institutions and how to avoid attention and persecution. On the other hand, in December 1914 the emperor dismissed Potiorek from his post, blaming him for the miserable outcome of the war against Serbia.[59] His successor was the highly motivated General Stjepan Sarkotić, whose intention was to break the military deadlock on the Balkan front and ensure peace and order within Bosnia.[60] By a series of administrative decrees he moved to regulate public order in new ways, but also retroactively to legalize the regime in existence since July 1914. So in 1915, he began discussions in Sarajevo and Vienna on how to organize political participation outside the suspended Bosnian Sabor so as to legitimize Habsburg rule without endangering its absolute power; however, the planned consultative council never met.[61]

Similarly, Sarkotić pressed for reforms of the Orthodox Church administration and the law on state–church relations. Already in October 1914 the Provincial Government had abrogated the Orthodox Church statute of 1905 because of its liberal rules, its broad social sphere of sanctioned influence and the huge participation of laymen. In fact, church structures such as parishes or the diocesan administration had ceased to operate after July 1914.[62] But the Sarajevo government argued for official suspension of the 1905 statute because church officials '[mis]used the autonomy granted to them in pursuing their extreme national and political targets'. Thus, during its ten-year existence, the church had developed 'into a subversive organization in its own country, into a bulwark of radical Serbdom [Serbentum], into a dangerous political weapon [Kampfmittel]' that carried 'the spirit of irredentism and high treason into the broad masses of the population'.[63] The church organization was called a 'dragon seed', a 'highly dangerous organism' and even the 'most influential organization throughout the country ... , a state within the state, whose troops are distributed in well-chosen positions'.[64] The argument was astonishingly simple and circular: the high number of imprisoned parish school teachers, Orthodox laymen and clerics served as proof of the so-called 'destructive tendencies of the autonomy [statute] of the Serb Orthodox Church'.[65] Orthodox religious organizations were therefore to be put under state control, and were not to benefit any longer from state support. The assumed collective disloyalty of an ethno-confessional community was thus also to be punished collectively. In this way the principle of equal treatment for all officially recognized religious groups within the empire was abandoned. Sarkotić soon proposed a new church statute for the Orthodox dioceses in Bosnia, strengthening the authorities' ability to control the church and eliminating to a large extent any lay participation.[66]

The Vienna-based Common Ministry of Finance, however, was quite sceptical about these plans to standardize relations in wartime Bosnia.[67] After all, Sarkotić also revealed a colonial arrogance when arguing for a revised church statute. To Vienna he wrote that

> it is in fact in the state's interest not to allow ecclesiastical-religious life to shrivel. Spiritual and moral barbarization of an entire lifestyle will easily spread, especially among the rural Orthodox population. And devastation in this field leads – as experience has shown – to a situation in which respect of state authority can only be maintained by the use of violence.[68]

Despite further consultations, the ministry in Vienna left the status of Bosnia's Orthodox Church unresolved, and delayed any solution until after the war. It was formally decided that all Serb schools were to be closed, although most of them had already stopped running since July 1914.[69] But Sarkotić in the end enacted no new church statute; instead, in July 1916 the supervisory law on religious administration was expanded by decree. In this way the Provincial Government returned to legal practices of the early 1880s and even intensified state control.[70]

Beside Sarkotić's largely fruitless legislation projects, he ruled in Bosnia mainly by symbolic decrees. In this manner his government in 1915 banned the cultural association *Prosvjeta*, an organization that since July 1914 had been moribund anyway.[71] He also opposed the official use of the Cyrillic alphabet, because it was 'used as an important national link and political weapon'. For Sarkotić there were numerous practical reasons for depriving the Cyrillic script of its public character and banning it from state offices and schools.[72] Again the Common Ministry of Finance was sceptical and warned of the negative impact on domestic and foreign policy.[73] But following Sarkotić's pleading, the ministry in November 1915 eventually consented to a decree that effectively banned the use of Cyrillic in public life.[74]

Sarkotić made similar efforts in another contentious arena – the terms to be used for the Orthodox denomination and Serb language. In line with the Habsburg administration until the late 1880s, the state again avoided the term 'Serbian Orthodox', using instead 'Oriental Orthodox' or 'Greek Orthodox'; likewise, officials turned against terming the local Slav language 'Serbo-Croatian' and introduced once again the denationalized term *Landessprache*.[75] Essentially, Sarkotić was a member of the military and loyal to the dynasty, possessing the mindset that nationalism and liberalism were responsible for the Monarchy's weakness. Originating from a Dalmatian Croatian family of army officers, his political views were anti-Serb and anti-Yugoslav, turning in the course of the war increasingly in a pro-Croatian direction.[76] Nevertheless, as governor and military commander of wartime Bosnia, he still sought to establish a regime based on a strictly a national military law, to weaken any accusations of injustice against any one national group.

The defeat of Serbia and Montenegro in the winter of 1915–16 did lead to a pacification of everyday life for Serbs in Bosnia-Herzegovina. Yet food supplies dramatically worsened in 1916, causing especially drastic results in mountainous regions like eastern Herzegovina where bad harvests even in peacetime had often led to food shortages. From the autumn of 1916 there was starvation and famine, with over a thousand deaths in the provinces in 1917.[77] Already that April, the Sarajevo government termed the food supply conditions in eastern Bosnia and Herzegovina as 'grim'.[78] Matters were exacerbated by the fact that in 1917 raids on villages and farmsteads along the Montenegrin border became more and more frequent. With the deterioration of the situation on the front, and growing numbers of deserters from the beginning of 1918, security in the hinterland noticeably worsened. The so-called Green cadres (*zeleni kadar*) of South Slav deserters from the Habsburg army partly terrorized the civil population, partly subsisted on the support of a sympathetic rural population. The security forces were barely able to control the situation and thus the number of refugees steadily grew again.[79]

Although violence was not exclusively linked to religious affiliation, it played an important and legitimizing role for the perpetrators. From the summer of 1918, mainly Orthodox people from Bosnia and Montenegro were plundering, expelling and murdering Muslims and Catholics in eastern

Bosnia and Herzegovina, causing a mass exodus of the non-Orthodox population. It was only with the arrival of Serbian troops in November 1918 that public order was slowly restored. These forces were invited into Bosnia by a newly established National Council of Bosnia-Herzegovina which acted as a government. It was the final act in the wartime orientation of many Serbs of Bosnia-Herzegovina, shifting almost continually towards the idea of unification with Serbia.

## Conclusion

The May crisis of 1913 and the July crisis of 1914 were watersheds for the Habsburg state with enormous impact. When Habsburg officials felt that the very existence of their empire was threatened, they reacted with war not only against foreign enemies but also within the state borders. Not distinguishing between foreign and domestic enemies was a core issue in the development of total war.[80] The empire proceeded radically to restructure its own principles of domestic administration. Strategic integration and a policy of balancing political demands through co-opting the elites of different confessional groups – this was replaced by a policy that clearly defined the enemies of the state and attacked them and their entire social milieu. Already before the war Austria-Hungary had abandoned its usual methods of managing the loyalties of imperial subjects, and had fast lost legitimacy among many Bosnian Serbs. In this respect Mitja Velikonja has noted correctly: 'For the first time in their history, a significant number of Bosnia-Herzegovina's inhabitants were persecuted and liquidated because of their national affiliation.'[81]

The state's repression, which in pre-war norms meant injustice towards one section of the population, wholly delegitimized the state among its Serb Orthodox inhabitants. Statutes and constitutions, religious and secular institutions, associations and political parties – the entire system of the enlightened Habsburg Monarchy – radically lost power, legitimacy and cohesion. And with the experience of violence, ethno-confessional loyalties were strengthened. As wartime progressed, obvious crimes by the Habsburg state against its own population strongly delegitimized its power while concomitantly legitimizing a future Yugoslav state order. Thus in the many visionary speeches made when the Kingdom of Serbs, Croats and Slovenes was formed on 1 December 1918, the sanctity accorded to the new common state and to Serbia as its midwife was accompanied by deep frustration and anger over Habsburg rule. The future state therefore was being envisaged as a clear counter-concept to the Habsburg state that was disappearing. This was illustrated by the Serb Orthodox bishop of Mostar, Petar Zimonjić, in an address he delivered when Serbian troops entered the town in November 1918. He pinpointed clear parallels between the trinity of God and the triune name of the new kingdom. The prospects for the common state were reflected in what society had lacked in the past:

> Our honourable Croat and Slovene brothers have accepted the flag of national liberation that you unfurled in Serbia, and have assisted our Serbs in defeating the main enemy of the Slavs – the German dragon and his allies – and preventing their return. And now Serbs, Croats and Slovenes, united in brotherly love, have founded in the name of the one Triune God a unified and triple-named Yugoslav state, in which peace and justice, brotherly concord, equality and freedom will prevail; ... where God will be honoured, the law will be executed, science and arts will blossom, and the splendid qualities of our dignified and gifted people will find unlimited and hitherto unexpected development.[82]

## Notes

1 See Wolfgang Höpken, 'Flucht vor dem Kreuz? Muslimische Emigration aus Südosteuropa nach dem Ende der osmanischen Herrschaft (19./20. Jahrhundert)', in Wolfgang Höpken (ed.), *Zwangsmigrationen in Mittel- und Südosteuropa* (Leipzig: Leipziger Universitäts-Verlag, 1996), 1–24; Bejtullah D. Destani (ed.), *The Balkan Wars: British Consular Reports from Macedonia in the Final Years of the Ottoman Empire* (London: I.B. Tauris, 2014).

2 Milorad Ekmečić, *Uticaj balkanskih ratova 1912-1913 na društvo u Bosni i Hercegovini: Radovi iz istorije Bosne i Hercegovine XIX veka* (Belgrade: Beogradski Izd.-Graf. Zavod, 1997), 414–18. For the perspective of a Herzegovinian Orthodox priest, see Spiro Lučić, *Ljetopis porodice Lučića i parohije Sutorinske od 1680. do 1930. godine*. (Herceg-Novi: Zavičajni Muzej, 2000), 139. See also the diary notes of Joseph Maria Baernreither, *Fragmente eines politischen Tagebuches. Die südslawische Frage und Österreich-Ungarn vor dem Weltkrieg* (Berlin: Verlag für Kulturpolitik, 1928), 163–8.

3 Report of the commander of the XV corps in Sarajevo, Johann von Appel to the War Ministry (hereafter KM), 19 December 1912, in Ludwig Bittner and Hans Übersberger (eds), *Österreich-Ungarns Außenpolitik von der Bosnischen Krise 1908 bis zum Kriegsausbruch 1914* (hereafter ÖUA), 8 vols (Vienna: Österreichischer Bundesverlag, 1930), V, 176–9. More generally, see Rudolf Kiszling, 'Die Entwicklung der österreichisch-ungarischen Wehrmacht seit der Annexionskrise 1908', *Militärwissenschaftliche Mitteilungen* 10/65 (1934): 798–800.

4 See Nikola Rakočević, *Crna Gora i Austro-Ugarska 1903–1914* (Titograd: Istorijski Institut SR Crne Gore, 1983), 119–33; Katrin Boeckh, *Von den Balkankriegen zum Ersten Weltkrieg. Kleinstaatenpolitik und ethnische Selbstbestimmung auf dem Balkan* (Munich: Oldenbourg, 1996), 46–8; Günther Kronenbitter, *'Krieg im Frieden'. Die Führung der k.u.k. Armee und die Großmachtpolitik Österreich-Ungarns 1906–1914* (Munich: Oldenbourg, 2003), 414–20; Alma Hannig, 'Die Balkanpolitik Österreich-Ungarns

vor 1914', in Jürgen Angelow (ed.), *Der Erste Weltkrieg auf dem Balkan. Perspektiven der Forschung* (Berlin: be.bra Wissenschaft, 2011), 35–56. For the plans of Vienna regarding domestic and foreign policy in May 1913, see the protocol of the Common Ministerial Council in Vienna, 2 May 1913: ÖUA, VI, 324–37.

5 Verordnung d. Landesregierung (Provisional Government: PG) für Bosnien und Herzegovina (BH), 2 May 1913, in: *Gesetz- und Verordnungsblatt für Bosnien und die Hercegovina* (hereafter GVBlBH) 1913, 127. Also, Verordnung d. LR für BH, 2 May 1913: ibid., 127–30. For the impact of the Scutari crisis in Bosnia and Herzegovina, see Hamdija Kapidžić, 'Skadarska kriza i izuzetne mjere u Bosni i Hercegovini u maju 1913. godine', in *Bosna i Hercegovina pod austrougarskom upravom. Članci i rasprave* (Sarajevo: Svjetlost, 1968), 155–97; Božo Madžar, 'Balkanski ratovi i iznimne mjere u Bosni i Hercegovini 1912–1913. godine', in *Godišnjak društva istoričara Bosne i Hercegovine* 35 (1984): 63–74.

6 Verordnung d. Landesregierung, 2 May 1913, 129. See also Božo Madžar, 'Represivne mjere austrougarske uprave protiv "Prosvjete"', in Sava Ćeklić (ed.), *Stotinu godina Društva 'Prosvjeta', 1902–2002* (Sarajevo: Prosvjeta, 2002), 147ff.

7 For the (Grenz-)Schutzkorps, see Ferdinand Schmid, *Bosnien und die Herzegovina unter der Verwaltung Österreich-Ungarns* (Leipzig: Veit, 1914), 262; Kapidžić, 'Skadarska kriza', 164–6; Ekmečić, *Uticaj balkanskih ratova*, 410–14; Robin Okey, *Taming Balkan Nationalism: The Habsburg 'Civilizing Mission' in Bosnia, 1878–1914* (Oxford: Oxford University Press, 2007), 248.

8 See, for example, the heroic and Habsburg-critical edition of the journal *Bosanska vila*, discussing the Balkan Wars in March 1914 (it appeared uncensored in Sarajevo): *Ratna Spomenica: Bosanska vila* 1-6/29 (1914).

9 See Rudolf Jeřábek, *Potiorek. General im Schatten von Sarajevo* (Graz, Vienna and Cologne: Styria, 1991), 46–8; Dževad Juzbašić, 'Die österreichisch-ungarische Okkupationsverwaltung in Bosnien-Herzegowina. Einige Aspekte der Beziehungen zwischen den Militär- und Zivilbehörden', *Prilozi Instituta za istoriju u Sarajevu* 34 (2005): 106–9.

10 See, for example, the newspaper articles: 'Die Ermordung des Thronfolgers. Potioreks Ausreden', *Arbeiter-Zeitung* 178/26 (30 June 1914), 1; 'Exzesse und Standrecht in Sarajevo', ibid., 2. Josef Redlich and Lajos Thallóczy also criticized Potiorek and his government in Sarajevo. Thallóczy noted, 'It seems like Potiorek could not prevent this, or he thought that they [the rioters] needed to let off steam [sich ruhig austoben sollen]': Ludwig Thallóczy, *Tagebücher. 23. VI 1914 – 31. XII. 1914* (eds. Ferdinand Hauptmann and Anton Prasch) (Graz: Universitätsverlag Graz, 1981), 15 (entry for 30 June 1914). Also Fritz Fellner and Doris A. Corradini (eds), *Schicksalsjahre Österreichs. Die Erinnerungen und Tagebücher Josef Redlichs. 1869-1936*, 3 vols (Vienna, Cologne and Weimar: Böhlau, 2011)), I: *Erinnerungen und Tagebücher 1869-1914*, 611: entry for 30 June 1914.

11 Vladimir Ćorović, *Crna knjiga. Patnje Srba Bosne i Hercegovine za vreme Svetskog rata 1914–1918* (Belgrade: Jugoslovenski Dosije, 1989 (1920)); Marko S. Popović, *Patnje Srba 1914.–1918. god. Sreza Mostarskog, Konjičkog,*

*Duvanjskog i Ljubuškog, prema izvještajima sveštenika: Spomenica Eparhije zahumsko-hercegovačke živim i upokojenim borcima za oslobođenje i ujedinjenje* (Niš: Sv. Car Konstantin, 1928), 72–4; Milorad Ekmečić, *Ratni ciljevi Srbije 1914* (Belgrade: Srpska Književna Zadruga, 1973), 165ff.; Đorđe Mikić, *Austrougarska ratna politika u Bosni i Hercegovini 1914–1918* (Banjaluka: Nezavisni univerzitet Banjaluka, 2011), 35ff, 42ff; Borivoje Milošević, 'Austrougarski zločini nad Srpskom pravoslavnom crkvom i sveštenstvom u Bosni i Hercegovini tokom Prvog svjetskog rata', in Vojislav Maksimović and Draga Mastilović (eds), *Bosna i Hercegovina u Prvom svjetskom ratu* (Gacko: Prosvjeta, 2015), 153–66. For accounts of wartime Herzegovina, see Borivoje Borozan (ed.), *Dolina Neretve, 1914–1918. godine. U dokumentima i literaturi* (Niš: Prosveta, 1992).

12 For the growing duality between civil and military power in Bosnia from 1908, see also Redlich's views: *Schicksalsjahre Österreichs*, I, 207.

13 Arhiv Bosne i Hercegovine, Sarajevo (Archive of Bosnia and Herzegovina: hereafter ABH) Common Ministry of Finance (CMF) – Presidium of the Office for the Affairs of Bosnia-Herzegovina (hereafter ZMF PrBH), 790/1914, KM (Krobatin) to CMF, 2 July 1914.

14 Ibid., CMF, Biliński to Krobatin, 3 July 1914. On this, see also Hamdija Kapidžić, 'Austro-ugarska politika u Bosni i Hercegovini i jugoslovensko pitanje za vrijeme Prvog svjetskog rata', in *Godišnjak Istoriskog Društva Bosne i Hercegovine*, 9 (1957): 10; Milorad Ekmečić, 'Žalosna baština iz godine 1914. Političke namjene sudskih procesa u Bosni i Hercegovini za vrijeme Prvog svjetskog rata', in Milorad Ekmečić, Đorđe Mikić, Dragoljub Živojinović and Nikola B. Popović (eds), *Politički procesi Srbima u Bosni i Hercegovini. 1914–1917* (Laktaši: Grafomark, 1996), 13.

15 Cf. for the stance of Biliński: Thallóczy, *Tagebücher*, 36 (7 July 1914); and John Leslie, 'The Antecedents of Austria-Hungary's War Aims: Policies and Policy-Makers in Vienna and Budapest before and during 1914', in Elisabeth Springer and Leopold Kammerhofer (eds), *Archiv und Forschung. Das Haus-, Hof- und Staatsarchiv in seiner Bedeutung für die Geschichte Österreichs und Europas* (Vienna: Verlag für Geschichte und Politik, 1993), 375–94.

16 Biliński to Landeschef Potiorek, 30 June 1914, in ÖUA, VIII, 229. Similarly, Thallóczy on Biliński's attitude: Thallóczy, *Tagebücher*, 11–13 (28–29 June 1914).

17 See the reports in ABH, ZMF PrBH 899, 965/1914.

18 According to data of the Provincial Government, between 28 June and 15 August 1914 there were 637 criminal cases connected with the assassination before civil courts in Bosnia, of which an above-average number stemmed from Herzegovina (PG to CMF, 17 August 1914: ABH, ZMF PrBH 1676/1914).

19 ÖUA, VIII, 288ff: CMF to PG (Potiorek), 3 July 1914; ABH, ZMF PrBH 931/1914, PG to CMF, 12 July 1914.

20 Verordnung des Gesamtministeriums, 25 July 1914: in *Reichsgesetzblatt* (RGBl) 1914, 825; Kaiserliche Verordnung, 26 July 1914, in RGBl 1914, 821ff. See also Stig Förster, 'Civil-Military Relations', in Jay M. Winter (ed.), *The Cambridge History of the First World War. Vol 2: The State* (Cambridge:

Cambridge University Press, 2014), 91–6; Mark Cornwall, 'Austria-Hungary and "Yugoslavia"', in John Horne (ed.), *A Companion to World War I* (Chichester: Wiley-Blackwell, 2010), 373; Christoph Führ, *Das k. u. k. Armeeoberkommando und die Innenpolitik in Österreich, 1914-1917* (Graz, Vienna and Cologne: Böhalu, 1968), 17–20.

21  Verordnung d. LR f. BH, 26 July 1914, in GVBlBH 1914, 295–9; Verordnung d. Landeschefs f. BH u. Armeeinspektors in Sarajevo, 26 July 1914, in GVBlBH 1914, 302–4; Verordnung, 25 July 1914, RGBl 1914, 815.

22  Jonathan Gumz, *The Resurrection and Collapse of Empire in Habsburg Serbia 1914-1918* (Cambridge: Cambridge University Press, 2009), 41ff; Redlich, *Schicksalsjahre Österreichs*, II, 24; T., M. (Toplica, Milan – that is, Pero Slijepčević), *Austro-Ugarska protiv svojih podanika* (originally Niš, 1915): re-published in Ćorović, *Crna knjiga*, 183–221, here 193.

23  See Chapter 11 in this volume. Also Führ, *Das k. u. k. AOK*; Matthew Stibbe, 'Krieg und Brutalisierung. Die Internierung von Zivilisten bzw. "politisch Unzuverlässigen" in Österreich-Ungarn während des Ersten Weltkrieges', in Alfred Eisfeld, Guido Hausmann and Dietmar Neutatz (eds), *Besetzt, interniert, deportiert. Der Erste Weltkrieg und die deutsche, jüdische, polnische und ukrainische Zivilbevölkerung im östlichen Europa* (Essen: Klartext, 2013), 87–106; Matthew Stibbe, 'Enemy Aliens, Deportees, Refugees: Internment Practices in the Habsburg Empire, 1914-1918', *Journal of Modern European History* 4/12 (2014): 479–99.

24  Data from Mile Stanić, 'Stradanje sveštenstva Zahumsko-hercegovačke eparhije u Prvom svetskom ratu', in Milorad Ekmečić (ed.), *Zbornik za istoriju Bosne i Hercegovine*, vol. 6 (Belgrade: SANU, 2009), 241–306; ABH, ZMF PrBH 1682/1914, PG to CMF, 12 October 1914.

25  Draga Mastilović, *Hercegovina u Kraljevini Srba, Hrvata i Slovenaca. (1918–1929)* (Belgrade: Filip Višnjić, 2009), 46ff; Đorđe Piljević, 'Doprinos Pera Slijepčevića u organizovanju dobrovoljaca u Prvom svjetskom ratu', in *Glasnik odjeljena društvenih nauka CANU* 12 (1998): 56ff.

26  For hostage-taking in Bosnia-Herzegovina as well as more generally in the Habsburg Empire, see T., M., *Austro-Ugarska*, 216; Ćorović, *Crna knjiga*; Ekmečić, *Ratni ciljevi Srbije*, 166. See also the reports of Orthodox priests after the war, in Arhiv Jugoslavije Belgrade (Archive of Yugoslavia: hereafter AJ), Ministry of Religion, 69-210-332; as well as the published reports of priests in Stanić, 'Stradanje sveštenstva', 241–306. The Serb writer from Mostar and deputy in the Bosnian parliament, Svetozar Ćorović (brother of the historian Vladimir Ćorović), was also a hostage in 1914 and 'accompanied' military trains. In 1919 he published a short autobiographic text about this: Svetozar Ćorović, *Beleške jednog taoca* (Belgrade, 1919), re-published in *Sabrana djela. Knj. 10* (Sarajevo: Svjetlost, 1967), 205–34.

27  Prota (archpriest) Stevan Pravica to Prota Patrikije Komadanović, Diocesan church court Mostar, 8 June 1919: in Stanić, 'Stradanje sveštenstva', 269ff.

28  ABH, ZMF PrBH 1715/1914, District administration (Bezirksamt) Višegrad to PG, 29 September 1914.

29  ABH, ZMF PrBH 1838/1914, Military Command Zagreb to KM, 2 November 1914 (emphasis in the original.) For perceptions of Serbs among Habsburg officers during the war, see Gumz, *The Resurrection*, 42ff; Daniela Schanes, *Serbien im Ersten Weltkrieg. Feind- und Kriegsdarstellungen in österreichisch-ungarischen, deutschen und serbischen Selbstzeugnissen* (Frankfurt am Main: Peter Lang, 2011).
30  ABH, ZMF PrBH 1410/1914, Flügelkommando Trebinje to Gendarmeriekorps, 13 August 1914. Similarly quoted in: ZMF PrBH 1682/1914. See also Ćorović, *Crna knjiga*, 91ff; T., M., *Austro-Ugarska*, 211; Popović, *Spomenica Eparhije*, 136.
31  ABH, ZMF PrBH 1682/1914, PG to CMF, 12 October 1914.
32  Decision of the PG to CMF, 4 December 1914, as well as confirmation from Vienna: ABH, ZMF PrBH 1788/1914. For this case see also Ćorović, *Beleške jednog taoca*.
33  Even Leon Biliński in his memoirs remembered the case of the priest's widow from Trebinje: Leon Biliński, *Wspomnienia i dokumenty, vol. 1: 1846-1914* (Warsaw: Hoesicka, 1924), 285.
34  Although Habsburg Serbs formed a large if not the largest group of interned Habsburg civilians, until today they have not been mentioned in basic works on wartime internment. Cf. for instance, Uta Hinz, 'Internierung', in Gerhard Hirschfeld, Gerd, Krumeich and Irina Renz (eds), *Enzyklopädie Erster Weltkrieg* (Paderborn and Munich: Schöningh, 2009), 582–4. Annette Becker also touches only briefly on the interned Serbs in occupied Serbia: Annette Becker, 'Captive Civilians', in Jay Winter (ed.), *The Cambridge History of the First World War. Vol. 3: Civil Society* (Cambridge: Cambridge University Press, 2014), 272.
35  In 1917 this was criticized by the president of the International Committee of the Red Cross: Becker, 'Captive Civilians', 260.
36  Gumz, *The Resurrection*, 40ff.
37  Already at the end of August 1914 there were 3,429 interned Bosnian Serbs in Arad according to the station commander of the fortress. According to the *Bozner Zeitung*, 1,400 detainees were additionally sent from the occupied town of Šabac. In 1917 the Landeschef of Bosnia spoke of 4,000 Serb detainees from Bosnia in Arad and several hundred in the camp of Žegar near Bihać in Bosnia proper. See Stibbe, 'Krieg und Brutalisierung', 95; *Bozner Zeitung (Südtiroler Tagblatt)*, 172/74 (25 August 1914), 1. Also 'Der Landeschef über die südslavischen Interpellationen. Eine Unterredung mit Seiner Exzellenz', *Bosnische Post* 173/34 (2 August 1917), 1ff.
38  Ćorović, *Crna knjiga*, 65–72; Srđan Budisavljević, *Stvaranje države Srba, Hrvata i Slovenaca. Povodom četrdesetgodišnjice jugoslovenskog ujedinjenja* (Zagreb: JAZU, 1958), 11–13; Mikić, *Austrougarska ratna politika*, 85ff; Andrej Mitrović, *Srbija u Prvom svetskom ratu*, 2nd edn. (Belgrade: Stubovi Kulture, 2004), 102ff. See the speech of the Reichsrat deputy, Ante Tresić-Pavičić, in October 1917: *Stenographische Protokolle über die Sitzungen der Abgeordneten des österreichischen Reichsrates im Jahre 1917 und 1918*, III (Vienna, 1918), 1669.

39  Stibbe, 'Krieg und Brutalisierung', 99ff.
40  See AJ, 69-250-378, 3. Eparhija Zahumlje-Herzegovina (hereafter ZH), Reports of priests from the diocese ZH; Stanić, 'Stradanje sveštenstva'.
41  The priest Stevan Šarenac wrote about this in 1919: 'Since that time [October 1915] they started to recruit internees into the army. Those who until that point had been enemies were now all of a sudden friends and protectors of the state': Stevan Šarenac to Prota Patrikije Popović, 21 May 1919, in Stanić, 'Stradanje sveštenstva', 256.
42  See Förster, 'Civil-Military Relations', 115ff.
43  Popović, *Spomenica Eparhije*, 136. See also Stanić, 'Stradanje sveštenstva', 302ff.
44  See on this subject, Kapidžić, 'Austro-ugarska politika u Bosni', 16ff.; Episkop žički Vasilije (Kostić), *Uloga Srpske Pravoslavne Crkve u Banjalučkom veleizdajničkom procesu*, 2nd edn (Kraljevo: Srpska Pravoslavna Eparhija Žička, 1970); *Veleizdajnički proces u Banjaluci 1915–1916. Zbornik radova s međunarodnog naučnog skupa, održanog 25-27. septembra 1986. g. u Banjaluci* (Banjaluka: Institut za istoriju, 1987); Ernest Bauer, *Der letzte Paladin des Reiches. Generaloberst Stefan Freiherr Sarkotić von Lovćen* (Graz, Vienna and Cologne: Styria, 1988), 96–102; Đorđe Beatović, *Veleizdajnički procesi Srbima u Austro-Ugarskoj* (Belgrade: Književne Novine, 1989); Ekmečić, *Politički procesi Srbima u Bosni i Hercegovini*.
45  See for example, 'Hinrichtung von Geiseln in Bosnien', *Bozner Zeitung* 166/74 (18 August 1914), 1.
46  *Stenographische Protokolle über die Sitzungen des Hauses der Abgeordneten des österreichischen Reisrates im Jahre 1917*, XXII. Session (Vienna, 1917), 712. Supplement.
47  Stefan Manz, Panikos Panayi and Matthew Stibbe, *Internment During the First World War: A Mass Global Phenomenon* (London and New York: Routledge, 2018), 1–18.
48  For the first months of war on the south-eastern front in Bosnia-Herzegovina, see Iljas Hadžibegović and Mustafa Imamović, 'Bosna i Hercegovina u vrijeme austrougarske vladavine (1878-1918)', in *Bosna i Hercegovina od najstarijih vremena do kraja Drugog svjetskog rata* (Sarajevo: Bosanski Kulturni Centar, 1998), 286–8; Gumz, *The Resurrection*, 44–61. See also the reports by Habsburg officials about the war crimes of Serbian troops on Muslim civilians in eastern Bosnia: ABH, ZMF PrBH 1715/1914, District administration Višegrad to PG, 29 September 1914; PG to CMF, 18 October 1914.
49  German-speaking colonists in Bosnia also entered these irregular units, which were also known as *Bürgerwehr* or *Schutzwehr*. The total number of members of the Schutzkorps was estimated at 11,000, of which probably 5,000 stemmed from Herzegovina. Later on these units were partly deployed on military fronts outside Bosnia. See Popović, *Patnje Srba 1914*, 74ff; Ekmečić, *Ratni ciljevi Srbije*, 170–5; Milorad Ekmečić, 'Planovi za gerilski rat 1914. godine', in *Radovi iz istorije Bosne i Hercegovine XIX veka.* (Belgrade: Beogradski Izd.-Graf. Zavod, 1997), 433ff; Mitrović, *Srbija u Prvom svetskom ratu*, 88ff; Mikić, *Austrougarska ratna politika*, 71–82.

50 See the reports about Schutzkorps atrocities, for example, in the village of Samobor: Miloš D. Slijepčević, *Samobor. Selo u gornjoj Hercegovini* (Sarajevo: ANUBiH, 1969), 19ff, 39. For the reports of Herzegovinian Orthodox priests: Stanić, 'Stradanje sveštenstva'. For an example of explicit 'Serbian' revenge on members of the Schutzkorps: 'Vom serbischen Kriegsschauplatz', *Meraner Zeitung* 20/49 (25 January 1915), 2.

51 See for example, AJ, 37-24-191-353, petition of the Orthodox parish of Čapljina to Prime Minister Milan Stojadinović, 27 March 1938.

52 For the influence of violence in moulding collective loyalties: Hannes Grandits, *Herrschaft und Loyalität in der spätosmanischen Gesellschaft. Das Beispiel der multikonfessionellen Herzegowina* (Vienna: Böhlau, 2008), 575–84; also Ipek Yosmaoğlu, *Blood Ties: Religion, Violence, and the Politics of Nationhood in Ottoman Macedonia, 1878–1908* (Ithaca: Cornell University Press, 2014).

53 For example, Thallóczy noted on 17 August 1914: 'Potiorek telegraphs that a lot of villages had to be burnt down near Avtovac [north-eastern Herzegovina].' (Thallóczy, *Tagebücher*, 111). For courts-martial of the Habsburg army: Gumz, *The Resurrection*, 33, 39.

54 ABH, ZMF PrBH 1715/1914, District administration Foča to PG, 23 September 1914.

55 For the case of executed hostages in Foča on 9-10 August 1914, see also T., M., *Austro-Ugarska*, 217; Ćorović, *Crna knjiga*, 50.

56 ABH, ZMF PrBH 1715/1914, District administration Foča to PG, 23 September 1914.

57 Ibid., PG to CMF, 18 October 1914.

58 Gesetz of 7 October 1914, in GVBlBH 1914, 497.

59 See Thallóczy, *Tagebücher*; Edmund von Glaise-Horstenau, 'In memoriam. Feldmarschall Krobatin und Feldzeugmeister Potiorek', *Militärwissenschaftliche Mitteilungen* 2/65 (1934), special supplement.

60 Jeřábek, *Potiorek*, 204–12. See, for example, Sarkotić's diary notes cited in Bauer, *Der letzte Paladin*, 47ff; Cornwall, 'Austria-Hungary and "Yugoslavia"', 375.

61 'Allerhöchste Entschließung', 9 October 1915: GVBlBH 1916, 109; Verordnung d. GFM, 22 October 1915 (ibid). See Kapidžić, 'Austro-ugarska politika u Bosni', 11–16; Bauer, *Der letzte Paladin*, 56–63, 93–5.

62 See Momčilo Isić, *Srpska crkva u Velikom ratu. 1914–1918* (Belgrade and Gacko: Filip Višnjić, 2014), 14–21; Radmila Radić, 'The Serbian Orthodox Church in the First World War', in Dragoljub R. Živojinović (ed.), *The Serbs and the First World War 1914–1918. Proceedings of the International Conference Held at the Serbian Academy of Sciences and Arts, Belgrade, June 13-15, 2014* (Belgrade: SANU, 2015), 263–85.

63 ABH, ZMF PrBH 1682/1914, PG to CMF, 12 October 1914.

64 Ibid.

65 Ibid.

66 ABH, ZMF PrBH 831/1915, 'Provisorisches Statut über die Regelung der Kirchenverwaltung der orient.-orth. Eparchien (Metropolien) in Bosnien und der Hercegovina' (n.d: 1915) (66 pages, 98§§).

67  ABH, ZMF PrBH 1682/1914, CMF to PG, 28 March 1915.
68  ABH, ZMF PrBH 831/1915, PG (Sarkotić) to CMF, 17 July 1915.
69  ABH, ZMF PrBH 831/1915: Conference about the PG's request on 17 July 1915 about the Serbian Orthodox Church and school autonomy, 17 August 1915. As far as possible Serbian Orthodox schools were to be converted into state schools and Orthodox parishes were to be compensated. For wartime Orthodox schools, see Božidar Madžar, 'Suspendovanje srpske crkveno-školske autonomie u Bosni i Hercegovini 1914-1915. godine', in *Veleizdajnički proces u Banjaluci 1915–1916*, 157–63.
70  Verordnung d. Landesregierung f. BH, 3 July 1916: in GVBlBH 1916, 153–156. See also Madžar, 'Suspendovanje srpske autonomije', 166–8.
71  Džaja, *Bosnien-Herzegowina 1878-1918*, 107; Madžar, 'Represivne mjere austrougarske'; Vojislav Maksimović, 'Srpsko prosvjetno i kulturno društvo "Prosvjeta" 1902–2002', in Radoslav Bratić, Vojislav Maksimović and Miloš Kovačević (eds), *Srpska proza danas. Sto godina 'Prosvjete' i njenih znamenitih ličnosti* (Bileća and Gacko: Prosvjeta, 2003), 192.
72  ABH, ZMF PrBH 121/1915, PG (Sarkotić) to CMF, 19 January 1915.
73  Already in October 1914 there were plans for this. See Thallóczy, *Tagebücher*, 264 (22 October 1914).
74  ABH, ZMF PrBH 534/1915, PG (Sarkotić) to CMF, 7 May 1915; Verordnung d. Landesregierung f. BH, 10 November 1915, in GVBlBH 1915, 291.
75  ABH, ZMF PrBH 1043/1915, PG to CMF.
76  On Sarkotić's outlook, see Mark Cornwall, 'The Habsburg Elite and the Southern Slav Question 1914-1918', in Lothar Höbelt and T. G. Otte (eds), *A Living Anachronism? European Diplomacy and the Habsburg Monarchy* (Vienna: Böhlau, 2010), 249, 260–70.
77  Ćorović, *Crna knjiga*, 172–7. In June 1919, Prota Stevan Pravica wrote that, 'In 1916 I had to bury 471 children, of whom over 400 died of hunger; your heart is oppressed, but you can't help them': Prota Stevan Pravica to Prota Patrikije Komadanović, Diocesan church court Mostar, 8 June 1919, in Stanić, 'Stradanje sveštenstva', 270.
78  ABH, ZMF PrBH 440/1917, PG to CMF, 25 April 1917, transmitting political situation reports for January/February 1917.
79  Mikić, *Austrougarska ratna politika*, 440–51, 458–63.
80  Förster, 'Civil-Military Relations', 91–6, 113–16.
81  Mitja Velikonja, *Religious Separation and Political Intolerance in Bosnia-Herzegovina* (College Station: Texas A&M University Press, 2003), 141.
82  Bishop Petar (Zimonjić) in Mostar, 15 November 1918, in *Vjesnik*, 1 April 1919, 4: cited in Sonja Dujmović, 'Srpska pravoslavna crkva u Bosni i Hercegovini i stvaranje nove države (Kraljevine Srba, Hrvata i Slovenaca) 1918. godine', *Historijska traganja* 3 (2009): 123.

# CHAPTER 14

# Remembering Franz Ferdinand and Sarajevo in interwar Czechoslovakia*

*Dagmar Hájková*

In 1919 Tomáš Garrigue Masaryk, first president of Czechoslovakia, paid a visit to his close friend, the lawyer and member of the Czech National Socialist Party, František Veselý in Benešov, around 50 kilometres south of Prague. When Veselý suggested taking Masaryk to visit the nearby Konopiště castle, part of Archduke Franz Ferdinand's estate, the president refused. He even rebuffed an offer to go to the surrounding forest – 'I will not go there, it belongs to Konopiště' – deciding to take the path past the woods instead.[1]

This anecdote illuminates the official attitudes that characterized the new state's rhetoric towards the Habsburg era and thus towards Franz Ferdinand. The empire – 'the enemy and oppressor' – was considered responsible for all injustices that had befallen the Czech nation.[2] The establishment of independent Czechoslovakia was seen as the end of 300 years of suffering under Habsburg domination and as redemption for defeat at the Battle of White Mountain in 1620, when the Roman Catholic Habsburgs had defeated the Protestant Bohemian forces. The official memory created by the new political elite after the foundation of the new state was built around the successful struggle of Czechs and Slovaks for independence, notably the 'resistance movement' at home and abroad, and the efforts of

---

*I am especially grateful to Andrea Talabér for enjoyable discussions on this issue and for her support in writing this chapter.

the Czechoslovak legionnaires who during the war had fought against the Habsburg army on the side of the Entente powers.[3]

As a result, within the independent state of Czechoslovakia the erasing of the Habsburg past took place at an organized, state-wide level that included not only monuments, statues and street names but also members of the Habsburg dynasty.[4] This process was generally referred to as 'de-Austrianization', meaning detachment from the former empire not only in the economic and administrative sphere but also in the ideological. The detachment was associated with a strict definition of 'us against them', making it more difficult for some national, religious and social groups within the state to identify with it. The term 'de-Austrianization' was introduced by the president himself on 28 October 1919 when he demanded a new de-Austrianized administration.[5] The following year, during the presidential speech delivered on his birthday (7 March), Masaryk elaborated: 'We all call for de-Austrianization. It is not just a matter of eliminating the [Habsburg] dynasty and constitutional forms, but the transformation of our entire *moral habitus*.'[6] The process affected the fundamental pillars of the Habsburg Monarchy, particularly the aristocracy and the Catholic Church. As a member of the Habsburg dynasty and an ardent Catholic, Franz Ferdinand became part of this de-Austrianization discourse.

This chapter focuses on the construction of the image of Franz Ferdinand in Czech society and in official memory after the First World War. The shaping of this image started after the archduke's death, mainly in Czechoslovak exile circles. After 1918, the anti-Catholic, anti-German and anti-aristocratic rhetoric of the state found its chief enemy in the Habsburgs. The figure of Franz Ferdinand perhaps naturally served as a useful antidote during the process of constructing a new Czechoslovak national identity. His image was created and confirmed at the ideological level with the help of newspaper articles, pamphlets, memoirs and historiography, which influenced public opinion, mostly in a scandalous fashion. The following analysis concerns those personal features of the archduke which were selected as unsuitable for the new republican values. We will also see how in practical terms the Habsburg heritage was diminished during the state land reform, and how a negative interpretation of Franz Ferdinand's activities was exploited during the nationalization of Habsburg properties. Finally, Konopiště castle is analysed as a 'site of memory'.

## Constructing a posthumous image of Franz Ferdinand

On Sunday 28 June 1914, a splendid Sokol performance in Brno was interrupted by news of the Sarajevo assassination. Almost immediately black flags were raised and the exercise stopped, although the audience was unaware of what was happening. In the middle of the training ground a discussion ensued: the Czech organizers wished to continue with the performance, while the representatives of the *Statthalterei* (the Moravian governor) wanted to suspend the event. In the end a compromise solution was reached; the Sokols finished the ongoing number after which the performance ended and the 60,000 gymnasts dispersed.[7]

The first reactions to the assassination in Czech society were connected to obligatory mourning. According to Czech newspapers, the whole of Prague was draped in black, and all theatre performances and concerts were cancelled.[8] *Lidové noviny*, a liberal newspaper, published an article entitled 'Our Mourning', which discussed the human tragedy and noted that 'nowhere in Europe has there been amassed so much passion, so many misunderstandings, such confusion and anarchy as in Austria'.[9] A local chronicler in the small, mostly Catholic central Bohemian town of Louňovice considered the assassination 'a tragedy and the result of perfidious plots by perverse revolutionaries and nihilists'.[10] Another tone to be found in the newspaper articles, besides condemnation, warned against anti-Serb pogroms and demonstrations.[11]

Despite the human sympathy expressed for the couple's orphans, no special memorial acts or demonstrations against the assassination took place. This lack of sympathy was influenced by many Czechs' pro-Slav feelings for Serbia. Franz Ferdinand was not generally considered to be popular, and according to the lawyer František Weyr and the writer Max Brod people failed to show deep mourning: his death was very soon forgotten.[12] One year later, the émigré politician Edvard Beneš recalled the situation after the assassination, writing in the exile periodical *La Nation Tchèque* that the Czechs had had no idea how to react to the Sarajevo events, and they could not foresee the consequences: 'They were asking whether they should rejoice over the Archduke's death, or whether they should fear the repercussions of this revolutionary act.' According to Beneš, there was clear uniformity in the negative approach to the ruling dynasty, with no signs of mourning among the people on 28 June 1914: 'The heir to the throne was a mystery for the Czechs. What they did know, did not earn their sympathy. ... [But] they also knew that he was not popular in Hungary, that he had been living for a long time in Bohemia and his wife was a member of the middle Czech aristocracy.'[13] Generally speaking, the news of the death of the heir apparent caused no great emotional reaction in the Bohemian lands; most Czech politicians remained silent.[14]

During the following years any memory of the Sarajevo assassination was overshadowed by the events of the war, the newspapers mainly reporting news from the trenches. In 1917 for instance, the Catholic newspaper *Čech* printed a very short report on page six reminding its readers of the 'sad third anniversary' of the assassination of the archduke and his wife. The article recollected that the event had led to the war against Serbia and consequently to the world war.[15] Franz Ferdinand's death was associated with the war as its pretext or starting point.[16] The lukewarm attitudes and little emotional interest presented in these articles generally corresponded to Czech public opinion within the Monarchy.

During the war a strongly negative image of the Habsburgs was fostered by Czech exile circles and émigrés. Since the dismembering of Austria-Hungary was a key point of the programme of the Czechoslovak National Council in Paris, an important aspect of Czechoslovak war propaganda was to paint the Habsburgs unfavourably as a disreputable family.[17] The cultivated image of Franz Ferdinand was that of a Catholic bigot, with politically and socially reactionary attitudes, whose accession to the throne would have resulted in policies of extreme Germanization and state centralization. And because of his friendly relations with the German Kaiser Wilhelm II, Franz Ferdinand was made responsible for the war. This sheds light on future narratives of Czech historical memory. At the same time the hostile image propagated by Czech émigrés was being undermined by myths about the tragic death of a devoted couple and by embryonic attitudes that fluctuated between disapproval, nostalgia and even sympathy.

Following the end of the war and the establishment of independent Czechoslovakia, Franz Ferdinand's image went through phases of both demonization and mockery. It fitted well with the republic's anticlerical and anti-Habsburg climate that was stronger in the Bohemian lands than in Slovakia. The Slovaks had found their enemy in the Magyars and were more neutral towards the former ruling dynasty in line with their overwhelming Catholicism.[18] How then was the anniversary of Sarajevo recalled in interwar Czechoslovakia? Whenever the precise date was remembered in the Czechoslovak press, it was usually for other reasons. Notably, the newspapers reported the commemorations held in Prague together with representatives of the South Slavs and Czechoslovak Sokols to mark Vidovdan – the anniversary of the Battle of Kosovo in 1389 that had led to medieval Serbia's annihilation.[19] Press articles also appeared about Gavrilo Princip, his friends and their fate, referring to them as martyrs, heroes or assassins. Especially in 1919, the newspapers published extensive stories depicting their tragedy because of the exhumation of their bodies that took place in June 1919 in Terezín (Theresienstadt).[20]

In discussions about the war, guilt was attributed to Austria-Hungary. Even in 1915 Masaryk had clearly stated his opinion about it in a declaration of the Czech Foreign Committee: 'There are now no doubts, that Austria-Hungary utilized the Sarajevo assassination unjustly against Serbia; Vienna and Budapest continued their anti-Slav politics.'[21] After the war, the publication of historical documents served as 'genuine' evidence for revealing alleged Habsburg plots. The circumstances of the assassination were recalled with the publication of documents that highlighted the relationship between the archduke and the German Kaiser. It was 'demonstrated' that

Franz Ferdinand, together with an aggressive Germany, had prepared the war at Konopiště castle in June 1914.

On this point, Czechoslovak interests coincided with those of the Western Allies. In 1919 Edgar Sisson, director of the foreign section of the US Committee for Public Information, sent the Czech-American Emanuel Voska to Vienna to make a search of the Austrian archives. Voska had served during the war as a spy for the British and the Americans as well as for the Czechoslovak émigré movement. His task in Vienna was to find out whether the Sarajevo assassination had been the result of a German-Austrian plot, with the goal of provoking a war.[22] In his memoirs, Voska recalled how he managed to 'borrow' the correspondence of members of the Habsburg dynasty, smuggling 'three wagons full of documents' out to Prague in February 1919. The material was photographed and the pictures were sent on to Paris for the use of the American delegation during the Paris Peace Conference.[23] Voska himself thought that he had discovered proof of the Habsburg dynasty's guilt. As he noted in 1936 in his memoirs,

> The capture of material from the Vienna Hofarchiv ... proved that the Habsburg dynasty was greatly responsible for the biggest world war, but it also provided our historians with enough documents to stop them from contemplating how events might have developed if Austria-Hungary had not fallen apart. ... The key members of the Peace Conference were convinced by these documents about the Habsburgs' responsibility for the war.[24]

Voska, however, was mistaken if he thought that these documents were crucial for proving Habsburg war guilt. His copies stayed untouched for two years before they were handed over to General Tasker Howard Bliss, a member of the US peace delegation. The US State Department felt that the documents delivered by Voska did not provide enough evidence for the theory that a plot was masterminded by Germans, Hungarians and Poles to provoke war through the archduke's murder. The documents had also been obtained illegally, with methods not endorsed by the American government.[25]

In 1923 four documents from Voska's 'borrowed' materials were published in an article in the history journal *Naše revoluce*. The article was concerned with the controversies surrounding Franz Ferdinand's personality and politics, and was intended as a response to a book by the historian Josef Pekař about Czechoslovak land reform, where the chapter on Konopiště was perceived as an apology to the archduke.[26] *Naše revoluce* reproduced four letters between Franz Ferdinand and Count Ottakar Czernin from the years 1905 to 1910, with Jaroslav Werstadt, editor of the journal and a pro-Masaryk historian, commenting that this correspondence was important for understanding the political ideas of the heir apparent. Werstadt also attacked his fellow historians Pekař and R. W. Seton-Watson for their idealized opinions of the archduke and the empire.[27] In fact, the published documents did not contain any surprising information.

Within Czech society, the general stance – bordering at times on the abusive – towards Franz Ferdinand was also reflected in literature. One of the most well-known examples comes from *The Good Soldier Švejk* written by Jaroslav Hašek and published in 1921. The book begins with the famous scene where the housekeeper Mrs Müller announces to Švejk: 'So they've killed our Ferdinand.' This rather personal-sounding message does not indicate any historical importance. Švejk replies in kind: 'Which Ferdinand, Mrs Müller? I know two Ferdinands. One of them does jobs for Průša the chemist, and one day he drank a bottle of hair oil by mistake; and then there's Ferdinand Kokoška who goes round collecting manure. They wouldn't be any great loss, either of 'em.' The housekeeper then describes the archduke: 'the one from Konopiště, you know, Mr Švejk, the fat, pious one.'[28] Her description demonstrates the main features that had become synonymous with Franz Ferdinand: wealth, religious piety and Konopiště castle. Paradoxically, the sentence 'So they've killed our Ferdinand' became popular, and even a century later was used in the Czech media in a positive way.[29]

Despite showing deep loyalty to the Monarchy, Švejk was later arrested. Talking to his cellmates at the police headquarters, he learnt why they too had been put in jail: 'Because of Sarajevo!' – 'Because of Ferdinand!' ... 'Because they did away with His Imperial Highness at Sarajevo.'[30] This image of Czech persecution was confirmed by both official memory and political practice. The characteristics underlined by Hašek – Franz Ferdinand as a fat, pious aristocrat – contrasted with the democratic republican ideals proposed by the slim Protestant president.

Most works about Franz Ferdinand attempted to present themselves as objective by quoting 'reliable sources'. Czech writer, dramatist and actor Emil Artur Longen, who was the first to adapt Hašek's novel for theatre, later wrote a play about Franz Ferdinand which he claimed was based on historical documents and eyewitness testimonies, therefore presenting a 'true story'. The storyline takes place in Konopiště in June 1914 during the visit of Kaiser Wilhelm II, when Sophie duchess of Hohenberg supposedly tells Wilhelm of a dream in which her husband becomes emperor and triumphantly marches into Belgrade. Wilhelm replies that this will indeed happen. When Franz Ferdinand then receives a warning from the Serbian king that it is dangerous to take part in the military manoeuvres, the archduke retorts that he is not afraid of the Serbian bogeyman and shouts: 'For God's sake, may nobody get in my way, there has to be a clear and large space ahead of me.'[31] The personalities of the couple in this play are shown in the worst possible light: immoral, greedy and power hungry. A novel, published in 1932 under the pen name Georges de Villa and with the title *Bouře na obzoru* (Storm on the Horizon), takes a similar approach to Franz Ferdinand. While advertisements for the book lured in prospective readers with suggestions of the heir's 'debauched' life, it contained references to real sources (the archduke's correspondence) and to alleged military negotiations in Konopiště.[32]

Probably the most well-known Czech novel about the archduke was published in 1935 by the writer Karel Nový under the title *Atentát* (Assassination).[33] It appeared within the context of other novels reflecting on the last years of Austria-Hungary, written by Robert Musil, Josef Roth and Karl Kraus; in 1932 a Czech translation of Bruno Brehm's novel *Apis und Este* was also published. Nový wrote from the perspective of the Slavs' movement for independence and the local events occurring in Konopiště; he had been born in the nearby town of Benešov and his negative attitudes towards the archduke were influenced by memories from his childhood.[34] During the years that it took him to write the novel, Nový used R. W. Seton-Watson's book about Sarajevo,[35] consulted with the Serbian Bohemist Jovan Kršić, and visited Yugoslavia.[36] In a non-fiction, documentary style he described the preparations for the assassination by Bosnian Serbs and expressed his sympathy for them. According to Nový the assassination was revenge against Serbia's oppressors and exploiters. Franz Ferdinand is portrayed as a supporter of war in order to destroy Serbia: 'To anyone who thinks of opposing us, we have the means of supreme power. Jails, bullets, ropes.'[37] In this account the heir apparent had plotted the war together with Wilhelm II in Konopiště.

Memoirs and stories of those close to the archduke and his family further supported a negative and comical characterization. Perhaps the most well-known memoir is that of Emanuel Rak, an uneducated guileless footman who had served at the Konopiště castle from 1910. Rak's memoir – published in 1932 – was edited by Jaroslav Veselý for final publication, and he (most likely) added emphasis to the anti-Habsburg sentiments. The memoir is reminiscent of Hašek's popular narrative; even the photograph on the cover brings to mind the appearance of Švejk. Rak's story balances between subservience and admiration towards the nobility, and between mocking and envious perceptions, with the strong social attitude of a man from a poor family with eleven children. When Wilhelm II visited Konopiště, Rak pictured the feast: 'Oh, the gentlemen had intelligence of the stomach! They ate Bouillabaisse, Caucasian shashlik, salads, ravioli, Toledo pheasants, spaghetti, minestrone, Polish chlodnik, Marengo chickens, lobster, crayfish, whatever a poor hungry man can imagine.'[38]

Following publication, other servants criticized Rak for his falsehoods, and he became the target of jokes from other employees. But Rak rebutted reproaches from his fellow servant Marie Hynková claiming that he had been forced to bend the truth: 'The masters have written that I just signed it and got paid.'[39] Thus, while Rak's memoir supported the official anti-Habsburg discourse of the First Republic, adding a personal touch to it, the defiance of the other servants and their experiences offered a clashing view. The social aspect of Rak´s memoir was further underlined during the communist era, when in 1964 the fiftieth anniversary of Franz Ferdinand's assassination was remembered. An article based on Rak's new recollections was published, noting that 'power, glory and wealth does not bring happiness'.[40] Rak's peculiar personality also attracted the writer Jindřiška Smetanová. Smetanová's conversation with Rak, at the time her neighbour in Prague's Malá Strana, became the topic of her short story published in 1967. During the conversation with Rak she intended to find out about Franz Ferdinand and the life in Konopiště. Rak duly leant Smetanová a handwritten manuscript – his unpublished memoirs – which she described as being little more than recollections about who ate what at the castle. Paradoxically, Rak himself was dubious about the possibility of publishing it but for different reasons: he believed that 'it was full of politics and Habsburgs'.[41]

Another book had been published in 1930 by the Czech traveller, hunter and adventurer Vilém Němec. It had the self-explanatory title *His Highness in Konopiště (Franz Ferdinand d'Este): His Rule-Over and Ravaging of the Konopiště Region, Various Stories, Memoirs and Adventures*.[42] Typically portraying Franz Ferdinand as a heartless and mad hunter, the author explained that all the information was based on his personal opinions and on stories circulating around the Benešov district. Němec and the publishers of these volumes duly reaped great financial profit from them for, beyond the aristocratic milieu, the archduke's morganatic marriage, his passion for hunting and his violent death were all enticing for any readership. Indeed, in 1996 Němec's book was re-published with a new subtitle to attract new readers – an 'unflattering portrait of the heir to the throne'.[43]

In the 1920s Masaryk's friend František Veselý had also entered the fray of anti-Franz Ferdinand studies with booklets about the heir apparent that questioned his 'Czechness'. Veselý pointed out that although Sophie duchess of Hohenberg hailed from the Czech noble family of Chotek, and despite rumours that the family had a good grasp of Czech, in fact none of them spoke any Czech. Veselý connected their poor knowledge of the Czech language with being prejudiced against Czechs.[44] The question of language proficiency was thus seen as a substantial proof of true Czechness. Veselý used his own personal knowledge, as well as testimonials from castle servants and estate administrators, publishing a series of short stories about Franz Ferdinand's greed, bad behaviour and severity towards servants and the local population. For example, he described in detail the lawsuits – actively pursued by the archduke – against any locals caught picking mushrooms on the Konopiště estate.[45]

Thus, across Czech interwar literature the figure of Franz Ferdinand was officially represented in an overwhelmingly negative light. Similarly, Czechoslovak newspapers like the centre-left *České slovo* described the archduke as 'a bloody devil' and an 'insane paralytic'.[46] This demeaning approach, stereotyping him as a fervent Catholic, an anti-Slavonic despot or a manic hunter, all corresponded to the official Czechoslovak programme of 'de-Austrianization'.

## Konopiště: A site of memory

Franz Ferdinand had bought Konopiště castle in 1886 from the noble Lobkowitz family, transforming it into a modern estate with parks, summer houses, sculptures, hunting grounds, flower gardens, greenhouses and ponds built over 250 hectares of land. Its rose garden with 200 types of roses (approximately 8,500 plants in 1910) attracted many visitors.[47] Yet before the war the estate had been shrouded in mystery, a closed park attracting the attention of the local population.[48] The archduke had created his own enclave by purchasing houses in the nearby village of Žabovřesky, rebuilding them in a Tyrolean style (Figure 14.1).

It is easy to rename bridges or streets, but it is not so easy to clear away buildings. Although statues connected to the Habsburg dynasty were destroyed after 1918, its residences such as Konopiště, Zákupy and Chlum u Třeboně remained. Konopiště castle and the park surrounding it therefore endured as a physical reminder of the assassinated heir. Indeed, Franz Ferdinand's idiosyncratic personality, his close connection to the highest political circles, his mysterious fate – all increased the castle's ghoulish attraction as a singular site of remembrance. After 1918, as we have noted, Konopiště also became a specific subject of historical discussion concerning

FIGURE 14.1 *Castle and hunting lodge of the Konopiště estate, 1901. Inscription reads: 'Both the castle of Archduke Franz Ferdinand in Konopiště and the deer park in which it is located are inaccessible to inhabitants of the town of Benešov which is about 10 minutes away' (author's possession).*

the start of the Great War. Based on Jaroslav Prokeš's observations, Czechs generally tended to view the plot to assassinate Franz Ferdinand as either a conspiracy theory fabricated in Vienna and Budapest – where people were now 'satisfied that the odious and dreaded heir is dead'[49] – or, rather ironically, as a plot designed at Konopiště by Kaiser Wilhelm and Franz Ferdinand himself in order to start a war.

Locals too believed that Konopiště castle was a place of worldly events. According to the post-1918 Konopiště village chronicle,

> the rose garden nearby the castle is considered by people as a place where consent was given for the world war. Others say that it was in the cork oak summer house or in the hunting lodge in the Black Forest. It is certain that Wilhelm II visited Konopiště castle twice and made an alliance with Franz Ferdinand in June 1914.[50]

Despite the rebuttal of all this speculation by the historian Josef Pekař, the myths endured. Historians and politicians, including the National Democrat Karel Kramář, backed the idea that Konopiště was a place of intrigue and war preparation. Thus Josef Otto Novotný wrote in his two-volume monograph on the 'resurrection' of Czechoslovak independence: 'In Konopiště there were negotiations ... between the Kaiser and the heir apparent about the war.' Novotný was convinced that the first assassination attempt had been prepared there to serve as a pretext for the attack on Serbia.[51] In August 1922, President Masaryk, too, in a bout of polemics with Kramář (his political rival), took up the issue in one article:

> Kramář has no doubts that the war was decided by Wilhelm and Franz Ferdinand at Konopiště, by the pawns on Europe's chessboard. ... It fits well with Kramář's way of thinking that the Sarajevo assassination was a mysterious act and somehow connected to the agreement in Konopiště. We are reading a fantastic story about the first, failed assassination attempt that was orchestrated [by Franz Ferdinand] and about the second that was real and surprising. What an amazing coincidence that both attackers, the would-be one and the actual assassin, met at the same time and place?[52]

Konopiště had also quickly become embroiled in the politics of the new state through the ideologically charged subject of land reform. In February 1919, the Municipal Office in Benešov asked the director of the Konopiště Estate to open up to the public a section of the park called Šiberna.[53] Jaroslav Thun, the trustee of Franz Ferdinand's children, declined this request, arguing that it would completely destroy the property.[54]

The Czechoslovak state treated the property of Franz Ferdinand in the same way as other Habsburg properties. The 1919 Land Control Act No. 215/1919 nationalized all property of the Habsburg-Lothringian family without compensation.⁵⁵ The Konopiště estate was also given under sequestration to the state, despite the fact that legally it belonged to Franz Ferdinand's children who were Hohenbergs and lacked any rights as members of the Habsburg family because of his morganatic marriage.⁵⁶ Thus the Land Control Act did not in fact cover the Konopiště estate. Even so, František Veselý saw the confiscation of the Hohenbergs' property as a remedy for the injustice caused to Konopiště's Bohemian owners by the seizure of their property after the Battle of White Mountain in 1620.⁵⁷

On 3 May 1919, with the state in control of the castle, an expert committee of the Ministry of Education visited to examine the furnishings. The committee's task included the allocation of all suitable furniture to the Czechoslovak legation in Yugoslavia, with the aim of reducing state expenditure by 'at least half million crowns'.⁵⁸ Antonín Kalina, a member of the committee and also Czechoslovakia's minister in Belgrade, wrote to Masaryk that the furniture selected for the legation actually improved the style of the interior of Konopiště castle. For with the new arrangement the castle looked more sophisticated, in contrast to the bad taste of its former owners. Thus, as with literary representations, the disparity between the former aristocracy and the current republican sensibilities was again highlighted. The bad taste in the castle's interior decoration – the cramming in of furniture – was supposedly incompatible with the Protestant simplicity of the republic. Kalina also complained that the orphans' aunt, Countess Chotek, was secretly manoeuvring to take away some of the more valuable pieces.⁵⁹

Despite the property's nationalization, the possibility that the Hohenbergs might return frightened the locals. In 1920, rumours that Konopiště and Chlum could remain in the possession of Franz Ferdinand's heirs caused demonstrations in Benešov and in Chlum u Třeboně. On 11 July, a meeting was organized by socialists in Benešov, where 600 people protested against returning Konopiště to the Hohenbergs; they even sent a petition to the government.⁶⁰ To establish that Franz Ferdinand's property was indeed part of the nationalization process, on 5 August 1921 the Czechoslovak Parliament passed an amendment, clarifying that property 'particularly of the former heir apparent Franz Ferdinand and his descendants' should be expropriated as well.⁶¹ During the debate on the amendment, the anticlerical radical Theodor Bartošek voiced his support, arguing that the castle was the place where the idea for the war had been hatched.⁶² These fundamental constitutional changes were part of the de-Austrianization phenomena of the First Czechoslovak Republic. The threat of a Habsburg return to Czechoslovakia served as a rhetorical ruse, making sure that the population would unify against the 'enemy'.

After 1918 many statues of members of the House of Habsburg or figures of the Catholic Church were destroyed in the Bohemian lands. Statues of Emperors Franz Joseph I and Joseph II and John of Nepomuk were demolished, not least because they had come to be seen as symbols of the Czech-German national conflict.⁶³ Not many memorials had been dedicated to the archduke.⁶⁴ In 1913 a column had been erected near Konopiště, in the small village of Poměnice – commemorating one of Franz Ferdinand's meetings with the German Kaiser – and in March 1914 a bridge named after him was opened in Prague⁶⁵ (Figure 14.2). However, shortly after the war the column's inscription plate was removed (the column is still there today and remains without a plate), and in 1920 the bridge was renamed after the Czech painter Josef Mánes. The column in Poměnice was preserved, since František Veselý was convinced that it would be good to retain such a memorial in the pure Czech countryside and to stain it with blood on memorial days.⁶⁶

While not named after the archduke, Konopiště castle was so closely connected to his memory that it could be considered his memorial. In the interwar republic, it became a tourist attraction. The park was opened to the public and although an entrance fee was charged the castle became a popular tourist destination for thousands of visitors each year, offering opportunities for business. Since the interiors still had the authentic furniture and decorations, visitors could survey the archduke's vast collections with the exhibits coming to characterize 'Franz Ferdinand's and his family's way of life, the social class he came from'. In his booklet about Konopiště, Veselý expressed the hope that the mindset that Franz Ferdinand represented belonged to the past and would never come back. He was also convinced that the castle was not suitable for habitation, especially not in a republican era that was heading towards democratic simplicity. For 'Konopiště ... was

**FIGURE 14.2** *The Archduke Franz Ferdinand Bridge in Prague, opened in 1914 (author's possession).*

a seat of aristocratic arrogance and pride that from now on has to serve the people, providing them with a lesson from history and refreshing their memory.'[67] This official negative approach towards the past era could not deter visitors' curiosity and admiration when they explored the castle and its surroundings.

## Franz Ferdinand: Habsburg nostalgia?

R. W. Seton-Watson remarked after the assassination of Franz Ferdinand that the heir apparent had been 'the most singular figure of the reigning dynasties of Europe'; 'he represented a progressive idea in the Europe of today.'[68] It is ironic then that today Franz Ferdinand is not remembered in popular memory for any of these qualities, but simply for his assassination that sparked the beginning of the Great War and the destruction of the Habsburg Empire. School textbooks and commemorations of the war all perpetuate this view, even though the conflict did not start for several weeks after the events in Sarajevo. In interwar Czechoslovakia, Franz Ferdinand was most definitely not the figurehead of any progressive idea of Europe; rather, he was exploited politically as part of an official anti-Habsburg and de-Austrianization agenda. In newspaper articles about the war, he was either completely ignored or he was depicted in a way that highlighted the abyss between the Habsburg Monarchy and the democratic First Republic. He was a bloodthirsty, mad hunter; mean and unstable; and a pious Catholic: the complete opposite of the Protestant and democratic character of the republic and its leader President Masaryk.

But changes in people's attitudes towards Austria-Hungary began with the dramatic developments of the Second World War and the following communist era.[69] Starting from the 1960s, the theatre performances of Jára Cimrman (a fictional character, presented as a universal genius) used the backdrop of the Austro-Hungarian Monarchy and were able to criticize the communist regime. In the 1983 film *Jára Cimrman Lying, Sleeping*, the character of Cimrman is a tutor to Franz Ferdinand's children and tries to destroy the Habsburg Empire by teaching them that the best form of government is that of a republic. With the help of the archduke's doppelgänger, Cimrman wants to force Emperor Franz Joseph to learn Czech and establish a state of 'Austria-Hungary-Czechia'. Just like his portrayal during the First Republic, the archduke is shown as a choleric and cruel personality.

After the fall of communism in 1989, interest in the Habsburg past and in Franz Ferdinand increased. The Habsburgs were no longer considered an 'enemy' but as a part of the nation's history. While historians were drawn to the archduke's vision of the future of the Monarchy, his relationship with Czech society and his morganatic marriage to a member of the Bohemian aristocracy, these themes were also attractive to the public.[70] In this narrative the Sarajevo assassination was accepted as a day of significant historical transition, with the term 'Sarajevo' becoming associated with fatalistic symbolism within Czech society.

In 2014, the centenary of the assassination of Franz Ferdinand was widely commemorated across the Czech Republic. Newspaper articles often paraphrased Hašek's sentence that 'they killed our Ferdinand', and exhibitions were held in Benešov, Konopiště, Třeboň and Prague. It is ironic that, with distance from the events of 1914, the popular feeling in his Czech locality of Konopiště also moved from antithetical and hostile to sympathetic and even a degree of pride in this famous local inhabitant. The town of Benešov and Konopiště castle both benefited from the association. While the town council in Benešov sponsored the publication of memoirs of the Czech servants in Konopiště, recalling the humanity of the murdered couple and their willingness to speak Czech with the domestic staff, the exhibition in the castle celebrated the marriage of Franz Ferdinand and Sophie Chotek, ignoring any negative aspects of their character.[71] For the anniversary commemorations, the sixth district of Prague had even intended to build a monument to Sophie since she had belonged to an old Bohemian noble family.[72] Despite protests from the public, a competition was announced and the jury chose several projects; the memorial was intended to be unveiled in the autumn of 2014 but eventually failed to come to fruition.

The attempts by the leaders of the First Republic to create a negative image of Franz Ferdinand that aligned with their project of de-Austrianization were only partly successful. The heir remained in popular memory in a mostly sarcastic and humorous way, through literary works and through his 'sites of memory'. The nationalization of Franz Ferdinand's property opened up his estate to the public – except during the Second World War when the castle served as an SS headquarters – and made his life accessible, through personal items, memorabilia and various other objects that the family had to abandon in 1919. The case of the heir apparent therefore highlights that the process of de-Austrianization was a more complicated and uncertain process than simply tearing down and erecting new statues and street signs, and creating a new symbolic identity. Contrary to intentions, the image created of Franz Ferdinand during the First Republic (and later) served to increase the interest in his personality; thus today his popular memory has become an intriguing blend of history and nostalgia.

## Notes

1 Ivan Herben and Josef Mach (eds), *T.G.M. Malé historky o velkém muži* (London: Čechoslovák, 1946), 95–7.
2 Masaryk's interview with *Tribune de Genève*, in Tomáš G. Masaryk, *Cesta demokracie. I. Projevy – články – rozhovory 1919–1920* (Prague: Masarykův ústav, 2003), 155.

3   The image of the independence movement was constructed by defining or self-defining who was rebellious. See Jan Hálek and Boris Moskovič, *Ve službách Maffie? Český domácí protirakouský odboj (1914–1918) v zrcadle ego-dokumentů* (Prague: Masarykův ústav, 2018).
4   Zdeněk Hojda and Jiří Pokorný, *Pomníky a zapomníky* (Prague: Paseka 1996); Cynthia Paces, *Prague Panoramas: National Memory and Sacred Space in the Twentieth Century* (Pittsburgh: University of Pittsburgh Press, 2009); Mark Cornwall, 'A Constructed and Divided Habsburg Memory', in Mark Cornwall and John Paul Newman (eds), *Sacrifice and Rebirth: The Legacy of the Last Habsburg War* (New York: Berghahn, 2016), 5.
5   Presidential address, 28 October 1919, in *Cesta demokracie I.*, 172.
6   T. G. Masaryk's speech on 7 March 1920, in *Cesta demokracie I.*, 233.
7   František Weyr, *Paměti 1: Za Rakouska 1879–1918* (Brno: Atlantis, 1999), 425.
8   'Druhý den po zdrcující zprávě', *Čech*, 30 June 1914, 2; 'Smuteční projevy z Prahy a obcí sousedních', *Národní listy*, 30 June 1914, 2.
9   'Náš smutek', *Lidové noviny*, 30 June 1914, 1.
10  Státní okresní archiv Benešov (State District Archive Benešov: hereafter SOAB), Chronicle of town Louňovice, 99.
11  Jan Galandauer, *František Ferdinand d'Este následník trůnu* (Prague, Litomyšl: Paseka, 2000), 316–17.
12  Weyr, *Paměti* 1, 425; Max Brod, *Život plný bojů* (Prague: Nakladatelství Franze Kafky), 76.
13  Edouard Bielsky [= Edvard Beneš], 'Les Tchèques et la guerre', in Dagmar Hájková and Pavel Horák (eds), *Edvard Beneš, Němci a Německo. Edice dokumentů 1* (Prague: Masarykův ústav a Archiv AV ČR, 2014), 208.
14  Ivan Šedivý, *Češi, české země a Velká válka 1914–1918* (Prague: Nakladatelství Lidové noviny, 2001), 23; Zdeněk Tobolka, *Politické dějiny československého národa od r. 1848 až do dnešní doby. Díl IV: 1914-1918* (Prague: Československý Kompas, 1937), 47–8.
15  'Smutné výročí', *Čech*, 28 June 1917, 6.
16  Similar opinions could be found in local chronicles. See, for example, Státní okresní archiv Opava (State District Archive Opava), Pamětní kniha obce Kyjovice, Pamětní kniha obce Píště; Státní okresní archiv Zlín, Kronika obce Polichno, Obecní kronika Mladová.
17  T. G. Masaryk, 'Degenerace Habsburků a Rakouska', in T. G. Masaryk, *Válka a revoluce. Články – Memoranda – Přednášky – Rozhovory 1914–1916*, ed. Karel Pichlík (Prague: Ústav T. G. Masaryka, 2005), 103–14.
18  Elena Mannová, 'Koncept loajality: Postoj k autoritám na Slovensku počas prvej světovej vojny', *Historický časopis* 55:4 (2007): 684, 691.
19  'Vidov dan', *Lidové noviny*, 28 June 1919, 2; 1 July 1920, 2; 'Ivan Meštrovič o myšlence Vidovdanského chrámu, *Lidové noviny*, 6 July 1919, 10.
20  'Po stopách mučedníků sarajevských', *České slovo*, 10 March 1919, 4–5; 'Exhumace sarajevských mučedníků', 9 July 1919, 2.

21 'Prohlášení Českého komitétu zahraničního', 14 November 1915, in Masaryk, *Válka a revoluce*, 138.

22 Rhodri Jeffreys-Jones, *American Espionage: From Secret Service to CIA* (New York: The Free Press; London: Collier Macmillan Publishers, 1977), 80–2. For Voska's wartime adventures, see Dagmar Hájková, *Emanuel Voska. Špionážní legenda první světové války* (Prague: Academia, 2014).

23 Emanuel Voska and Will Irwin, *Spy and Counterspy* (New York: Doubleday, Doran & Co., 1940), 297; 'Paměti kapitána Em. V. Vosky', *Jas*, X, no. 9 (1936): 8.

24 'Paměti kapitána Em. V. Vosky', *Jas*, 8.

25 Jeffrey-Jones, *American Espionage*, 83.

26 Josef Pekař, *Omyly a nebezpečí pozemkové reformy* (Prague: Vesmír, 1923).

27 'Dva představitelé Rakouska: František Ferdinand a Otakar Černín: Několik dokumentů', *Naše revoluce* 1:1 (1923): 43.

28 Jaroslav Hašek, *The Good Soldier Schweik* (London: Penguin, 1958), 11.

29 Petr Třešňák, 'Proč nám zabili Ferdinanda', *Respekt* 26, 23–26 July 2014, 50–6; Jiří Bakala, 'Tak nám zabili Ferdinanda', *Britské listy*, 28 June 2014. https://legacy.blisty.cz/art/18749.html; TV Nova, Zabili nám Ferdinanda, 28 June 2014, http://tn.nova.cz/clanek/zpravy/zahranici/tak-nam-zabili-ferdinan da-je-to-presne-100-let.html; Prague 1 organized a performance 'Tak nám zabili Ferdinanda' https://www.praha1.cz//cps/doprava-a-parkovani-45556. html; Czech TV24, Historie.cs, 'Tak nám zabili Ferdinanda', 28 June 2014, https://www.ceskatelevize.cz/porady/10150778447-historie-cs/2144528014 00022-tak-nam-zabili-ferdinanda

30 Hašek, *Good Soldier Schweik*, 22.

31 Arthur Longen, *Frant. Ferd. d'Este (Konopišťská růže). Čtyři jednání ze života zavražděného následníka rakouského trůnu před vzplanutím světové války* (Prague: František Švejda, 1925), 30–1.

32 Georges de Villa, *Bouře na obzoru. František Ferdinand d'Este* (Prague: Čas. Světová literatura, 1932).

33 Karel Nový, *Sarajevský atentát* (1935; Prague: Československý spisovatel 1980). The novel was re-published several times, with the last, eighth edition appearing in 1982. What is remarkable is that the story was continuously 'updated' to suit the contemporary political situation. From 1952, the editions ended with the words of Lenin about how the First World War had been transformed from an imperial war into a revolution (368).

34 Karel Nový, 'Vzpomínky na mládí', *Panorama* 25 (1950): 5.

35 R. W. Seton-Watson, *Sarajevo. Studie o vzniku veliké války* (Prague: Melantrich, 1929).

36 Miloš Pohorský, 'Války a zápasy', in Nový, *Sarajevský atentát*, 380.

37 Nový, *Sarajevský atentát*, 32.

38 Jaroslav Veselý, *Jak se Emanuel Rak ze Štěchovic dostal k arcivévodovi na Konopiště. Životní příběhy českého člověka u dynastie* (Prague: Jan Naňka, 1932); Luboš Velek, 'Ve službách "Vysokého pána" I.', *Sborník vlastivědných prací z Podblanicka* 38 (1998): 221–44.

39 Lukáš Pavlík, *Ve službách konopišťského pána. Zaměstnancem nejen na zámku Konopiště v Čechách* (Benešov: Muzeum umění a designu Benešov, 2013), 102.

40 'Jak to bylo před padesáti lety. Z pamětí Emanuela Raka, komorníka na Konopiši', *Zemědělské noviny*, 27 July 1964, 3.

41 'Jak se dostal Emanuel Rak ze Štěchovic na Konopiště', in Jindřiška Smetanová (ed.), *Ustláno na růžích* (Prague: Československý spisovatel, 1967), 82–90.

42 Vilém Němec, *Vysoký pán konopišťský (arcivévoda Frant. Ferdinand d´Este): jeho vláda a řádění na Konopišťsku, různé příběhy, paměti a dobrodružství* (Prague: Nákladem vlastním, 1930).

43 Vilém Němec, *Vysoký pán konopišťský, aneb Nelichotivý portrét následníka trůnu Františka Ferdinanda d'Este* (Jihlava: Madagaskar, 1996).

44 František Veselý, *Konopiště a Hohenbergové* (Prague: Melantrich, 1924), 8–10.

45 František Veselý, *Konopiště. Vzpomínky, příspěvky k charakteristice* (Prague: Jan Dubský, 1921), 34–5.

46 Jaroslav Klofáč, 'Před 15 lety. Sarajevský atentát – Velký sokolský slet v Brně', *České slovo*, 6 July 1929, 2; 'K pětiletému výročí sarajevského atentátu', *České slovo*, 27 July 1919, 1; 'Konopiště', *České slovo*, 27 March 1919, 3.

47 Miroslav Brožovský, *Konopiště: průvodce* (Prague: Středisko památkové péče, 1981), 101.

48 In June 1914, the park was opened for two days to the public for the first time.

49 Jaroslav Prokeš, *Obrázkové dějiny naší samostatnosti* (Prague: Nakladatelství české grafické unie, 1930), 237!

50 SOAB, Konopiště, AO village chronicle 1926–37, 16. One close collaborator of Masaryk, the *Times* journalist Henry Wickham Steed, wrote about the 'Konopiště pact' and his opinions were publicized by Czech exiles from as early as 1916. Steed based his exaggerated statements on information given to him by an anonymous informant. See Henry Wickham Steed, 'The Pact of Konopischt', *Nineteenth Century and After* 79 (1916): 253–73; 'Nineteenth Century and After – H. W. Steed: Le Pacte de Konopiste', *La Nation Tchèque* I (1915–1916): 337–8; Adolf Žipek, *Domov za války. Díl I* (Prague: Pokrok, 1929), 19–20. For a recent attempt to resurrect this myth, see John Zametica, *Folly and Malice: The Habsburg Empire, the Balkans and the Start of World War One* (London: Shepheard-Walwyn, 2017), 425–39.

51 J. O. Novotný, *Vzkříšení samostatnosti československé I.* (Prague: Topič, 1932), 82.

52 Tomáš G. Masaryk, 'Pět přednášek Karla Kramáře o zahraniční politice', in Tomáš G. Masaryk, *Cesta demokracie. II. Projevy – články – rozhovory 1921–1923* (Prague: Masarykův ústav, 2007), 318.

53 Archiv Ústavu T.G. Masaryka Prague (Archive of the Masaryk Institute: hereafter AÚTGM), fond TGM-R, box 468: Municipal Office Benešov to director of Konopiště estate, 10 February 1919.

54 Ibid., Jaroslav Thun to Municipal Office Benešov, 27 February 1919.

55 Mark Cornwall, 'National Reparation? The Czech Land Reform and the Sudeten Germans 1918–38', *The Slavonic and East European Review* 75:2 (April 1997): 259–80.

56 Jan Galandauer, 'První sirotci Velké války', *Středočeský sborník historický*, 22–23 (1996–97): 114.
57 Veselý, *Konopiště*, 73.
58 AÚTGM, fond TGM-R, box 468, Report of the Committee of the Ministry of Education and National Enlightenment, 3 May 1919. The hunting lodge was used as a summer house by the Yugoslav minister Ivan Hribar: 'Vzpomínka na náš výlet do Konopiště', *České slovo*, 7 July 1919, 9.
59 AÚTGM, fond TGM-R, box 468, Antonín Kalina to T. G. Masaryk, 22 May 1919.
60 Veselý, *Konopiště*, 68; SOAB, fond District Office, box 4, Report of District political committee on meeting in Benešov, 13 July 1919.
61 Digital parliamentary library: http://www.psp.cz/eknih/1920ns/ps/stenprot/08 3schuz/s083009.htm
62 Galandauer, *František Ferdinand d'Este*, 328.
63 Nancy M. Wingfield, *Flag Wars and Stone Saints: How the Bohemian Lands Became Czech* (Cambridge, MA: Harvard University Press 2007), 156.
64 The only memorial dedicated to Franz Ferdinand was erected in Sarajevo on 28 June 1917 and named *Sünhnedenkmal* (memorial of reconciliation) in German and *Spomenik umorstva* (memorial of murder) in Serbo-Croat. This monument was dismantled at the end of the 1918 and placed in the local museum. See Petr Novák, 'Připomínky sarajevského atentátu a jeho proměny', in Martin Čížek, Antonín Kudláč, Luboš Velek, Vít Vlnas, Jiří Vykoukal (eds), *Poslední staročech. K 70 narozeninám Jiřího Raka* (Prague: Masarykův ústav a Archiv AV ČR, Charles University, 2017), 184.
65 *Věstník hlavního města Prahy* 21 (1914): 42; Jan Galandauer, 'Husův národ a most Františka Ferdinanda', *Historie a vojenství* 44 (1995): 14.
66 Veselý, *Konopiště*, 75–6.
67 Ibid., 66–7.
68 R. W. Seton-Watson, *Sarajevo: A Study in the Origins of the Great War* (London: Hutchinson & Co, 1926), 80; and Arthur J. May, *The Passing of the Hapsburg Monarchy 1914-1918*, 2 vols (Philadelphia: University of Pennsylvania Press, 1966), I, 27–8. May, however, also mentioned that others such as Henry Wickham Steed 'had little faith in Francis Ferdinand' and had even quipped that the archduke's disappearance was 'a godsend to the dynasty' (ibid., 27).
69 Luboš Velek, 'Habsburská monarchie v moderní době', in Dagmar Hájková and Pavel Horák (eds), *Republika československá 1918–1939* (Prague: Nakladatelství Lidové noviny, 2018), 13.
70 Jiří Pernes, *Život plný nepřátel, aneb dramatický život a tragická smrt následníka trůnu Františka Ferdinanda d'Este* (Prague: Iris, 1994); Jan Galandauer, *František Ferdinand d'Este* (Prague: Svoboda-Libertas, 1993); Jiří Pernes, *O trůn a lásku. Dramatický život a tragická smrt Františka Ferdinanda d'Este* (Prague: Brána, 2007).
71 Jiří Chramosta, *Spojeni v životě i ve smrti* (Libice: Gloriet, 2014).
72 http://www.praha.eu/jnp/cz/o_meste/mestske_casti/praha_6/galerie_vystavuje_ 45_navrhu_pomniku.html

# SELECTED FURTHER READING

Afflerbach, Holger and Stevenson, David (eds), *An Improbable War? The Outbreak of World War I and European Political Culture Before 1914* (New York: Berghahn, 2007).
Biondich, Mark, *Stjepan Radić, the Croat Peasant Party, and the Politics of Mass Mobilization, 1904–1928* (Toronto: University of Toronto Press, 2000).
Boeckh, Katrin and Rutar, Sabine (eds), *The Balkan Wars from Contemporary Perception to Historic Memory* (New York: Palgrave Macmillan, 2016).
Bridge, F. R., 'British Official Opinion and the Domestic Situation in the Hapsburg Monarchy, 1900–1914', in B. J. C. McKercher and D. J. Moss (eds), *Shadow and Substance in British Foreign Policy 1895–1939* (Edmonton: University of Alberta Press, 1984), 77–113.
Bridge, F. R., *The Habsburg Monarchy Among the Great Powers, 1815–1918* (New York: Berg, 1990).
Clark, Christopher, *The Sleepwalkers: How Europe Went to War in 1914* (London: Allen Lane, 2012).
Cornwall, Mark, 'Serbia', in Keith Wilson (ed.), *Decisions for War 1914* (London: UCL Press, 1994), 55–96.
Cornwall, Mark, 'The Habsburg Elite and the Southern Slav Question 1914–1918', in Lothar Höbelt and T. G. Otte (eds), *A Living Anachronism?: European Diplomacy and the Habsburg Monarchy* (Vienna: Böhlau, 2010), 239–70.
Cornwall, Mark, 'Loyalty and Treason in Late Habsburg Croatia: A Violent Political Discourse Before the First World War', in Jana Osterkamp and Martin Schulze Wessel (eds), *Exploring Loyalty* (Göttingen: Vandenhoeck & Ruprecht, 2017), 97–120.
Dedijer, Vladimir, *The Road to Sarajevo* (London: Macgibbon & Kee, 1967).
Godsey Jr., William D., *Aristocratic Redoubt: The Austro-Hungarian Foreign Office on the Eve of the First World War* (West Lafayette, IN: Purdue University Press, 1999).
Gumz, Jonathan E., *The Resurrection and Collapse of Empire in Habsburg Serbia, 1914–1918* (Cambridge: Cambridge University Press, 2009).
Hajdarpasic, Edin, *Whose Bosnia?: Nationalism and Political Imagination in the Balkans, 1840–1914* (Ithaca, NY: Cornell University Press, 2015).
Höbelt, Lothar, 'Austria-Hungary and the Balkan Wars, 1912–13', in Jean-Paul Bled and Jean-Pierre Deschodt (eds), *Les guerres balcaniques 1912-1913* (Paris: Presses universitaires de Paris-Sorbonne, 2014), 131–44.
Leslie, John, 'The Antecedents of Austria-Hungary's War Aims: Policies and Policy-Makers in Vienna and Budapest Before and During 1914', in Elisabeth Springer

and Leopold Kammerhofer (eds), *Archiv und Forschung. Das Haus-, Hof- und Staatsarchiv in seiner Bedeutung für die Geschichte Österreichs und Europas* (Vienna: Verlag für Geschichte und Politik, 1993), 307–94.

MacKenzie, David, *Apis, The Congenial Conspirator: The Life of Colonel Dragutin T. Dimitrijević* (New York: Columbia University Press, 1989).

Miller, Nicholas, *Between Nation and State. Serbian Politics in Croatia Before the First World War* (Pittsburgh: University of Pittsburgh Press, 1997).

Miller, Paul, '"The First Shots of the First World War": The Sarajevo Assassination in History and Memory', *Central Europe* 14:2 (2016): 141–56.

Milojković-Djurić, Jelena, *Tradition and Avant-Garde: Literature and Art in Serbian Culture 1900–1918* (New York: Columbia University Press, 1988).

Mitrović, Andrej, *Serbia's Great War 1914–1918* (London: Hurst, 2007).

Okey, Robin, 'A Trio of Hungarian Balkanists: Béni Kállay, István Burián and Lajos Thallóczy in the Age of High Nationalism', *The Slavonic and East European Review* 80/2 (April 2002): 234–66.

Okey, Robin, *Taming Balkan Nationalism: The Habsburg 'Civilizing Mission' in Bosnia, 1878–1914* (Oxford: Oxford University Press, 2007).

Otte, T. G., *July Crisis: The World's Descent into War, Summer 1914* (Cambridge: Cambridge University Press, 2014).

Scheer, Tamara, 'Denunciation and the Decline of the Habsburg Home Front During the First World War', *European Review of History: Revue européenne d'histoire* 24 (2017): 214–28.

Seton-Watson, R. W., *Sarajevo: A Study in the Origins of the Great War* (London: Hutchinson, 1925).

Stergar, Rok and Scheer, Tamara, 'Ethnic Boxes: The Unintended Consequences of Habsburg Bureaucratic Classification', *Nationalities Papers* 46:4 (2018): 575–91.

Stibbe, Matthew, 'Enemy Aliens, Deportees, Refugees: Internment Practices in the Habsburg Empire, 1914–1918', *Journal of Modern European History* 4/12 (2014): 479–99.

Wank, Solomon, 'The Archduke and Aehrenthal: The Origins of a Hatred', *Austrian History Yearbook* 33 (2002): 77–104.

Williamson, Samuel R., 'Influence, Power, and the Policy Process: The Case of Franz Ferdinand, 1906–1914', *The Historical Journal* 17 (1974): 417–34.

Williamson, Samuel R., *Austria-Hungary and the Origins of the First World War* (New York: St Martin's Press, 1991).

# INDEX

Page numbers in *italics* refer to illustrations
FF = Franz Ferdinand

Aehrenthal, Alois Lexa von  59, 61, 65, 76 n.16, 78 n.44, 166
  relations with FF  21, 23–4, 27, 29, 66
Alaupović, Tugomir  113, 114
Albania  50, 133–4, 135, 153, 155, 158, 184
Aleksandar Karadjordjević, regent of Serbia  8, 127, 131, 140
Aleksandar Obrenović, king of Serbia  3, 127, 128, 131–2, 185
Andrić, Ivo  108–9
Apis, *see* Dimitrijević, Dragutin
Appel, Johann Freiherr von  85, 91, 93, 97 n.13
aristocracy (Croatian)
  conservatives  70–2 (*see also* Rauch)
  definition and values  57–8
  economic adaptability  59, 60, 69, 70
  political importance  58
  political/national orientations  61–2, 64, 66–8, 73–4
  Serb nobility  57, 61, 68–9, 70, 73
Auffenberg, Moritz von  61, 67, 68, 76 n.15, 77 n.23, 86, 87
Austria-Hungary (Habsburg Monarchy)
  and Balkan Wars  6, 50, 87, 110, 152–6, 211, 253–4
  as a European Great Power  3–4, 33, 43, 46, 59, 84, 153, 156, 158–9, 165, 166, 177, 192
  fails as *Rechtsstaat*  6, 210, 226
  in July crisis  151, 166–7
  ultimatums issued to Serbia  134, 144, 153, 174, 189, 192

Babunović, Vukašin  111
Badaj, Alexander  211
Bahr, Hermann  59
Balkan League  152, 154, 157, 189, 190, 253
Balkan Wars  6, 28, 50, 110, 133, 135, 152–6, 184, 186, 209
Banjaluka  13 n.31, 85, 135, 261
Bardolff, Carl von  23
Bašagić, Safvet  114
Bauer, Antun  208
Beck, Max Wladimir von  21, 23
Beck-Rzikowski, Friedrich  69
Belgrade  50–1, 109, 110, 112, 126, 129, 132, 134, 138, 144, 188, 220
  Bosnian students in  117, 126–7, 140–3
  as South Slav mecca  3, 48, 64, 68
Belošević, Stjepan  218
Belvedere, *see* Franz Ferdinand
Benešov  274, 280–4, 287
Berchtold, Leopold von  18, 24, 27, 28, 32, 151–3, 155–6, 157–8, 159, 186
  in July crisis  151, 166, 176, 189, 190, 192
Bernatzik, Edmund  23
Bethmann Hollweg, Theodor von  168–9, 174, 176
Biliński, Leon  104, 114, 152, 166, 254, 255–6
Bjelovučić, Nikola Zvonimir  44
Black Hand (*Crna Ruka*), *see* Ujedinjenje ili Smrt
Bombelles, Josip  61, 73, 81 n.68
Bombelles, Marko  41, 73

Bosnia-Herzegovina, *see also* Common
    Ministry of Finance; *Mlada Bosna*
  administration of   83, 91, 95, 255,
    257
  annexation (1908)   3, 4, 24, 29,
    43, 51, 59, 62, 67, 84, 86, 94,
    109, 132–3
  army organization in   84–5, 86
  in Balkan Wars   253–4
  and a 'Bosnian' identity   83, 84,
    91–3, 95
  Catholics (Croats) in   83, 86, 87,
    89, 104, 254
  education in   92–3, 104–8
  as a Habsburg colony   103–4
  hostage taking (wartime)   257–61,
    262, 269 n.26
  language policy in   82–96
  Muslims   83, 84, 85–9, 90–1,
    93–6, 104, 105, 106, 107, 109,
    111, 254, 261, 264
  Orthodox (Serbs) in   83, 86, 87,
    90, 107, 109, 254–66
  population statistics   86, 94, 105,
    106
  Sabor (assembly)   86–7, 94, 113,
    152, 254, 262
  Schutzkorps   254, 261, 271 n.49,
    272 n.50
  state of emergency imposed   254–6
  wartime arrests and internment
    257, 260–1, 270 n.37
  wartime violence/atrocities against
    Serbs   255–6, 256, 258–9,
    261–2, 265
Brandsch, Rudolf   26
Brătianu, Ion   154, 176
Brooks, Sydney   195
Brosch von Aarenau, Alexander   21,
  23, 24, 27, 29
Budisavljević, Srdjan   137, 219,
  224–5
Bulgaria   28–9, 50, 51, 152, 154,
  155–6, 157, 158, 184
Bülow, Bernard von   31

Čabrinović, Nedeljko   110, 115, 141,
  243
Carol, king of Romania   28–9, 154
Cartwright, Fairfax   184, 185–6

Čerović, Božidar   114
Chernyshevsky, Nikolai   110, 112, 140
Chlumecky, Leopold von   24, 42
Chotek, Sophie, duchess of
    Hohenberg   23, 27, 29, 31,
    34 n.6, 187, 198, 199, 257,
    276, 281
  assassination   1, 125
  character   18, 31, 279
  funeral   33, 234, 236
  memorialization of   287
Ciganović, Milan   137, 141, 142
Cimrman, Jára   286
Clam-Martinic, Heinrich   26, 27
Clark, Christopher   2, 102, 126,
  127, 235
Clément-Simon, Louis   51
Common Ministry of Finance   84,
  93, 95, 119 n.9, 254, 255,
  263–4, *see also* Biliński; Kállay;
  Thallóczy
Conrad von Hötzendorf, Franz   4, 8,
  21–3, 22, 24, 32, 52, 153, 156,
  166, 175
Ćorović, Vladimir   114, 269 n.26
Cristea, Miron   25
Croatia-Slavonia, *see also* aristocracy;
    Croat-Serb Coalition; *Nagodba*;
    Sabor
  'absolutism' in   211
  capitalist ventures in   60, 61,
    69–70
  idea of 'Greater Croatia'   5, 41, 42,
    44, 64, 73
  *pravaši* (state-right politicians)   41,
    44, 49, 210, 212, 223, 224
  Serbs in   6, 57, 62, 64–7, 71, 72,
    210, 219–25, 226
Croat-Serb Coalition   65, 66, 68,
    76 n.19, 216
  agreement with Hungarian
    government   66, 211
  and Croatian aristocracy   61,
    66–7, 69–71, 73
  formation   5, 60
  relations with Skerlecz   209,
    211–15, 217–19
  Serb Independent Party   64, 68,
    209, 211, 219
  in wartime   223–4, 225, 226

Crowe, Eyre   185, 188–9, 192
Csicserics, Maximilian   61, 69
Cuvaj, Slavko   50, 211, 212
Cvijić, Jovan   77 n.31, 127
Czechs /Czechoslovakia   26, 30, 31, 42, 60, 88, 103, 108, 113, 186, *see also* Konopiště
  FF reputation reassessed   287
  monuments to FF   285, *285*
  negative portrayal of FF in literature   279–81, 286
  reaction to Sarajevo assassination   275–6
Czernin, Ottokar   24, 27, 32, 150, 157, 177 n.1, 278

Dalmatia   5, 42, 84, 106, 110, 111, 141, 260, 261
Danzer, Carl M.   24, 30
Daruváry, Géza   64, 65
De Bunsen, Maurice   186, 188–9
Dedijer, Vladimir   2, 40–1, 42, 47, 48, 103, 108, 109, 141, 233
Delegations   44, 46, 54 n.22, 186
denunciations   64, 105, 222, 223, 224, 257, *see also* Trieste
De Panafieu, Hector André   51
Dimitrijević, Dragutin ('Apis')   110, *131*, 134, 136–7, 138, 140, 142–3, 280
  in Black Hand   130, 133, 135, 142
  character   130–1
  role in FF assassination   51, 126, 141–2, 144
Dimović, Danilo   152
Drašković, Ivan   70, 76 n.14, 79 n.46
Drašković, Josip   61, 67–8, 70, 76 n.14, 78 n.43, 79 n.46
Dvor   65, 221

Edward VII, king of Great Britain   184, 186
Eichhoff, Johann   23
Erdödy, Stjepan   61, 70–2, 81 n.68

Ferdinand, tsar of Bulgaria   29, 155–6
Foča   261–2
France   28, 29, 32, 130, 132, 153, 171–2, 174, 176, 186, 187, 188, 189, 192

Frank, Josip   25, 36 n.34, 61, 64, 65, 67, 76 n.20, 78 n.42
Franz Ferdinand, archduke   *xii*, 151, 154, 156, 159, 208, 209, 211, 234, *see also* 'Greater Austria'
  abused after his death   221, 222, 238–9, 242, 257
  assassination   1, 17–18, 103, 110, 158, 226, 233, 275–6, 286
  and Belvedere circle   19–27, 30, 33
  and Catholic church   20, 25, 26, 29, 275
  character   2, 9, 18, 30–2, 198, 277, 279, 281
  and Croatian aristocracy   41, 56, 61, 62, 73
  and diplomatic network   23–4, 27
  favours peace   23, 28
  funeral   33, 208, 234, 237, 239, 243
  hostility to Magyars   20, 23, 24, 25–6, 28, 42, 46, 48
  links to Austrian press   24
  memorialization of   10, 226–7, 231 n.85, 285, 287, 291 n.64
  military connections   19–23, *20*, 22, 76 n.15
  morganatic marriage   23, 31, 187
  plans for his reign as emperor   6, 19, 25, 27, 33, 39–52, 66, 165, 235
  political network   21, 23–6, 41, 61
  relations to Serbia/Serbs   7, 25, 32, 39, 42, 48, 50–2, 227 n.8, 254
  and trialism   25, 40–52, 66
  view of crowned heads of Europe   28–9
Franz Joseph, Habsburg emperor-king (1848–1916)   1, 20, 45, 59, 64, 73, 92, 150–1, 159 n.2, 187, 211, 216, 218, 223, 234, 235, 239, 284
  attitude to war   150
  in July crisis   152–4, 158
  rejects constitutional change   41, 52
  relationship with FF   19–20, *20*, 21, 23, 27–8, 29–30
  visits Bosnia   86
Franz Salvator, archduke   207

Friedjung, Heinrich 62, 185, 188
Funder, Friedrich 24

Gaćinović, Vladimir 108, 109–10, 111, 112, 114, 115, 136
George V, king of Great Britain 29, 186–7, 194–5, 196, 201
Germany 11, 40, 130, 149, 167, 171, 184, 194, 195
  and Balkans 28, 156, 157
  in July crisis 159, 168–70, 172–3, 174, 175, 177, 192, 193
Golubović, Mustafa 109
Gooch, G. P. 104
Goremykin, I. L. 171
Gospić 207–8, 222, 230 n.56
Grabež, Trifko 141
Gračac 65, 220–1
Grba, Rade 62
Great Britain 28, 157, 169, 170, 171
  British views of FF 187, 195, 196–9
  declares war on Austria-Hungary 194
  in July crisis 172–3, 174, 187–93
  relations with Austria-Hungary 184–202
  severs diplomatic relations with Serbia 129, 185
'Greater Austria' 25, 40–3, 45, 46, 47, 48–9, 62, 64, 208
Grey, Edward 153, 172–3, 176, 188, 193–4, 196
  on Austria-Hungary 186, 191–2, 194, 197–8
  on Serbia 190, 191

Hajdaparsic, Edin 83
Hanau, Heinrich 49
Hašek, Jaroslav 238, 279, 280, 287
Hellenbach, Dioniz 61, 67
Hercigonja, Rudolf 220–1
Hinković, Hinko 223
Hodža, Milan 25
Hohenlohe, Gottfried 27
Hohenlohe, Konrad, prince 27, 237
Horváth, Edmund von 48
Hoyos, Alexander 151–2, 159, 167, 168
Hruban, Moric 46

Hungary/ Hungarians 4, 5, 12 n.18, 23, 61, 84, 86, 116, 151, 260, *see also* Thallóczy; Tisza
  and FF 20, 25, 26, 28, 29, 30, 40, 41–2, 47, 48, 49, 276
  relations with Croatia 210–18, 219–20, 222, 225, 226 (*see also* Nagodba)

Ilić, Danilo 110, 112, 115, 144
Italy 23, 32, 40, 195, 235, 241, 246–7

Jagow, Gottlieb von 169, 176
Janković, Božidar 133–4
Jeftanović, Gligorije 50–1
Jeftić, Borovije 108
Jeglič, Anton Bonaventura, prince bishop 45, 47
Jelačić, Janko 61, 64
Jews 26, 59, 60, 70, 234, 254, 257
Josipović, Géza 66
Jovanović, Slobodan 130
Joyce, James 242
Jukić, Luka 108
July crisis (1914), *see under individual countries*

Kalina, Antonín 284
Kállay, Benjámin 84–5, 91–2, 93, 94, 95, 96, 104–5, 108, 113, 116, 119 n.10
Kann, Robert A. 24, 52
Karl, Habsburg emperor-king (1916–1918) 17, 27, 226, 260
Karlin, Andrej, bishop 236–7
Khuen-Héderváry, Károly 66, 68, 76 n.15, 108, 210
Klemenčič, Ivanka 40
Kočić, Petar 108, 109, 110, 113, 116, 120 n.31
Kodrić, Alojz 245
Kokovstov, V. N. 171
Konopiště (castle of FF) 274, 282, 282–6
  confiscated by state 283–4
  meeting of FF and Wilhelm II 179 n.25, 278, 279–80, 283, 290 n.50
Korošec, Anton 45–6

Kosmić, Scherif 88–9, 94
Kosovo, battle (1389) 109, 111, 158, 277
Kramář, Karel 283
Kranjčević, Ivan 52
Kranjčević, Mica 207–8, 221
Kristóffy, József 25, 27
Kropotkin, Peter 110, 112, 140
Kršnjavi, Isidor 67, 231 n.76
Krupp, Marcel 132, 138
Kulmer, Miroslav 60, 61, 69–70, 74, 80 n.58, 81 n.68

Lammasch, Heinrich 23
Lányi, József, bishop 26
Latour, Vinzenz 26
Leopold Salvator, archduke 61, 69, 76 n.15
Liechtenstein, Alois, prince 41
Linder, Georg 26
Ljubljana 45, 60, 237
   Croatian-Slovene assembly (1912) 49
Longen, Emil Artur 279
Lueger, Karl 26, 49

Magdić, Pero 218, 224
Mahnić, Anton, bishop 49
Malobabić, Rade 136–7, 141, 142
Maniu, Iuliu 25
Marković, Svetozar 110
Mary, queen of Great Britain 187, 196, 201
Masaryk, Tomáš 108, 274, 275, 277, 283, 284, 286
Mažuranić, Bogoslav 217
Medaković, Bogdan 58, 62
Mehmedbašić, Muhamed 109–10
Mensdorff-Pouilly-Dietrichstein, Albert 153
   and British royal family 186–7, 194–5, 199, 201, 202
   and departure from London 194–6, 200–2
   in July crisis 188, 189–92, 193, 196–200
Meštrović, Ivan 111
Mihalović, Antun 60, 69, 79 n.52, 226
Milanković, Milutin 127

Miller, William 104
Milner, Alfred 104
Mitrinović, Dimitrije 108
Mitrovica 135, 222, 226
*Mlada Bosna* (Young Bosnia) 102–18
   Austro-Hungarian attitude to 112–14
   definition 103, 108, 140
   ideology 107–12, 115–16, 117
   Russian/Marxist influence 103, 108, 110, 112, 140
   and Yugoslavism 108, 110–11, 141
Moltke, Hermann von 159
Montenegro 3, 4, 51, 111, 162 n.38, 258–9, 260, 261, 264
   in Balkan Wars 153, 155, 254
Mostar 85, 107, 113, 136, 255, 259, 265
Muslims, *see* Bosnia-Herzegovina
Musulin, Aleksandar 61, 76 n.16

*Nagodba* (1868) 58, 75 n.5, 208, 213, 214, 218–9, 223, 224, 226, 228 n.15
   violations of 210, 212, 216
Nardelli, Nicola 106
*Narodna Odbrana* (People's Defence) 109, 136, 137, 140, 142, 143, 147 n.53
   formation 133
Němec, Vilém 281
Nicholas II, tsar of Russia 29, 174
Nicolson, Arthur 185, 189–90, 192, 193, 196
Nietzsche, Friedrich 108, 110
Nikita, king of Montenegro 153, 155, 161 n.17, 254
Nikolić (Podrinski), Vladimir 41, 60, 67, 68, 69, 70
Nový, Karel 280

'Octavius' (author of *Gross-Habsburg*) 163–5, 167, 177 n.1
Otočac 208, 221
Ottoman Empire 3, 51, 84, 86, 104, 127, 157, 158, 170, 177
   in Balkan Wars 50, 138, 154, 253–4
   and Serbia 133, 134, 135, 136, 137, 141

Paar, Eduard von 69
Paléologue, Maurice 171
Parežanin, Vidak 259, 260
Pašić, Nikola 51, 155, 211
　aspirations against Austria-Hungary 50, 52
　and crisis with army in Serbia 127, 128–9, 130, 134, 137–8, 142, 144
Pastor, Ludwig 26
Pavlović, Dimitrije 135–6, 137
Pejačević, Teodor 61, 69, 81 n.68, 216
Pekař, Josef 1, 278, 283
Petar Karadjordjević, king of Serbia 50, 129, 131, 140, 147 n.61
'Pig War' (1906–11) 132
Poincaré, Raymond 171–2, 174, 176, 189
Popović, Dušan 210, 219, 226
　arrested at start of war 224
Popovici, Aurel 25
Potiorek, Oskar 109, 113, 114, 254, 256, 257, 262, 267 n.10, 272 n.53
Prague 1, 108, 111, 276, 277, 281, 285, 287
*pravaši, see* Croatia; 'state right'
Pravica, Stevan 258, 273 n.77
Pribićević, Milan 137, 147 n.54
Pribićević, Svetozar 209, 211, 218, 219, 226
　in wartime 223–4
Pribićević, Valerijan 209, 219, 223–4, 229 n.44
Princip, Gavrilo 108, 109, 112, 116, 142, 158, 257
　assassinates FF 1, 177, 233
　in Belgrade 107, 117, 140–2, 144
　memorialization of 10, 103, 118 n.5, 125–6, 143, 277
　trial 7, 111, 141, 143
　and Yugoslav vision 5, 51–2, 111, 141
*Prosvjeta* 116, 254, 264
Protić, Stojan 135, 139, 142
Putnik, Radomir 139, 140, 142, 143, 144

Radić, Stjepan 215, 216–7, 226
'railway pragmatic' (Croatia) 211, 212, 213, 214–5, 229 n.37
Rajačić, Josif 68
Rak, Emanuel 280–1
Rathenau, Walter 176
Rauch, Pavao 25, 36 n.34, 58, 63, 70, 75 n.9, 81 n.68
　as ban of Croatia 62–6, 77 n.27, 212
Redlich, Josef 1, 185, 257
Regent, Ivan 246, 249 n.14
Reichsrat (Austrian parliament) 26, 41, 43, 45, 47, 261
Riedel, Richard 23
Rijeka (Fiume) 41, 45, 152, 216, 218
Romania 3, 24, 28, 29, 30, 50, 154, 155–6, 158, 194
Romanians
　and FF 25, 29, 33, 42, 48, 66
Rudolf, Habsburg crown prince 19, 31, 36 n.44
Russia
　in Balkans 3, 6, 51, 135, 138–9, 185
　and FF 27–9, 32
　in July crisis 167, 170–4, 175, 188, 189–93

Šabac 135, 136, 137, 270 n.37
Sabor (Croatian assembly)
　pre-war 57–8, 61, 69, 74 n.2, 75 n.6, 211, 212–3, 216, 217–18, 219
　wartime 224, 225–6
Samassa, Paul 25
Sandžak of Novi Pazar 134–5, 261
Sarajevo (city) 10, 86, 88, 91, 92, 105, 106, 109–10, 126, 255
Sarkotić, Stjepan 8, 262–4
Sazonov, S. D. 170, 171, 174–5, 176
Schäfer, Jakob 220
Schebeko, N. N. 189
Schönaich, Franz 21
Schopenhauer, Arthur 108, 110, 112
Schwarzenberg, Karl, prince 26, 41, 46

Scutari (Shkodër)   133, 153, 155, 254
Serbia
  deteriorating relations with Austria-Hungary   131–4, 135
  idea of 'Greater Serbia'   3, 5–8, 10, 39, 42, 49, 52, 64, 86, 155, 184, 185, 209, 219–20, 225
  influence of 1903 regicides   128–31
  intelligence network in Bosnia   134–8, 143
  military aid to Sarajevo plotters   126, 140–2
  political-military crisis in 1914   138–44
  'rogue state' theory   126
  and war guilt   126, 190
Serbs, see Bosnia; Croatia; Serbia
Seton-Watson, R. W.   62, 103, 125, 185, 211, 278, 280, 286
  his solution to Southern Slav Question   5–6, 7, 52
Sieghart, Rudolf   19
Silva-Tarouca, Ernst   26
Skerlecz, Ivan   208, 216, 225, 226–7, 228 n.28
  appointed ban of Croatia   58, 66, 212
  attempted assassination of   220
  loyal to Tisza   209, 212–14
  relations to Croat-Serb Coalition   209, 213, 217–18, 219, 223, 224, 226
  struggle with military in Croatia   222
  tours Croatia   218
Skerlić, Jovan   111, 112, 128, 139, 140
Skupština (Serbian parliament)   128, 129, 130, 139
Slijepčević, Pero   257
Slovaks   277
  and FF   25, 33, 42, 66
Slovenes   49–50, 67, 113, see also Trieste
  views of FF reform plans   40, 43–7
Smetanová, Jindřiška   281
Sokol clubs   65, 225, 254, 275–6, 277

Sosnosky, Theodor von   24
Southern Slav Question   1–11, 56, 66, 83, 95
  Habsburg views of   3–4, 7, 8, 50, 208
  as major cause of First World War   2–3, 10–11
  solutions to   4–6, 6–7, 8, 10, 39, 40–9, 51, 52, 59, 66, 79 n.52
Spalajković, Miroslav   50–1
Spinčić, Vjekoslav   41
Spitzmüller, Alexander von   23, 27
Starčević, Mile   61, 77 n.20, 212, 228 n.30
'state right' (Croatia)   5, 45, 47, 61, 67, 208, 209, 212
Steed, Henry Wickham   185–6, 191, 290 n.50, 291 n.68
Stefanović, Dušan   138, 139, 142
Steinacker, Edmund   26
Stodola, Cornel   25
Strandman, Basil de   134–5, 137
Stürgkh, Karl   151, 152, 237
Supilo, Frano   216–17
Šušteršič, Ivan   43, 45, 47, 152
  relations with FF   46–7
Szápáry, Friedrich   167
Szögyény, László   168

Tamaro, Attilio   246
Tankosić, Vojislav   141–2
Tarnowksi, Adam   156, 157
Thallóczy, Lajos   105–6, 107, 113, 118, 267 n.10, 272 n.53
Thun, Franz   26
Thun, Jaroslav   26–7, 46, 283
Tisza, István   66, 151, 211–13, 214–15, 218, 219, 220
  and 'expropriation' of Croatian coast   216
  and FF   24, 28
  view of Southern Slav Question   8, 66
  visits Zagreb in 1914   213
  and wartime Croatia   222, 223, 224, 226, 230 n.64
Todorović, Kosta   136
Tomašić, Nikola   60, 61, 66, 71, 76 n.15

treason, traitors   30, 73, 207, 219, 223, 242, 245, 258, 263
  wartime trials   7, 210, 220, 221–2, 224–5, 230 n.59, 257, 261
  Zagreb high treason trial   58, 62, 64, 65, 137, 185, 209, 210, 219–20, 224
trialism   5, 8, 40–5, 46, 47, 49, 51, 52, 66, 67
Trieste
  arrests and denunciations   239–40, 241, 242, 243
  Italian nationalists in   235, 240, 241, 245–6, 247–8
  press response to Sarajevo murders   234–5
  Slovene inhabitants   234, 235, 241, 243–6, 246–8, 252 n.67
  socialists   235, 242, 246, 248
  violence in   243, 244, 247–8
  and war mobilization   235, 239, 240, 243
Triple Alliance   167, 192, 235, 247
Tschirschky, Heinrich von   30
Turba, Gustav   24
Tuzla   85, 107, 114, 136, 243
Tyrrell, William   191, 195

*Ujedinjenje ili Smrt* (Union or Death: Black Hand)   51, 109, 130, 133, 135, 142, 144
Ušeničnik, Aleš   44–5

Vaida-Voevod, Alexandru   25
Valerio, Alfonso   235–6
Varaždin   64, 73, 76 n.17, 218, 221, 222, 224, 229 n.36
Vasić, Milan   136, 137, 147 n.53
Veselý, František   274, 281, 284, 285
Vidaković, Miloš   112
Vienna   18, 19, 31, 43, 73, 105, 108–9, 278

Viviani, René   171–2, 176, 181 n.51
Voska, Emanuel   278

war guilt   102–3, 126, 149–50, 277, 278
War Ministry (Austro-Hungarian *Kriegsministerium*)   20, 83, 85, 255, 256, 257
  and language policy in Bosnia   90, 91–5, 96
Werstadt, Jaroslav   278–9
Wierer, Rudolf   52
Wilhelm II, Kaiser of Germany   156, 168, 169
  relations with FF   28, 32, 179 n.25, 277, 279–80, 283

Yugoslavia (Kingdom of Serbs, Croats and Slovenes)   8, 52, 70, 111, 128, 141, 265–6, 280, 284
  commemoration of Sarajevo event   103, 125–6
Yugoslav idea   5–7, 8, 41, 45, 59, 66–7, 68, 72, 73–4, 108, 110–11, 141, 212, 219, 234, 243, 266

Zagreb   44, 64, 65, 68, 69, 76 n.15, 111, 208, 213, 220
  as a new South Slav capital   5, 6, 43, 48
  students   105, 108, 110, 112
  violence after Sarajevo murders   72
  in wartime   222–5, 230 n.68
Zametica, John   142, 179 n.25
Zanantoni, Eduard   61
Žerajić, Bogdan   109
Zimonjić, Petar, bishop   265–6
Žitomislić monastery   255
Žolger, Ivan   25, 47
Zurunić, Teodor   114
Zweig, Stefan   17–18, 31, 238